Picasso's Guernica

Picasso's Guernica

Illustrations · Introductory Essay · Documents · Poetry · Criticism · Analysis

Edited by

ELLEN C. OPPLER

SYRACUSE UNIVERSITY

W · W · NORTON & COMPANY

New York · London

PRINTED IN THE UNITED STATES OF AMERICA.

FIRST EDITION

Library of Congress Cataloging-in-Publication Data
Oppler, Ellen C.
    Guernica: illustrations, introductory essay,
documents, poetry, criticism, analysis.
    (Norton critical studies in art history)
    Bibliography: p.
    1. Picasso, Pablo, 1881-1973. Guernica. 2. Picasso,
Pablo, 1881-1973—Criticism and interpretation.
I. Title.   I. Series.
ND553.P5A66   1987   759.4   86-28662

ISBN 0-393-01950-0
      0-393-95456-0   ppk.

W. W. Norton & Company, Inc., 500 Fifth Avenue, New York, N. Y. 10110

W. W. Norton & Company Ltd., 37 Great Russell Street, London WC1B 3NU

1 2 3 4 5 6 7 8 9 0

Contents

CONTENTS

Preface

It would be foolhardy to assume that one could select in a single handy volume all worthwhile materials written about *Guernica*. Picasso surely is the most-discussed artist of our century, with countless books and articles in several languages written about him; and *Guernica* is his painting that has generated a vast literature of commentary and criticism.[1] It is not necessarily his best painting, nor the most innovative or stylistically influential.[2] Yet it is Picasso's "masterpiece," with all that this term implies. *Guernica* fulfills the requirements that Kenneth Clark demands of a masterpiece:

> It is not merely a superb piece of technical skill, it is the record of a profound and prophetic experience. * * * it represents, or symbolizes, a society in the throes of destruction, as convincingly as Raphael's *School of Athens* represents a society in perfect equilibrium. * * * it is above all the work of an artist of genius who has been absorbed by the spirit of the time in a way that made his individual experience universal.[3]

The "prophetic experience" was Picasso's response to the bombing of Guernica. On the fiftieth anniversary of this historic event, we must recall that it was the first methodical attack against civilians, an ominous prelude to the great conflict that would soon engulf the world. Some of the painting's background, therefore, was political. The anthology began to organize itself. Documents about the Spanish Civil War were essential; recollections by the very squadron commanders who bombed Guernica are translated and published here in English for the first time. Since Picasso was sympathetic to the Spanish Republic and to the cause of international Communism—while continuing to paint in the modernist style the latter rejected—a selection of Marxist criticism became relevant.

---

1. See Selected Bibliography.

2. The most innovative would be *Les Demoiselles d'Avignon* of 1907. Picasso himself preferred *The Dance* (or *Three Dancers*) of 1925 to *Guernica* because it is "more a real painting" by itself "without any outside considerations" (comments made in 1965 when the Tate Gallery acquired the picture; partly quoted by John Russell in *The Meanings of Modern Art* [New York, 1981] p. 289).

3. *What Is a Masterpiece?* (London, 1979; New York, 1981), p. 44; also published in *Portfolio* (Feb./ Mar. 1980, p. 53), where a reproduction of *Guernica* heads the essay (p. 42). Inspired by Clark's essay, *Art News* attempted an opinion poll of experts (only 14 of 27 scholars consulted were willing to tackle the question [Avis Berman, "What Makes a Masterpiece?" *Art News*, March 1980, pp. 128–32]). Walter Cahn, author of *Masterpieces: Chapters on the History of an Idea (Princeton, 1979)* provided especially useful observations (p. 132), as did Ann Sutherland Harris who emphasized the "staying power" of a masterpiece, its ability to be "endlessly revealing, when one discovers new significance at each encounter" (p. 132). According to many of these criteria, *Guernica* is indeed a masterpiece of our century.

Mark Roskill, on the other hand, after devoting his concluding chapter to *Guernica*, argues that the question has not yet been settled "whether *Guernica* really is a masterpiece in the same full sense as the greatest works in the past" (*What Is Art History?* [London and New York, 1976], p. 180).

PREFACE

My aim was to compile a one-volume, yet comprehensive, anthology for students of the arts and humanities, of interest also to the general reader, and with useful texts and documentation for the specialized Picasso scholar. I therefore included statements by Picasso that have been frequently reprinted elsewhere, as well as a selection of less accessible poetry and drama that relate to the painting. Parts IV and V were givens: how *Guernica* was experienced first in Paris and London before it was sent to New York in 1939, and how it affected America. During the latter part of its 40-year sojourn in this country, *Guernica* again was politicized; it became a popular antiwar symbol against U.S. military involvement in Southeast Asia.

Part VII—the core of the *Guernica* essays—presented many problems of selection, and I regret that several interesting articles or chapters of books had to be omitted because of space limitations or because permission to publish was denied. The *Art Journal,* for instance, between winter 1964–65 and winter 1973–74 published half a dozen essays of varied—indeed debatable—interpretation. These are cited in the bibliography and are readily available in every college and metropolitan city library. Finally, it seemed appropriate to bracket *Guernica* with Picasso's works that are inseparable from it: the private and public etchings that are its preludes—*Minotauromachy* and *Dream and Lie of Franco*—and its great coda, *The Charnel House.*

Over the years, my greatest inspiration has been the authors of my selections. I am deeply indebted to them for their generous permission to publish, and for rewarding opportunities to discuss our common interests. I am saddened by the fact that in too many cases I can no longer give them this book with my inscription. I offer it to them and to my parents, in memoriam, with gratitude and affection. My students in Picasso classes and graduate seminars helped directly by sampling the anthology and tracking down details of research, as well as indirectly, since I prepared for them (and students elsewhere) a book that would instruct and delight. I am indebted especially to three scholars in the field; Dr. Catherine Freedberg, for her extraordinary generosity in sharing materials, and Professors Sandra Coyner and Josephine Withers for their attentive reading of the manuscript. My research was greatly facilitated by cooperative European and American professionals in museums and publishing houses. It would have been impossible without the Museum of Modern Art and the inestimable resources of its library, the helpful staff of the Registrar's Office, and Frances Keech and Richard Tooke of Rights and Reproductions.

My special thanks also go to Randall Bond and Barbara Opar, our art librarians at Syracuse University; to Dorcas MacDonald, the efficient chief of Interlibrary Loan Services; to the Photo Center; to the Humanities Typing Service of the College of Arts and Sciences; and particularly to my designer and former student, Barbara Jones, who helped realize my vision of harmoniously coordinated text and illustrations. Finally, I am grateful to my editors and the fine production staff at W. W. Norton.

ELLEN C. OPPLER
1987

List of Illustrations

Guernica Studies, States, and Postscripts

NOTE: *Guernica* studies are pencil, crayon, ink, or gouache on paper, except as indicated.
Paintings are oil on canvas, except as indicated.

Illustrations for the Introductory Essay

Illustrations for Anthology Selections

Note on the Captions

A precise date indicates that Picasso actually dated the work, frequently marking with roman numerals the sequence on a given day. For such "undated" works as Nos. 59 or 60, for instance, dates assigned by Zervos and others are cited.

For dimensions, height precedes width. Measurements furnished by the owners are recorded and may vary by fractions of an inch or centimeter from previously published dimensions. (For the *Guernica* studies, MoMA's measurements in inches and the Prado's slightly differing measurements in centimeters are given here.) Documentation includes the major catalogues identified in the Selected Bibliography. For Zervos, *Z.XI:9* indicates plate 9 in volume 11. Arnheim (A.); Geiser (G.) or Bloch (B.) for graphic works; and Spies (S.) for sculpture are cited.

Frontispiece.   Picasso with *Guernica* completed. Published 13 July 1937 in Ce *Soir*. Photo by David Seymour (Magnum)

Photo on p. 139.   Picasso working on *Guernica*. 1937. Photo by Dora Maar; courtesy *CdA*

Foldout.   *Guernica*. Early May to 4 June 1937. Oil on canvas, 11'5½" x 25'5¾" (3.49 x 7.77 m). Prado (Casón del Buen Retiro), Madrid

THE ILLUSTRATIONS

1. *Composition Study.* 1 May 1937 (I). Pencil on blue paper, 8¼ x 10⅝″ (21 x 26.9 cm). Z.IX:1; A.1; Prado (Casón) 108

2. *Composition Study.* 1 May 1937 (II). Pencil on blue paper, 8¼ x 10⅝″ (21 x 26.9 cm). Z.IX:2; A.2; Prado (Casón) 109

3. *Composition Study*. 1 May 1937 (III). Pencil on blue paper, 8¼ x 10⅝″ (21 x 26.8 cm). Z.IX:3; A.3; Prado (Casón) 110

4. *Horse*. 1 May 1937 (IV). Pencil on blue paper, 8¼ x 10⅝″ (21 x 26.9 cm). Z.IX:4; A.4; Prado (Casón) 111

5. *Horse*. 1 May 1937 (V). Pencil on blue paper, 8¼ x 10½″ (21 x 26.8 cm). Z.IX:5; A.5; Prado (Casón) 112

3

6. *Composition Study*. 1 May 1937. Pencil on gesso on wood, 21 ⅛ x 25½″ (53.7 x 64.7 cm). Z.IX:10; A.6; Prado (Casón) 113

7. *Head of a Horse*. 2 May 1937 (I). Pencil on blue paper, irregular right edge, 8¼ x 6″ (21 x 15.5 cm). [Measurements sometimes switched with No. 8.] Z.IX:6; A.7; Prado (Casón) 114

8. *Head of a Horse*. 2 May 1937 (II). Pencil on blue paper, 10½ x 8¼″ (26.9 x 21 cm). Z.IX:7; A.8; Prado (Casón) 115

10. *Composition Study*. 2 May 1937. Pencil and oil on gesso on wood, 23⅝ x 28¾″ (60 x 73 cm). Z.IX:8; A.10; Prado (Casón) 117

9. *Head of a Horse*. 2 May 1937. Oil on canvas, 25½ x 36¼″ (65 x 92.1 cm). Z.IX:11; A.9; Prado (Casón) 116

11. *Horse and Bull.* Undated; early May 1937. Pencil on tan paper, irregular shape, 8⅞ x 4¾" (22.7 x 12.1 cm). Z.IX:9; A.11; Prado (Casón) 118

12. *Composition Study.* 8 May 1937 (I). Pencil on white paper, 9½ x 17⅞" (24.1 x 45.7 cm). Z.IX:13; A.12; Prado (Casón) 119

13. *Horse and Mother with Dead Child.* 8 May 1937 (II). Pencil on white paper, 9½ x 17⅞" (24 x 45.5 cm). Z.IX:12; A.13; Prado (Casón) 120

6

14. *Mother with Dead Child*. 9 May 1937 (I). Pen and ink on white paper, 9½ x 17⅞″ (24 x 45.3 cm). Z.IX:14; A.14; Prado (Casón) 121

15. *Composition Study*. 9 May 1937 (II). Pencil on white paper, 9½ x 17⅞″ (24 x 45.3 cm). Z.IX:18; A.15; Prado (Casón) 122

16. *Mother with Dead Child on Ladder.* 9 May 1937 (III). Pencil on white paper, 17⅞ x 9½" (45.3 x 24 cm). Z.IX:16; A.16; Prado (Casón) 123

17. *Mother with Dead Child on Ladder.* 10 May 1937 (V). Pencil and color crayon on paper, 17⅞ x 9½" (45.7 x 24.4 cm). Z.IX:15; A.21; Prado (Casón 128)

18. State I (first record of work on the canvas). 11′5½″ x 25′5¾″ (3.49 x 7.77 m). Photographed 11 May 1937

19. *Horse.* 10 May 1937 (I). Pencil on white paper, 9½ x 17⅞" (24.1 x 45.6 cm). Z.IX:17; A.17; Prado (Casón) 124

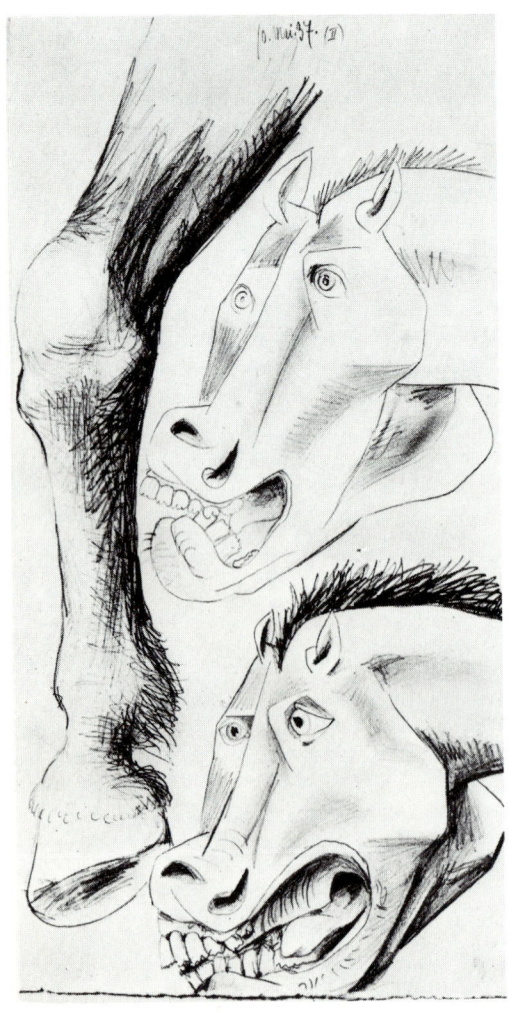

20. *Leg and Heads of a Horse.* 10 May 1937 (II). Pencil on white paper, 17⅞ x 9½" (45.4 x 24.3 cm). Z.IX:21; A.18; Prado (Casón) 125

21. *Head of a Bull with Human Face.* 10 May 1937 (III). Pencil on white paper, 17⅞ x 9½" (45.4 x 23.9 cm). Z.IX:20; A.19; Prado (Casón) 126

10

22. *Horse.* 10 May 1937 (IV). Pencil and color crayon on white paper, 9½ x 17⅞″ (24.2 x 45.6 cm). Z.IX:19; A.20; Prado (Casón) 127

23. *Bull with Human Face.* 11 May 1937. Pencil on white paper, 9½ x 17⅞″ (23.9 x 45.5 cm). Z.IX:23; A.22; Prado (Casón) 129

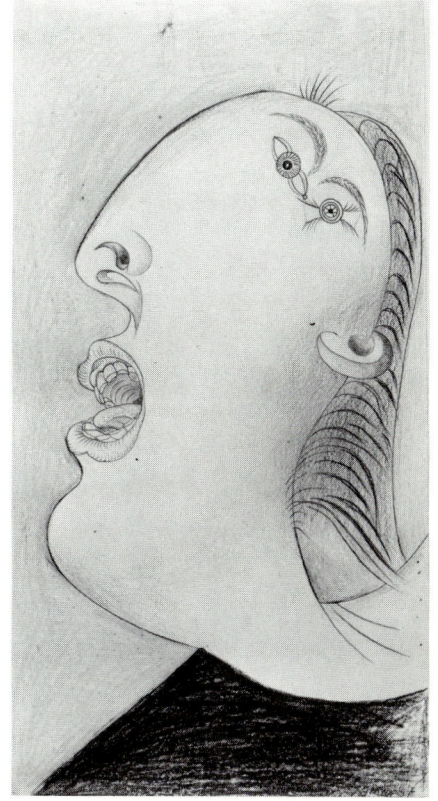

24. *Head of a Woman.* 13 May 1937 (I). Pencil and color crayon on white paper, 17⅞ x 9½″ (45.4 x 24 cm). Z.IX:22; A.23; Prado (Casón) 130

11

26. *Hand of a Warrior with Broken Sword.* 13 May 1937 (II). Pencil on white paper, 9½ x 17⅞″ (23.9 x 45.4 cm). Z.IX:24; A.24; Prado (Casón) 131

25. *Mother with Dead Child.* 13 May 1937 (III). Pencil and color crayon on white paper, 9½ x 17⅞″ (23.9 x 45.5 cm). Z.IX:25; A.25; Prado (Casón) 132

12

27. State II. Undated; photographed around 13 May 1937

28. State III. Undated; photographed between 16 and 19 May 1937

13

29. *Head of a Bull.* 20 May 1937. Pencil and gray gouache on white paper, 9¼ x 11½″ (23.1 x 29.2 cm). Z.IX:28; A.26; Prado (Casón) 133

30. *Head of a Bull with Studies of Eyes.* 20 May 1937. Pencil and gray gouache on white paper, 9¼ x 11½″ (23.2 x 29.2 cm). Z.IX:29; A.27; Prado (Casón) 134

31. *Head of a Horse.* 20 May 1937. Pencil and gray gouache on white paper, 11½ x 9¼″ (29 x 23.1 cm). Z.IX:27; A.28; Prado (Casón) 135

32. *Head of a Horse.* 20 May 1937. Pencil and gray gouache on white paper, 9¼ x 11½″ (23.1 x 29.1 cm). Z.IX:26; A.29; Prado (Casón) 136

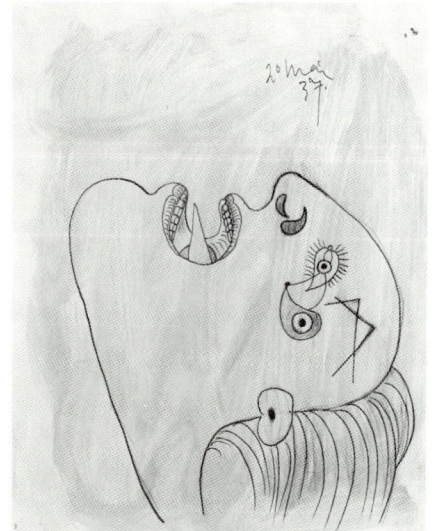

33. *Head of a Woman.* 20 May 1937. Pencil and gray gouache on white paper, 11½ x 9¼″ (29 x 23.2 cm). Z.IX:32; A.30; Prado (Casón) 137

34. *Head of a Weeping Woman.* 24 May 1937. Pencil and gray gouache on white paper, 11½ x 9¼″ (29.2 x 23.1 cm). Z.IX:31; A.31; Prado (Casón) 138

35. *Head of a Weeping Woman.* 24 May 1937. Pencil and gray gouache on white paper, 11½ x 9¼″ (29.2 x 23.2 cm). Z.IX:33; A.32; Prado (Casón) 139

36. *Head.* 24 May 1937. Pencil and gray gouache on white paper, 9¼ x 11½" (23.1 x 29.3 cm). Z.IX:30; A.33; Prado (Casón) 140

37. State IV. Undated; photographed between 20 and 24 May 1937

38. State V. Undated; photographed around 27 May 1937

39. *Head of a Weeping Woman.* 27 May 1937. Pencil and gray gouache on white paper, 9¼ x 11½″ (23.2 x 29.3 cm). Z.IX:36; A.34; Prado (Casón) 141

40. *Falling Man.* 27 May 1937. Pencil and gray gouache on white paper, 9¼ x 11½″ (23.2 x 29.3 cm). Z.IX:34; A.35; Prado (Casón) 142

18

41. *Mother with Dead Child.* 28 May 1937. Pencil, color crayon, and gray gouache on white paper, 9¼ x 11½" (23.2 x 29.3 cm). Z.IX:38; A.36; Prado (Casón) 143

42. *Mother with Dead Child.* 28 May 1937. Pencil, color crayon, gray gouache, and hair on white paper, 9¼ x 11½" (23.1 x 29.2 cm). Z.IX:37; A.37; Prado (Casón) 144

43. *Head of a Weeping Woman*. 28 May 1937. Pencil, color crayon, and gray gouache on white paper, 9¼ x 11½" (23.2 x 29.3 cm). Z.IX:35; A.38; Prado (Casón) 145

44. *Head of a Weeping Woman*. 31 May 1937. Pencil, color crayon, and gray gouache on white paper, 9¼ x 11½" (23.2 x 29.3 cm). Z.IX:39; A.39; Prado (Casón) 146

45. State VI. Undated; photographed around 1 June 1937

20

46. *Head of a Weeping Woman.* 3 June 1937. Pencil, color crayon, and gray gouache on white paper, 9¼ x 11½" (23.2 x 29.3 cm). Z.IX:40; A.40; Prado (Casón) 147

47. *Head of a Weeping Woman.* 3 June 1937. Pencil, color crayon, and gray gouache on white paper, 9¼ x 11½" (23.2 x 29.3 cm). Z.IX:44; A.41; Prado (Casón) 148

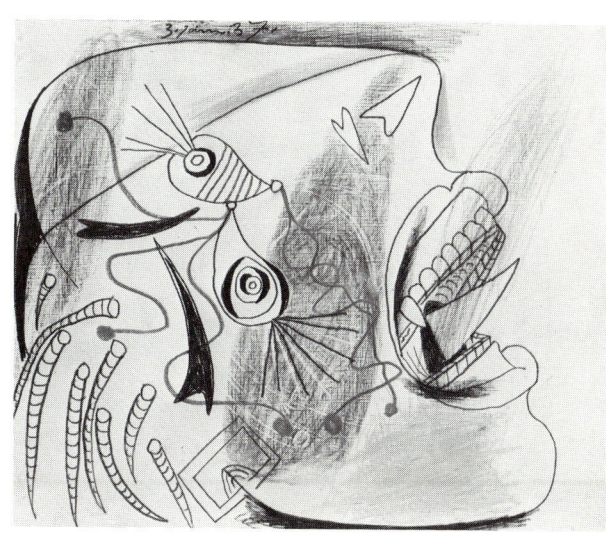

48. *Head of a Weeping Woman.* 3 June 1937. Pencil, color crayon, and gray gouache on white paper, 9¼ x 11½" (23.2 x 29.3 cm). Z.IX:41; A.42; Prado (Casón) 149

21

49. *Head of a Warrior and Horse's Hoof.* 3 June 1937. Pencil and gray gouache on white paper, 9¼ x 11½" (23.2 x 29.2 cm) Z.IX:45; A.43; Prado (Casón) 150

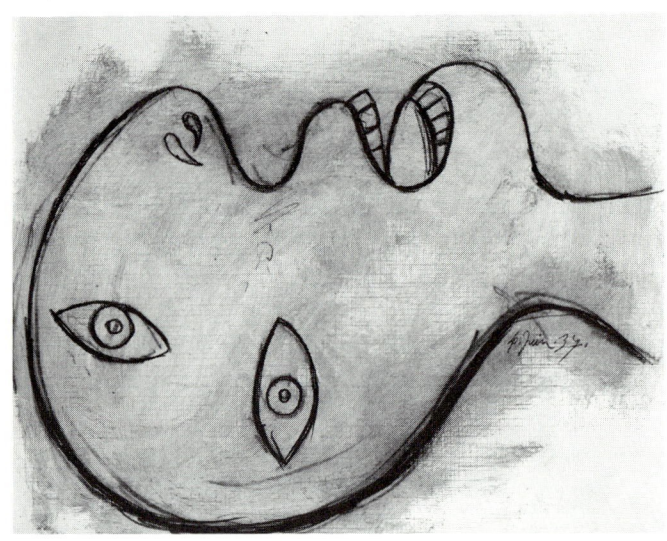

50. *Head of a Warrior.* 4 June 1937. Pencil and gray gouache on white paper, 9¼ x 11½" (23.2 x 29.2 cm). Z.IX:42; A.44; Prado (Casón) 151

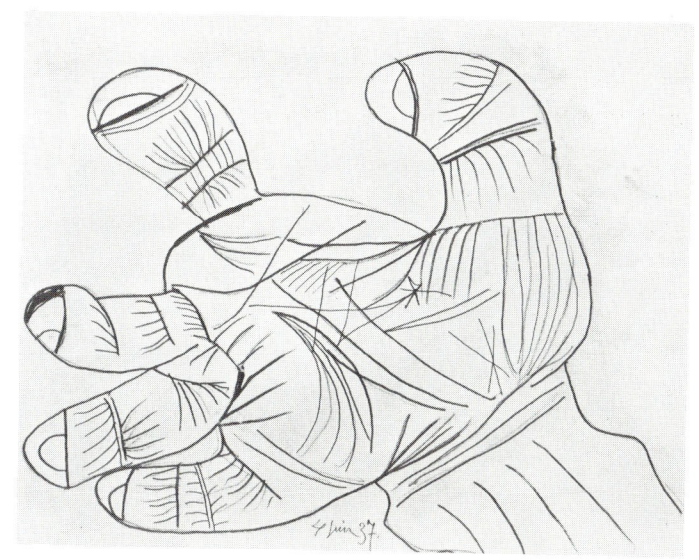

51. *Hand of a Warrior*. 4 June 1937. Pencil and gray gouache on white paper, 9¼ x 11½" (23.2 x 29.2 cm). Z.IX:43; A.45; Prado (Casón) 152

52. State VII. Undated; photographed around 4 June 1937

53. Detail of *Guernica*

24

54. Detail of *Guernica*

55. *Dream and Lie of Franco.* 7 June 1937. Etching and aquatint. See No. 110

56. *Head of a Weeping Woman.* 8 June 1937. Pencil and gray gouache on white paper, 11½ x 9⅛" (29.1 x 23.2 cm). Z.IX:48; A.46; Prado (Casón) 153

57. *Head of a Weeping Woman.* 8 June 1937. Pencil, color crayon, and gray gouache on white paper, 11½ x 9¼" (29.1 x 23.2 cm). Z.IX:46; A.47; Prado (Casón) 154

26

58. *Head of a Weeping Woman.* 13 June 1937. Pencil, color crayon, and gray gouache on white paper, 11½ x 9¼" (29.1 x 23.1 cm). Z.IX:47; A.48; Prado (Casón) 155

59. *Head of a Weeping Woman.* Undated; Prado: 15 June 1937, Zervos and Arnheim: 26 June. Pencil, color crayon, and oil on canvas, 21⅝ x 18⅛" (55 x 46.3 cm). Z.IX:54; A.52; Prado (Casón) 159

60. *Head of a Weeping Woman.* Undated; Prado: 15 June; note on back: 19 June 1937. Pencil and gouache in color on cardboard, 4⅝ x 3½″ (11.7 x 8.8 cm). Z.IX:53; A.49; Prado (Casón) 156

61. *Head of a Weeping Woman with Handkerchief.* 22 June 1937. Oil on canvas, 21⅝ x 18⅛″ (55 x 46.3 cm). Z.IX:52; A.50; Prado (Casón) 157

62. *Head of a Weeping Woman with Handkerchief.* Undated, mid-June 1937. Oil on canvas, 21⅝ x 18⅛″ (55 x 46.3 cm). Z.IX:51; A.53; Los Angeles County Museum of Art (Gift of Mr. and Mrs. Thomas Mitchell)

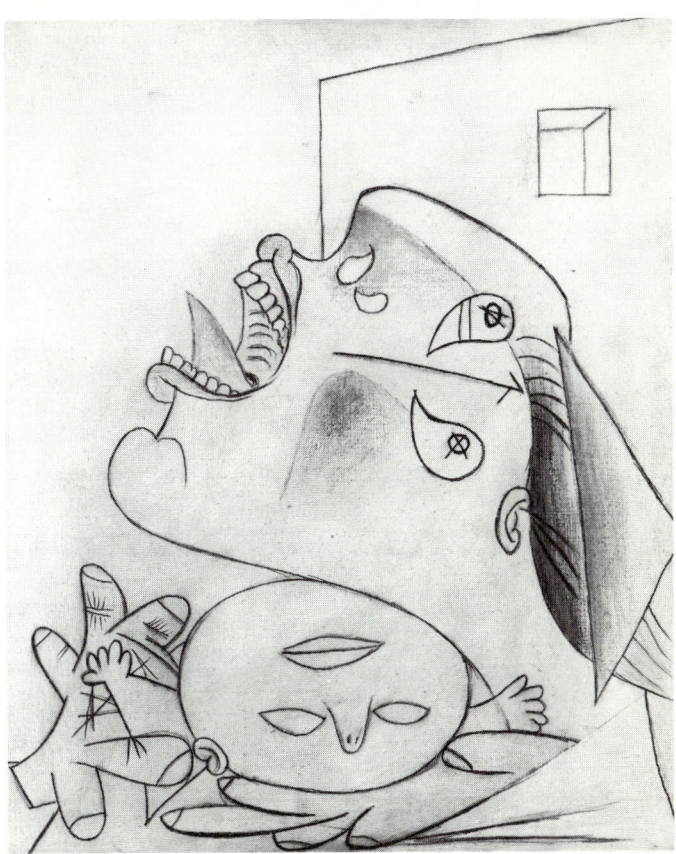

63. *Mother with Dead Child.* 22 June 1937. Pencil, color crayon, and oil on canvas, 21⅝ x 18⅛″ (55 x 46.3 cm). Z.IX:49; A.51; Prado (Casón) 158

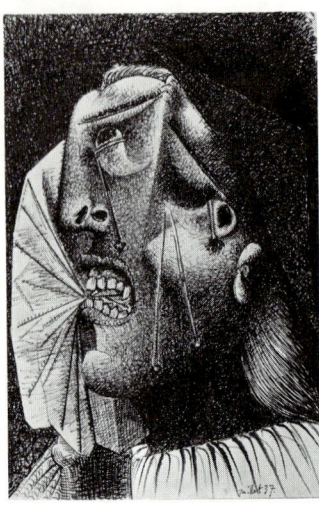

64. *Weeping Woman.* 2 July 1937. Etching (scraper) with aquatint, 3rd state, No. 6/15. 27¼ x 19½″ (69.2 x 49.4 cm). B.1.333; A.54; Prado (Casón) 160; Baer 62

66. *Weeping Woman with Handkerchief.* July 1937 (Prado: 4 July). Pen and ink on white paper, 10 x 6¾″ (25.3 x 17.1 cm). Z.IX:56; A.56; Prado (Casón) 162

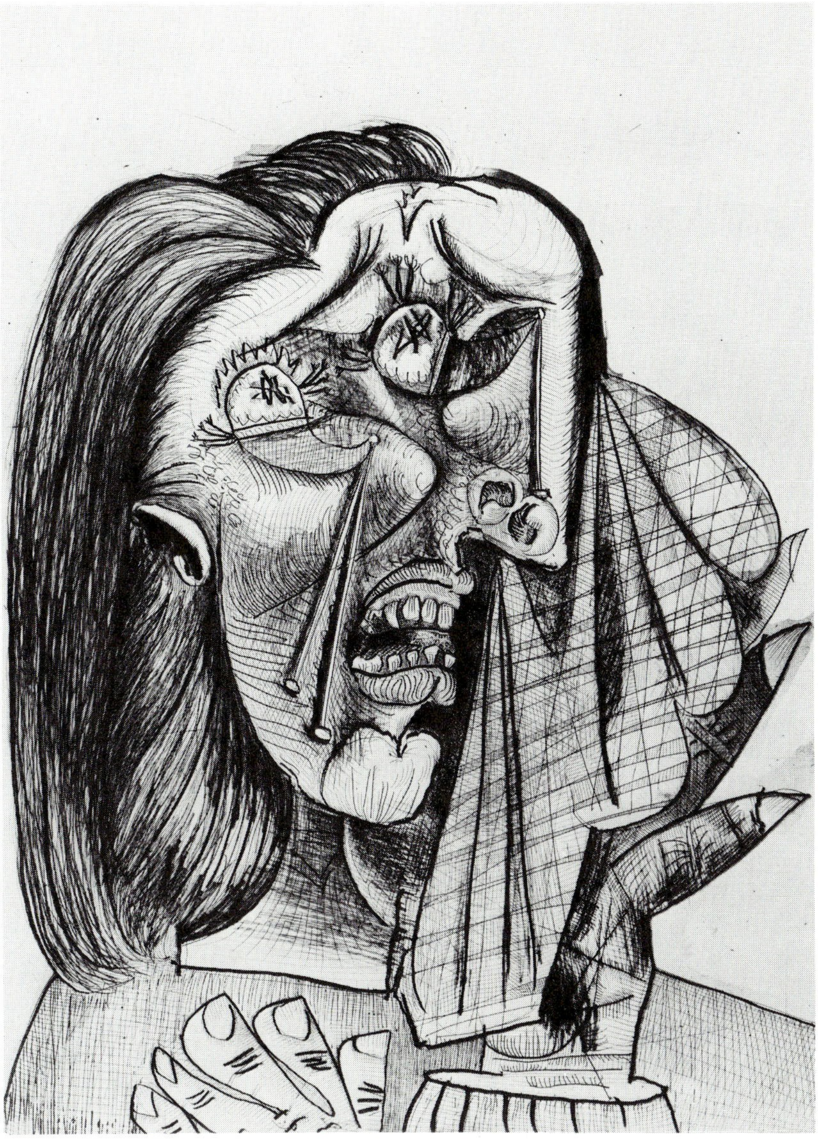

65. *Weeping Woman.* 2 July 1937. Etching (scraper and drypoint) with aquatint, 6th state, No. 4/15. 27¼ x 19½″ (69.2 x 49.4 cm). B.1.333; A.55; Prado (Casón) 161; Baer 63

67. *Weeping Woman with Handkerchief.* 6 July 1937. Pen and ink on tan paper, 6 x 4⅝″ (15.2 x 11.5 cm). Z.IX:57; A.57; Prado (Casón) 163

31

68. *Mother with Dead Child.* 26 September 1937. Monochrome oil on canvas, 51¼ x 76¾″ (130 x 194.3 cm). Z.IX:69; A.58; Prado (Casón) 164

69. *Weeping Woman.* 12 October 1937. Pen and ink and pencil on cream paper, 35⅜ x 23″ (90.1 x 58.4 cm). Z.IX:74; A.59; Prado (Casón) 165

70. *Weeping Woman with Handkerchief.* 13 October 1937. Pen and ink and oil on canvas, 21⅝ x 18⅛″ (55 x 46.3 cm). Not in Zervos; A.60; Prado (Casón) 166

33

71. *Weeping Woman with Handkerchief.* Undated; 17 October 1937. Oil on canvas, 36¼ x 28⅝" (92 x 72.6 cm). Z.IX:77; A.61; Prado (Casón) 167

72A. *Weeping Woman with Handkerchief.* 18 October 1937. Oil on canvas, 21⅝ x 18⅛" (55 x 46 cm). Not in Zervos. Musée Picasso, Paris (MP 165)

72B. *Weeping Woman.* 18 October 1937. Oil on canvas, 21⅝ x 18⅛" (55 x 46 cm). Not in Zervos. National Gallery of Victoria, Melbourne, Australia. Acquired with the generous assistance of the Jack and Genia Liberman Family and the Donors of The Art Foundation of Victoria. (See page 82, note 62.)

73. *Weeping Woman*. 26 October 1937. Oil on canvas, 23⅝ x 19¼″ (60 x 49 cm). Z.IX:73.
Private collection, England

74. *Weeping Woman.* 28 October 1937. Oil washes and black ink on paper, 15¾ x 10¾" (40 x 26 cm). Z.IX:76; Fogg Art Museum, Harvard University, Cambridge, Mass. (1940 Purchase—Francis H. Burr Memorial Fund)

75. *Suppliant Woman.* 18 December 1937. Gouache and India ink on wood, 9½ x 7¼" (24 x 18.5 cm). Not in Zervos. Musée Picasso, Paris (MP 168)

37

Chronology

Focuses on *Guernica*'s creation and exhibition history and pertinent international events *(italicized)*. Turning points in Picasso's life and art were selected from Jane Fluegel's essential chronology in *Picasso Retrospective 1980* and the various biographies; important documentation also in *Guernica–Legado Picasso*.

1881   October 25: Picasso born in Málaga, Spain.

1895   September: family settles in Barcelona; Picasso enters Fine Arts Academy.

1900   October: first visit to Paris; again in 1901, 1902.

1904   Spring: settles in Paris; Fernande Olivier his mistress to 1911.

1906   Summer in Gosol, Spain, with Fernande.

1907   Spring/summer: *Les Demoiselles d'Avignon;* meets Braque and future dealer Kahnweiler.

1909   Summer with Fernande in Barcelona, Horta de Ebro (annual visits to Spain, 1909–13).
       General strike in Barcelona, anticlerical arson and massacres; repression; execution of Francisco Ferrer (Oct. 13).

1914   *August 3: Germany declares war on France; Spain remains neutral.* Picasso isolated in Paris: Braque, Derain, Apollinaire at the front; Kahnweiler in Switzerland; Eva (mistress since 1911) dies December 1915.

1917   January: visit to Barcelona; February–March with Ballets Russes in Rome; meets ballerina Olga Koklova; *Parade* opens in Paris (May 18); summer in Spain: *Parade* in Madrid (June 23–30); July–November in Barcelona with Olga (*Parade* opens Nov. 10).

1918   July 12: marries Olga. November 9: Apollinaire dies of influenza.
       November 11: armistice; end of World War I.

1921   February 4: son Paulo born.
       Summer at Fontainebleau: *Three Musicians, Three Women at the Spring.*

1923   Summer: meets André Breton.

1925   June: expressionist *The Dance (Three Dancers).*
       November: joins exhibition, "La Peinture Surréaliste."

1927   January: meets Marie-Thérèse Walter.
       Fall/winter: etchings for *Le Chef-d'oeuvre inconnu* by Balzac.

1930   *January 28–30: resignation of Primo de Rivera; more moderate government in Spain.*
       February: *Crucifixion;* later completes *Woman in a Garden* sculpture in studio of Gonzalez.

1931   *March: Constitution restored in Spain, general elections.*
         April 14: King Alfonso XIII leaves Spain and Republic is established.

1932   *Head of a Woman* sculpture; *Girl before a Mirror; Crucifixion* drawings (Sept.–Oct.).

1933   *January: radical uprisings in Barcelona; April and November: municipal and parliamentary elections in Spain, increased rightist strength; December: syndicalist-anarchist uprising in Barcelona.*
         Spring: etchings, *The Sculptor's Studio.*
         June: first issue of *Minotaure,* with collage cover by Picasso.
         Woman with Vase sculpture completed at Boisgeloup.
         August 18–25 in Barcelona with Olga and Paulo.
         September: bullfight drawings and paintings at Boisgeloup.

1934   *April: general strike in Barcelona.*
         Early summer: continues bullfight theme at Boisgeloup.
         Late August to mid-September: trip through Spain (San Sebastián, Burgos, Madrid, Toledo, Barcelona) with Olga and Paulo.
         October: conservative cabinet formed in Spain; insurrection and repression of miners in Asturias.

1935   Zervos, "Conversation with Picasso."
         Spring: *Minotauromachy* etching.
         June: marital crisis and final separation from Olga.
         September 5: María de la Concepción (Maya) born to Marie-Thérèse [see p. 106, note 120].
         November: Sabartés returns, becomes personal secretary; Picasso stops painting and writes poetry.

1936   *February 16: general elections in Spain; victory of Popular Front.*
         Spring: important Picasso retrospective in Spain—Barcelona (Jan. 18–28), Bilbao (Feb.), Madrid (May).
         March–April: Picasso with Marie-Thérèse at Juan-les-Pins. 32 Picasso works in "Cubism and Abstract Art," MoMA, New York.
         Popular Front election victory in France (Léon Blum cabinet, June 5).
         July 14: Picasso's design used for curtain, *14 juillet* by Romain Rolland.
         July 17–18: Spanish Civil War begins. Military uprising in Spanish Morocco; garrisons in Seville, Cádiz, Burgos; Barcelona resists takeover (July 19); Junta of National Defense (Franco) established in Burgos (July 23).
         August: fall of Mérida, Badajoz; murder of García Lorca.
         Summer in Mougins above Cannes; liaison with photographer Dora Maar.
         September 19: Picasso is named director of the Prado.
         November: Republican government flees to Valencia; International Brigades reach Madrid (Nov. 7–8); Battle for Madrid.

1937   January 8: *Dream and Lie of Franco,* etching and poem (figs. 109, 110, 147A, 147B).
         Picasso accepts commission for a painting in the Spanish Pavilion, Paris Exposition.
         February 8: fall of Málaga.
         Late February: cornerstone laid for Spanish Pavilion.

April 18: one of Picasso's several visits to the Exposition (see fig. 162A).

April 26: Guernica bombed.

April 28: Guernica occupied by Franco troops; French press coverage begins.

May 1, May Day: Picasso draws 6 initial studies for *Guernica* painting.

May 3–8: civil strife in Barcelona.

May 9: Picasso completes last compositional study (fig. 15) before drawing on large canvas itself.

May 11: first photograph of *Guernica* canvas (state I, fig. 18).

May 12–13: state II (fig. 27) photographed; study for state III (fig. 28).

May 20: studies of head of horse, bull; state IV (?).

May 27: studies of falling man, weeping woman (figs. 39, 40); state V (?).

May 28: Picasso is paid 150,000 francs for *Guernica*.

June 4: last two studies of warrior-statue (figs. 50, 51); state VII; *Guernica* is virtually completed.

June 7: Picasso adds four final scenes to *Dream and Lie of Franco* (fig. 55).

June 19: fall of Bilbao.

July 12: inauguration of Spanish Pavilion at Paris Exposition.

July, September, October: Picasso continues *Guernica* postscripts.

November 25: International Exposition closes, having received 33 million visitors.

1938   *January 11: heavy bombardment of Barcelona.*

March 16–17: Barcelona bombed 8 times.

Spring: *Guernica* included in exhibition of French art (Picasso, Matisse, Braque, Laurens; organized by Galerie Rosenberg, Paris) in Kunstnernes Hus, Oslo; Liljevach Konsthall, Stockholm; Statens Museum for Kunst, Copenhagen.

October to January 1939: *Guernica* and studies shown in England for Spanish war relief. New Burlington Galleries, London (Oct. 4–28); Leeds, Liverpool, Manchester; Whitechapel Art Gallery, London (31 Dec. 1938 to mid-Jan. 1939); returned to Paris.

1939   *January 26: Barcelona falls to Franco troops.*

March 28: Madrid falls; hostilities cease March 29.

April 1: United States recognizes Franco government.

May 1: *Guernica* and studies arrive in New York aboard ship *Normandie*.

May 4–27: *Guernica* exhibition at Valentine Gallery for Spanish war relief.

August–October: *Guernica* exhibition on fund-raising tour: Los Angeles, Stendhal Gallery (Aug. 10–21); San Francisco Museum of Art (Aug. 28–Sept. 18); Chicago Arts Club (Oct. 1–10).

August 23: German–Soviet Nonaggression Pact.

September: World War II begins: German troops invade Poland; Great Britain and France declare war on Germany (Sept. 3).

15 November 1939 to 7 January 1940: *Guernica* and studies included in exhibition, "Picasso: Forty Years of His Art," MoMA, New York.

1940   Picasso retrospective travels with *Guernica* and studies: Chicago Art Institute (Feb. 1–Mar. 3); St. Louis, City Art Museum (Mar. 16–Apr. 14); Boston, Museum of Fine Arts (Apr. 26–May 25); San Francisco Museum of Art

(June 25–July 22); Cincinnati Museum of Art (Sept. 28–Oct. 27); Cleveland Museum of Art (Nov. 7–Dec. 8); New Orleans, Isaac Delgado Museum (20 Dec. 1940–17 Jan. 1941).

May 12: German troops invade France at Meudon.

June 13: Paris is occupied; armistice is signed June 22.

1941 Picasso retrospective with *Guernica* continues: Minneapolis Institute of Arts (Feb. 1–Mar. 2); Pittsburgh, Carnegie Institute (Mar. 15–Apr. 13).

Summer: *Guernica* at MoMA, "Masterpieces of Picasso," (July 16–Sept. 7). *Guernica* at Fogg Art Museum, Cambridge (Sept. 24–Oct. 20); Columbus, Gallery of Fine Arts (Nov. 4–30).

December 7: Japanese attack Pearl Harbor: United States enters World War II.

1942 *Guernica* in Cambridge, Fogg Art Museum (June 26–Sept. 15); thereafter, continuing display at MoMA, New York.

1943 May: meets Françoise Gilot.

1944 March 5: Max Jacob dies in concentration camp at Drancy.

June 26–September 10: Picasso exhibition includes *Guernica* studies at Mexico City, Society of Modern Art.

August 25: Liberation of Paris.

October 5: Picasso announces membership in French Communist Party.

October 6: Salon d'Automne (Salon de la Libération), Paris, includes 74 Picasso paintings, 5 sculptures—his first participation in a group exhibition.

Winter 1944–45: interviews with Jerome Seckler.

1945 March: interview with Simone Téry.

Late April; Liberation of Nazi concentration camps, newsphoto coverage.

Picasso paints *The Charnel House.*

May 8: V-E Day, end of World War II in Europe.

August 6: atomic bomb dropped on Hiroshima; Japan surrenders Aug 14.

1947 May 15: Claude born to Françoise and Picasso.

1948 August 25: Picasso leaves for First World Peace Congress in Wroclaw, Poland.

1949 April 19: Paloma born to Françoise and Picasso.

April 20–23: World Peace Congress in Paris; Picasso's "peace dove" lithograph as poster.

1950 *June 25: Korean conflict breaks out.*

October: Picasso attends World Peace Congress in Sheffield, England; "peace dove" in flight used for poster.

November: awarded Lenin Peace Prize for painting.

1951 Attends World Peace Congress in Rome.

1952 Studies for *Guernica* tour U.S., September 1952–March 1956.

1953 May–July 5: major Picasso retrospective (including *Charnel House*) at Galleria Nazionale d'Arte Moderna, Rome.

End of September: with Claude and Paloma, Françoise Gilot leaves Picasso.

October–November 20: *Guernica* added to Picasso retrospective at Palazzo Reale, Milan.

13 December 1953 to 20 February 1954: *Guernica* also in Picasso retro-

spective at Museu de Arte Moderna (II Bienal), São Paulo, Brazil.

June: first portrait of Jacqueline Roque (*Madame Z*).

1955 February: Olga Picasso dies.

Summer: *Guernica* in Picasso retrospective at Musée des Arts Décoratifs, Paris (June–Oct.)

October 25–December 26: Picasso retrospective travels to Haus der Kunst, Munich.

1956 Picasso retrospective with *Guernica* continues: Rheinisches Museum, Cologne (30 Dec. 1955–29 Feb. 1956); Kunsthalle Hamburg (Mar. 10–Apr. 29).

Summer: *Guernica* and studies shown at Palais des Beaux Arts, Brussels (May–June): Stedelijk Museum, Amsterdam (July 14–Sept. 30); National-museum, Stockholm (Oct. 19–Dec. 2).

October 25: Picasso's 75th birthday. First retrospective in Museum of Modern Art, Moscow (until mid-November).

1957 Summer: *Guernica* and studies in "Picasso: 75th Anniversary Exhibition," MoMA, New York (May 22–Sept. 8); show travels to Chicago Art Institute (Oct. 29–Dec. 8).

1958 Anniversary exhibition with *Guernica* and studies continues to Philadelphia Museum of Art (Jan. 8–Feb. 23). This is *Guernica*'s final loan exhibition; constant travel has weakened the huge canvas. Thereafter it remains at MoMA "on extended loan," but the studies continue to travel.

1961 March 2: Picasso marries Jacqueline Roque.

1962 May 1: awarded Lenin Peace Prize again.

Winter: *Guernica* studies shown in Japan: Museum of Western Art, Tokyo (Nov. 3–Dec. 23).

1963 January–March: *Guernica* studies in Kyoto (Jan. 16–Feb. 17); Kurume, Kyushu (Feb. 23–Mar. 10); Nagoya (Mar. 16–31).

1964 *Guernica* studies in Canadian exhibition, "Picasso and Man," Art Gallery of Toronto (Jan. 11–Feb. 16) and Montreal Museum of Fine Arts (Feb. 27–Mar. 31).

1966 October 25: Picasso's 85th birthday. Two *Guernica*-related paintings in major retrospective, Grand Palais, Paris (19 Nov. 1966—12 Feb. 1967).

1967–1970 *Guernica* again becomes antiwar symbol during U.S. military action in Southeast Asia.

1968 Franco approves "Operación Retorno"—*Guernica*'s "return" to Spain.

1969 October: Pérez Embid publicly announces that Spain should receive *Guernica*.

1970 September: Picasso confirms agreement with MoMA for *Guernica*'s future in a democratic Spain.

1971 Summer: all *Guernica* studies shown in "The Artist as Adversary" exhibit, MoMA, New York (July 1–Sept. 27).

1973 April 8: Picasso dies in Mougins, France, age 91; burial at Château de Vauvenargues.

1974 February 28: Shafrazi sprays "Kill Lies All" on *Guernica*.

1975 *November 20: Franco dies in Madrid, just under age 83.*

November 22: Juan Carlos is crowned constitutional monarch.

1977 *June 15: first general elections in Spain since civil war: victory for right-centrist coalition of Premier Adolfo Suarez.*

1978   *December: democratic constitution adopted in Spain.*

1980   Summer: Picasso retrospective in New York (May 22–Sept. 16), MoMA's 50th anniversary celebration anticipating Picasso's centennial of 1981; it is the last exhibition featuring *Guernica* in New York.

1981   February: Picasso's lawyer, Roland Dumas, approves *Guernica*'s transfer to Spain.

        September 9: *Guernica* and studies are turned over to Spanish Minister of Culture in New York; departure aboard Iberia plane.

        October 25: Picasso's centennial celebrations throughout Spain.

        "Legado Picasso" exhibition—*Guernica*, 60 studies, and *Dream and Lie of Franco*—opens to the public in the Casón del Buen Retiro, Madrid.

        November 5: great Picasso retrospective opens at Museo Español de Arte Contemporaneo, Madrid (Nov.–Dec. 1980).

1982   January–February: Picasso retrospective continues in Museo Picasso, Barcelona.

1987   Plans for moving *Guernica* to an attractive modern art center have become public just as this book goes to press. The Centro de Arte Reina Sofía, an eighteenth-century hospital on Calle de Santa Isabel not far from the Prado, is being renovated into a handsome site for temporary exhibitions: one of the 1987 shows marked this fiftieth anniversary, "The Spanish Pavilion at the International Exhibition in Paris, 1937." The vast structure (a "building of truly majestic proportions and vistas" suggestive of both "a palace and a monastery") will be further modernized to house the Prado's growing collection of twentieth-century art, with works by Picasso and his friends Juan Gris and Joan Miró providing a handsome showcase for *Guernica. (See New York Times, 12 July 1987, sec. 2, p. 29.)*

Guernica—Its Creation, Artistic and Political Implications, and Later History

In 1937, Picasso was asked to design a mural for the Spanish Pavilion at the international exposition in Paris. The result was *Guernica*—named after a Basque town that had been bombed some months before, during this first year of the Spanish Civil War. It is Picasso's best-known painting and one of the masterpieces of our time. Yet it is a problematic work, stylistically complex, with images difficult to decipher, whose meaning is unclear.

We are pulled swiftly into the picture by a monstrous foot on the right and by the bloated knee of a woman running, stumbling toward a light flashing diagonally across dark houses. The powerful arm of another woman with the classic profile of a tragic mask thrusts an old-fashioned oil lamp into the center; above, a flattened ceiling lamp with bare electric bulb shoots shrapnel rays and black spiky shadows onto a stricken horse. Jaws open, dagger-tongued, paint-saliva dripping, its newsprint coat pierced, slashed, the horse screams toward a black-and-white bull whose eyes are calm, level. He threatens—no, shelters—a woman with crazed tear-drop eyes, wailing over an infant, eyes blank, nose flopped over, dead. Below, a huge hand crisscrossed with lines of fate: a fallen rider/soldier/shattered statue, eyes askew, severed arm clutching a ghostly flower and splintered sword, stretching across the canvas. We are back with the running woman. Above her stumbling leg, a woman hurtles from a burning house, flames regular as dragon's teeth gnawing at her, at dark timber, an open door—the balanced counterpart of the bull and grieving mother.

Amid shattered and jumbled debris, *Guernica*'s figures are reduced to vivid silhouettes against black and somber grays: paper cutouts, posterlike, resembling the stark images of news photos or flickering newsreels. The picture is unlike anything Picasso had painted before, unlike the brilliant Cubist still lifes or sensuous nudes and telling portraits of the previous decades. Why did this master of personal imagery suddenly paint a monochrome twenty-six-foot canvas for an official exposition pavilion? Why did Picasso—hitherto apolitical and a Spanish expatriate in Paris—accept a commission from the Spanish government? And why did he name it after a small provincial town he had never seen? Our search for answers must first take us to public events, to international politics and the military incidents of the civil war.

Spain has had a turbulent history during Picasso's lifetime: defeat in the Spanish–American War of 1898, revolutionary strikes and anarchist uprisings (three prime ministers assassinated), military dictatorships in the 1920s. When the Spanish Republic finally was established in 1931, every possible social, economic, and political problem confronted the new government. Numerous conservative and reactionary interest groups resisted democratic reforms: wealthy landholders, the privileged church, and the militarists, monarchists, and adherents to the Falangist party (patterned after

Fascist prototypes in Germany and Italy). After two years, these right-wing factions gained government control through national elections. In February 1936, however, a left-of-center Popular Front uniting Republicans, Socialists, labor unions, Communists, and even anarchists won a decisive electoral victory. Thereafter, rightist plots against this Republican government intensified, led by regular army generals, especially General Francisco Franco, victorious commander of the Foreign Legion during the Moroccan campaigns of the 1920s and future chief of Nationalist Spain.[1]

The Spanish Civil War erupted late on 17 July 1936 as a coordinated revolt of army chiefs in Spanish Morocco and in garrison towns of mainland Spain: La Coruña and Burgos in the north, Salamanca, and southern Córdoba, Seville, and Cádiz (see fig. 76). By late July, the right-wing Insurgents controlled one third of the country. After bitter street fighting, however, Barcelona—home of Picasso's family since 1895—remained a Republican stronghold, as did Valencia and other areas of eastern, central, and southern Spain. The Basque provinces in the north, with the crucial seaport Bilboa, also resisted military takeover. Madrid held firm: the capital was the last city to surrender in late March 1939 when the civil war finally ended. The conflict had torn the country apart for nearly three years, taking an estimated 500,000 to 800,000 lives.[2]

The civil war did not remain an internal Spanish struggle. From the beginning, Hitler and Mussolini helped the Insurgents: Nazi transport planes airlifted Moorish troops to the mainland, the famous German Condor Legion attacked Madrid and the Basque cities with bombers and fighter planes, and "volunteer" troops assisted their Spanish ally. In November 1936, the two Fascist dictators recognized the Nationalists[3] as the official government of Spain with Franco as head of state (caudillo being roughly equivalent to il duce and der Führer).

Only the Soviet Union sided openly with the Republic, sending military advisers, pilots, and Russian materiel (sold for precious Spanish gold, however) and organizing Communist-directed International Brigades of volunteers. The Western democracies remained officially neutral, swayed by influential conservative power groups, despite protests from young intellectuals, leftists, and idealists who passionately sided with the Spanish Republic.[4]

1. A one-paragraph summary of the complex causes and events culminating in the war, of course, must be a vast oversimplification. For in-depth studies, see Gerald Brenan and background chapters by Gabriel Jackson and Hugh Thomas; Hugh Purcell's 128-page illustrated overview is remarkably effective; Robert Payne has published important primary sources.
    Note: Full citations for relevant books and frequently used references are given in the Selected Bibliography. Authors cited in these footnotes also have been indexed.

2. See Thomas (1977), pp. 926–27, for casualty estimates.

3. Labels for the two sides reflect the writers' sympathies. Historians term the Franco forces "Rebels" or "Insurgents" until "Nationalists" becomes the neutral term. The government forces are "Loyalists" or "Republicans," though the Franco side always called them "the Reds."

4. In the United States and France, President Franklin Roosevelt and Socialist Premier Léon Blum favored Republican Spain but gave in to conservative pressures. The American mood was pacifist and isolationist after the First World War and the Depression years. In England it was the era of appeasement and "peace at any price," and the Conservative Baldwin and Chamberlain governments instinctively favored the Franco Nationalists and what was interpreted as an attempt to restore law and order.

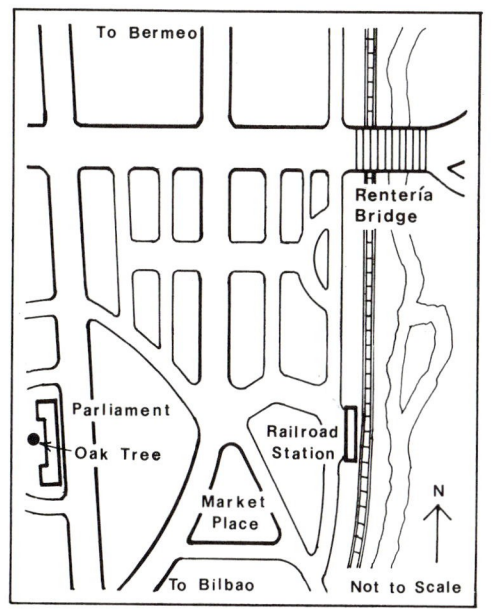

76. *Map of Guernica and Spain*. March 1937. (Adaptation and design by Oppler and Margo Bury)

It is only against this background of official government neutrality—despite much popular sympathy for the Republic and strong convictions that European Fascism must be stopped in Spain—that the present generation of young people can understand what the civil war, now a half century ago, meant to their counterparts during the 1930s. The Spanish Civil War inflamed and divided some American groups as bitterly as the war in Vietnam or American involvement in Central America, civil rights, and racial and feminist issues have engaged later generations. During the 1960s and 1970s, in fact, when thousands of young Americans battled with police and went to jail or exile over the war in Southeast Asia, *Guernica* again became an inspiring peace symbol (figs. 128A, 128B, 129, 154, and 155).

Young people had made enormous sacrifices for Spain in the 1930s. Some 3,000 Americans crossed the Atlantic, made the illegal and hazardous trip from France to Spain, and fought for the Republic in guerrilla groups or the International Brigades. Inadequately equipped and trained, few escaped being wounded; about a third of the volunteers were killed. The idealism of this generation dying for a great cause, opposing official positions they considered immoral and insane, was recorded by some of the best writers of the time. Ernest Hemingway's *For Whom the Bell Tolls* (1940), George Orwell's *Homage to Catalonia* (1938), André Malraux's *Days of Hope* (*L'Espoir*, 1938), countless poems, and important films have immortalized this passionate and tragic period.[5]

The extraordinary battle for Madrid in late October 1936 brought foreign involvement to a dramatic climax. While German and Italian planes bombed Madrid, Russian fighter planes counterattacked to protect the city. The Republican government escaped to Valencia, convinced that Madrid could not hold out, as Insurgent forces marched towards the capital. Suddenly, on 8 November 1936, the first units of the International Brigades arrived, singing revolutionary songs: there were German veterans of the First World War and from Nazi concentration camps, British machine gunners, Poles, Hungarians, Yugoslavs, and Spanish anarchists. The battle raged for ten days; then the concentrated assault ended, and both sides dug in for the duration of the war. The famous battle cry that had resounded from the barricades and over Radio Madrid and had stirred sympathizers in Paris, London, and New York had come true: "*No pasarán!*" (They shall not pass!)[6]

As the Spanish Civil War intensified, Picasso and his friends became deeply involved; some true activists indeed volunteered to fight in Spain. The Republican government recognized Picasso as Spain's greatest living painter by naming him director of the Prado Museum. It was a symbolic and tragic gesture: by late 1936 the museum was an empty shell in the beleaguered capital, its priceless treasures evacuated to the relative safety of Valencia (later stored in neutral Switzerland). Christian Zervos, director of *Cahiers d'Art* which regularly produced Picasso's works, sped down to Valencia to inspect the Prado treasures and published his findings in the magazine.[7] Picasso's closest friend among the poets, Paul Eluard, no doubt expressed

---

5. See part III; Weintraub, *The Last Great Cause*, and others in Selected Bibliography. Films about the war include *For Whom the Bell Tolls*, *To Die in Madrid*, and Buñuel's *España 36*.

6. La Pasionaria (Dolores Ibarruri, fig. 141) became the Communist heroine of resistance with her radio broadcasts against the Insurgents beginning in July 1936: "It is better to die on your feet than to live on your knees! No pasarán!"—echoing the slogan of Verdun (Thomas [1961], p. 140).

7. *Cahiers d'Art* (1938), p. 312; also p. 92, below, for the Paris exhibition of medieval art rescued from the Catalonian churches and museums.

the feelings of the group with his verses about the battle for Madrid (just as some months later his poem would commemorate the Guernica incident):

November 1936[8]

Look at the builders of ruins at work
They are rich patient methodical black stupid

But they are doing their best to be left alone on earth
They are on the edge of humanity and cover it with filth
They flatten to the ground mindless palaces.
One gets used to everything
Except to these leaden birds
Except to their hatred of everything radiant
Except to yield to them.

Even if Picasso had not been a Spaniard, he might have been caught up in the wave of sympathy that the war raised in Paris, as it did around the world. But he was very much a Spaniard, proudly retaining his Spanish citizenship throughout his self-imposed exile in France during the Franco era. Picasso never again returned to Spain after 1934.

The tragic events affected him even more since he had recently strengthened personal ties with his homeland. After an absence of sixteen years, he visited Spain again during the summers. The 1933 trip to Barcelona inspired violent oil paintings, fantastic drawings (fig. 108), and etchings of the bullfights—prophetic of Guernica's symbolic content. When he returned to Barcelona in 1934, his family and friends must have described the recent turmoil: a paralyzing general strike in April 1934; in December 1933, ten days of street fighting during anarchist-syndicalist uprisings. Picasso renewed other ties with his Spanish past in 1935 when he sent for Jaime Sabartés, the friend of his youth, to keep him company as secretary and confidant. His disastrous marriage having ended in separation, Picasso again spoke Spanish and the Catalan dialect in his Paris apartment.

Finally, Picasso achieved artistic recognition also in Spain—at least by the avant-garde in Barcelona, Madrid, and Bilboa. The Friends of the New Art (Amigos de los Artes Nuevas—ADLAN) staged his first one-man show since his youth: a crack express train arriving in Barcelona thirty years late, was Salvador Dali's apt description.[9] Timed to coincide with the national elections in February 1936, the exhibition opening in Barcelona dramatically celebrated Picasso and victory of the Popular Front coalition. ADLAN and Josep Lluis Sert, its energetic young president, championed innovation; they selected Picasso's challenging Cubist and Surrealist works instead of showing the popular Blue, Rose, or Neoclassic periods. ADLAN also exhibited the

8. Eluard, Oeuvres complètes, vol. I (Paris 1968), p. 801 (ECO trans.). First published in L'Humanité, included in a precious limited edition, Solidarité (April 1938), with etchings by Picasso, Miró, and others to raise funds for the Spanish Republican war effort.

9. Dali's invitation to the Picasso retrospective was read over Radio Barcelona (as was a message from Gonzalez); the tardy express train is frequently exaggerated to an improbable 40-year delay (Daix, p. 263, and Cabanne, p. 281, with lively account of the various manifestations). Sert gave a newspaper interview; Eluard spent a month in Spain, lecturing in Madrid and Barcelona. See Jean-Charles Gateau, Eluard, Picasso et la peinture: 1936–1952 (Geneva, 1983), especially pp. 14–15. The special Picasso number of Cahiers d'Art reprinted these texts (vol. no. 7–10, 1935—though actually published in 1936; see also McCully, pp. 191–96).

art of Joan Miró and Alexander Calder, and staged plays and poetry readings by García Lorca. A year later, as architect of the Spanish Pavilion, Sert was equally courageous and innovative, not deferring to popular taste, but calling on these same artists to contribute modern works to the building.[10]

The Spanish Republic's commission for a large mural in its pavilion was yet another way his native country honored Picasso. When Sert completed his architectural plans with his associate Lluis Lacasa in early January 1937, Picasso was ready for his official visitors. He had been working on cartoonlike etchings that indisputably expressed his contempt for General Franco (figs. 109 and 110). Sert recalled how Picasso read the accompanying poem (pp. 184–85) "with such extraordinary enthusiasm and force and violence," that he could vividly imagine the commissioned mural:

> cries of children cries of women cries of birds cries of flowers
> cries of timbers and of stones cries of bricks cries of
> furniture.[11]

The enormous canvas required a larger studio, which Picasso found in a 17th-century town house near an ancient quai of the Seine. In recent years, Jean-Louis Barrault had rehearsed plays in the spacious "attic" of No. 7, rue des Grands-Augustins, and Contre-Attaque—a short-lived political group of leftist intellectuals—had met there.[12] By a marvelous coincidence, Balzac had described this very building for scenes of his *Unknown Masterpiece (Le Chef d'oeuvre inconnu)* and completed his final revision in 1837, precisely 100 years before Picasso created his *well-known* masterpiece.[13] Balzac's tale was one of Picasso's favorite stories, one he had embellished with etchings and drawings in a deluxe 1931 edition.[14] For Picasso, given to superstition, these were good omens: he would paint his 20th-century masterpiece in a historic setting haunted by fascinating ghosts.

Nevertheless, Picasso did not begin working for several months, uncertain of a suitable subject. To understand his problem, two points need emphasis: his usual handling of commissions, and the basically apolitical nature of his art. The way he "illustrated" Balzac's text is characteristic: he gave Vollard twelve etchings of the artist and his model, most of which neatly fit Balzac's story; an irrelevant bull-and-horse image was thrown in as well. Nor did he specifically design the famous *Peace Dove* poster of 1949. He simply had his Communist friend Louis Aragon look through

10. See pp. 70 and 72. The assassinated poet García Lorca was especially honored in the pavilion.

11. The poem and etchings, promptly christened *Dream and Lie of Franco,* were sold for Spanish war relief. See pp. 184 and 338, below.

12. Organized by the writer Georges Bataille, Contre-Attaque included Paul Eluard and Dora Maar— Picasso's new mistress since early 1936—who thus knew about this suitably large studio space. See Sidra Stich, "Picasso's Art and Politics in 1936," *Arts Magazine,* October 1983, p. 116 and notes 27–29, p. 118, for rich background information). Pierre Daix emphasized that Dora Maar's role in this politicization should not be underestimated (note 3, p. 273).

13. The historic studio was Picasso's home throughout the war. It was frequently photographed by Brassaï, the best source about the studio's history (*Picasso and Company,* pp. 44–45).

14. Edition of 340, Ambroise Vollard publisher, 1931, with 12 etchings of 1927, and a 1931 table of contents; ill. Bloch, 82–94. Cf. Dore Ashton's imaginative essay, *A Fable of Modern Art* (New York, 1980).

77. *Picasso in His Studio.* May 1937. Photo by Dora Maar (courtesy *CdA*)

recent lithographs that, fortuitously, included an appropriate pigeon.[15] The commission for the Spanish Pavilion obviously required more serious commitment and a clearly worked-out message.

Kahnweiler, Picasso's friend and dealer, once described the artist as the most apolitical man he had known. Asked about his politics—soon after they had met in 1907—Picasso replied (surely tongue-in-cheek): "In Spain there is a king: I am a royalist."[16] The critic Maurice Raynal, however, recalled Picasso's "bitter and

15. See p. 250, note 2, below. Cabanne describes this incident most amusingly (p. 407).
16. Kahnweiler, *My Galleries and Painters*, p. 108.

78. *Press Coverage of Guernica Bombing.* Collage by Oppler and Barbara Jones

outspoken indignation in 1909," when the anarchist intellectual Francisco Ferrer was summarily executed in Spain.[17] Picasso's youthful associations in Barcelona and Paris and his own temperament made him sympathetic to anarchism; in his revolutionary art and unconventional life-style, Picasso was a long-time rebel—one might say an anarchist. During the 1930s in Paris, Picasso was close to the Surrealist poets who had joined the French Communist Party in January 1929, convinced that revolutionary art and thought must go with revolutionary politics. In December these intellectuals, who prized their personal and artistic freedom above all, left the Party *en masse*, quickly disillusioned by rigid Party discipline and ideological dogmatism, but most remained Communist sympathizers.[18] Picasso's new friends of 1936, Paul Eluard and Dora Maar, were among the most politically committed; and as exiled Spaniards working for a Republican victory reached Paris, Picasso was politicized also. The basic dilemma remained, however: How could the creative person follow the dictates of art and yet serve a political cause? Picasso had to resolve this problem for himself: paint the inspiring work his French and Spanish friends expected, but without compromising his standards and endangering his artistic freedom.

Although it has always seemed that Picasso procrastinated until May Day with his *Guernica* studies, he was actually considering subjects so different from *Guernica* that they have remained a closely guarded secret until after his death.[19] The treasures of the Picasso Museum in Paris include drawings of the theme that obsessed Picasso much of his life, that indeed *was* Picasso's life: "the artist in the studio" (fig. 162B). As Reinhold Hohl has brilliantly argued, it was Picasso's way of fighting death and the horrors of the civil war (p. 313, below). Though it was apolitical, this celebration of the creative artist would have been appropriate for the Spanish Pavilion. When the cornerstone was placed during a ceremony in late February, the Spanish ambassador emphasized that the building would demonstrate the people's triumph with all weapons necessary for victory, "those of liberty, of culture, of work."[20] The 40-foot sculptural shaft guarding the entrance, for instance, was abstract and only its inspirational title conveyed a clear message: *The Spanish People Have a Path That Leads to a Star* (fig. 83).

The bombing of Guernica gave Picasso a new universal subject. On the afternoon of 26 April 1937, Nazi planes flying for General Franco bombarded the town and machine-gunned people fleeing from collapsing and burning houses. Full newspaper coverage reached Paris on 28 and 29 April (fig. 78) when Picasso probably read the stirring and now-famous account by the London *Times* correspondent G. L. Steer, translated in *L'Humanité* and reprinted on pp. 160–63. On May first—while

17. Raynal, *Picasso* (Geneva, 1953), p. 84; for Ferrer, see Egbert, *Social Radicalism*, p. 325.

18. See Gershman, especially ch. 4 on Surrealism and politics.

19. Zervos hinted at Picasso's dilemma (p. 207, below, and reproduced beach scenes that anticipate *Guernica*'s elongated proportions [Z.VIII:336, 337, 339]). But to publicize other studies—and we don't know whether Picasso showed them to his friends—would have detracted from *Guernica*'s impact. The familiar theme of the artist's studio, and especially a woman artist in fig. 162B, might not have seemed relevant. Stimulated by Spies's discussion of the pre-*Guernica* ideas (note 3, p. 314, below), Ludwig Ullmann suggests some alternate interpretations of these drawings, including exploratory studies for a political sculpture, possibly intended for the Spanish Pavilion ("Zur Vorgeschichte Picassos *Guernica*," *Kritische Berichte* I (1986), pp. 4–25.

20. *Guernica–Legado Picasso* (Madrid, 1981), p. 151; an essential source for *Guernica* studies, with color reproductions and anthology of the hitherto unpublished documents (hereafter, *Guernica–Legado*).

parades celebrated labor's traditional May Day—Picasso began working in a furious burst of creativity: six sketches in one day (figs. 1–6).

After the destruction of Coventry, Rotterdam, Dresden, and Hiroshima, one may wonder about this universal outrage over an air raid that became "the most notorious event of the whole war."[21] Fifty years ago, however, it was the first saturation bombing of a civilian center, and Guernica was a very special town. This ancient capital of the Basques, whose origins are shrouded in the legends of prehistory, was honored throughout Spain as the oldest center of democracy. It had also become a military objective in the Nationalist drive toward Bilboa, the modern industrial port city. The Basque provinces were stubbornly Loyalist enclaves in the north; General Emilio Mola in March 1937 had threatened the Basques with extinction if they did not surrender.[22] German planes and pilots of the Condor Legion carried out Mola's threats and supported advancing Nationalist troops. Yet the bombing raid did *not* destroy specific military objectives in Guernica: the railroad station, the crucial bridge over the Mundaca River, and a small-arms factory on the outskirts of town. (See Fig. 76 and pp. 165–68 for recollections of the Nazi chief of staff and the very pilots who dropped the bombs.) The Nazi military were unaware of Guernica's historical significance; for them it was an opportunity to test new planes and the effectiveness of incendiary bombs—effective in terrorizing people and destroying towns largely built of wood.[23]

Surprised by outraged reaction in Western Europe and America—countries that were committed to staying out of the conflict—Berlin and Franco's headquarters tried to escape responsibility for the raid. The latter devised the unlikely explanation that the Basques themselves, before evacuating Guernica, had destroyed their historic town as a propaganda move to gain international support.[24] The leftist press in Paris sought to increase French sympathy and involvement by dramatizing the incident with photographs and captions such as these in *L'Humanité*:

> Nothing left to chance in the Fascists' atrocious extermination of the noncombatant population. Well-attended market, full churches, populated quarters, those are the preferred objectives of the murderers. Above, some women—mothers no doubt—slaughtered during the bombardment.

Wildly contradictory stories thus filled the Parisian newspapers while Picasso continued working on the mural that would immortalize the city and make the name *Guernica* symbolize the barbaric destructiveness of war for decades to come.[25]

21. Raymond Carr claimed in *The Spanish Tragedy* (London, 1977), p. 187: "Guernica gave rise to more column inches of bitter controversy than Hiroshima; it inspired poetry and Picasso's most famous painting."

22. Handbills dropped on the Basque cities, quoted by Thomas (1977), p. 616.

23. Hermann Goering, commander in chief of the German air force, admitted during the war-crimes trials that he welcomed the opportunity to test "experimental fighter units, bombers, and anti-aircraft guns . . . under combat conditions" in Spain; he constantly rotated German "volunteers" so that "the personnel, too, might gather a certain amount of experience" (*International Military Tribunal: The Trial of the Major War Criminals* [Nuremberg, 1947–49], vol. IX, pp. 280–81, testimony of 14 March 1946).

24. Soon after Franco troops occupied Guernica on 29 April, foreign correspondents were invited to inspect the alleged effects of arson and dynamiting; the Nationalist pamphlet *Guernica: Being the Official Report* . . . published their findings. For a thorough, essential study of international press and propaganda, see Southworth, *Guernica! Guernica!*

25. See part V about the Vietnam era. Writers on either political side have, indeed, speculated that without Picasso's *Guernica*, the bombing might have become simply one of the many "Fascist atrocities" or incidents in the war (Carr, p. 188).

We have become accustomed to seeing *Guernica* in a museum (fig. 139A) or in reproduction, divorced from the time and place for which it was created. Only by imagining *Guernica* in its intended setting, in the Spanish Pavilion in Paris, at the very height of the Spanish Civil War, can we understand its extraordinary impact at the time.

The official name of the 1937 fair established its theme: International Exposition—Arts and Technology in Modern Life. The various pavilions, flying bright flags, created a festive panorama along the Seine and in the Trocadero gardens with splashing fountains (fig. 79). Here, the Exposition Universelle of 1900 had first attracted Picasso to Paris. Across the Seine stood the Eiffel Tower, historic landmark from the 1889 exposition. In the center of this harmonious vista, however, the two enormous structures of Nazi Germany and Soviet Russia glared at each other like "pretentious stone dragons" (the painter André Lhote's vivid term). The exposition was an international propaganda forum where conflicting ideologies confronted each other even as they clashed on Spanish soil.

79. *The Exposition Universelle.* Photo from *Architectural Forum* (September 1937)

The three rigid, overpowering pilasters of the Nazi pavilion soared to a height of some 117 feet, climaxed by an enormous German imperial eagle clutching a swastika within a laurel wreath (fig. 80).[26] At two million dollars, it was rumored to be the most expensive structure of the exposition. The American architectural historian Henry-Russell Hitchcock considered it "certainly the worst building in Paris," at once reactionary and inhuman in its impossible scale.[27]

The Soviet Pavilion was not quite as monstrous and inhumane. Its bold image was Vera Mukhina's colossal sculpture of stainless steel: a young worker and peasant woman, energetic and windblown, carrying the hammer and sickle of the Soviet revolution (figs. 81A and 81B).[28] This striking confrontation between Nazi Germany and Soviet Russia, recognized as an ominous and prophetic message, haunted visitors to the fair: "It is this militant pair of pavilions that one sees at every turn overshadowing the modest efforts of the more numerous democracies."[29]

One of these was the Spanish Pavilion (figs. 82, 83, 84) not far from the Nazi building. Spain also carried a message to the fairgoers and to the world: a young Republic struggling for its very survival. Sert, the 35-year-old Catalan architect, city planner, and ADLAN chief, was responsible for design and construction assisted by Lluis Lacasa (see p. 198). For practical economy they had assembled the entire pavilion from standard prefabricated elements of readily available commercial materials. The structural steel skeleton remained exposed, trimmed deep red and white. The walls were covered with plywood, textured Celotex, and with gray, corrugated asbestos. The main hall and courtyard were paved with rough cement squares; natural straw matting carpeted the exhibition floors on the two upper levels (figs. 88–92).

The color scheme was kept light and neutral, predominantly light gray and natural straw shades, with occasional deep red and white accents, harmonizing with the landscape surroundings and providing a quiet background for art objects and displays. This simple color scheme and use of unpretentious commercial materials— contrasting with elegant marbles and lavish decorations in many other pavilions— led some observers to conclude that the Spanish Pavilion had remained unfinished: a poignant reminder of a nation at war. Works of modern art of the highest quality, however, inside and around the building more than compensated for the lack of precious materials. The artists freely contributed their work to the Republican cause, although they received necessary supplies and materials. Joan Miró, for instance,

26. Albert Speer, Hitler's architect and designer of the pavilion, observed in his memoirs that the French had deliberately arranged this Nazi-Soviet confrontation. Having discovered secret Russian designs, he could top the Soviet building where "a sculptured pair of figures . . . [was] striding triumphantly toward the German pavilion. I therefore designed a cubic mass, also elevated on stout pillars, which seemed to be checking the onslaught, while from the cornice of my tower an eagle with a swastika in its claws looked down on the Russian sculptures. I received a golden medal for the building; so did my Soviet colleague" (Speer, *Inside the Third Reich* [New York, 1970], p. 81).

27. *Architectural Forum*, September 1937, p. 163. The architectural journals include the best critical and photographic documentation of the exposition.

28. It obviously impressed Picasso very much (see fig. 161 and Hohl's discussion, pp. 314–16). Forty years later, Mukhina's towering sculptural group was still considered exemplary for Communist art since it personified "Soviet society boldly advancing towards its chosen goal and inspired in its march by the ideals of freedom and humanism" (*Art in the Soviet Union* [Leningrad, 1978], p. 23, frontispiece and fig. 98).

29. *Architectural Record*, October 1937, p. 81.

80. *The Nazi Pavilion.* Architect, Albert Speer. Photo from *Exposition Universelle.* Paris, 1937

81A. *The Soviet Pavilion.* Entrance and front view. Architect, Boris M. Iofan. Photo from *Exposition Universelle.* Paris, 1937

81B. *The Soviet Pavilion.* Side view. Architect, Boris M. Iofan. Photo from *Exposition Universelle.* Paris, 1937

83. *The Spanish Pavilion*. Entrance and side; sculpture by Alberto Sánchez. Photo, courtesy Sert

82. *The Spanish Pavilion*. Architect, Josep Lluis Sert. Photo from Kollar Photographic Archives, Paris

85. Julio Gonzalez. *Montserrat*. 1937. Iron, 64″ (162.5 cm) high. Stedelijk Museum, Amsterdam

84. The Spanish Pavilion. Entrance with *Montserrat* by Julio Gonzalez. Photo from Kollar Photographic Archives, Paris

87. Picasso. *Woman with Vase*. Created summer 1933. Cast cement, 86½" (219.7 cm) high. S.135. Photo, courtesy *CdA*

86. Picasso. *Head of a Woman*. Created 1932. Cast cement, 50⅝ x 21½ x 24⅝" (128.5 x 54.5 x 62.5 cm). S.133. Photo, courtesy *CdA*. (Plaster original, Museum of Modern Art, New York; see also No. 157)

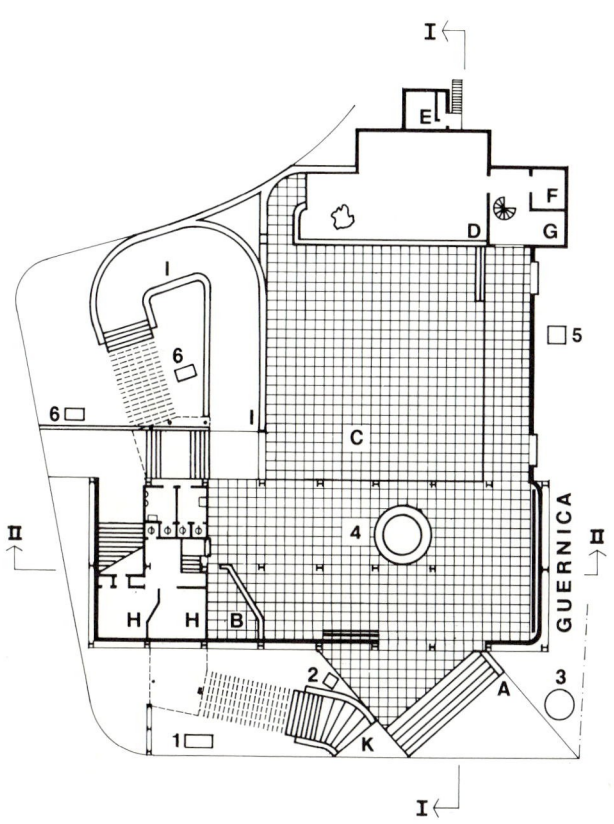

Pavilion:

    A. Main Entrance
    B. Book Sales and Display
    C. Patio–Auditorium
    D. Stage
    E. Projection Booth
    F. Dressing Room
    G. Bar
    H. Administration
    I. Ramp to Third Floor
    K. Main Exit

I & II. Sections I–I & II–II.
    See Fig. 91.

Sculpture:

    1. Picasso, Head of a Woman
    2. Gonzalez, Montserrat
    3. Alberto Sánchez, The Spanish
       People Have a Path Which
       Leads to a Star

    4. Calder, Mercury Fountain
    5. Picasso, Woman with a Vase
    6. Other Sculpture

Scale

88. *Spanish Pavilion*, ground plan. Courtesy Sert; redrawn by Margo Bury

89. *Spanish Pavilion,* interior. Photo, courtesy *CdA*

90. *Spanish Pavilion,* interior. Photo, courtesy Sert

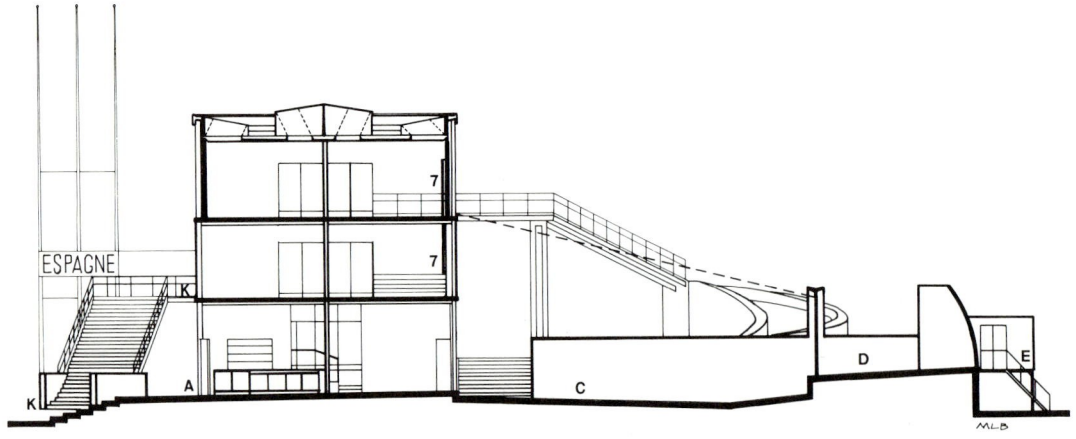

Longitudinal Section I-I

A. Main Entrance
C. Patio — Auditorium
D. Stage
E. Projection Booth
K. Main Exit
M. Floor Ends
N. Interior Stairs

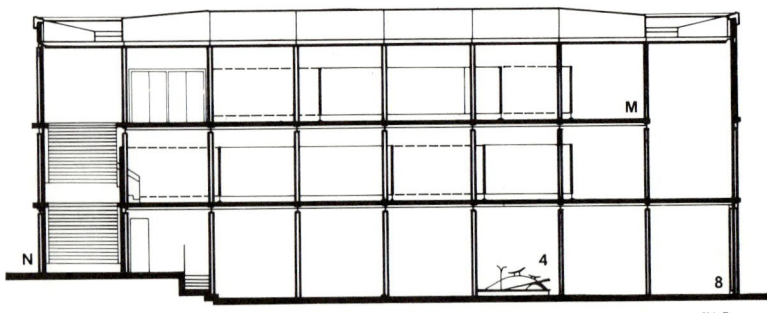

7. Miró, The Reaper
4. Calder, Mercury Fountain
8. Picasso, Guernica

Scale

Transverse Section II – II

91. *Spanish Pavilion*, sections. Design by Margo Bury

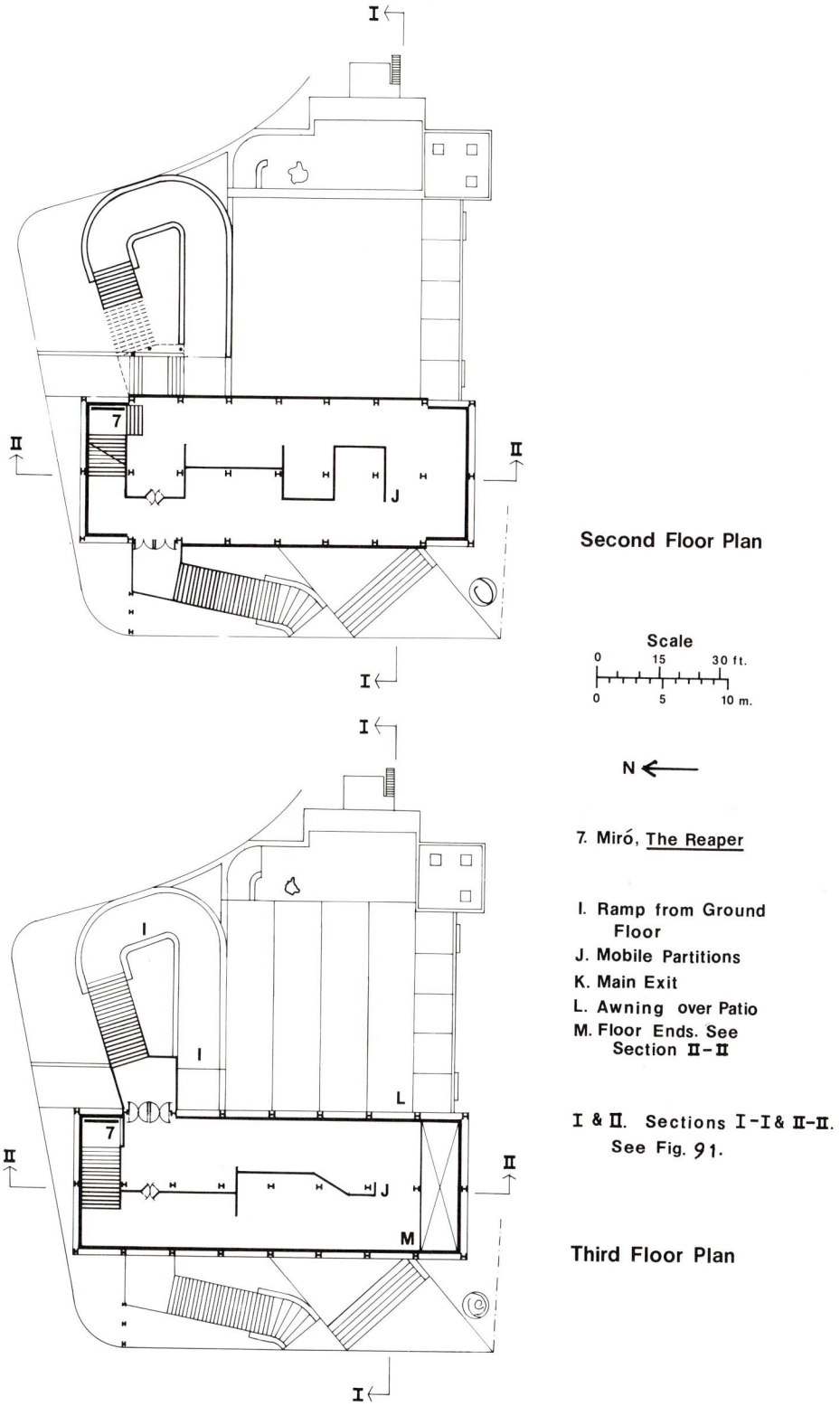

Second Floor Plan

Scale

0   15   30 ft.

0   5   10 m.

N ←

7. Miró, <u>The Reaper</u>

I. Ramp from Ground
   Floor
J. Mobile Partitions
K. Main Exit
L. Awning over Patio
M. Floor Ends. See
   Section II-II

I & II. Sections I-I & II-II.
   See Fig. 91.

Third Floor Plan

92. *Spanish Pavilion,* two upper floors. Courtesy Sert; redrawn by Margo Bury

painted directly on the Celotex paneling (fig. 93A). Picasso, somewhat reluctantly, on 28 May 1937 accepted 150,000 French francs for *Guernica*—roughly $7,000—modest compensation that formalized the Spanish Republic's ownership and certainly paid for the enormous canvas and the buckets of paint needed to cover it.[30]

Visitors approaching the short west side of the pavilion saw photomontages with frank propaganda slogans on the red-and-white facade. To the right of the main entrance loomed Alberto Sánchez's surrealistic totem pole of twisting concrete (fig. 83);[31] to the left, between portico and exit stairs stood the life-size *Montserrat* by Picasso's Catalan friend, Julio Gonzalez (figs. 84 and 85). Named after the revered "serrated mountain" near Barcelona and "Our Lady of Montserrat, Patroness of Catalonia," the structure depicted a proud Spanish peasant, a sickle in her right hand, a heavily gowned baby looking like a defensive shield on her left arm. The *Montserrat*, welded of iron in a deliberately realistic style, was extremely popular with the general public, who easily responded to her direct human appeal.[32]

In contrast to this secular madonna, Picasso's large sculptures must have puzzled visitors, for they lacked any direct reference to the Spanish conflict. In fact, they were inspired by Picasso's voluptuous young mistress Marie-Thérèse and created between 1931 and 1933, "under the sign of Nimba, Baga goddess of fertility"—his

30. Picasso was reluctant to receive *any* remuneration (Fernández-Quintanilla, *La Odisea del "Guernica" de Picasso*, p. 102, and *Guernica–Legado*, appendix 3 (28 May 1937 letter). In fact, Picasso gave more than 400,000 francs to Spanish refugee relief (Barr, p. 212). He could be extremely generous, while at the same time insisting on the highest prices for his work (see William Rubin's observations to Catherine Freedberg, cited in her dissertation, *The Spanish Pavilion at the Paris World's Fair of 1937* (p. 658, note 41).

Sert (in my 1970 interview and 1979 letter) and Larrea (1970 letter) claimed that they could not recall any financial payments. It now appears that Republicans in exile kept an unwritten agreement not to confirm Picasso's remuneration. To publicize the payment could have strengthened Franco's claim that *Guernica* legally belonged to Spain. Reports of Picasso's "symbolic payment" first leaked out in 1970 (Talón, *Arde Guernica*, p. 22). For his *New York Times* article in 1978, Markham telephoned the painter Josep Renau—the Spanish Republic's director-general of fine arts in 1937 and preparator of the pavilion's exhibitions—who confirmed the alleged 150,000-franc payment.

Finally in October 1981 with *Guernica* safely installed in Madrid, Fernández-Quintanilla, the Spanish diplomat who tracked down the actual documents for the disputed payment, published his findings in *La Odisea* (ch. 10, and pp. 194–204; some documents also reprinted in appendixes 3–7, *Guernica–Legado*). Picasso's 150,000 francs, however, represented only 3.5 percent of the roughly 4.3 million francs that the Spanish embassy in Paris spent on cultural and propaganda affairs between October 1936 and May 1937. (The great film director Luis Buñuel, for instance, received 554,000 francs to finance his work.)

31. The 40-foot column, Alberto's most famous piece (everyone called him Alberto), was lost after the fair. Born in 1888, Alberto was trained as a painter, then turned to sculpture with Surrealist influence during the 1930s; after the Franco victory he immigrated to the Soviet Union where he died in 1962. Freedberg includes informative material about this less well-known artist (ch. 4).

32. Gonzalez during the 1930s had been welding some of his most innovative abstract pieces; the semirealistic *Montserrat* in a popularly accessible style thus was a deliberate choice. See the superb exhibition catalogue by Margit Rowell, *Julio Gonzalez* (New York: The Solomon R. Guggenheim Museum, 1983), pp. 166–67. This exhibition also revealed how the *Maternité* theme had fascinated the artist for some 30 years (see the 1906 drawings, figs. 37 and 38, and the 1914–18 painting [fig. 8], and how this theme fused in his imagination with that of the young peasant woman [figs. 86, 87, 90a, 93]). For other good illustrations and discussion of this imagery, and its contribution to the Spanish Pavilion as a "visible rallying point for Republican Spain," see Josephine Withers, *Julio Gonzalez: Sculpture in Iron* (New York, 1978), p. 94, figs. 115–22.

93A. Joan Miró at work on *The Reaper* in the Spanish Pavilion. Photo, courtesy *CdA*

recently acquired African shoulder mask.[33] *The Head of a Woman,* 50 inches tall and elevated even higher on a pedestal near the exit staircase, presented curiously different configurations of head and body parts as one walked around her (figs. 86 and 157). To the thoughtful viewer, however, the piece could express human vitality, sexual and artistic creativity, and an optimistic message for the future. Two large heads and a bust of a woman also stood in the upper exhibition hall of the pavilion.[34] Picasso's other outside piece, an enigmatic and nearly faceless *Woman with a Vase,* guarded the southern wall of the building (fig. 87). Her naked forms are primeval; the irregular deformations and rough surface suggest a weathered icon with a ritual vessel, excavated from some ancient tomb, perhaps even a primitive oil lamp (evoking kinship with *Guernica's* lamp). The figure was especially meaningful for Picasso; she now marks his grave at Vauvenargues. He kept a cast in his personal collection, clearly tagged: "This sculpture belongs to the Spanish Republic."[35]

Immediately inside the airy portico, the visitor faced the large, complex, and puzzling *Guernica* mural that nearly filled the south wall at the right (figs. 88 and 89). Instead of an inspiring call to arms for all to hear, the gray-white and black composition held a terrifying jumble of faces and limbs, massacred animals and human beings, all painted in a difficult modern style. At the left was an information and sales area with a large photograph of Spain's great martyred poet, García Lorca, identified "shot at Granada."[36] For the central area, the American sculptor Alexander Calder constructed an ingenious abstract fountain: mercury not water splashed down chutes and mobile plates into a basin—silvery mercury from the Almadén mines, one of Spain's valuable resources.[37]

From this main entrance hall one walked onto an open patio auditorium (with adjustable awning roof of red-and-white striped canvas for rainy days) where one could watch films, lectures, folk singers and dancers, demonstrations of crafts, and also relax at an informal café bar. A handsome tree retained from the garden site cast decorative shadows against the awning (fig. 90). One reached the top floor, via exit door onto an inclined ramp, to see a permanent art exhibition (including Picasso's

33. William Rubin, *"Primitivism" in 20th-Century Art* (New York, 1984), p. 325 ff. Dates for these monumental sculptures are being revised. The earliest and most naturalistic head (Spies 128) and the *Bust of a Woman* (Spies 131) are related to the painting, *The Sculptor,* dated 7 December 1931. That Picasso completed the third piece, the sexually charged head (Spies 132), and the most monumental of the heads (Spies 133) all within the same month seems unlikely. See *Picasso 1980,* pp. 284–89, for illustrations and dates (also p. 459). In the first edition of his *Sculpture of Picasso,* Spies dated all four: 1932; in his 1983 revision he assigns 1931 to all four. Christa Lichtenstern's *Picasso, "Tête de Femme"* (Frankfurt, 1980) is an intelligent study of the third piece. See also Albert Elsen, "The Many Faces of Picasso's Sculpture," *Art International,* Summer 1969, especially pp. 31–34, and 76.

34. See the fine installation shot in *Architect and Building News,* 13 June 1937, p. 194. The five Picasso sculptures are clearly identified for the first time in ch. 5 of Freedberg's dissertation and book.

35. Illustrated and cited by David Douglas Duncan, *The Silent Studio* (New York, 1976), pp. 20 and 61; see also André Malraux, *Picasso's Mask* (New York, 1974), pp. 242–43, for a poetic description of the grave site. The original cement casts of the largest head and a smaller one are now in the Picasso Museum at Antibes (Dor de la Souchère, *Picasso in Antibes* [New York, 1960], pp. 13, 15, 16). The original plaster of the largest head (fig. 157) is in the Picasso Museum in Paris; the "intermediary plaster" (Spies 133:Ib) is in MoMA, a 1982 gift of Jacqueline Picasso.

36. See Chipp, 1980, p. 108; Freedberg's study (p. 424 and fig. 15), and also p. 177, below.

37. Like Alberto's column, Calder's fountain disappeared after the fair; a reconstructed model and photographs of the 1937 installation were shown in the Whitney Museum's exhibition, "Calder's Universe" (New York, 1976–77). For Calder's analysis of the fountain, see Phyllis Tuchman's master's thesis or her essay, "Alexander Calder's Almaden Mercury Fountain," *Marsyas/Studies in the History of Art,* XVI (1972–73), pp. 97–107.

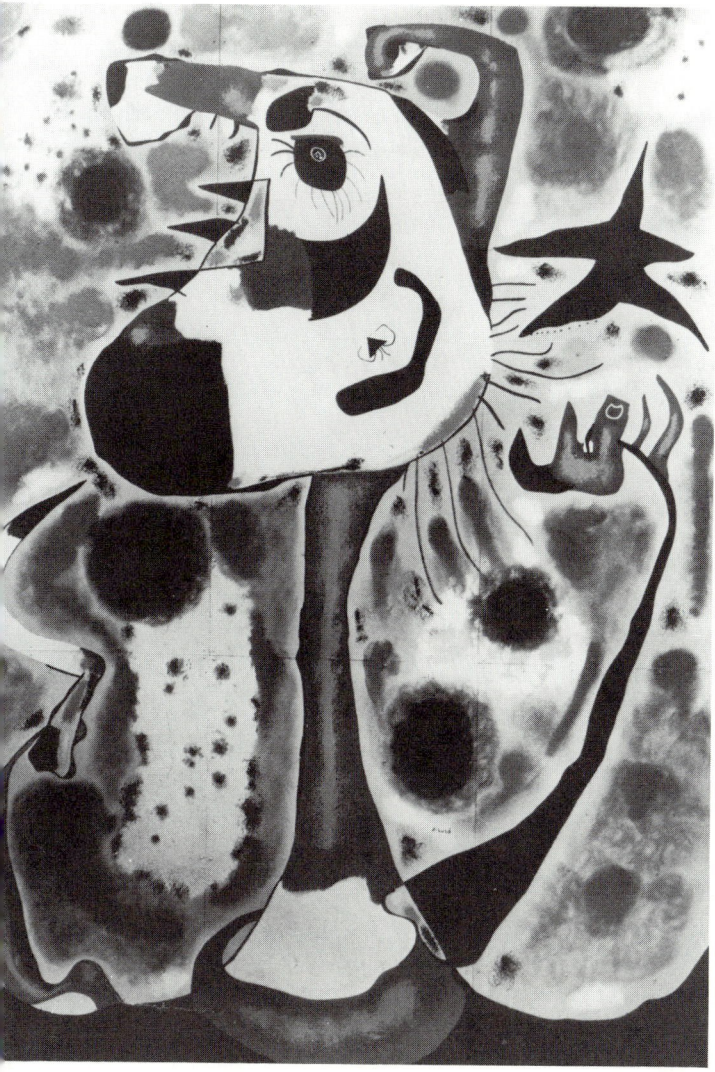

93B. Joan Miró. *The Reaper*. 1937. Mural on Celotex, now lost. Photo, courtesy *CdA*

three sculptures) and changing shows of topical drawings, graphic arts, and posters emphasizing the war. There were local handicrafts and regional products, pottery and folk costumes; the Basque section featured Eluard's poem "The Victory of Guernica," with photographs of the devastated town and its sacred oak tree.

Inside, the stairs led to the middle floor (figs. 91 and 92) whose exhibitions contrasted the Republic's accomplishments in education, social welfare, and industry with effective photomontages of the civil war. Joan Miró's picture, *The Reaper* (fig. 93B) dominated the landing between the two floors. Its brilliant color and semi-abstract figure struck some viewers as pure decoration; others recognized a tormented form with defiantly clenched fist against menacing dark shapes.[38] Like

38. According to James Thrall Soby, the title probably derives from the Catalan song of liberation, "The Reapers" (*Joan Miró* [New York, 1959], p. 88). Miró's mural was yet another casualty of the war. Its colors can be deduced from the contemporaneous *Still Life with Old Shoe*—Miró's sorrowful, explicit image of his war-torn homeland (color plate in Soby, p. 89, and *Miró in the Collection of The Museum of Modern Art* [New York, 1973], p. 72).

Guernica, Miró's painting was ambiguous: a modernistic, decorative panel, yet also an emotional response to the war. And like Picasso (whose *Dream and Lie of Franco* was sold at the information desk), Miró also designed a frankly political color stencil for sale: a huge clenched fist derived from the more abstract *Reaper,* with the clearly lettered message: AIDEZ L'ESPAGNE (Help Spain—fig. 94).

94. Joan Miró. *Aidez l'Espagne.* 1937. Stencil printed in color, 9¾ x 7⅝" (24.8 x 19.4 cm). Photo, courtesy *CdA*

Guernica and much of the art around the Spanish Pavilion featured modernist, semiabstract styles, thereby celebrating individualism and freedom of expression, in marked contrast to the regimented, obvious propaganda art of the Fascist and Soviet pavilions. Miró's handwritten declaration on his poster-flyer opposed the "spent forces" of the Fascists to the "boundless creative will" of the Spanish people.[39] He meant the "present struggle" of the war, but he also spoke for the Spanish Pavilion at its best. Nevertheless, "certain Spanish politico-social authorities" sharply (but not openly) criticized *Guernica,* as "wholly inadequate for the wholesome mentality of the proletariat."[40] Public criticism of *Guernica* would obviously have hurt the Republican cause. But there was noticeable silence in the French Communist press: photographs of *Guernica* were reproduced with a minimum of comment.[41] This explains why

39. "In the present struggle I see, on the Fascist side, spent forces; on the opposite side, the people, whose boundless creative will gives Spain an impetus that will astonish the world."

40. Larrea, p. 72. These political leftists (but esthetic conservatives) considered removing *Guernica* and replacing it the next year with social-realist paintings of the civil war. For financial and political reasons, international plans to reopen the exposition in 1938 were abandoned and the pavilions were dismantled after the fair closed on 25 November 1937. (See also Freedberg's study, chs. 2 and 3.)

41. In covering the opening of the Spanish Pavilion on 12 July, *L'Humanité* merely stated that the crowd "was looking with interest at the big painting by Pablo Picasso, *The Massacre of Guernica . . .*" (the title usually given by the Communist and left-wing press). *Ce Soir* commented that the mural "translates in the astonishing style of its creator what he has termed 'the abominable outrage which the Spanish people are suffering.'"

95. Guernica exhibited at Whitechapel Gallery, London; speaker at opening ceremony (December 1938): Captain Clement Attlee, future prime minister of Labour government. Photo, courtesy Sir Roland Penrose

early admirers of *Guernica* took pains to make the painting accessible to "the proletariat," the construction workers of the pavilion, in fact; and emphasized that ordinary people responded to *Guernica* (pp. 204–205 and 214–15).

Political debates followed *Guernica* wherever Picasso sent it abroad, as fundraiser for Spanish war relief (see Chronology). In 1938, it was shown in London first at the elegant New Burlington Galleries, then at Whitechapel Gallery in the working-class East End (fig. 95), where four times as many admissions were recorded as at the New Burlington Galleries: "The misgivings of those who imagined that Picasso's work would mean nothing to the working classes have proven false," Roland Penrose, organizer of the tour, noted with satisfaction.[42] Nevertheless, the basic question remained, which an American soldier familiar with *Guernica* in New York since 1939 asked Picasso in 1944: "Why do you paint in such a way that your expression is difficult for people to understand?" (p. 149). A decade later, East German critics who saw the painting in West Germany repeated this question, so fundamental to Marxist-Stalinists:

> But why does a great artist, who thinks politically and who had decided to fight politically, paint pictures with political intent that remain ineffectual or work in the wrong direction for the very people to whom they are supposed to say something?[43]

Picasso would have responded as he answered the young American: "I paint this way because it's a result of my thought. I have worked for years to obtain this result. . . . I can't use an ordinary manner just to have the satisfaction of being understood" (p. 149).

☐ ☐ ☐

Having seen *Guernica* in its historical setting and from a visitor's viewpoint, let us now concentrate on the work itself. Picasso carefully dated his preparatory studies, even numbering them sequentially within a day, to document not just "the result of [his] thought," but its very process.

The first compositional study is fascinating and poignant in its shorthand vision (fig. 1). A rapid pencil sketch on blue paper, it already includes the final protagonists: the woman with the lamp, a wounded horse and summarily drawn fallen victims, and the bull with a winged creature on his back. The main horizontals and verticals have been established instantly. As Picasso had observed in 1935, "basically a picture doesn't change, . . . the first 'vision' remains almost intact."[44] Two compositional sketches divide figure 2; the lower clarifies the bull's rider: a tiny Pegasus, winged steed of the poets. Figure 3 suggests "a first return to the kindergarten,"[45] a young child's fantastic scrawls playing with the horse. A beautifully drawn horse

42. *London Bulletin,* January–February 1939, p. 59.

43. Heinz Lüdecke, "Phänomen und Problem Picasso," *Bildende Kunst* 5 (1955), p. 343 [ECO trans.]; the discussion continued through several issues of the magazine into 1956 (p. 400). See part VI for explorations of the Marxist-Leninist debates.

44. P. 143, below, and Arnheim's analysis, p. 286, below.

45. Russell, p. 145. Mary Gedo concludes that the Guernica incident restimulated Picasso's childhood trauma of the 1884 earthquake (see p. 83, below). Curiously, she sees the "airborne" horse in the upper left as "an animated bomber," its "rectangular opening like the bomb bay of an airplane" (*Picasso: Art as Autobiography*, pp. 178–81).

dying in agony follows another childish stick creature (figs. 5 and 4). Picasso summarized the first day's work on a sturdy surface: pencil on wood whitened with gesso (fig. 6). A single dead warrior with classical helmet has replaced many victims; Pegasus leaps from the slashed horse whose screaming head awkwardly joins the bull's hindquarters at center stage. The jumbled composition is emotional but unsuccessful: "much organizing remains to be done."[46]

The next day Picasso continued working on the horse, twice drawing its head with dagger-tongue and extruding teeth, then painting it in oil (figs. 7, 8, 9, followed by undated fig. 11).[47] Again he summarized the day's work on gessoed wood: another transitional composition with the horse's head suddenly lowered in pain (fig. 10 and p. 286 for fuller discussion). After completing eleven drawings and paintings in two days, Picasso rested for five days, perhaps escaped from Paris, gathering strength for his next burst of activity.[48]

On 8 and 9 May, Picasso adopted elongated rectangles of a 5:9 ratio (figs. 12 and 15) closer to the actual canvas (roughly 5:11 proportion). He concentrated on the mother fleeing with her dead infant (figs. 13 and 14), very possibly affected by news reports about Spanish refugees reaching France. Later, this configuration was separated into the falling and stumbling women on the right of the canvas, and the grieving mother on the left. The crucial compositional study of 9 May (fig. 15) recalls specific newspaper reports and photographs of women and victims, and a city aflame; the bull and wheel suggest Guernica's traditional market day. In symbolic protest, clenched fists confront deserted black doorways and jagged house fronts like stage sets. Next, Picasso used colored crayons for a woman and her dead child escaping down a ladder (fig. 17); these primary colors—yellow, green, blue, cadmium red, and magenta—also depict other studies of maternal nightmares and screaming women.[49] One might assume from the dated studies that Picasso again rested between 13 and 20 May, but that was not the case. By 11 May, he had begun painting on the large canvas. He continued drawing, however, working out details for the canvas, or exploring a particular protagonist.

On 11 May, Dora Maar photographed the outlines that Picasso had drawn on a canvas so tall—close to 11'6" by 25'6"—that it had to be slightly tilted (figs. 18 and 77). This was the only dated shot, unfortunately. Nevertheless, the seven photographed states of the work in progress and the preparatory studies that *are* dated provide an extraordinary record of a great artist's creative process and "the metamorphoses of a picture" (Picasso's words, p. 143). On the canvas, Picasso had greatly improved upon the cluttered composition of 9 May (fig. 15). He consolidated the raised arms with clenched fists into one powerful central accent: the defiant anarchist salute adopted by the Spanish Loyalists. Having first retained the frontally facing

---

46. Arnheim, p. 40; cf. Russell p. 151. Even a genius can make inadequate drawings!

47. The decisions by Arnheim (p. 48) and Russell (p. 159) to place the *undated* drawing around the second day's work are convincing.

48. Picasso has explained his working rhythm: "For me, creation first starts by contemplation, and I need long, idle hours of meditation. It is then that I work most" (Simonne Gauthier, "Picasso," *Look* 32 [10 Dec. 1968], p. 38). Some time also must have been spent stretching the big canvas.

49. Before *Guernica–Legado* reproduced all the studies in full color, Arnheim's 1962 frontispiece (our fig. 17) was a rare color plate. It is interesting that after the one colored drawing of a horse (fig. 22), Picasso used these bright crayons only for studies of suffering women (figs. 24, 25, 41–44, 46–48).

bull from the 9 May study, he swung the head around into a more forceful silhouette.[50] He clarified forms that would survive the many changes of the next weeks: for three of the women, the warrior's hand with the splintered sword, and the body of the horse.

In this first photographed state, Picasso outlined in great detail the architectural background, the roof and windows of the burning house, and drew directional lines of almost mathematical precision. He divided the canvas with verticals on either side of the exact center: the hard edge of the house and oil lamp, extending its axis downward, and sending a shaft of light diagonally across the fleeing woman. With several slanting lines on the left, this established the central triangle, a motif that he repeated on either side, with sharp triangles unexpectedly set on their points. Many of these divisions remained throughout the painted states and give *Guernica* its sense of geometry.

Could Picasso have been toying with the classical system of proportions—the golden section—that has fascinated architects from ancient Egypt to Le Corbusier and painters from Leonardo to Seurat and Juan Gris?[51] One does discover forms in *Guernica* that *approximate* golden sections and triangles (as one might find in any large and complex composition) since the $\overset{A}{\cdot}\text{-----}\overset{B}{\cdot}\text{--------}\overset{C}{\cdot}$ ratio is an esthetically satisfying division that artists do discover spontaneously. But one cannot imagine Picasso patiently calculating and measuring golden sections on the *Guernica* canvas or plotting geometric forms with mechanical instruments; neither his temperament nor intuitive working methods were suited to these procedures.

In the second state (fig. 27), Picasso transformed the powerful clenched hand from state I into a "fistful of grain" against a sunflower sun (p. 350, below). Had he retained this central motif, Picasso would have created the symbol that his Marxist critics demanded: a triumphant and hopeful gesture promising ultimate victory to the Loyalist cause and regenerative growth under a Spanish sun. Picasso rejected such an obvious, easily read human symbol. Only the gentlest promise of future life remains in the final painting; growing out of the rubble near the warrior's sword is a tiny flower whose petals were formed from the swollen fingers of a dead woman.[52]

50. These changes prove that Picasso had worked on the canvas before the so-called First State was photographed (cf. Russell, pp. 247 and 251).

51. Although Picasso's absolute lack of interest and schooling in even simple arithmetic is well documented (Penrose [1958], pp. 30–31), he could have known of a recent study, *Le Nombre d'or: les rythmes, les rites* (Paris, 1931, 2 vols.) by Matila Ghyka, a Rumanian naval officer and diplomat in Paris. (Condensed, poorly edited, and translated as *The Geometry of Art and Life* [New York, 1946; Dover paper ed., 1977]; the book is still popular in the classroom and in artists' studios.) See also William I. Homer, *Seurat and the Science of Painting* (Cambridge, Mass., 1964); and William A. Camfield, "Juan Gris and the Golden Section," *Art Bulletin*, March 1965, pp. 128–34—lucid proof with diagrams that Juan Gris was the single artist in the 1912 Section d'Or exhibition "with serious commitment to geometrical proportions." Camfield's article is comprehensible even to mathematical illiterates like myself; the golden section is expressed by these equations: $\frac{AB}{BC} = \frac{BC}{AC} = \frac{0.618}{1.000} = \frac{1.000}{1.618}$.

The author of the latest attempt at "golden-sectioning" *Guernica* (Oriol Anguera, *Guernica al Desnudo* [Barcelona, 1979], p. 55) should have heeded Camfield's caveat that photographic distortions or too-small scale (a crucial point considering *Guernica's* size) can impair proper calculations and that this "complex, flexible system of proportion in the hands of an overzealous investigator can be manipulated to cover almost any thesis" (p. 131).

52. Russell begins his prologue with a detail of this small plant and quotes from T. S. Eliot, *The Waste Land:*

What are the roots that clutch, what branches grow
Out of this stony rubbish?

The raised arm has disappeared in state III (fig. 28) and the solar halo, balanced by a crescent moon on the left, is flattened to an ellipse. The heap of fallen victims is condensed into one figure, turned around, his head facing downwards and overlapping the horse's hoof. Though the head of the horse remains embedded in the cluttered center, its head is turned around and now faces upwards. Beginning with this state and consistently thereafter, Picasso painted flat, angular planes of gray in and around the light triangle in the center, helping to differentiate the entangled limbs and giving the central area its cubistic look.

State IV reveals a crucial change (fig. 37); two drawings of horse's heads, dated 20 May (figs. 31 and 32), have prepared the way for that. Picasso dramatically raised the head of the horse, returning to his initial vision of 1 May. He drew its head and neck in perspective and modeled them as sculptural form, thereby distinguishing them clearly from the surrounding flat shapes and emphasizing the commanding role of the horse. A mortally wounded animal, screaming in agony and rage, has replaced the uplifted arm with clenched fist. Picasso's compositional decisions have effected significant changes in meaning.

State V shows that Picasso continued working on the horse and also refined the woman falling from the burning building with its now schematic flames (fig. 38). The photograph could be dated around 27 May, when Picasso drew the falling man (fig. 40), bearded and resembling the artist's alter ego (p. 147, below).

By state VI (fig. 45) Picasso experimented again with color and textures, reattaching collage elements he had first tried out in state IV: a patterned kerchief, wallpaper gown, and red tears for the running woman. Now the falling woman also received a checkered dress and the grieving mother an ornate wallpaper covering.[53] (I do not believe, however, that Picasso seriously considered disrupting the restrained color scheme expressive of Guernica's somber message.)

A final decisive change in state VII securely dates it around drawings of 3–4 June (figs. 49, 50, 51). Picasso turned up the warrior's head to face the bull. The beautiful dehumanized profile and neatly squared-off neck transform the warrior into a statue and strengthen Guernica's base line. Above, Picasso resolved another spatial problem, turning the area previously filled by the bull's hindquarters into a table, and outlined a shrieking bird (fig. 53) around the light fragment of the bull's shoulder saved from state II. Is this an ordinary kitchen table with all its familiar and comforting associations, or is it a sacrificial altar as in figure 111?[54] Picasso added a single 20th-century detail, a bare electric bulb in a utilitarian ceiling fixture as in a student's

---

53. These collaged elements in states IV and VI (figs. 37 and 45) but not in state V (fig. 38) have become problematic. I have followed the sequence first recorded by Zervos, accepted also by Larrea, Russell, and Arnheim in his 1962 and 1980 editions (while the first paper edition in 1973 brought the two collaged states together [our figs. 38, 37, and 45], perhaps a printer's error). The Prado's Guernica–Legado places the two collaged states together in sequence of our figs. 37, 45, and 38—an acceptable solution. But the two collaged states need not follow each other. Compared to state IV, the slightly higher position of the wallpaper "garment" indeed suggests that Picasso had removed the paper and then attached it anew. And surely the "unveiling ceremony" (pp. 200–203) would have been Picasso's last dramatic gesture.

In the spring of 1938, the collage technique rekindled Picasso's imagination: he constructed the huge (nearly 10 × 15′) design for a tapestry, Women at Their Toilette, filling the studio wall that Guernica had vacated, and despite their bright colors and ostensibly cheerful subject, the gestures and evocative features of the women recall their cousins in Guernica (see color plate in Picasso 1980, p. 357, and Musée Picasso: Catalogue sommaire, p. 29 and p. 123).

54. Cf. Max Raphael, p. 156, and Rubin, p. 350, below, in relation to the Charnel House.

or poet's attic (fig. 96), or a bureaucratic office. The life-enhancing solar disk of state II is degraded into a dangerous light sending off shrapnel rays, an unblinking eye with mechanical pupil—a mockery of the all-seeing eye traditionally signifying the Godhead.[55] The floor also received Picasso's attention. Squared off into a grid pattern that suggests tiles of a kitchen or an outside courtyard, it reinforces the ambiguity of the indoor/outdoor setting while effectively linking *Guernica*'s space with its setting, the cement squares of the pavilion (fig. 89 and p. 319, below). Picasso included a precisely drawn arrow—emblem of Franco's Falangists flattened to the ground?

Guernica now was nearly completed. At an unveiling witnessed by friends, Picasso ceremoniously removed the wallpaper swatches and the last red tear (pp. 201–2). Already by state VII, however, he had introduced painted texture with the hairy pattern of the horse that has suggested newsprint to many observers.[56] He now clothed the grieving woman in a striped skirt and as a final gesture outlined a door with doorknob at the far right—half opening the door to his monumental painting—and the work was finished in that first week in June.[57]

☐ ☐ ☐

96. Picasso. *The Poet's Attic* *(Interieur à la femme endormie)*. 18 December 1936. Oil on canvas, 38 x 51" (97 x 130 cm). Z.VII:309. Perls Galleries, New York

55. The multivalent sun/eye/lamp has produced some imaginative commentary, partly summarized by Russell, p. 324, including the "degraded sun" motif linked to Mithraic rites, first discussed by Penrose (1958), p. 273. Other interesting associations in William Darr, "Images of Eros and Thanatos," p. 343.

56. Dora Maar in a recent interview revealed that she had helped Picasso with these tedious brush strokes (John Richardson, "Your Show of Shows," *New York Review of Books*, 17 July 1980; a perceptive essay, reprinted also in McCully, pp. 278–84).

57. Lydia Gasman interprets the door as an important death symbol in such works as Picasso's *Three Dancers* of 1925, and the doorknob as his "handle" on death, his way of controlling *Guernica*'s disaster (*Mystery, Magic and Love in Picasso, 1925–1938*, pp. 731 and 743). As for Picasso's feelings about finishing, in effect finishing *off* a painting, see p. 351, below. When Alfred Barr asked Picasso how long he had worked on *Guernica*, he was characteristically noncommittal, but a final date of around 4 June is now generally accepted (*Picasso 1980*, p. 342).

During these five weeks of intense creativity, Picasso reached back to draw on his own work as much as he found inspiration in past masters. In his Blue period at the beginning of the century, he had discovered the expressive power of a single dominant color endlessly modulated, just as he voluntarily limited his palette to muted earth tones during his great innovative period of Analytical Cubism. Paintings of the next decades, such as the large *Milliner's Workshop* of 1926 or the intimate *Poet's Attic* of 1936 (fig. 96) anticipate *Guernica*'s grisaille and collage-like forms in the idiom of Synthetic or Biomorphic Cubism. Yet Cubism is only one of the stylistic sources, most evident in the central triangle. Prototypes for the flattened, emotionally distorted figures appear as early as 1907—in Picasso's first breakthrough painting *Les Demoiselles d'Avignon*—and as recently as in his 1925 masterpiece, *The Dance* (or *Three Dancers*). In the earlier 1920s, paintings of exuberantly running women, wildly contorted acrobats, bathers with ballooning limbs, and then a decade later, the classical profile and pliant erotic body of Marie-Thérèse—all of these prepared the way for *Guernica*'s figuration.[58] (Other specific sources will be discussed below.)

After he had finished his work on *Guernica*, Picasso on 7 June took up again his etching plate for the *Dream and Lie of Franco* and filled the four empty spaces with pictures of anguished women with their children (fig. 55) drawn in the expressive style of the *Guernica* studies. The creative momentum carried Picasso well past the summer; in October 1937 he was still painting and etching what Barr termed "postscripts" (figs. 69–74). Even before *Guernica* was finished, however, Picasso improvised on certain themes. Not all drawings are studies for the painting, strictly speaking; some are autonomous works. Especially poignant is the study of 28 May (fig. 42), a mother rushing from a flaming building, her dead child pierced by a huge arrow (the arrow that returns to *Guernica*'s floor?). Picasso glued a wad of hair to the paper, creating a very human level of reality. Picasso twice varied this image for the *Dream and Lie* additions, and also included his other recurring theme, the weeping woman. In the many drawings, the woman's agony is externalized: black, red, or magenta lines scratch out tears streaming down her face or suggest raw, exposed nerve endings. Features and background splotches are scribbled with the colored crayons and the very technique of children's drawings. In this connection, Penrose quoted Picasso's comments upon visiting an exhibition of children's drawings, "When I was their age, I could draw like Raphael, but it took me a lifetime to learn to draw like them."[59]

An elaborate etching with aquatint (figs. 64 and 65), several drawings, watercolors, and oil paintings in full color (figs. 58–62, 66–74), created in June, July, and October 1937, record Picasso's obsession with the weeping woman, tearing at the handkerchief between her teeth, her head covered with a peasant's kerchief or an incongruously fashionable hat associated with the elegant Dora Maar.[60] Intelligent,

---

58. For illustrations, see *Picasso 1980* (note especially pp. 228, 238, 256, 262, 280, 288, 291–93). Frank Russell includes a good discussion of Cubism and Picasso's other styles (p. 288, note 8), terming *Guernica* a kind of encyclopedia of Picasso (p. 289, note 10). See also John Russell on other "pre-echoes" for *Guernica* (*The Meanings of Modern Art*, p. 288).

59. Penrose (1958), p. 275, quoting a 1956 letter by Herbert Read. See pp. 304 and 345, for two modern artists' appreciation of Picasso's drawings.

60. Penrose described how he acquired the most famous of these weeping women (fig. 73) painted the day after Picasso's birthday in 1937 (*Scrap Book* [London and New York, 1981] p. 88, reprinted also by McCully, p. 211). Gedo offers an intriguing clue to the kerchief's significance for Picasso, citing his memories of the traumatic 1884 earthquake: "My mother was wearing a kerchief on her head. I had never seen her like that" (p. 178; quoting Sabartés, *Picasso*, p. 5). At the same time, it is the traditional peasant's kerchief as seen on Gonzalez's *Montserrat* (fig. 85).

sensitive, and politically committed, she was "essentially 'the weeping woman' "[61] for Picasso, and he gave her one of these paintings (a variant of our fig. 61) painted in ghostly white, muted grays, and blue. For his own collection, he retained two later versions of October 1937. The one has entered the Picasso Museum in Paris (fig. 72A), the other (fig. 72B), inherited by his granddaughter Marina, was sold and has brought the *Guernica* legacy to Australia.[62]

And finally in 1944–45, the deportation and death of friends[63] followed by news reports and photographs of horrendous atrocities in Nazi concentration camps forced Picasso once more to respond directly to contemporary events. *The Charnel House* (fig. 167 and p. 348, below) is the great tragic epilogue to *Guernica*. It is again a very large canvas (roughly 6½' by 8'), again painted with somber monochrome in an expressionistic style derived from Cubism, but simpler, more legible, and thus (for some) more successful than *Guernica* (p. 346, below). While *Guernica* was a commissioned public statement, *The Charnel House* was Picasso's private expression of grief. Lacking the former's mystifying symbolism, "the picture shows us nothing but the stark reality of our murderous, suicidal age. . . . a pietà without grief, an entombment without mourners, a requiem without pomp."[64]

□   □   □

In *Guernica*, the human and animal figures are both fact and symbol—sometimes an uneasy combination of the two. They are the subject of this next section. We are closest to reportage and experienced reality with the women at the far right. Having read the newspaper accounts about the fires that swept through Guernica after the bombing, Picasso envisioned a woman frantically trying to escape with her infant down a ladder or falling helplessly from the burning house. At some point, Picasso actually identified with the woman, for even after he had outlined her on the canvas, his surprising study of 27 May (fig. 40) depicts a falling man wearing his favorite striped jersey and the curly beard of the sculptor, one of the artist's surrogates during the 1930s (as in *Minotauromachy* [fig. 165] for instance, or fig. 116).

The woman fleeing below and painfully, clumsily stumbling to her knees also appears to be a realistic figure, yet at the same time may have very personal meanings for Picasso. She flees with her child in several preparatory studies (figs. 12, 13, 14); her cloaked form and heavy breasts have suggested advanced pregnancy to some viewers. Recent proponents of psychobiography may be justified in their claims

61. Dora Maar's *Weeping Woman* (Z.IX:50) was hung together with Penrose's version in the comprehensive Picasso retrospective of 1960 (Arts Council of Great Britain [London], p. 47).

62. For the 18 October 1937 dating of both, see Duncan, *Picasso's Picassos* (p. 225) and color plate 133 for fig. 72A: against a mauve background, grisaille features tortured by black lines and light paint scratched down to the bare canvas. For fig. 72B, see *Marina Picasso*, plate 43, also with unusual color contrasts of soft pink flesh shaded with olive and leaf greens. Sold to the National Gallery of Victoria for Australian $1.6 million, the museum's most valuable painting in August 1986 was held political hostage. So-called Australian "cultural terrorists" intent on achieving greater support for artists and on embarrassing the government, stole the painting and, when officials held firm, returned it unharmed 17 days later.

63. Max Jacob, Picasso's oldest friend from his first years in Paris, on 28 February 1944 was arrested and deported to the French concentration camp at Drancy where he died six days later. The poet Robert Desnos, a member of the French Resistance, lived near Picasso when he was arrested on 22 February 1944, deported to Buchenwald, then to Terezin (Theresienstadt); he died of typhus in June 1945 (Brassaï, pp. 114–15).

64. Penrose (1958), p. 318; he quotes from Barr's concluding phrases (p. 250).

that Picasso here remembered his mother, about to give birth to his sister Lola, during the catastrophic earthquake that rocked Málaga in December 1884. It is not simply the private "exorcism" of a childhood trauma, however: "In his effort to imagine the first massive aerial bombardment on the European continent, Picasso searched his own past for an analogous experience. The metaphor, earthquake-bombing, came naturally to him."[65] After Picasso transferred her dead infant to the mother on the opposite side, he freed her arms to reach out in the classic gesture of grief and supplication (as in fig. 97).[66] No longer simply the victim of the Guernica bombing (or the traumatic earthquake), she became typological, representing all victims, and partaking of a long artistic tradition.

Many historical prototypes with appropriate themes come to mind: Raphael's fresco in the Vatican, *The Fire in the Borgo* (fig. 163), the impassioned figures in Michelangelo's *Last Judgment*, and Guido Reni's *Massacre of the Innocents* (fig. 98)— Guernica as a modern slaughter of the innocents.[67] One also thinks of Poussin's

97. Young woman mourning student shot at Kent State University. May 1970. Photo by John Filo, © Valley News Dispatch, Tarentum, Pa.

65. John O. Jordan, "A Sum of Destructions: Violence, Paternity, and Art in Picasso's 'Guernica,' " p. 6. While both Jordan and Gedo begin with Picasso's vivid recollection of his early "cataclysmic" experience, as told to Sabartés (note 60, above), hers is the more literal-minded and simplistic interpretation of the material.

66. In this famous document of students shot during antiwar protests at Kent State University, the young mourner quite naturally assumes the classic pose immortalized in art.

67. Cf. note 41, above: *The Massacre of Guernica.*

98. Guido Reni. *Massacre of the Innocents*. c. 1611. Oil on canvas, 105½ x 67" (268 x 170 cm). Pinacoteca, Bologna. (Alinari Art Reference Bureau)

several versions of the massacre and his *Rape of the Sabine Women* (figs. 99A and 99B), or of David's sequel, *The Battle of the Romans and Sabines* (fig. 100)—all French masters of the classical tradition whom Picasso admired. Formal and thematic correspondences abound among these paintings with their typical diagonal sweep of dramatic gestures. Heads raised in agony and mouths opened wide also derive from the tragic masks of antiquity or the raving Maenads of ancient Greece (p. 293, below). By quoting these venerable images, Picasso evoked historical and artistic associations that can deepen and enrich our response to *Guernica*.

99A. Nicolas Poussin. *Massacre of the Innocents*. c. 1628–29. Oil on canvas, 57⅞ x 67⅜″ (147 x 171 cm). Musée Condé, Chantilly. Photo Giraudon

99B. Nicolas Poussin. *Rape of the Sabine Women*. c. 1635. Oil on canvas, 61 x 82½″ (154.6 x 210 cm). The Metropolitan Museum of Art, New York. (Harris Brisbane Dick Fund, 1946)

101. Pierre Paul Prud'hon. *Justice and Divine Vengeance Pursuing Crime*. 1808. Oil on canvas, 8′ x 9′7″ (2.44 x 2.92 m). The Louvre, Paris. Photo Giraudon

100. Jacques Louis David. *Battle of the Sabines and Romans*. 1799. Oil on canvas, 12′8″ x 17′ (3.86 x 5.2 m). The Louvre, Paris. Photo Giraudon

Every art lover soon discovers favorite links with older art, and these many sources may all be quite valid,[68] so long as we respect Picasso's basic intent, best expressed in the preparatory studies, his work as a whole, and confirmed by his occasional comments (pp. 148–51, for instance). He obviously did not intend the precise political allegory claimed by some writers,[69] since he carefully removed contemporary clues and strenuously resisted Seckler's political interpretations (p. 148, below). Nor is it likely that Rubens's *Consequences (or Horrors) of War* (fig. 160) provided the paramount inspiration for *Guernica* as is currently being claimed,[70] since we have scant information in the vast Picasso literature that Rubens especially concerned him. Gifted with an extraordinary visual memory, Picasso was the greatest curator of his private "museum without walls"; he freely admitted selecting from past masters whatever suited his purpose.[71] But, surely, that does not mean that he needed an old-master prototype for every single form and image in *Guernica!*[72]

The mother howling to the heavens at the far left shares with her counterpart on the right a painfully elongated neck, distorted profile, jagged eyebrow, tear-drop eyes, and nostrils dislocated in anguish. Here is the most extreme human suffering: a pointed tongue like that of the horse or bellowing bull pierces her open mouth; her shock of hair echoes the horse's tail—all suggesting that her agony reaches an elemental creature level beyond human restraint and endurance. This final version of the many women with injured or dying infants that Picasso tried out in drawings has come to represent all mothers who have sacrificed their children throughout legend and recorded history. This archetypal mother became a favorite protest image

68. See Anthony Blunt's many suggestive comparisons and illustrations, Robert Rosenblum's observations (in *Ingres* [New York, 1967]), and Frank Russell's vividly documented study. One also sees striking analogies between *Guernica* and *War* by Henri Rousseau—an artist whom Picasso knew and admired—but the whereabouts of this impressive painting between 1894 and the 1940s are a mystery (Carolyn Lanchner and William Rubin, *Henri Rousseau* [New York, 1984], p. 70 and note 126). Picasso, however, knew the lithograph of it, published on bright orange paper in *L'Ymagier* of 1895, which he *owned*. I owe this information to Lydia Gasman who studied the former archives of the Société Picasso that belong now to the Musée Picasso; the astonishing wealth and range of Picasso's book collection, when published, will be of the greatest interest to Picasso scholars.

69. Carla Gottlieb in her 1964/65 article in the *Art Journal*, for instance, and, more recently, Eberhard Fisch, *Picasso, Guernica—Eine Interpretation* (Freiburg, Basel, Wien, 1983). Relentlessly, he pursues to their illogical conclusion the similarities between Picasso's 1 May *Guernica* study (fig. 6) and Baldung Grien's 1544 woodcut, *The Bewitched Groom*, discussed by Werner Spies in *Marina Picasso*, pp. 29–31. The witch and her flaming torch becomes Picasso's woman with the lamp—in the final painting—interpreted as destructive fury, Lucifer, and ultimately, the Fascist dive bombers!

70. First suggested with proper qualifications by Masheck (pp. 306–7, below), it has become *Picasso's "Guernica" after Rubens's "Horrors of War"* (Philadelphia: The Art Alliance Press, 1984) by Alice Doumanian Tankard, with a concluding section: "Picasso on the Art Historian's Couch" thrown in; but nowhere does she explain how Picasso came to depend totally on the Rubens painting, in the Palazzo Pitti in Florence, or on an engraving perhaps, which might explain the mirror-image reversal of the protagonists. Yet I have found only two notes that Picasso was interested in Rubens: an early letter of 1897 after he visited the Prado (Cabanne, p. 41) and the old reproduction of an amorous couple (p. 150). Nevertheless, the "Rubens connection" is a current favorite also in Spain (ABC, 23 Oct. 1981; and Santiago Sebastián Lopez, *El Guernica y otras obras de Picasso; Contextos Iconograficos* (Universidad de Murcia, 1984), pp. 94–104.

71. Ashton, p. 51.

72. After I made this comment, I came across Arnheim's sane and succinct review of the books by Fisch and Tankard. He asks what exactly we gain from this "search for antecedents . . . the favorite sport of art historians today" and worries "when we detect a tendency among scholars to take care of an artist and his work and be done with them by referring them back to their forerunners" (*Leonardo* 18/2 [1985], p. 116).

The most extreme example of this quest, with bizarre interpretation of "hidden images" is Mel Becraft's *Picasso's Guernica: Images within Images* (New York: Vantage Press, 1983); ever more idiosyncratic sources have been included in an expanded edition of 1987.

103. François Rude. *La Marseillaise.* *(Departure of the Volunteers of 1792).* 1833–36. Arc de Triomphe, Paris. Stone, approx. 42 x 26' (128 x 79 cm). Photo by H. S. Bryant

102. Frédéric Auguste Bartholdi. *Liberty Enlightening the World.* (Statue of Liberty). 1885. Pont de Grenelle, Paris. Bronze, approx. 37'6" (11.4 m) from base to tip of torch. Photo by M. L. Trachtenberg

DIE FREIHEIT KÄMPFT IN IHREN REIHEN

Nach Delacroix

104. John Heartfield. *Freedom Fights in Their Ranks*. Photomontage published in *Die Volks-Illustrierte* I (Prague), 19 August 1936

of the late 1960s and 1970s, symbolizing the mothers of Southeast Asia at war (fig. 129). She recalls the Christian Mary, the *mater dolorosa* of the *Pietà,* mourning the crucified Christ on her lap. Reference to that tradition, and the contrast with Picasso's secular Madonnas of his youth and of the 1920s (celebrating the birth of his first-born child), give this image its special poignancy.

While these three *Guernica* women exist both as naturalistic figures and as archetypes, the woman with the lamp makes little sense in realistic terms. She thrusts her old-fashioned lamp through the window,[73] "to shed light" on the disastrous scene, to "enlighten" the world. The very words demand symbolical and spiritual interpretation. This woman with the classical profile of a tragic mask functions like a Greek chorus: witness and commentator.[74] As Nemesis—the Greek goddess of vengeance—she recalls an allegorical prototype in the Louvre: Prud'hon's *Justice and Vengeance Pursuing Crime* (fig. 101).[75] She personifies History and Truth,[76] and her light is the beacon of Liberty (fig. 102).[77] She leads the people into battle urging the volunteers into revolutionary war, as *La Marseillaise* (fig. 103) and as *Freedom [She] Fights in Their Ranks* (fig. 104).[78] Picasso surely identified with this woman's symbolic gesture (as in Peter Saul's irreverent variation, fig. 134): he too would bring to light the horrors of war and reveal the truth about the attack on Guernica.

But why are *Guernica's* human protagonists all women?—the fallen warrior-statue (and perhaps the dead infant) being the only male figures. We can find answers in historical fact, in the conventions of symbol and allegory, and in certain consistent traits of Picasso's art. In wartime, women and children and old men were primary victims of air raids (a point that the leftist press regularly emphasized, fig. 78, photo at lower left, and p. 57, above). On the symbolic plane, women traditionally person-ify Liberty and Truth[79] and denote a Greek chorus of witnesses, as our many refer-ences to the art of the past have shown.[80] Finally, Picasso was primarily a painter of women, on whom he projected his greatest joys and anxieties. During the decade preceding *Guernica*—the period of Surrealism and a time when his private life was in great turmoil—Picasso created extraordinary images of his radiant beloved or his tormenting wife Olga transformed into nightmarish apparitions. One may speculate

73. Nonetheless, there was a real prototype: the big kerosene lamp in the Boisgeloup sculpture studio, which lacked electricity (Brassaï, p. 19).

74. See Brendel, p. 294, below. Slightly earlier, the candle had functioned in comparable symbolic ways in Picasso's fantastic bullfights (figs. 108 and 165).

75. Fermigier's telling comparison is persuasive, despite obvious stylistic differences between Picas-so's and Prud'hon's paintings (his fig. 166 and p. 264).

76. See Read and Hohl, especially pp. 218 and 318, below.

77. I am indebted to Marvin Trachtenberg who generously shared his excellent photograph from *The Statue of Liberty* (New York, 1976, fig. 6). Picasso, of course, knew this quarter-scale replica of Bartholdi's *Liberty Enlightening the World* (the original title) near the Pont de Grenelle, beyond the 1937 exposition site.

78. To document his stance at the outbreak of the Spanish Civil War, the German anti-Fascist artist John Heartfield here combined a reproduction of Delacroix's 1830 masterpiece, *Liberty Leading the People,* with recent news photographs of Loyalist fighters.

79. See Marina Warner, *Monuments and Maidens: The Allegory of the Female Form* (New York, 1985) for a fascinating historical and feminist overview, from Liberty, Victory, and Wisdom to *nuda veritas.*

80. Some exceptions from preceding decades: beggars, blind men, and acrobats abound in the Blue and Rose periods; Picasso painted Cubist portraits of male friends, dealers, and musicians; occasional portraits and male figures reappear in his 1920s Neoclassicism.

that *Guernica*'s women exemplify his well-known ambivalence toward women, treating them as "goddesses or doormats,"[81] idealized symbol of maternal or erotic love, or helpless victim.

Of the other human figures, the fallen soldier underwent a startling metamorphosis, and also evokes far-ranging associations: Greek pedimental warriors or academic plaster casts, the sleeping soldier in Grünewald's *Resurrection* of Isenheim, and the dead or dying in Géricault's *Raft of the Medusa* and Delacroix's *Liberty*.[82] In actuality, he could be a Basque militiaman, but his lance and classical helmet (fig. 6) soon transformed him into a casualty of battles throughout history. He conveys a bitter message in the final version: instead of holding a modern rifle, he clutches an ineffectual, splintered wooden sword (fig. 26). He is not even a human soldier, but after the 4 June drawing (fig. 50) he is transformed into a toppled statue. His dismembered limbs echo the classical fragments and disembodied portrait busts that Picasso included in many earlier still lifes (fig. 105). Is it the end of the outmoded academic-

105. Picasso. *Studio with Plaster Head.* Summer 1925. Oil on canvas, 38⅝ x 51⅝" (98 x 131 cm). Z.V:445. The Museum of Modern Art, New York

---

81. Gilot, p. 84. Picasso thus exemplifies a male tendency, observed by Freud, to split love into the sacred and profane, to respect the mother-surrogate and to sexually desire the prostitute ("On the Universal Tendency to Debasement in the Sphere of Love," *Contributions to the Psychology of Love*, II [1912], Freud Standard Edition, vol. 11, p. 183).

Since around the time of Picasso's death, scholars have felt increasingly free to discuss his ambivalence toward women; e.g., the books by Gedo, Fermigier, Cabanne, or the frank studies of *Les Demoiselles d'Avignon* by Leo Steinberg (*Art News*, Sept. and Oct. 1972) and William Rubin (*Art Bulletin*, Dec. 1983).

82. See Russell, pp. 82, 88, and 89; also Proweller's article.

classical tradition or more profoundly, the collapse of civilization as we know it?[83]

The recumbent figure is no less intriguing stylistically. As the archetypal victim, he derived from the heap of sprawling men and women who cluttered up the early compositional studies and *Guernica* states. By 4 June, Picasso dramatically reversed the head and rounded its contours, apparently quoting from an 11th-century manuscript in the Spanish Mozarabic tradition (fig. 106), the Commentary on the Apocalypse from Saint Sever. This treasure of the Bibliothèque Nationale was exhibited from July 1937 through January 1938, hence too late to have inspired *Guernica's* fallen warrior, as has been speculated.[84] But Picasso already knew and admired the Saint Sever Apocalypse and had paraphrased elements from it for his *Crucifixion* of 1930 (fig. 112), having just seen Georges Bataille's illustrated article in *Documents* (1929).[85] Whatever stimulated Picasso to remember the Apocalypse manuscript in 1937—possibly the ongoing exhibition of Catalan art with manuscripts from this same heritage—the flood victim of the Biblical catastrophe provided a fitting detail for Picasso's vision of a modern apocalypse.[86]

With his usual attention to detail, Picasso carefully inscribed strong lines on the palms of each *Guernica* figure, even on the small hands of the dead infant and the

106. *The Flood* from the *Apocalypse of Saint-Sever*. 1028–1072. MS. lat. 8878, fol. 85 recto. 14⅞ x 11" (36.5 x 28 cm). Bibliothèque Nationale, Paris

83. Jordan correctly points out (p. 5) that the principal "bearer and transmitter" of this academic tradition was, of course, Picasso's own father, expanding his frequently impressive psychoanalytical discussion of "Picasso's paternal myth"—played out not only in *Guernica*, but in much of his life and art, in terms of "rebellion and accommodation, innovation and tradition." (Most readers, however, may be unwilling to follow him throughout, especially in his interpretation of the bull.)

84. By Blunt, p. 54, and Decio Gioseffi, *Domus*, October 1966, p. 3. The Saint Sever manuscript is one of eight variations on the Apocalypse of Beatus of Liebana, BN Lat. 8878.

85. See Ruth Kaufmann's convincing arguments.

86. Possibly Picasso's friend Tériade, who reproduced *Guernica* in his first issue of *Verve* (Dec. 1937), discussed his plans to include sumptuous color plates of the Saint Sever manuscript in the second issue.

compressed left hand of the lamp bearer. The open palm of the warrior-statue invites particular scrutiny; it is a curiously displaced right hand at the far left and with outsized fingernails, as well as internal lines. Especially in the preparatory drawing of 4 June (fig. 51), these are not casual or abstract decorative configurations,[87] but simplified and exaggerated renditions of Picasso's right hand, fortunately captured in plaster during the *Guernica* decade.[88] Picasso was fascinated by his hands and recorded them frequently: in these plaster casts and in drawings. In 1936 he imprinted his palm on an etching plate so that one can read the major lines, and in a 1947 photograph he displayed his two open palms as if ready for divination.[89] We know that he was superstitious and that friends of his youth, Max Jacob and Alfred Jarry, and later the Surrealists were fascinated by parapsychology and the occult.[90] In the early 1900s, Max Jacob initiated him into the mysteries of palmistry and foretold his future with comments that were carefully safeguarded in Barcelona and are now in that city's Picasso Museum.[91] A brief exploration of Picasso and palmistry thus is in order.[92]

Around two drawings of Picasso's left hand, Max Jacob first noted some fundamentals of palmistry, then offered several interpretations that no doubt pleased his friend. He observed Picasso's "magnificent" heart line; a prominent Mount of Mercury (below the little finger), indicating intelligence; emphatic lines leading toward the Mount of Apollo (below the ring finger) dedicated to inspiration and the arts; and finally, an unusual cluster of lines joining the strong line of fate or destiny, a "living star" resembling "the first spark of a firework display" that appeared "only in predestined individuals." But Max Jacob also saw a life line ending at age 68 after serious illness—an ominous prophesy that Picasso no doubt remembered as he entered his sixties and in 1943 created his memorable sculpture, the *Death's Head*.[93]

87. Arnheim comments on the "starlike pattern" within a hand that itself "approaches the shape of a regular star pattern" (p. 106). Russell sees "the star of the stigmata" in the painted hand (p. 239; also p. 267).

88. Brassaï, *Picasso and Company*, plate 41; also plates 34–40. Spies has revised his dating of 1943 (1971 edition) for these significant plaster hands to 1937—contemporaneous with *Guernica* (1983 edition: Nos. 220, 220A–C, 221, and 224).

89. The 1936 etching for Eluard's *Barre d'appui* is Bloch 295a. Sabartés reproduces the 1947 photograph (*Picasso: Documents iconographiques* [Geneva, 1954] plate 156); he adds perceptive comments to 1919 drawings of Picasso's hands, plates 123–25.

90. Everyone who knew him well has described Picasso's rituals of superstition (e.g., Penrose, p. 344; Gilot, pp. 230–32); see also Gasman's dissertation, pp. 36–91, and throughout this important study. For Jarry, see Roger Shattuck, *The Banquet Years* (New York, 1961), chapters 7 and 8.

91. Patrick O'Brian in 1976 published a partial translation of Max Jacob's two sheets in his biography, pp. 486–87. They were finally reproduced by Josep Palau i Fabre in *Picasso—The Early Years, 1881–1907* (New York, 1981), p. 326, where he dates them 1902/1903—a period of close friendship between Picasso and Max Jacob. (My quotations come from these two sources.)

92. William Rubin once observed in conversation that it might be rewarding "to read" the palms in *Guernica;* I am glad to have followed his suggestion. For an introduction to the subject, see "palmistry" in *Man, Myth and Magic: The Illustrated Encyclopedia of Mythology, Religion and the Unknown* (New York, London, Toronto, 1983). *Cheiro's Language of the Hand* (pseud. of Count Louis Hamon [1866–1936]), with its clear charts, do-it-yourself instructions, and "Cheiro's" palmistry readings of international celebrities was enormously popular from the 1890s to the 1930s and could have been known in the Picasso circle. A revised edition of 1895 in New York followed the author's first private printing of 1884; editions and printings appeared in rapid succession—the 6th in 1897, 14th in 1910, 25th in 1935.

93. Leo Steinberg imaginatively exploited Max Jacob's ominous prophesy in his essay, "The Skulls of Picasso," included in *Other Criteria: Confrontations with Twentieth-Century Art* (New York, 1972), p. 121 and note 5, reprinted from *Art News*, October 1971. It was the first publication of the palmistry reading.

Significantly, in both the preparatory drawing (fig. 51) and the *Guernica* painting, Picasso straightened out and cut short the life line (the line closest to the thumb, which usually curves around the Mount of Venus). In the drawing, the thumb recalls his own "head-strong thumb,"[94] but in the final painted version, it has shriveled to lifeless proportions. The drawing also includes Picasso's repeated vertical lines that testify to a flow of energy, but are now checked by horizontal bands, especially at the enlarged, isolated index finger (the Finger of Jupiter, said to reveal leadership qualities). Picasso removed these energetic verticals from the painted hand in *Guernica*. The monstrously enlarged ring finger, dedicated to Apollo and the arts, is flabby and bloated in death.

□ □ □

While the human protagonists of *Guernica* embody personal and historical allusions, Picasso's ambiguous animal symbols raise some fundamental problems of interpretation. Seen naturalistically, they could be farm animals since Guernica was an agricultural center with a weekly market reported in progress when the bombing began. But few viewers would stop at this simple-minded explanation (though the bull does look like a good-natured barnyard creature in some sketches, figs. 6, 12, and 15). Rather, commentators identify bull and horse with the *corrida,* Spain's national ritual and fiesta and equate these antagonists of the bullfight with the military opponents of the civil war. To American eyes, especially, the bull was the villain of the piece, symbol of Franco and Fascist brutality; horse and women seemed to fall victim to "the unleashed furies of the bull."[95] Even the Spaniard Marrero saw a "threatening bull" triumphing "over the work of desolation and chaos" (p. 173, above). When Seckler suggested such an interpretation to Picasso in 1944, however, the artist agreed politely that the bull could represent brutality, the horse the people, but he protested strenuously when Seckler argued for Fascist implications in a related still life (fig. 145): "No, the bull is not fascism, but it is brutality and darkness," Picasso explained carefully (p. 148).

Picasso thus lent credence to commentators who associate *Guernica* with the bullfight and its ritual moral drama: the matador, dressed in his sparkling *traje de luces* (suit of light), triumphs with human reason and skill over dark animal forces, over instinct and brute strength of the fighting bull. Such profoundly Spanish meanings were of course in Picasso's blood, and he may consciously have chosen the bull-and-horse imagery as appropriate to the Spanish Pavilion. For *Guernica,* these totemic animals could immediately locate events as taking place in Spain.

Picasso's earliest memories were of his father taking him to bullfights in Málaga; his first drawings of 1890 include a bullfight.[96] Later, however, Picasso transformed the bullfight into an arena where his imagination enjoyed free play and where he

94. Brassaï's comments for plate 41 of the right hand. In his portentous reading of Picasso's left hand, Max Jacob had seen "no strength of will" in the short thumb. Shown Brassaï's photograph (without revealing the subject) a palmist in 1983 volunteered this description: "a real bull thumb." She was convinced that Picasso had made the 4 June 1937 drawing from his right hand and suggested the interpretations I have used.

95. Sidney and Harriet Janis, "Picasso's 'Guernica'—A Film Analysis with Commentary," *Pacific Art Review* 1 (1941–42) p. 22. Ad Reinhardt cited this interpretation from their book, *Picasso—The Recent Years: 1939–1940* (New York, 1946), p. 234, below. For good background material on bulls and bullfights see Marrero.

96. Illustrated in Juan Cirlot, *Picasso: Birth of a Genius* (London, New York, 1972), p. 12, and *Picasso 1980,* pp. 16–17.

107. Picasso. *Gored Horse.* Summer 1917. Charcoal on canvas, 31½ x 40⅝″ (80.2 x 103.3 cm). Museo Picasso, Barcelona

108. Picasso. *Bullfight (Bull Disemboweling a Horse).* Summer 1934. India ink on wood, 12⅜ x 16″ (31.5 x 40.7 cm). Z.VII:215. Musée Picasso, Paris

became "the toreador of painting."[97] He usually omitted human agents altogether and reduced the drama to a struggle between the two animals. It is a very personal vision with strong sexual implications: the fierce black bull attacking, in effect raping, the gentle white horse (fig. 108). After Picasso's visits to Spain, this imagery in 1934–35 recurred with increasing frequency and intensity in his works, thus emerging quite naturally in the first *Guernica* sketches.

But is a bullfight depicted or even suggested in the mural? Is the bull goring the horse? Can he be held responsible for the fallen warrior or the weeping mother? Does he engage in his characteristic attacks anywhere in the preparatory sketches or stages of the mural? Clearly not. Instead, he stands aloof from his traditional foe, the screaming horse, and actually seems to be sheltering the lamenting mother. He remains calm also in the preparatory drawings (except in fig. 10 where he leaps away). Finally, the bullfight does not make sense as a metaphor for the Guernica bombing, as Max Raphael argued persuasively:

> It is possible to interpret the bullfight as the freeing of a society from its brute forces, blind instincts, etc.—a kind of sacrificing of the lower instincts through the intelligence and vigilance of the matadors. The bombing raid, on the contrary, is an attack by blind instinct, by the unredeemed urges of stupidity and brutality.[98]

In contrast to *Guernica*'s ambiguities, the bullfights in *Dream and Lie of Franco* are unmistakable (figs. 109 and 110 and pp. 342–43). Reading from right to left, as the episodes were drawn before the metal plates were reversed for printing, in scene 5 and 14 a vigilant bull attacks a caricatured Franco, embodiment of Fascist stupidity and lower instincts. In the 13th vignette, a noble bull haloed by sun rays confronts a vile, toothy Franco head, crowned to show the general as usurper to the Spanish throne. Here are Picasso's most spontaneous thoughts expressed in January 1937, before he had officially accepted the *Guernica* commission. Throughout these cartoons, the bull is a benevolent and vital image; he stems the onslaught of the *Caudillo* and survives the catastrophies of war depicted in the final scenes. As each vanquished bull in the *corrida* is replaced by a new animal, the bull becomes "the symbol of the enduring force of life, the only power capable of eternal survival."[99] This is indeed the totem, the very soul of Spain, and I believe that this symbolic bull of the etchings is also the bull of *Guernica*.

The studies for the painting confirm such an interpretation. The bull is idealized to "god-like perfection" with a "sublime human head," or represented as "a powerful, imperturbable monument"[100] (figs. 21, 23, 29). In the completed work he maintains this steadfast gaze through human eyes—level eyes not distorted or dislocated like those of other protagonists. They are schematic forms of Picasso's own eyes recognizable from early self-portraits and photographs.[101] Picasso not only delights

97. Ramon Gomez de la Serna, *Cahiers d' Art 7* (1932), pp. 124–25.

98. Raphael, *Demands of Art*, p. 150.

99. Penrose in *Picasso in Retrospect*, p. 170.

100. Arnheim's descriptions, pp. 70, 78. Russell has documented a striking resemblance between this "sublime head" (fig. 23) and Picasso's lovely portrait of Dora Maar (p. 202).

101. Details of the eyes from the 1907 portrait and from the *Guernica* bull dramatized this point on the cover of *Art Journal*, winter 1973–74, the issue that contained Chipp's fine study. See also Penrose, *The Eye of Picasso* (New York, 1967).

in the corrida's evocative imagery, but he has adopted the bull, the emblem of Spain, as his personal totem.

This personal identification provides the key to several otherwise mystifying still lifes with sculpted bull's heads. The features of one such humanized horned beast, painted exactly one week before the Guernica bombing, strikingly resemble Picasso's own; the sculpture often joins other traditional symbols of the artist's world—a candle, book, and palette. When Picasso discussed the *Still Life with Black Bull's Head* (fig. 145), he refused to identify the bull with Fascism, but termed it "brutality and darkness" (p. 148). According to Lydia Gasman, who has analyzed these and others as Spanish Civil War Still Lifes (frequently relating them to specific battles), Picasso believed that through his art he could "magically" affect the outcome of the war. In the black-bull still life, painted when the crucial Battle of the Ebro was beginning, Picasso thus fought with his symbolic weapons against the "brutality and darkness" of the war.[102] Yet we also can see Picasso in that very bull, revealing the dark and brutal strength of his nature. There is no ambiguity in the last and most haunting of these still lifes: now there is only the palette and a pathetic bull's head on a table, within a claustrophobic space and in shadowy grays that anticipate *The Charnel House* (fig. 167). Picasso sadly admitted defeat of the Republican cause, as the final Campaign for Catalonia was to begin in December 1938.[103]

Picasso has not depicted an allegorical bullfight that can be resolved into a logical interpretation without ambiguities. If such were the case, the horse would have to be a malevolent element. As antagonist to the noble bull, the horse could symbolize the Franco forces, as Larrea argued. It is a possible interpretation, since the picador-carrying horse of the *corrida* is not an admirable creature, neither man's agricultural helper nor the aristocratic steed of chivalry. Certain segments of *Dream and Lie of Franco* require this negative reading: Franco arrives on a nasty, sagging horse; toward the end, the radiant bull disembowels an obscene equine creature.

The horse, however, is a multivalent symbol for Picasso. Several horses in the etching bear positive connotations. In Scene 12, a lovely white horse cradles a bleeding man, mirroring the pose of the mother with her wounded child in scene 17; the bearded man recalls Picasso's alter ego, the sculptor, and the Christ-like figure in *Minotauromachy* (fig. 165). Franco's other steeds are winged horses—like Pegasus of the Muses—pursued, vanquished, and arousing our sympathy (scenes 8 and 10). In the second *Guernica* study (fig. 2), Pegasus elegantly rides the bull; in the last composition of 1 May (fig. 6), it escapes from the wounded horse, signifying its

102. See Gasman's chapter XVI, especially pp. 1207–1310. The still life of 19 April 1937, erroneously entitled *Negro Sculpture before a Window,* is reproduced in Barr, p. 198; Duncan includes a related painting of 27 November 1938, *Candlestick, Open Book, Palette and Negro Sculpture,* in color (*Picasso's Picassos,* p. 155). Our black-bull still life, while usually associated with the Spanish Civil War, also could have had a private significance for Picasso. As he was contemplating the slaughter in his native land, he may have thought of that other great war that brought a very personal loss, the death of Apollinaire in November 1918—just as he commemorated the death of Gonzalez in late March 1942 in *Still Life with Steer's Skull* (*Picasso 1980,* p. 372; dated 5 Apr. 1942).

103. Sensitive reproduction of this monochrome painting in Schiff (1985), p. 87; he characterized it "as one of Picasso's saddest works, all the more poignant because of the beauty of the draftsmanship." (Good use of Gasman's interpretation in his introduction, p. 8, and pp. 84, 85, 87.)

109. Picasso. *Dream and Lie of Franco*, I. 8 January 1937. Etching and aquatint, 12⅜ x 16¾" (31.4 x 42.1 cm). B.297; Prado (Casón) 168. Syracuse University Art Collections

110. Picasso. *Dream and Lie of Franco,* II. 8–9 January, 7 June 1937. Etching and aquatint, 12⅜ x 16¾″ (31.4 x 42.1 cm). B.298; Prado (Casón) 169. Syracuse University Art Collections

immortal soul and hence promising future life.[104] Just as Picasso rejected the blatant political imagery tried in early photographed states, he removed Pegasus, symbol of poetic inspiration. References to classical mythology, no doubt, seemed too complex and inappropriate for a public statement. But the spiritual function and even the first position of Pegasus above the bull is assumed by the shadowy bird (fig. 53).

The *Guernica* horse clearly is an agonized creature, viciously attacked by several weapons and suffering multiple wounds. Picasso prepared more studies of the horse than of other figures, concentrating especially on its expressive head. In the final state, it is linked visually to the screaming mother. Picasso revealed to Larrea that the horse generally represented a woman in his life (p. 284, below), and evidence for this meaning abounds in Picasso's surrealistic works such as *Minotauromachy*. Nevertheless, Picasso briefly tried other connotations: the erect phallic neck in figures 2 and 6 has been seen as a male symbol.[105] Whatever it represents specifically, the agonized horse arouses our sympathy and we identify with its suffering—perhaps more keenly and on a more deeply instinctual level than with the women's pain. Lifted in a terrified scream, its head has replaced the raised fists of states II and III (figs. 27 and 28). This embodiment of suffering seemed a truer and more universal image for the central position, and Picasso in state IV (fig. 37) reclaimed the characteristic view he had drawn in the studies (figs. 6–9, 31–32). He emphasized its body with texture and shaded its head and neck into three-dimensional form, unique among the flat silhouettes. The horse's role as artistic and emotional focal point is assured. The horse has become a symbol of the universal victim, and its agonized screams continue to be heard.

The meaning of the bird in *Guernica* is as elusive as that of bull and horse, though it has attracted less critical notice. It appeared already in the first sketch, alighting on the back of the bull. Picasso briefly transformed it into Pegasus with the connotations of artistic imagination and immortality discussed above. In the first photographed state (fig. 18), a bird escapes from the flaming building, another falls among the victims in the lower right. These are soon covered, but in the penultimate state VII (figs. 52 and 53) the bird reappears on a table between bull and horse[106] and shrieks to the heavens from its wide-open beak.

What sort of bird is it? Its dark outlines around a triangular streak of light are difficult to decipher. It does not look like a dove, yet *that* has become a frequent and plausible identification. One thinks of Picasso's father the painter of pigeons, of the prodigy's first drawings and the 1901 *Child Holding a Dove,* of late photographs with Picasso's winged pets.[107] Closer to *Guernica* are the two doves in *Minotauromachy* and the cruelly *Caged Birds* of early 1937. Picasso's most famous bird was the lovely white pigeon, a pet transformed into the celebrated 1949 peace poster (p. 250, below). A *L'Humanité* cartoon of 28 April 1937 shows a peace dove bleeding

---

104. Cf. Arnheim, p. 32, and Russell, p. 151. Might Picasso not have known the verses that Marrero reproduces on p. 55 (without identification, unfortunately)? "Horse that in thirty paces / will die on the sand . . . / Your soul will go flying / while your legs are dying. / Fly, little dead horse! / The soul has no reins, / and the wind no whips / nor the angels spurs."

105. See Runnquist, and Rubin, p. 350, below.

106. Cf. Rubin, *idem,* and Russell, p. 267.

107. For reproductions, see *Picasso 1980,* pp. 16 and 42, and magnificent photographs of Picasso's pets in Duncan, *Goodbye Picasso,* pp. 37, 84, and 85.

111. René Dubosc. "At the New Roman Forum: The Sacrificial Altar." Cartoon published in *L'Humanité,* 28 April 1937

and decapitated on a sacrificial altar prepared by the Fascist dictators (fig. 111).[108] The *Guernica* bird has been similarly politicized into a peace dove.

In the Bible, the dove of the Holy Ghost signifies resurrection and eternal life; the dove that returned to Noah with an olive branch gave proof that the flood had abated, heralding hope and the promise of victory. (Would the *Guernica* bird be a good omen of victory, of Spain's survival?) Picasso outlined the bird in early June, when he recalled the Apocalypse manuscript for his warrior-statue. In the illumination of the Flood (fig. 106), a clearly labeled "Colomba" perches in her olive tree, in the same left-hand area as a similar bird in *Guernica* and in Picasso's *Crucifixion* of 1930 (fig. 112).

The chicken, and especially the cock, interested Picasso first as a barnyard animal, later as sacrificial victim associated with mythic rites.[109] Though not identifiable visually as a cock, the *Guernica* bird may indeed have been one in Picasso's imagination. In February 1938, during the desperate battle for Teruel, Picasso painted a violent, ritualistic *Girl with a Cock,* reportedly symbolizing "the destruction of helpless humanity by the forces of evil."[110] He marked the defeat of Republican Spain in April 1939 with the cruel *Cat and Bird*—the victim remarkably like the *Guernica* bird. In an enigmatic drawing of August 1936 that Picasso kept in his private collection, a large generic bird (most resembling a water fowl, not a bird of prey) holds center stage, comes between a horned creature, a faun (despite the traditional title of Minotaur), and an agitated white horse that seems to trample the bird. It is the triad of *Guernica* animals, reminding us that Picasso's private symbols resonate throughout his art of the mid-1930s.[111]

108. See Tuchman's 1983 article for other cartoons that might have stimulated Picasso.

109. The sun bird—eagle or cock—closely associated with the sacred bull in Mithraic sacrifice, fascinated the Picasso circle; see Penrose (1958), p. 273, and Kaufmann, p. 558; also Campbell, *Creative Mythology,* pp. 216–17.

110. Barr, pp. 212–14 and 265, quoting the sculptor Meric Callery who had acquired the painting from Picasso; though reluctant to sell, he was eager to donate the funds to Spanish war relief. Further illustrations and discussion in Willard E. Misfeldt, "The Theme of the Cock in Picasso's Oeuvre," *Art Journal,* Winter 1968–69, pp. 146–54, 165.

111. Illustrated in *Picasso 1980,* p. 335, below our fig. 116 (both in color), which it resembles stylistically and thematically; the *Cat and Bird* is on p. 363. Gasman sees the bird as Picasso's symbol for his new love, Dora Maar (pp. 1524–26).

Finally, if we let Picasso have the last word about his animal symbolism hoping for precise clarification, we will be disappointed. Asked to resolve several conflicting interpretations, he "explained" his images in characteristic fashion:

> But this bull is a bull and this horse is a horse. There's a sort of bird, too, a chicken or a pigeon, I don't remember now exactly what it is, on a table. And this chicken is a chicken. Sure, they're symbols. But it isn't up to the painter to create symbols; otherwise, it would be better if he wrote them out in so many words instead of painting them. The public who look at the picture must see in the horse and the bull symbols which they interpret as they understand them. There are some animals. These are animals, massacred animals. That's all, so far as I'm concerned. It's up to the public to see what it wants to see.[112]

With these disarmingly simple words, Picasso touched on important truths about art and its symbols, their power to affect each of us differently, according to our life experiences. Picasso was not about to verbalize his intent—even if he had wanted or been able to spell out *Guernica*'s many levels of meaning, from the public/political to the personal and largely subconscious. The enduring magic and power of *Guernica* for many viewers derive from its complex imagery, endlessly suggestive of multiple overlapping, even contradictory, interpretations.

Jimmy Ernst poignantly described how *Guernica* worked its magic on him when he visited his divorced parents in Paris. His initial response was political, having heard about the bombing attack and "having lived in close proximity to terror, violence and hatred" in Hitler's Germany, as teenage son of a Jewish mother and Max Ernst, whom the Nazis had branded "degenerate artist." After repeated viewings, however, the painting touched him at a deeper, more personal level and helped him become reconciled with his painter-father and with painting itself, which he had stubbornly rejected until then:

> It reached into your own secret well of universal recall regardless of the particular history that had brought it about. The artist, all of him, uninhibited by any preconceived dicta of communication, had engaged in an intense projection of his own private language. * * * My father's work unreeled like a kaleidoscope somewhere behind my eyes.[113]

After a picture is finished, Picasso observed in 1935, "it still goes on changing, according to the state of mind of whoever is looking at it" (p. 143, below). Were his feelings about the *Guernica* protagonists, the animals evoking the warring factions in Spain, already ambivalent as he was painting, or did they change with the bloody defeat of the Republic? At least in April 1944, during the relentless Allied bombing of Nazi-occupied Europe that preceded the Normandy invasion, he made this bitter comment:

> I heard a story about a young girl who was hurled against a wall by the explosion of a bomb. She hung there, flattened against the wall, like a bas-relief on a background of blood. All these scenes of horror remind me of the carnage and atrocities of the Spanish Civil War . . . Guernica . . . The Spaniards are alone in their love of violence and cruelty—they love to see it flow, to run; the blood of the horses, the blood of the bulls, the

---

112. From the MoMA Symposium on *Guernica*, pp. 13–14; also Ashton (crucial sentence omitted), p. 155. Barr had requested Kahnweiler to seek Picasso's response to the contradictory interpretations of Seckler and Larrea (pp. 148 and 284, below); when he read Kahnweiler's reply and reassurance, "That is exactly what he said," the audience laughed, of course.

113. *A Not-So-Still Life: A Memoir by Jimmy Ernst* (New York, 1984), pp. 86–90.

blood of men. Whether they are "whites" or "reds," whether it is priests or communists who are tortured and burned there is always the same pleasure in seeing the flow of blood. In that particular realm, there is no one who can top the Spaniards. . . .[114]

Whatever his imagery meant to Picasso, his own work and occasional spoken comments such as these provide our best clues for interpretation. Related drawings, etchings, and paintings—some already cited, others to follow—best illuminate *Guernica's* content.

□ □ □

According to William Rubin, *Guernica's* diverse imagery is unified into a meaningful structure, "resolved into a single harmonious triad" by considering three universal myths or traditions—"the collective archetypal dream symbols in narrative form."[115] These are the Spanish national ritual of the bullfight discussed above, the Christian heritage of the Crucifixion, and the classical Mediterranean myth of the Minotaur.[116]

In 1930 Picasso had painted the *Crucifixion* (fig. 112) with the bright Spanish colors and simplified forms of medieval Catalan frescoes and Mozarabic manuscripts, adding disconcerting apparitions in his skeletal "bone" style. The imagery evokes private nightmares as well as religious experiences of the most primitive kind. Two years later he played Surrealist variations on Grünewald's *Crucifixion* from the Isenheim Altarpiece with a fascinating sequence of drawings.[117] When he began the studies and states of *Guernica*, Picasso clearly drew on this earlier material for iconographic and expressive content, and even for specific details. The broken bodies of the crucified thieves prefigure the *Guernica* victims, the ghostly gray and white of the central Crucifixion announce the grisaille of the mural, the open-jawed screaming head anticipates the horse and grieving women. Furthermore, *Guernica's* tripartite structure resembles a Christian triptych altarpiece: a central Crucifixion and side panels with a *mater dolorossa* on the left and a hysterically grieving Magdalene on the right, her raised arms imploring the heavens. The dying horse, victim of nameless brutality, has replaced Christ on the cross. Picasso has created a secularized Crucifixion.

Amidst the distorted figures of his *Crucifixion*, Picasso has included a tiny, realistically drawn horseman, more picador than Roman centurion, thereby aligning the taurine drama to the Christian one. For a Spaniard it is a familiar association; to this day, bullfights take place on Sundays and on major church holidays. Picasso's priceless definition of a perfect Sunday in the Spanish style was "mass in the morning,

114. Brassaï, p. 116.

115. Rubin, *Dada and Surrealist Art,* pp. 290–309. See also Read and Campbell, part VIII.

116. Writers usually have focused on one or the other theme, whereas Rubin has interrelated them effectively. In his "scenarios" for the *Guernica* drama, Russell has expanded upon Rubin's tripartite schema.

117. Illustrations and detailed discussions by Rubin, Kaufmann, and Penrose (*Picasso in Retrospect,* pp. 182–87); already in his 1958 biography, Penrose had termed the *Crucifixion* an important forerunner of *Guernica* (p. 236). When Picasso visited the Barcelona Museum in 1934, he admired the newly installed Catalan Romanesque frescoes as "an invaluable lesson for the moderns" (from an 8 Sept. 1934 newspaper account reprinted in McCully, p. 189).

112. Picasso. *Crucifixion*. 7 February 1930. Oil on wood, 19¾ x 25⅞" (50 x 65.5 cm). Z.VII:287. Musée Picasso, Paris

113B. Picasso. *Christ as Matador*. 2 March 1959 (XV). Ink and brush, sketch book I, 14½ x 10⅝″ (37 x 27 cm) book size. Z.XVIII:347. Picasso Estate

113A. Picasso. *Christ as Matador*. 2 March 1959 (IX). Ink and brush, sketch book I, 14½ x 10⅝″ (37 x 27 cm) book size. Z.XVIII:342. Picasso Estate

bullfight in the afternoon, whorehouse in the evening."[118] In a private sketchbook of early 1959, Picasso reflected on the peculiarly Spanish association between the two great rituals. The crucified Christ, victim of man's brutality, becomes a matador; using his loincloth to distract the bull, he sides with the stricken horse, victim of animal brutality, its head extended as in *Guernica* (figs. 113A and 113B).[119]

Corrida and Crucifixion, interrelated and sacred to Spain, represent Picasso's native heritage; the Parisian Surrealists introduced him to the Minotaur, the third mythical force that determined *Guernica*'s composition. The legendary beast took charge of Picasso's imagination in 1933, after he had designed the first cover of the elegant new magazine, *Minotaure* (fig. 114). The hybrid creature fascinated the Surrealists: the bull-man stood for irrational forces and the vitality of the creative subconscious. His labyrinth home, designed by the first artist and architect, Daedalus, became a metaphor for the dark secrets of the mind and a mysterious world apart from everyday reality.

Minotaur replaces Harlequin and the sculptor as Picasso's favorite alter ego in works of the 1930s that include memorable self-portraits in disguise. The 1933 charcoal drawing (fig. 115), for instance, hauntingly suggests a human spirit imprisoned behind the bull's mask. The identity of that humanized beast is revealed in an autobiographical painting (and related drawing) of April 1936 that Picasso retained in his personal collection: *Minotaur Moving His House*.[120] Earlier, the mythical creature had appeared helpless and blinded by his love for the little blond girl (Marie-Thérèse) who guides him (fig. 164 and p. 328, below). In several gouache drawings of May 1936, Minotaur is mortally wounded and finally dies, dressed as Harlequin (fig. 116)—a curious melange of private meanings and political gesture like the defiant clenched fist that could make a suitable curtain for Romain Rolland's rousing drama, *Le 14 juillet*.[121]

Picasso climaxed his minotaurean fantasies in 1935 with his large, mystifying etching *Minotauromachy* (fig. 165). It has long been recognized that this important composition adumbrates *Guernica*, that its mirror image (the way Picasso drew it on the metal plate before reversal in printing) prefigures the painting (fig. 117). This

---

118. Gilot, p. 243, with her comment that while he "had no trouble getting along without the first and last of these," the bullfight remained one of his passions. Significantly, Geneviève Laporte begins her memoirs by recalling Picasso's love of bullfighting, which surprised her, considering his feeling for animals (p. 1). He attempted several explanations: that witnessing the survival of a Mithraic cult thrilled him (p. 2, perhaps to impress her?); or that it was a pretty spectacle (p. 78), *Sunshine at Midnight: Memories of Picasso and Cocteau*, trans. and annotated by Douglas Cooper (New York, 1975 [Paris, 1973]).

119. From *Picasso: Toros y Toreros*, facsimile reproductions of three sketchbooks with essay by Georges Boudaille and excellent commentary by the bullfighter Luis Miguel Dominguín (New York, 1961).

120. Illustration and the artist's exasperated explanation to Duncan: "And the horse isn't gored—she's having a baby!" (*Picasso's Picassos*, pp. 86–87). Picasso's household routine was indeed disrupted by 1936: his marriage finally dissolved and Marie-Thérèse gave birth to his first daughter on 5 September 1935. Maya herself provided this corrected birth date for Brigitte Baer (p. 331, note 4, below). See also the exhibition catalogue, *Picasso Intime: Collection Maya Ruiz-Picasso* (Hong Kong Museum of Art, 1982, with delightful, hitherto unpublished Picasso letters).

121. Although it is usually assumed that Picasso simply selected an existing more-or-less appropriate work for the curtain design (Penrose, *Picasso in Retrospect*, p. 192), Daix has hinted at a political struggle between good and evil (p. 265). Sidra Stich has argued convincingly for an exact political interpretation celebrating the recent Popular Front victory in France (like the earlier election results in Spain). She sees the "human barricade" of the bearded elder and radiant youth as "a coalition of defiant figures who boldly confront a bestial menace"—the hybrid bird-man signifying Fascism, with the head of a bird of prey, a vulture or the eagle of the Roman and German empires (*Arts* Magazine, Oct. 1983, p. 115).

115. Picasso. *Bull's Head (Minotaur)*. 1933. Charcoal, 20⅛ x 13⅜" (51 x 34 cm). Z.VIII:137. Musée Picasso, Paris

114. Picasso. Maquette for the cover of *Minotaure*. May 1933. Collage of pencil on paper, corrugated cardboard, silver foil, ribbon, wallpaper painted with gold paint and gouache, paper doily, burnt linen leaves, tacks, and charcoal on wood. 19⅛ x 16⅛" (48.5 x 41 cm). Not in Zervos. The Museum of Modern Art, New York (gift of Mrs. Alexandre P. Rosenberg)

correspondence is of the utmost importance. It suggests that the *Minotauromachy* schema engaged Picasso's psyche at profound levels and that unconscious processes drew Picasso to this familiar composition while he was working on *Guernica*. His first study recalls the etching; then he experimented with alternatives before reverting to the older schema. *Guernica* thus resonates with the many associations that *Minotauromachy* elicits. Interpretations of the etching range from the most personal— Freudian readings of Picasso's anxieties and private life—to the universal, to transformations of ancient Mediterranean mythologies and Jungian archetypes of the collective unconscious (see part VIII).[122]

The protagonists in the two dreams coincide exactly. The bison-headed Minotaur prefigures *Guernica*'s bull, the wounded horses share poses and central positions, the flower-child with candle suggests the woman with the lamp, and the bearded man on the ladder corresponds to the falling woman and to mothers escaping down ladders in preparatory drawings. This man with a white loincloth is often termed Christ-like, an archetypal Wise Man (p. 333, below). He could also be a self-portrait: Picasso's civilized and spiritual self, while the Minotaur is the artist's dark alter ego— brutal, sexually aggressive, vital and creative, at times also pathetic.

The critic Robert Melville compared *Minotauromachy* to a pack of Tarot cards whose separate figures are brought together into a permanent configuration, "separable elements which yet have every appearance of inevitability," and he termed it Picasso's best contribution to collage, "a collage of his own images."[123] The same

116. Picasso. *Composition with Minotaur* (Curtain for *Le 14 juillet* of Romain Rolland). 28 May 1936. India ink with gouache, 17¼ x 21½" (44 x 54.5 cm). Z.VIII:287. Musée Picasso, Paris

122. An important early study of this theme is Runnquist's *Minotauros*. See also Russell's ch. 3, Chipp's first essay, and Gloria K. Fiero, "Picasso's Minotaur," *Art International*, Nov.–Dec. 1983, pp. 20–23 (good illustrations with bibliography).

123. Melville, *View*, 1942, reprinted in Schiff's anthology, p. 92.

117. Picasso. *Minotauromachy* (No. 165) reversed, as drawn, and *Guernica*.

can be said of *Guernica*. Collage-like, *Guernica*'s forms are cut up and recombined into a new composition. Its separate images, symbols, and indeed whole mythologies overlap, are reshuffled, and recombined into a unified structure. Picasso's mythical and imaginary figures, charged with emotion and private meanings, work their magic in the etching and in the great painting as well:

> How can anyone enter into my dreams, my instincts, my desires, my thoughts, which have taken a long time to mature and to come out into the daylight, and above all grasp from them what I have been about—perhaps against my own will? (Picasso, 1935, p. 145, below.)

□ □ □

The fascinating debate, whether or to what extent Picasso was a Surrealist cannot be resolved in this essay.[124] His closest friends were Surrealist poets and he participated in Surrealist manifestations and exhibitions. Yet he carefully explained to Seckler that he was not a Surrealist, that he had "never been out of reality," and was always concerned with "the essence of reality" (p. 149, below). So were the Surrealists. But they expanded their definition of reality to include visions discovered "with the eyes closed," as André Breton demanded.[125]

The Surrealist poets and their ideas affected Picasso profoundly during the *Guernica* decade. The year he created his mythic *Minotauromachy*, Picasso also wrote Surrealist poetry in the best stream-of-consciousness manner—colorful words, evocative phrases, and incongruous metaphors are strung together without interrupting punctuation.[126] A similar poetic outburst provides jarring commentary for his grotesque *Dream and Lie of Franco* (fig. 147B and pp. 184–86), thereby breaking down, "as the Surrealists so passionately longed to do, distinctions between thought, writing and visual imagery."[127] John Golding concludes his perceptive evaluation of Picasso's Surrealism by acknowledging that *Guernica*, as a large public statement inspired by a contemporary event, "militates against much that Surrealism stood for."

> And yet the debt of *Guernica* to Surrealism has perhaps never been sufficiently emphasized. The expressive distortions, the ability to render states of emotions by the use of a few calligraphic markings, the conventions used to evoke grief and horror, these were features of Picasso's art that had been developed during the years of his association with the movement; in the last analysis the work owes as much to the primitive sources of Surrealism as it does to a knowledge of the traditions of classical art. And Picasso's method of work, his ability to think aloud in images, to contradict himself and change his mind in mid-stream, to fuse such a multitude of widely diverse iconographic material in a single work, speak eloquently of the Surrealist experience.[128]

124. Among the best explorations of this topic are by Rubin, Rosenblum (reprinted in Schiff), the essays by Golding and Penrose in *Picasso in Retrospect*.

125. Rubin, *Dada and Surrealist Art*, p. 279.

126. Published in *Cahiers d'Art* 10 (1935) (pp. 49–55, with laudatory essays by André Breton, "Picasso poète"). See also p. 184, below. Gasman's analysis of Picasso's other writings is subtle and perceptive ("The Mourlot Texts" [1941] and *The Four Little Girls* [1968], which have received little critical attention).

127. Golding, p. 119.

128. Ibid., p. 120.

Indeed, Picasso achieved with *Guernica* what the Surrealist poets rarely accomplished: a political stance furthering leftist-revolutionary ideals without compromising his artistic freedom and stylistic integrity (p. 56, above). The bombing of Guernica stimulated Picasso to become totally involved in a historic event. For him it was what Breton celebrated as "the ideal moment in which man is a prey to a particular emotion, is suddenly caught up by the 'stronger than himself,' and thrust, despite his bodily inertia into immortality."[129]

□   □   □

Picasso's *Guernica* floored me. When I saw it first at the Dudensing Gallery, I rushed out, walked about the block three times before coming back to look at it. And then later I used to go to the Modern every day to see it.[130]

Lee Krasner has vividly recaptured that first impact of *Guernica* in New York. She was not alone in selecting Picasso for a survey of "most admired" 20th-century masters. Artists of diverse styles and generations cited *Guernica:* Jack Levine ("the most pivotal single painting"), Jack Youngerman ("it's hard to get around *Guernica,* the epitome of Picasso"), and Seymour Lipton admired its "fusion of form and meaning," its "inventive esthetic structure . . . inseparable from the substance of the reality of our time."[131]

Guernica reached New York at a crucial moment for American artists who were polarized between realism and abstraction. Social realists and admirers of the Mexican muralists expressed their leftist convictions often in conservative styles, while avant-garde abstractionists appeared divorced from the urgent concerns of the age. Critical both of the Mexicans' "cultural provincialism" and the "socially sterile geometric abstractionists,"[132] Stuart Davis adopted a modernist idiom for recognizably contemporary subjects in his WPA projects and public murals. He therefore reacted immediately and enthusiastically to *Guernica,* first reproduced in the 26 July 1937 issue of *Life* magazine, praising it as "one of the greatest formal syntheses in the history of art painting."[133] A decade later, he downgraded Picasso's subject matter ("not a condition for *Guernica's* greatness") while justifying its strength: "Art knocks you out on a physical level, without showing you its Passport. The impact of *Guernica* rests on that basis. The emotional and intellectual concern of Picasso for his Subject are there."[134]

129. Breton's Second Manifesto of Surrealism (1929) quoted by Golding, p. 120. See also *Surrealists on Art,* Lucy R. Lippard, ed. (New York, 1970), pp. 27–35.

130. Grace Glueck, "The 20th-Century Artist Most Admired by Other Artists," *Art News* 75th anniversary issue, November 1977, p. 89. (Dudensing ran the Valentine Gallery.) Other responses to *Guernica's* first showing in New York discussed by Dore Ashton, *The New York School: A Cultural Reckoning* (New York, 1973), p. 102.

131. *Art News,* pp. 90, 103, and 91; Picasso was the most frequently named artist, followed closely by Matisse.

132. From the unpublished notebooks of Davis, quoted by John R. Lane, *Stuart Davis: Art and Art Theory* (New York: The Brooklyn Museum, 1978), notes 29 (entry of 30 Sept. 1937) and 31 (entry of 24 Mar. 1937)

133. Ibid., p. 39, quoting Davis's notation of 29 July 1937, with visual juxtaposition of his 1939 murals and *Guernica.*

134. Statement for the 1947 symposium at the Museum of Modern Art reprinted by Diane Kelder, *Stuart Davis* (New York, 1971), p. 177.

Guernica's impact on Jackson Pollock also was immediate and dramatic. More precisely, the effect of *Dream and Lie of Franco* and the *Guernica* studies, rather than the finished painting, shows in Pollock's 1939–40 drawings that he gave his Jungian psychoanalyst for clues to his inner turmoil, his own dreams and nightmares (figs. 118A and 118B).[135] Pollock's dialogue with *Guernica*-related material extends well into the mid-1940s, as he absorbed Picasso's imagery and, more important, his expressive, often crude and childlike lines, thereby liberating himself for his stylistic breakthrough (fig. 119).[136] Many other artists have admired the painful immediacy and primitive force of Picasso's studies. Robert Motherwell considers them "much greater than the painting itself"; for Walter Bannard, the drawings and Abstract Expressionism "were cousins."[137] Others also have linked Pollock's innovative style

118A. Jackson Pollock. Untitled. c. 1939–40. Pencil and colored pencil on paper, 13 x 10¼" (33 x 26 cm). O'Connor 516. Maxwell Galleries, San Francisco

118B. Jackson Pollock. Untitled. c. 1939–40. Colored pencil on paper, 15 x 11" (38.1 x 27.9 cm). O'Connor 540. Maxwell Galleries, San Francisco

135. *Jackson Pollock: Psychoanalytical Drawings* (New York, 1970); this book by C. L. Wysup and the exhibition at the Whitney Museum in New York were criticized for lack of esthetic value and scholarship, and questionable medical ethics (*New York Times*, 16 Oct. 1970, p. 48). See also the review by Lawrence Alloway reprinted in his *Topics in American Art Since 1945* (New York, 1975), pp. 58–61.

136. *War*, the picture illustrated, is especially indebted to *Guernica* studies. Though later inscribed "1947," it is usually dated 1944. For color illustration, see Bernice Rose, *Jackson Pollock on Paper* (New York, 1969), p. 36; discussion also in her *Jackson Pollock: Drawing into Painting* (New York, 1980), notes 28 and 30, p. 26. Francis V. O'Connor and Eugene V. Thaw, *Jackson Pollock: A Catalogue Raisonné of Paintings, Drawings, and Other Works* (4 vols., New Haven and London, 1978) is an essential reference.

137. Pp. 304 and 345, below. This preference for the direct, intimate mode of drawing—versus the finished, more public painting—is fairly typical of 20th-century taste. Indeed, much painting since Impressionism has assumed the personal touch and "unfinished" look of the sketch.

to earlier Cubism, and consider his breakthrough as important for art of the later 20th century as Cubism had been for the first half.[138] After *Guernica* and the studies, and also *The Charnel House* temporarily for exhibition (p. 139, below), had been sent to Spain, the historic space in the Museum of Modern Art was turned over to the masters of Abstract Expressionism, and Jackson Pollock's magnificent *One* (Number 31, 1950; 8'10" by 17'5½") took over the wall space that *Guernica* had vacated.

Guernica's influence on the generation of Abstract Expressionists is often suggested but difficult to document with precision, except for the drawings just discussed. During the 1930s, John Graham, Arshile Gorky, Lee Krasner, Jackson Pollock, and Willem de Kooning all admired Picasso's work—first in *Cahiers d'Art* reproductions, and then as it was increasingly exhibited in New York. After *Girl before a Mirror*, for instance, was exhibited in 1936 and then acquired by the Museum of Modern Art in 1938, Picasso's curvelinear or biomorphic Cubism appeared in many American paintings (fig. 120, for instance).[139] Similar abstracted forms could also

119. Jackson Pollock. *War.* 1944 (later inscribed 1947). Brush, pen, and black ink, and crayon on paper, 20¾ x 26" (52.7 x 66 cm). O'Connor 765. The Metropolitan Museum of Art, New York (gift of Lee Krasner Pollock)

138. E. A. Carmean, *American Art at Mid-Century: The Subjects of the Artist* (Washington, 1978), pp. 145–47, includes good summary of discussions by Clement Greenberg, William Rubin, and others.
139. See Alloway, "The Biomorphic '40s," in *Topics*, pp. 17–24; also Irving Sandler, *The Triumph of American Painting* (New York, 1970), p. 20.

120. Lee Krasner. *Composition*. 1943. Oil on canvas, 30 x 24" (76.2 x 61 cm). National Museum of American Art, Washington, D.C.

have been derived from *Guernica*, itself an amalgam of Picasso's earlier styles.

After 1928–30, Gorky had virtually apprenticed himself to Picasso and was nicknamed the "Picasso of Washington Square";[140] he represented the younger generation at a panel discussion when *Guernica* was first shown in New York. Gorky may already have reacted to the *Guernica* issue of *Cahiers d'Art* with his *Enigmatic Combat* and the *Khorkom* paintings (1937–38), "but the Picasso influence on them ultimately stems from earlier work."[141]

The New York avant-garde had admired Picasso so much during the 1930s that reaction was inevitable, even necessary to forge a new style. Lee Krasner tells an amusing anecdote about Pollock's ambivalent admiration for this artistic father figure. Hurling a book on Picasso to the ground, he yelled: "God damn it, that guy missed nothing!" She elaborated: "There's no question that he admired Picasso and at the same time competed with him, wanted to go past him."[142]

140. Sandler, p. 47, citing Meyer Schapiro and Harold Rosenberg. Gorky proudly told his future dealer in 1932: "I was *with* Cézanne for a long time, and now naturally I am *with* Picasso" (Julian Levy, *Arshile Gorky* [New York, 1966], p. 56; frequently quoted).

141. Jim M. Jordan and Robert Goldwater, *The Paintings of Arshile Gorky: A Critical Catalogue* (New York and London, 1982); Jordan's note 177, p. 101. Diane Waldman in her *Arshile Gorky: A Retrospective* (New York, 1981) sees *Guernica* in "the clenched fists, contorted face, flame-like forms" of the late work, *They Will Take My Island* (1944; p. 57 and Cat. Nos. 180, 181); her introduction thoroughly surveys Picasso influences on Gorky's various styles.

142. Interview with B. H. Friedman reprinted from *Jackson Pollock: Black and White* (Marlborough-Gerson Gallery, New York, March 1969); the incident happened before 1945 when the couple moved out to the Hamptons. Pollock's library included both 1939 and 1946 editions of Barr's *Picasso*, three other Picasso monographs (Paris, 1928 and 1930; London, 1930), and the Janis book of 1946 (O'Connor's documentation in vol. IV, p. 187 ff.).

The younger Ad Reinhardt honored *Guernica* in his popular didactic/satirical illustrations for the newspaper *P.M.* (fig. 152B) that helped to support him while he forged his abstract painting style. His straightforward treatment of *Guernica*, with perceptive and lyrical descriptions, in January 1947 document Reinhardt's admiration (or at least, respect) for the painting at that time. It is an attitude that he and other modernist artists evidently shared with *P.M.*'s editors and readers who were politically left wing but conservative in matters of art (p. 232, below). By the late 1950s, however, *Guernica* had come to represent a historic masterpiece in a cubist-expressionist style that the younger Americans rejected. But it had been there, in New York, a huge presence, a big canvas that helped inspire ever-larger American paintings.[143] It was a standard of European achievement against which to measure oneself.

Thomas Hess stated it well: "Even if *Guernica* was sneered at, it stuck in the back of the mind." Though it "was generally disliked and virtually ignored . . . nevertheless, the image of those big, torn black shapes must have lived in every artist's subconscious."[144] De Kooning's collages and paintings of 1946–48, for instance, seem indebted to *Guernica*'s flat shapes and distorted anatomies, especially when executed in black and white (fig. 121).[145] Black and white characterized much work around 1950, and though it would appear to be a delayed reaction, *Guernica* may have contributed to this style in artists as diverse as de Kooning, Pollock, Barnett Newman, Robert Motherwell, and Louise Nevelson.[146] Years later, when Newman created his *Stations of the Cross* (1958–66), primarily in black on white, he elucidated this religious cycle by speaking about Picasso's monochrome and thereby revealing, perhaps, why others also favored those somber shades: "In the large tragic theme of this kind, when Picasso does *Guernica*, he cannot do it in color. He does it in black and white and gray."[147]

Motherwell's *Elegies to the Spanish Republic* are so frequently linked to *Guernica* that the artist, doubtless tired of the comparison, has categorically denied the connection: "They [*Guernica* and Miró's *Still Life with Old Shoe*] simply exercised no influence, period."[148] The origins of Motherwell's celebrated image (fig. 122)—

143. For a connection between *Guernica* and the increasing size of American canvases, see Eugene Goossen, "The Big Canvas," *Art International*, November 1958; and William Rubin, "Jackson Pollock and the Modern Tradition," *Artforum*, March 1967, pp. 34–36, where he also stresses "affinities with the late Monet."

144. Thomas B. Hess, *Barnett Newman* (New York, 1971), pp. 68 and 60.

145. Other examples in Hess, *Willem de Kooning* (New York, 1968), pp. 48–49, 52–61; see also Lawrence Alloway, "Sign and Surface: Notes on Black and White Painting in New York," *Quadrum* 9, (1960), p. 51. When Selden Rodman visited de Kooning's studio in 1956, he saw a *Guernica* postcard amidst piles of magazines, scraps of drawings, and beer cans (*Conversations with Artists* [New York, 1957], p. 101).

146. David S. Rubin surveys *Guernica*'s role in the catalogue, *Black and White Are Colors: Paintings of the 1950s–1970s* (Claremont, CA, 1979), pp. 9–13; good use of sources. Questioned about *Guernica*'s effect on Pollock's black drawings/paintings, Lee Krasner commented, "If so, it was an awfully slow burn—say, twenty years" (Friedman interview, note 142, above). Louise Nevelson's preference for painting her wood constructions black, white (and gold) might even be traced to *Guernica*: "I really feel that it touched me as any creative painting. Now, why? First, the color. Black, gray, and white. And then the way he used form." See Nevelson, *Dawns + Dusks* (taped conversations with Diana MacKown [New York, 1976], p. 68).

147. Hess, *Newman*, p. 100, from "Conversation" of 1966.

148. From an October 1977 conversation with E. A. Carmean, quoted in his admirable essay on the elegies in *American Art at Mid-Century*, p. 101.

121. Willem de Kooning. *Painting.* 1948. Enamel and oil on canvas, 42⅝ x 56⅛″ (108.2 x 142.5 cm). The Museum of Modern Art, New York (Purchase Fund)

122. Robert Motherwell. *Elegy to the Spanish Republic, 70.* 1961. Oil on canvas, 69 x 114″ (175.3 × 289.6 cm). The Metropolitan Museum of Art, New York (anonymous gift)

explored throughout his life, in close to 150 variations—partly justify his denial. It began as "linear automatism," a structured doodle to decorate (not illustrate) an unpublished poem by Harold Rosenberg in 1948. When Motherwell enlarged his *Ink Sketch* a year later, it reminded him of a temple, which he dedicated to García Lorca and his masterful "Lament" (pp. 177–83), and christened it *At Five in the Afternoon* (1949). "To be more concise," he explained, "the 'temple' was consecrated to a Spanish sense of death, which I got most of from Lorca, but from other sources as well."[149] Motherwell had come of age, turned 21, when the Spanish Civil War broke out; he heard André Malraux speak in San Francisco at a fund-raising rally for the Spanish Republic, and became deeply involved. Yet the *Elegies* developed a full decade after this Liberal cause was lost—hence the image must have expressed profoundly personal meanings over the years. Again, the artist himself states it best:

> The "Spanish Elegies" are not "political" but my private insistence that a terrible death happened that should not be forgot. They are as eloquent as I could make them. But the pictures are also general metaphors of the contrast between life and death, and their interrelation.[150]

Guernica may not have influenced the *Elegies* directly, but the comparison is inevitable; they relate to the same Spanish conflict, and invoke the struggle between life and death with their looming shapes and light-and-dark contrasts. To our contemporary sensibility, to Motherwell himself, the effect of his art is "more tragic, Picasso's more melodramatic."[151] A persuasive argument is that Motherwell was making a critique of *Guernica*, interpreting it "in a more abstract format." Indeed, each of the younger Americans with their monumental black-and-white paintings may have been trying "to make *Guernica* over in his own image."[152]

In contrast to these avant-garde painters, many realist and figurative artists saw *Guernica* as an exemplar. Ben Shahn frequently praised *Guernica* in conversation,[153] but there was no specific influence. We see his characteristic expressive style already in 1931–32, in his famous studies of the Sacco-Vanzetti case. An artist also might return to a figurative mode in order to convey a political message to a wider public. The sculptor David Smith, for instance—close friend of Pollock's and Motherwell's later in life—by 1939–40 already had created impressive abstract pieces, yet he undertook a unique essay of social protest: "a series of medallions which were against the perils or evils of war, against inhuman things."[154] He developed his Medals for

149. Ibid., p. 98, from a conversation of 17 August 1977.

150. From "A Conversation at Lunch," Smith College, January 1963, reproduced in Frank O'Hara, *Robert Motherwell* (New York, 1965), p. 54.

151. From Motherwell's letter to me, 10 June 1974. He was describing a slide lecture that compared *Guernica* and his *Elegy No. 70* in the Metropolitan Museum (fig. 122), one of his personal favorites, as are the versions in the Cleveland Museum and in Buffalo's Albright-Knox Art Gallery.

152. Observations by Robert Hobbs in his Ph.D. dissertation, "Motherwell's Concern with Death in Painting" (1975), pp. 233–34, as quoted by Carmean, note 30, p. 120. See also Bradford R. Collins, "The Fundamental Tragedy of the *Elegies to the Spanish Republic,* or Robert Motherwell's Dilemma," *Arts Magazine,* September 1984, pp. 94–97.

153. Rodman,*Conversations,* pp. 223, 228. During the 1947 *Guernica* symposium at MoMA, Shahn admitted that *Guernica* might be an interesting painting, but condemned it as a poster and piece of propaganda for mass use—much to the delight of the audience (MoMA typescript, pp. 73 and 74).

154. *David Smith by David Smith,* Cleve Gray, ed. (New York, 1968), pp. 27 and 61, from autobiographical notebooks.

123. David Smith. *Medals for Dishonor: Propaganda for War.* 1939–40. Bronze, 9½ x 11⅜ x ⅞″ (23.8 x 28.9 x 2.24 cm). Hirshhorn Museum and Sculpture Garden, Washington, D.C.

124. Louis Hechenbleikner. *The War, Plate II: Europe.* 1945. Wood engraving, 9¼ x 13⅜″ (23.5 x 34 cm). Library of Congress, Washington, D.C. (First Purchase Prize, 1945)

Dishonor from an astonishing range of sources: German propaganda medallions of 1914–18 seen in the British Museum, Sumerian cylinder seals, classical Greek coins, and American comics. The bullfight imagery of the *Medal for Dishonor: Propaganda for War* (fig. 123) also recalls Goya and Picasso's *Dream and Lie of Franco*. Like Picasso, Smith added poetic commentary to his preparatory drawings and for the exhibition catalogue: "The speakers part the mind and offer red apples while Radio parts the ether with shrieks and emotional bombings."[155] By the end of the war, *Guernica* had become so familiar, through reproductions and constant traveling exhibitions, that an artist could simply quote its imagery to signify the war in Europe (fig. 124).[156]

Rico Lebrun also needed to come to terms with the recent war, with "the constantly repeated history of man's blindness and inhumanity."[157] After drawing and painting some 200 variations on the Crucifixion theme from 1948 to 1950, he rapidly completed a huge triptych (fig. 125A, really a Deposition) in six weeks—just over

125A. Rico Lebrun. *Crucifixion (Deposition)*. 1950. Triptych, Duco on Upson board, 16 x 26' (4.88 x 7.93 m). Syracuse University Art Collections

155. Ibid., p. 30. See also *Medals for Dishonor* exhibition catalogue (Willard Gallery, NYC, Nov. 1940), and a superb analysis by Rosalind Krauss; cf. p. 276, below.

156. The Austrian-born artist, Louis Hechenbleikner (1893–1983), was trained in Düsseldorf and Munich, specialized in printmaking, and taught at Queens College, New York, from 1939 to his retirement in 1963.

157. James Thrall Soby, quoting the artist in *Rico Lebrun Drawings* (Berkeley, California, 1960), p. iv. Born 1900 in Naples, Lebrun immigrated to America in 1924, lived in New York, then California—where he probably saw *Guernica* on its 1939 tour (see Chronology).

the time that Picasso spent on *Guernica*. In scale and proportions the triptych's horizontal section, 11'4" by 26 feet, nearly duplicates *Guernica*'s dimensions (11'5½" by 25'5¾"); the central panels extend to a height of 16 feet. The gray/black/brown tonalities, cubistic planes, and expressionist distortions—even specific figures—quote *Guernica* (the sleeping soldier on the left, the horse on the right). The Calvary cycle provided Rico Lebrun with a traditional narrative framework familiar to the widest public. Formal allusions to Picasso's modern antiwar statement forced the viewer to experience his *Crucifixion* within a 20th-century context.[158]

Guernica, in effect, is replacing the Crucifixion as an icon of cruelty and inhumanity for our secular age. And just as Picasso enriched his painting with multiple references to Christian and classical imagery, certain artists have set an emotional tone and suggested levels of meaning by quoting or subtly referring to *Guernica*. The

125B. Rico Lebrun. *Figures at the Cross*. 1950. Charcoal on Upson board. 60 x 40" (152 x 102 cm). Syracuse University Art Collections

158. The Crucifixion cycle includes paintings of machine guns and burning tanks. Lebrun freely acknowledged *Guernica*'s influence and kept a reproduction of it, worn with handling and push pins, in his studio. He was impressed by its power to reach common people: "My sister tells me that there is a reproduction of it in home after home in Italy" (interview, *Art Digest*, 1 May 1951). See Ellen C. Oppler, *Rico Lebrun: Transformations/Transfiguration*, exhibition catalogue (Syracuse University, 1983), especially pp. 8–9.

Italian Communist Renato Guttuso, for instance, in *The Triumph of War* (1966, fig. 126) featured the *Guernica* horse amidst helmeted monsters and splintery forms suggesting bayonets and shrapnel; it is a more appropriate homage than his Picasso banquet of 1975 where awkwardly literal quotations from Picasso's famous paintings surround a photographic likeness of the master.[159]

Rudolf Baranik, an American artist of strong social and political convictions who rejects simple, realistic protest art, often cites *Guernica*.[160] His *Napalm Elegies* of 1969–74 (fig. 127) evolved from his personal, poetic works of the 1950s (*White*

126. Renato Guttuso. *The Triumph of War*. 1966. Oil on canvas, 52¾ x 74″ (135 x 190 cm). Galleria Toninelli, Milan

159. For background on this primarily socialist-realist artist and long-time admirer of Picasso's, see Egbert, *Social Radicalism*, pp. 693–97; more recent work is illustrated in exhibition catalogues: *Guttuso* (Paris, 1971; Berlin, 1972; Frankfurt, 1975).

160. In lectures and conversation. Born 1920 in Lithuania, Baranik first saw *Guernica* in 1939, just after immigrating to Chicago, and again in 1948 in New York, after military service abroad; for years, a reproduction hung in his studio.

Silence or *Black Sleep*). They incorporate photostat and newspaper collages of Vietnam victims, evoking memories of other victims: the petrified corpses of Pompeii and of *Guernica:*

> *Guernica* was topical-timely, but even then one sensed its timeless quality. . . . The sound Guernica does not evoke any more the small Basque town bombarded by the Luftwaffe. Instead, these three syllables, an outcry, carry a meaning transcending the specific. Napalm is more than a jelly substance used by the U.S. Air Force in Viet Nam. . . .[161]

When Baranik wanted to make an obvious "topical-timely" statement he designed antiwar posters with *Guernica*'s fallen warrior (figs. 128A and 128B).

By the 1960s and 1970s, *Guernica* was familiar to an ever-widening American public. It is still a popular reproduction, sold poster-size, on college campuses. Its associative powers, instantly suggesting unjust wars and terror bombings, worked effectively in protest art, posters, and actual demonstrations against U.S. involvement in Vietnam (figs. 129, 154, 155 and pp. 236–43). The simplified, cartoon-like figures that antagonized the Abstract Expressionists endeared *Guernica* to the Pop generation.[162] Its well-known composition could be adapted, and bring profounder asso-

127. Rudolf Baranik. *Napalm Elegy White Silence*. 1970. Oil and collage on canvas, 70 x 80" (179.5 × 205 cm). Collection of the artist

161. From interview with Irving Sandler, in Rudolf Baranik, *Napalm Elegy* (Rutgers, N.J., 1973), pp. 11–12.

162. Adolph Gottlieb commented: "Esthetically I am jarred by the disemboweled horse and by the figure gesturing to the sky . . ." (Rodman, *Conversations*, p. 89); Ad Reinhardt in 1967 still spoke for his generation by likening *Guernica* to cartoons, p. 237, below.

128A. Rudolf Baranik. *Angry Arts Against the War in Vietnam.* 1967 poster, 25¼ x 20½″ (64.1 x 52 cm). Collection of the artist

128B. Rudolf Baranik. *Stop the War in Vietnam Now!* 1967 poster, 19 x 28¼″ (48.2 x 71.8 cm). Collection of the artist

129. Pat Conant. *The Great Society*. 1967. Gesso-cut print, artist's proof, 18 x 21" (45.7 x 54 cm). E. C. Oppler collection

ciations to topical cartoons: *Guernixa*, brilliantly spoofing the Nixon administration's Watergate coverup (fig. 130),[163] or the joyous celebration of democratic elections in Spain (fig. 131), quite literally the dawn of a new era, with Franco at last the fallen warrior and all other protagonists grinning broadly.

163. The personages of *National Lampoon*'s "Surprise Poster #6," May 1974: Former President Nixon hides Trojan-horse fashion; his former Vice-President Agnew is the woman with the lamp-telephone; an imperturbable, pipe-smoking bull / former Attorney General Mitchell; his wife Martha Mitchell as horse, forever telephoning; Presidential secretary Rosemary Woods hopelessly tangled up in dictaphone tapes; hidden microphones everywhere; fallen-warrior / Presidential counsel John Dean; White House staffer John Ehrlichman dragging a foot-in-mouth Magruder. Undoubtedly there are numerous other cartoons: the French journal *Lui* in April 1971 derided Franco's appointing Prince Juan Carlos as his successor, shown rising from a pyre of *Guernica* fragments; President Reagan's slashing budget cuts were cartooned into *Guernica* scaffolding (*Washington Post*, 7 March 1981).

124

131. Eugène Mihaesco. *VOTE.* 1977. Crayon drawing, 4⁵⁄₁₆ x 10⅛" (11 x 25.5 cm). Published in *The New York Times,* "The Week in Review," 19 June 1977. Courtesy Mihaesco

130. Randall Enos. *Guernixa (Surprise Poster No. 6).* Published in *National Lampoon,* May 1974

125

132. Josep Guinovart. *Operación Retorno*. 1970. Whereabouts unknown.

Franco's ill-advised attempts to "repatriate *Guernica*" (pp. 153–55) fairly demanded lampooning, and Spanish artists rose to the occasion. The Catalan Josep Guinovart in 1967 and 1970 had fabricated mixed-media constructions (*Homage to Picasso* with *Guernica* references); in *Operación Retorno* (fig. 132, also of 1970) he decried the painting's political manipulation and commercialization. He scattered cutout *Guernica* figures across the land as vivid advertisements, the bull transformed into the ubiquitous sign for Spanish cognac; a distant billboard demands, "Buy your GUERNICA."[164]

Two young artists from Valencia, who have been collaborating since 1964 as an artistic/political "chronicling team" (signing their work, Equipo Crónica), painted eight variations on *Guernica*'s attempted "recovery." Despite their banal Pop style, they are provocative political commentators: *Guernica* fragments are strewn along a field, are dished up banquet-style, serve for target practice, drip blood on pristine wall socles, or break through commercial coverup packaging;[165] leaping off the canvas and thrusting the lamp (of liberty and truth) toward an official delegation, they protest this *Visit* (fig. 133) to the prison-like museum.

164. Born 1927 in Barcelona, Guinovart already showed considerable political courage in 1951 with eight etchings for a limited-edition *Homage to García Lorca*. See Cesáreo Rodríguez-Aguilera, *Guinovart* (Madrid, 1971), for reproductions, and the World of *Josep Guinovart* (Fine Arts Museum of Long Island, New York, 1987).

165. The *Guernica* sequence (1969–70) by Rafael Solbes (b. 1940) and Manuel Valdés (b. 1942) is fully illustrated in Thomas Llorens, *Equipo Crónica* (Barcelona, 1972); also in *Guernica* (Berlin, 1975), with perceptive commentary, pp. 70–71, 77–80.

133. Equipo Crónica. *The Visit*. 1969. Acrylic on canvas, 47¼ x 47¼" (122 x 122 cm). Private collection, Spain

For these Pop artists, *Guernica* belongs to everyday visual experience, accessible through the mass media. Like the cityscape and commercial products of our industrial age, it is their raw material, fair game for artistic improvisation. Indeed, some feel that this overexposed image needs recharging and that the viewer must be shocked into seeing it anew, either as a work of art or as a political statement. Shocking, indeed, are Peter Saul's lurid, fluorescent colors and pneumatic forms (fig. 134), whereby he has "updated" *Guernica*. He considered it "Pop Art, before Pop," and "helped [Picasso's] picture to be interesting to us now by giving it my style," he modestly explained.[166]

Another California artist of that same generation,[167] Tom Marioni, applied his particular talents—as minimalist sculptor turned performance and installation artist—to make American viewers experience *Guernica* anew, after the painting had left for Spain.[168] He taught his students how to enlarge a photograph of *Guernica* to full scale for an exhibition that they organized, "Art Against War," to open on 26 April 1983, anniversary of the Guernica bombing. Incorporating this group project,

134. Peter Saul. *Liddul Gurnica*. 1973. Acrylic on canvas, 72 x 121" (182.9 x 307.3 cm). Photo by Ric Pollitzer, courtesy Allan Frumkin Gallery

166. Peter Saul in Jean Lipman and Richard Marshall, *Art about Art* (New York, 1978), p. 122. There are two versions by the California painter (born 1934): *Saul's Guernica* preceded *Liddul Gurnica*. Note the comic-style labels: "Paablow" carrying the torch of "cooobizzm" near the lamp of "inspeer a shun."

167. In a 1984 letter to me, Marioni emphasized that he was born in May 1937, just when Picasso was painting *Guernica*. He has won three artist fellowships of the National Endowment for the Arts and a Guggenheim Foundation grant, and has staged his installations from California to Europe and Japan.

168. Quotations are from my telephone interview and from John Yau's preface to the catalogue, *Awards in the Visual Arts 3* (Southeastern Center for Contemporary Art, Winston-Salem, 1984; an exhibition that traveled from the San Antonio Museum of Art to the Cranbrook Academy Art Museum).

135A. Tom Marioni. *Observation Platform*. 1983–84. Oil on canvas and wood construction with 1,000-watt yellow light; 11½ x 25½' canvas (3.5 x 7.7 m) and 3' (tapering to 2'6") x 30' platform (.9 x 9.14 m). Collection of the artist

135B. Tom Marioni. *Observation Platform*. Close-up

Marioni constructed a 30-foot *Observation Platform* (figs. 135A and 135B) with planks that resonate, xylophone-fashion, as people walk slowly across the boards to study the painting.

Viewers have reported varied and often quite contradictory experiences. To some, the scaffolding suggests that the painting has just been completed; or that they are examining an artifact from ancient history, just excavated; that they are being "asked to perform an autopsy on a victim of history."[169] They feel that they have ascended the hangman's gallows, become targets for an executioner. Illuminated by a 1,000-watt yellow flood light, they find themselves on stage, quite literally in the spotlight, participating in a dramatic event with *Guernica* as backdrop. It is a startling reminder that in our television culture, war seems to be "happening elsewhere." Marioni has forced his viewers (whatever their individual response) to participate physically in his installation and to interact with *Guernica*.

In 1972, *Guernica* inspired the Italian Enrico Baj to construct an enormous commentary on a Milanese police scandal. Some years earlier, he had paraphrased *Les Demoiselles d'Avignon* and *Guernica* as elaborate collages with that amusing mix of homage and competition whereby Picasso previously had tackled Manet and Velázquez. Into a life-size *Guernica* collage, gaily decorated with upholstery fringe, tassels, buttons, and medals, he introduced the enemy missing in *Guernica*: tragicomic military monsters of his own invention.[170] Baj's lighthearted parodies turned deadly serious with his huge, 10-by-39-foot construction, *The Funeral of the Anarchist Pinelli* (figs. 136A and 136B)—a latter-day Sacco-Vanzetti case in Milan—citing *Guernica* (with Carlo Carrà's *Funeral of the Anarchist Galli* of 1910–11).[171] Arrested

136A. Enrico Baj. *The Funeral of the Anarchist Pinelli.* 1972. Mixed media construction, 12' 5½" x 39' 6½" (3.8 x 12 m). Private collection, Milan

169. Ibid. With *Guernica's* permanent installation in Spain, more than one American artist is painting his own life-size copy. Joseph Mashek has reproduced the painting by Mike Bidlo in progress at a Los Angeles art gallery in October 1984 ("Two Blasts-from-the-Past in Picasso [And, Yes, Marcel, You Too]: Notes on Retroactive Influence," *Arts Magazine*, March 1985, p. 132). A full-scale tapestry of *Guernica*, authorized by Picasso, has been in the Nelson A. Rockefeller collection.

170. In a December 1977 note to me, Baj identified "three marching personages who represent, in real and symbolic terms, the Nazism and destructive brutality of militarism . . . conceited, vulgar, grotesque, ready to march and trample on anything." See Herbert Lust's excellent essay and reproductions in the catalogue raisonné, *Enrico Baj* (by Enrico Crispolti, Turin, 1973): "PICABAJ, Kitsch Combine—The Picasso Period (1967–1971)," p. xii.

171. Ibid., "Pinelli—Crucifixion Without God (1972)" pp. xiv–xv; also p. 21, translation from the *Pinelli* catalogue that was censored in Milan. By horrendous coincidence (or plan?), the Italian police commissioner in 1969 most implicated in Pinelli's death was shot the day, 17 May 1972, that Baj's *Pinelli* exhibit was to open that night in the Palazzo Reale, Milan; it was canceled. The show was widely exhibited, however, in major European museums in 1973–75 (Rotterdam, Stockholm, Düsseldorf, Antwerp).

136B. Enrico Baj. *The Funeral of the Anarchist Pinelli.* 1972. Etching with aquatint, 15¾ x 34⅝"
(40 x 88 cm). Museum Boymans-van Beuningen, Rotterdam

in December 1969 for terror bombing of a bank (later traced to neo-Fascists), Pinelli
hurtles (is pushed?) to his death from a window at police headquarters, his body
recalling the falling woman of *Guernica.* His widow and children, like Picasso's
"cardboard characters," have stepped out into three-dimensional space—onto the
vast theatrical stage, which some critics have wished for *Guernica,* and that Picasso
also seems briefly to have envisioned.[172] It is a worthy progeny of *Guernica.* Will
others follow, now that Picasso's work has been reaching new spectators in the
Prado?

□ □ □

Guernica is not precisely in the Prado Museum among Picasso's illustrious forebears.
Its current resting place is in the neighboring Casón del Buen Retiro under Prado
administration (figs. 137 and 138).[173] Historical ironies abound: *Guernica* is installed
in the 17th-century ballroom of King Philip IV under Italian ceiling frescoes depicting
the *Allegory of the Golden Fleece.*[174] The grandiose gardens behind the royal residence, which were once on the outskirts of Madrid, have become the Retiro Park,
popular excursion spot for Madrileños and tourists alike. And while newspaper
headlines welcomed a "liberated *Guernica*" to Madrid,[175] the politically sensitive

172. See figure 162B and Hohl's discussion, pp. 317–20, below. Bannard spoke of Picasso's "cardboard characters" and imagined *Guernica* constructed in three dimensions (p. 303, below).

173. William Rubin emphasized that Picasso "on three or four occasions" discussed *Guernica's*
final installation in Madrid "under the aegis of the Prado Museum" (19 May 1980 letter, *Guernica–
Legado,* p. 168. Cf. also pp. 154–55, below.) For future installation plans, see p. 44, above.

174. The Casón was built in 1637–38, with Luca Giordano's ceiling decorations added in 1692.
Remodeled during the past century with a Neoclassical facade, it became the Museum of Nineteenth
Century Art. (See Jonathan Brown and J. H. Elliot, *A Palace for a King: The Buen Retiro and the Court of
Philip IV* [New Haven and London, 1980] especially pp. 74, 214, 239, 244, and 252, for the history of
the Casón, one of only two structures remaining from the ruined palace complex.)

175. "El 'Guernica' en Libertad," *Pueblo,* 10 September 1981.

131

137. *Guernica* canvas being installed in the Casón, Madrid, October 1981. Photo, courtesy Pittsburgh Press

138. Crowds lining up to see *Guernica* in the Casón, Madrid, 25 October 1981. Photo by Torremocha, courtesy *Hoja del Lunes*

132

139A. *Guernica* in The Museum of Modern Art, New York, 1980. Photo by E. C. Oppler

139B. *Guernica* with civil guard in the Casón, Madrid, October 1981. Wide World Photo

133

painting, together with its 60 preparatory studies and the *Dream and Lie of Franco*, is hardly free. It needs stringent security measures against terrorists of the right and left, and Basque separatists for whom it remains a special symbol. *Guernica* is encased in a bulletproof glass box, safely and hygienically sealed from the public, as in a transparent coffin or as reliquary for a sacred icon.[176] Metal detectors, closed-circuit television, and armed civil guards screen the spectators (fig. 139B). Would Picasso be happy in this setting? a Spanish cartoonist wondered (fig. 140).

—Máximo—

140. Máximo. Picasso in Madrid. Cartoon published in *El País*, 25 October 1981

    Guernica has come full circle. The painting had started out in 1937 in a highly charged political setting, then spent years as a refugee in America where its historic origins gradually grew less important. It became Picasso's masterpiece to the American public,[177] and a less successful late work to the avant-garde. Politicized again during the Vietnam era, *Guernica* has now been welcomed in Spain, again first as a political symbol. Yet its immaculate installation keeps the public at a safe 6-foot distance and in effect encourages esthetic distance. The painting as a work of art and Picasso's "masterpiece" gradually may again overshadow the political statement.

    The Spanish minister of culture Iñigo Cavero formally opened the *Guernica* installation by inviting dignitaries "to receive this great work of art as a messenger of peace and harmony among Spaniards."[178] Indeed, among the many celebrities were witnesses of *Guernica*'s Spanish Republican past: the architect Josep Lluis Sert and Josep Renau, the former director of fine arts, and most poignantly, "La Pasionaria" (Dolores Ibarruri), the great Communist orator of the civil war, now in her mid-80s and back from exile in Moscow since 1977, when the Spanish Communist Party was again legalized (fig. 141).

    The opening for the general public attracted an estimated 4,000 visitors; it began on Sunday, October 25, Picasso's 100th birthday. There were exhibitions and celebrations in Málaga, Barcelona, and elsewhere in Spain. Features about *Guernica* and

---

176. For Douglas Cooper's more positive response, see p. 321, below.

177. "The triumph of *Guernica* was to a large extent a popular triumph" (Clark, *What Is a Masterpiece?*, p. 44; see also my preface, p. xiii, above.

178. Ya, 25 October 1981, p. 39; cf. his statement at the brief transfer ceremony in New York, referring to reconciliation, "common cultural patrimony of humanity and a message of peace" (*New York Times*, 10 Sept. 1981, C20).

Picasso dominated the weekend editions of the press. One of the world's largest commemorative postage stamps was issued (fig. 142).[179]

This certainly was Picasso's homecoming in a specifically artistic sense as well. Quite aware that "the magnitude of Picasso's love for Spain is comparable only to the ignorance in Spain about Picasso,"[180] the Museum of Contemporary Art in Madrid and the Picasso Museum of Barcelona mounted the first Picasso retrospective in Spain since 1936. Some 140 important paintings and sculpture borrowed from European and American museums and private collections finally enabled Picasso's compatriots to experience the great range and quality of his art.[181]

141. La Pasionaria in front of *Guernica*, Madrid, October 1981. AP Photo

179. Which triggered angry protests in the Spanish press: it had been printed from an old painted copy of *Guernica*, not a recent photograph! (See *El Periódico*, 9 Feb. 1982, p. 19.) Compare this mammoth stamp with one issued 1966 in Czechoslovakia to mark the 30th anniversary of the International Brigades' entry into the civil war (fig. 143).

180. The diplomat Fernández-Quintanilla (cf. p. 154, note 5, below) quoted in the *New York Times*, 11 September 1981. Books about Picasso, however, have been published at an impressive rate. Every major Guernica study has been translated: Arnheim and Larrea already in 1976 and 1977; Russell in 1981; Cabanne's lively biography was translated in 1982. Several Spaniards have published their interpretations: Josep Palau i Fabre, the leading Picasso scholar, *El Guernica de Picasso* (1979) and *Picasso vivent* (1983); Joaquin de la Puente, *El Guernica: historia de un cuadro* (1983); and the award-winning book by Carlos Rojas, *El Mundo mitico y magico de Picasso* (1984); see also notes 51 and 70.

Interviewed upon *Guernica*'s departure, William Rubin also emphasized how *Guernica* could change Spain's attitude toward modern art, could "annihilate the last vestiges of parochialism" in the arts and become a symbol of national reconciliation, "the final act in the closing of the Civil War" (*New York Times*, 10 Sept. 1981, p. 21).

181. *Picasso, 1881–1981: Exposición Antólogica* (Madrid, 5 Nov.–Dec. 1981; Barcelona, Jan.–Feb. 1982). MoMA sent 15 major works, including *The Charnel House*; Moscow and Leningrad contributed 8 important paintings, something that international politics prevented MoMA from realizing in the Picasso 1980 retrospective.

Thus already during the first weeks in Madrid, *Guernica* was accomplishing its political and artistic mission of reconciliation. Nearly half a century after it began, the most bitter of civil wars had finally ended, symbolically, with the repatriation of its last important exile—a veteran canvas, much-traveled, fragile and scarred. And through *Guernica* with its studies—and with well over 100 works in the museum retrospective—Picasso at last also returned to his homeland.

144.

143.

142.

**DOCUMENTS
POETRY
CRITICISM
ANALYSIS**

I.
PICASSO STATEMENTS

Picasso's friends agree that while he loved to talk about art, and often did, with "quick flashes of insight and wit," he was most reluctant to have his thoughts trapped on paper.[1] His biographer, Roland Penrose, also emphasized the difficulties of recording Picasso's conversations that relied "on glances, expressions, gestures, a quick laugh which introduces a relative absurdity and above all on the reactions of his listeners to ambiguities and paradoxes which can become the threshold of new ideas."[2]

Nevertheless, Picasso occasionally submitted to lengthy interviews and informally approved what had been recorded. A 1935 conversation with Christian Zervos, editor of the influential *Cahiers d'Art,* begins our selections: it provides glimpses of Picasso's creative process especially pertinent for *Guernica*. During another interview Picasso discussed *Guernica* with an American soldier in 1944–45. A brief 1945 interview with a French journalist actually has a unique *written* statement by Picasso. This part[3] ends with Picasso's instructions to his lawyer about *Guernica*'s future.

1. Ashton, quoting the poet Michel Leiris, in her introduction to *Picasso on Art,* p. xviii. She cites other friends of Picasso's who emphasize his reluctance to be quoted directly, and the difficulty of catching the right cadence of his speech. While she was debating whether to include passages from Gilot's *Life with Picasso,* "they all said the tone was never right and reminded [her] that Picasso was not given to lectures and disquisitions" (p. xxvii). Douglas Cooper, however, praised Geneviève Laporte's memoirs for capturing "the authentic voice of Picasso himself talking . . . the rapid switches of tone . . . the patient explanations, the impetuosities of his thinking, the unpredictability of what he might say next" (from his preface, p. xi).

2. Penrose (1958), p. 366 with Picasso's warning: "You mustn't always believe what I say. Questions tempt you to tell lies, particularly when there is no answer."

3. Picasso's Surrealist poem appears in part III; quotations from alleged political statements are included in parts V (p. 225) and VI (p. 251).

Christian Zervos
Conversation with Picasso—[1935]*

Christian Zervos interviewed Picasso at his Boisgeloup estate in 1934–35 while collecting material for the special Picasso issue of *Cahiers d'Art*. He modestly omitted his part in this verbal give-and-take with Picasso: brusque "one-liners" follow longer philosophical thoughts in unexpected juxtaposition, very much in the style of a black-and-white collage, or indeed like a study for *Guernica*. In context, also, the conversation illuminates *Guernica* in the Surrealist vein of the 1930s; note Picasso's recurring talk about the mysteries of the creative process and the supremacy of feelings, for instance. Many comments proved to be prophetic for *Guernica:* Picasso's desire to have "the metamorphoses of a picture" recorded photographically, and his observations "that basically a picture doesn't change, that the first 'vision' remains almost intact," whereas the picture "goes on changing, according to the state of mind of whoever is looking at it." And finally, his exasperated exclamation: "How can you expect an onlooker to live a picture of mine as I lived it?"

We might adopt for the artist the joke about there being nothing more dangerous than implements of war in the hands of generals. In the same way, there is nothing more dangerous than justice in the hands of judges, and a paintbrush in the hands of a painter. Just think of the danger to society! But today we haven't the heart to expel the painters and poets from society because we refuse to admit to ourselves that there is any danger in keeping them in our midst.

It is my misfortune—and probably my delight—to use things as my passions tell me. What a miserable fate for a painter who adores blondes to have to stop himself putting them into a picture because they don't go with the basket of fruit! How awful for a painter who loathes apples to have to use them all the time because they go so well with the cloth. I put all the things I like into my pictures. The things—so much the worse for them; they just have to put up with it.

In the old days pictures went forward toward completion by stages. Every day brought something new. A picture used to be a sum of additions. In my case a picture is a sum of destructions. I do a picture—then I destroy it. In the end, though, nothing is lost: the red I took away from one place turns up somewhere else.

*From "Conversations avec Picasso," *Cahiers d'Art* 10 (1935), pp. 173–78; trans. based on Myfanwy Evans's in Barr, pp. 272–74, and reprinted by permission of The Museum of Modern Art. The statement has been frequently anthologized (e.g., Chipp, *Theories of Modern Art,* and Ashton).

Born 1889 in Greece, educated in Alexandria and Paris (Sorbonne dissertation on a Neoplatonic philosopher), Zervos is best known for his monumental undertaking of cataloguing Picasso's complete works: 23 volumes were published from 1932 to 1971; the project was continued after his death in 1970.

It would be very interesting to preserve photographically, not the stages, but the metamorphoses of a picture. Possibly one might then discover the path followed by the brain in materializing a dream. But there is one very odd thing—to notice that basically a picture doesn't change, that he first "vision" remains almost intact, in spite of appearances. I often ponder on a light and a dark when I have put them into a picture; I try hard to break them up by interpolating a color that will create a different effect. When the work is photographed, I note that what I put in to correct my first vision has disappeared, and that, after all, the photographic image corresponds with my first vision before the transformation I insisted on.

A picture is not thought out and settled beforehand. While it is being done it changes as one's thoughts change. And when it is finished, it still goes on changing, according to the state of mind of whoever is looking at it. A picture lives a life like a living creature, undergoing the changes imposed on us by our life from day to day. This is natural enough, as the picture lives only through the man who is looking at it.

At the actual time that I am painting a picture I may think of white and put down white. But I can't go on working all the time thinking of white and painting it. Colors, like features, follow the changes of the emotions. You've seen the sketch I did for a picture with all the colors indicated on it. What is left of them? Certainly the white I thought of and the green I thought of are there in the picture, but not in the places I intended, nor in the same quantities. Of course, you can paint pictures by matching up different parts of them so that they go quite nicely together, but they'll lack any kind of drama.

I want to get to the stage where nobody can tell how a picture of mine is done. What's the point of that? Simply that I want nothing but emotion to be given off by it.

Work is a necessity for man.

A horse does not go between the shafts of its own accord.

Man invented the alarm clock.

When I begin a picture, there is somebody who works with me. Toward the end, I get the impression that I have been working alone—without a collaborator.

When you begin a picture, you often make some pretty discoveries. You must be on guard against these. Destroy the thing, do it over several times. In each destroying of a beautiful discovery, the artist does not really suppress it, but rather transforms it, condenses it, makes it more substantial. What comes out in the end is the result of discarded finds. Otherwise, you become your own connoisseur. I sell myself nothing.

Actually, you work with few colors. But they seem like a lot more when each one is in the right place.

Abstract art is only painting. What about drama?

There is no abstract art. You must always start with something. Afterward you can remove all traces of reality. There's no danger then, anyway, because the idea of the object will have left an indelible mark. It is what started the artist off, excited his ideas, and stirred up his emotions. Ideas and emotions will in the end be prisoners in his work. Whatever they do, they can't escape from the picture. They form an integral part of it, even when their presence is no longer discernible. Whether he likes it or not, man is the instrument of nature. It forces on him its character and appearance. In my Dinard pictures and in my Pourville pictures I expressed very much the same vision. However, you yourself have noticed how different the atmosphere of those painted in Brittany is from those painted in Normandy, because you recognized the light of the Dieppe cliffs. I didn't copy this light nor did I pay it any special attention. I was simply soaked in it. My eyes saw it and my subconscious registered what they saw: my hand fixed the impression. One cannot go against nature. It is stronger than the strongest man. It is pretty much to our interest to be on good terms with it! We may allow ourselves certain liberties, but only in details.

Nor is there any "figurative" and "non-figurative" art. Everything appears to us in the guise of a "figure." Even in metaphysics ideas are expressed by means of symbolic "figures." See how ridiculous it is then to think of painting without "figuration." A person, an object, a circle are all "figures"; they react on us more or less intensely. Some are nearer our sensations and produce emotions that touch our affective faculties; others appeal more directly to the intellect. They all should be allowed a place because I find my spirit has quite as much need of emotion as my senses. Do you think it concerns me that a particular picture of mine represents two people? Though these two people once existed for me, they exist no longer. The "vision" of them gave me a preliminary emotion; then little by little their actual presences became blurred; they developed into a fiction and then disappeared altogether, or rather they were transformed into all kinds of problems. They are no longer two people, you see, but forms and colors: forms and colors that have taken on, meanwhile, the *idea* of two people and preserve the vibration of their life.

I deal with painting as I deal with things, I paint a window just as I look out of a window. If an open window looks wrong in a picture, I draw the curtain and shut it, just as I would in my own room. In painting, as in life, you must act directly. Certainly, painting has its conventions, and it is essential to reckon with them. Indeed, you can't do anything else. And so you always ought to keep an eye on real life.

The artist is a receptacle for emotions that come from all over the place: from the sky, from the earth, from a scrap of paper, from a passing shape, from a spider's web. That is why we must not discriminate between things. Where things are concerned there are no class distinctions. We must pick out what is good for us where we can find it—except from our own works. I have a horror of copying myself. But when I am shown a portfolio of old drawings, for instance, I have no qualms about taking anything I want from them.

When we invented cubism we had no intention whatever of inventing cubism. We wanted simply to express what was in us. Not one of us drew up a plan of campaign, and our friends, the poets, followed our efforts attentively, but they never dictated to us. Young painters today often draw up a program to follow, and apply themselves like diligent students to performing their tasks.

The painter goes through states of fullness and evaluation. That is the whole secret of art. I go for a walk in the forest of Fontainebleau. I get "green" indigestion. I must get rid of this sensation into a picture. Green rules it. A painter paints to unload himself of feelings and visions. People seize on painting to cover up their nakedness. They get what they can wherever they can. In the end I don't believe they get anything at all. They've simply cut a coat to the measure of their own ignorance. They make everything, from God to a picture, in their own image. That is why the picture-hook is the ruination of a painting—a painting which has always a certain significance, at least as much as the man who did it. As soon as it is bought and hung on a wall, it takes on quite a different kind of significance, and the painting is done for.

Academic training in beauty is a sham. We have been deceived, but so well deceived that we can scarcely get back even a shadow of the truth. The beauties of the Parthenon, Venuses, nymphs, Narcissuses, are so many lies. Art is not the application of a canon of beauty but what the instinct and the brain can conceive beyond any canon. When we love a woman we don't start measuring her limbs. We love with our desires—although everything has been done to try and apply a canon even to love. The Parthenon is really only a farmyard over which someone put a roof; colonnades and sculptures were added because there were people in Athens who happened to be working, and wanted to express themselves. It's not what the artist *does* that counts, but what he *is*. Cézanne would never have interested me a bit if he had lived and thought like Jacques Émile Blanche, even if the apple he painted had been ten times as beautiful. What forces our interest is Cézanne's anxiety—that's Cézanne's lesson; the torments of Van Gogh—that is the actual drama of the man. The rest is a sham.

Everyone wants to understand art. Why not try to understand the songs of a bird? Why does one love the night, flowers, everything around one, without trying to understand them? But in the case of a painting people have to *understand*. If only they would realize above all that an artist works of necessity, that he himself is only a trifling bit of the world, and that no more importance should be attached to him than to plenty of other things which please us in the world, though we can't explain them. People who try to explain pictures are usually barking up the wrong tree. Gertrude Stein joyfully announced to me the other day that she had at last understood what my picture of the three musicians[1] was meant to be. It was a still life!

How can you expect an onlooker to live a picture of mine as I lived it? A picture comes to me from miles away: who is to say from how far away I sensed it, saw it, painted it; and yet the next day I can't see what I've done myself. How can anyone enter into my dreams, my instincts, my desires, my thoughts, which have taken a long time to mature and to come out into the daylight, and above all grasp from them what I have been about—perhaps against my own will? * * *

Jerome Seckler
Picasso Explains—[1945]*

A young American soldier, part of the first troop contingent to liberate France, was determined to meet Picasso: he had studied *Guernica* and argued about it after it reached New York in 1939. He painted in his free time, and had admired Picasso's wartime paintings, in the Liberation Salon of October 1944. Jerome Seckler did see Picasso twice in 1944–45, and the artist approved the interview for publication. This delightfully vivid and conscientious account includes important comments by Picasso.

1. [*Three Musicians*, painted summer 1921 in two versions (Philadelphia Museum of Art and MoMA) illustrated in *Picasso 1980*, pp. 230 and 231.]

*Reprinted with the kind permission of the author from *New Masses*, 13 March 1945, pp. 4–7. Frequently republished; initially in Barr, with perceptive comments, p. 268; in Chipp, and Ashton.

How amusing it is to watch Seckler try yet fail to draw political interpretations from Picasso! Seckler obviously had Marxist convictions at that time.[1] During the symposium at The Museum of Modern Art in 1947, however, he admitted candidly: "When I interviewed Picasso, I made the same mistake that Mr. Larrea is making now in looking for precise political labels. Picasso made it very clear to me that such labels were not to be found in *Guernica*."

For the past ten years my friends and I had discussed, analyzed and rehashed Picasso to the point of exasperation. I say exasperation because very simply it was just that. The only conclusion we could ever arrive at was that Picasso, in his various so-called "periods," quite accurately reflected the very hectic contradictions of the times, but only reflected them, never painting anything to increase one's understanding of these times. Various artists and critics who make their living by putting labels on people identified him with a wide variety of schools—surrealist, classicist, abstractionist, exhibitionist and even contortionist. But beyond this lot of fancy nonsense, these people never did explain Picasso. He remained an enigma.

Then came the bombshell. In the midst of the last agonized hours of Loyalist Spain, Picasso painted his *Guernica* mural, and with this mural emerged as a powerful and penetrating painter of social protest. But there was only the *Guernica*. Up to the time France entered the war there were no echoes in Picasso's painting of the furious protest that had produced the *Guernica*. Then came France's military disaster and her humiliating occupation by the Germans. Nasty stories circulated about Picasso. That he was living well in Paris under the Germans; that he played ball with the Gestapo, which in return permitted him to paint unmolested. That he was selling the Nazi fakes—works he signed, but which were actually painted by his students. Still another that he was dead. From 1940 until the liberation of Paris, Picasso remained a figure completely surrounded by mystery and obscurity.

Then in October following the liberation came the electrifying news that Picasso had joined the Communist Party.

In that same month, liberated Paris held a gigantic exhibition of contemporary French art, one room of which was especially devoted to Picasso—seventy-four paintings and five sculptures, most of them executed during the occupation. The exhibition startled me. It was the Picasso of the *Guernica*, painting powerfully, painting beautifully, painting of life and hope.

I was so excited by Picasso's work I determined to see him. Through a young French artist who knew him I managed to get his address. At his studio I was told, after a whispered conversation in another room, that Picasso was "not at home." His secretary explained, "Picasso has not painted for two months what with all that was happening, and now he wants to settle down and do some work." But finally my young artist friend arranged a meeting for me, and at 11:30 of a Saturday morning I arrived at his studio, was ushered in and told to wait.

Picasso occupies the top two floors of a definitely unpretentious place, a four-story building close to the Seine. To get up to his studio one enters one of the holes in the wall that pass for doorways and climbs three flights up a narrow winding stairway with bare walls and worn wooden steps. This has been his home and his

---

1. Seckler's Marxist sympathies may be inferred from his close friendship with Vernon Clark, whose essay appears in part VI.

studio for the past eight years. You enter directly into one of the studios, a room with several easels, paintings, books—without order. As I waited I noticed one of his recent paintings on an easel, of a metal pitcher on a table. Tacked above the painting was a small pencil sketch of the composition, which the painting duplicated down to the last line and detail. Though it was only a quick sketch, he had followed it so closely that when he crossed lines at the corner of a table he also crossed them in the painting.

I asked his secretary if Picasso had had trouble with the Germans. "Like everyone," he said, "we had hard times." Picasso was not permitted to exhibit. Once the Gestapo came and accused Picasso of being in reality a man called Leipzig. Picasso simply insisted, "No, I am Picasso, that's all." The Germans did not bother him after that, but they kept a close watch on him at all times. Nevertheless, Picasso maintained a close contact with the underground resistance movement.

After about ten minutes, Picasso came down from the upstairs studio and approached me directly. He gave me a quick glance, looked me squarely in the eyes. He was dressed in a light gray business suit, a blue cotton shirt and tie, a bright yellow handkerchief in his breast pocket—small hands but solid. I introduced myself and Picasso offered me his hand immediately. He had a warm, sincere smile, and spoke without restraint, which put me at once at ease.

I explained that I had always been interested in his work, but that he had always puzzled me, and how I felt suddenly at his recent exhibition that I understood what he was trying to say. I wanted to know him personally, and to ask him if my analyses of his paintings were correct, and if they were, to write about them for America. Then I described for Picasso my interpretation of his painting *The Sailor*, which I had seen at the Liberation Salon. I said I thought it to be a self-portrait—the sailor's suit, the net, the red butterfly showing Picasso as a person seeking a solution to the problem of the times, trying to find a better world—the sailor's garb being an indication of an active participation in this effort. He listened intently and finally said, "Yes, it's me, but I did not mean it to have any political significance at all."

I asked why he painted himself as a sailor. "Because," he answered, "I always wear a sailor shirt. See?" He opened up his shirt and pulled at his underwear—it was white with blue stripes! [Cf. fig. 40.]

"But what of the red butterfly?" I asked. "Didn't you deliberately make it red because of its political significance?"

"Not particularly," he replied. "If it has any, it was in my subconscious!"

"But," I insisted, "it must have a definite meaning for you whether you say so or not. What's in your subconscious is a result of your conscious thinking. There is no escape from reality."

He looked at me for a second and said, "Yes, it's possible and normal."

Picasso then asked if I were a writer. I told him the truth—I was not a writer, had never written before. That by vocation I worked in lumber. I was a painter too, but only by avocation, because I had to make a living. Picasso laughed and said, "Yes, I understand." Then asked if I had his consent to write an article about him.

"Yes," he said, and then added, "For which paper?"

I told him the *New Masses*. He smiled and answered, "Yes, I know it."

He looked at the open door. There were several people waiting for him. "Let's go upstairs to the studio for a moment," he said. So we climbed the stairs to the large studio where he actually does his painting. The room was neat and clean. It didn't have the dusty, helterskelter appearance of the room downstairs.

I told Picasso that many people were saying that now, with his new political affiliations, he had become a leader in culture and politics for the people, that his influence for progress could be tremendous. Picasso nodded seriously and said, "Yes, I realize it." I mentioned how we had often discussed him back in New York, especially the *Guernica* mural (now on loan to the Museum of Modern Art in New York).[2] I talked about the significance of the bull, the horse, the hands with the lifelines, etc., and the origin of the symbols in Spanish mythology. Picasso kept nodding his head as I spoke. "Yes," he said, "the bull there represents brutality, the horse the people. Yes, there I used symbolism, but not in the others."

I explained my interpretation of two of his paintings at the exhibition, one of a bull, a lamp, palette and book [fig. 145]. The bull, I said, must represent fascism, the lamp, by its powerful glow, the palette and book all represented culture and freedom—the things we're fighting for—the painting showing the fierce struggle going on between the two.

"No," said Picasso, "the bull is not fascism, but it is brutality and darkness."

I mentioned that now we look forward to a perhaps changed and more simple and clearly understood symbolism within his very personal idiom.

"My work is not symbolic," he answered. "Only the *Guernica* mural is symbolic. But in the case of the mural, that is allegoric. That's the reason I've used the

145. Picasso. *Still Life with Black Bull's Head*. 19 November 1938. Oil on canvas. 38¼ x 51¼" (97 x 130 cm). Z.IX:240. Private collection

2. [From 1939 to 1981, when it was sent to Spain.]

horse, the bull and so on. The mural is for the definite expression and solution of a problem and that is why I used symbolism.

"Some people," he continued, "call my work for a period 'surrealism.' I am not a surrealist. I have never been out of reality. I have always been in the essence of reality [literally the "real of reality"]. If someone wished to express war it might be more elegant and literary to make a bow and arrow because that is more aesthetic, but for me, if I want to express war, I'll use a machine-gun! Now is the time in this period of changes and revolution to use a revolutionary manner of painting and not to paint like before." He then stared straight into my eyes and asked, *"Vous me croirez?"* (Will you believe me?)

I told him I understood many of his paintings at the exhibition, but that quite a few I could not figure out for myself at all. I turned to a painting of a nude and a musician that had been in the October Salon, set up against the wall to my left. It was a large distorted canvas, about five by seven feet. "For instance this," I said, "I can't understand it at all."

"It's simply a nude and a musician," he replied. "I painted it for myself. When you look at a nude made by someone else, he uses the traditional manner to express the form, and for the people that represents a nude. But for me, I use a revolutionary expression. In this painting there is no abstract significance. It's simply a nude and a musician."

I asked, "Why do you paint in such a way that your expression is so difficult for people to understand?"

"I paint this way," he replied, "because it's a result of my thought. I have worked for years to obtain this result and if I make a step backwards (as he spoke he actually took a step back), it will be an offense to people (the French was just that, *offense*) because that is a result of my thought. I can't use an ordinary manner just to have the satisfaction of being understood. I don't want to go down to a lower level.

"You're a painter," he continued; "you understand it's quite impossible to explain why you do this or that. I express myself through painting and I can't explain through words. I can't explain why I did it that way. For me, if I sketch a little table," he grabbed a little table just alongside to illustrate, "I see every detail. I see the size, the thickness, and I translate it in my own way." He waved a hand at a big painting of a chair at the other end of the room (it had also been in the Liberation Salon), and explained, "You see how I do it.

"It's funny," he went on, "because people see in painting things you didn't put in—they make embroidery on the subject. But it doesn't matter, because if they saw that, it's stimulating—and the essence of what they saw is really in the painting."

I asked Picasso when I could see him again, and he said he would be glad to see me any time I wished. We shook hands and I left.

I found it difficult to visit Picasso again as promptly as I wished, but on a Saturday morning some weeks later I paid him a second call. Picasso received me in his bedroom, where, when I entered, I could hear him discussing political problems to be solved within the unity of the Allies with several friends. As soon as he saw me he came over, smilingly shook hands and greeted me, *"Bonjour! Ça va bien?"* Again he was so simple and sincere that I felt as though I had known him for years. He apologized for receiving me in his bedroom. "I've had to organize myself in this little room," he said, "with my dog, my papers, my drawings, my bed, because I was freezing downstairs." His hands as usual were expressively accompanying his words, like those of an orchestra conductor's. For a small room, it certainly was crammed full. The unmade bed, several bureaus, a slanting drawing table and a large gently-eyed dog all revolved about a little coal stove, capped by a pot of water. Scattered on the bed and table were seven or eight large etchings in color which he had just finished—with bright reds, blues, and yellows laid down in mass. On the bed also were five or six newspapers, including *L'Humanité*. Resting on a bureau on the wall was an etched zinc plate with two prints from it, of a lemon and a stemmed wineglass, done in the same beautiful bright colors. Over another bureau was an old photogravure of a Rubens—a man and woman bursting with love, very richly and sensitively done. On another wall was a small Corot landscape.

I brought out my report of our first interview and we went over it together. The article being in English, I had to translate into French. Everything was agreeable to him, but in translating what he had said about the bull, palette and lamp painting, I must have slipped in my French and he misunderstood me, thinking I was quoting him as saying the bull represented fascism.

"No," he protested, "it doesn't represent fascism."

I explained what he had said was that it did not represent fascism but that it did represent darkness and brutality. "But that's just the point," I said. "You make a distinction between the two. But what distinction can there be? You know and the people of the world know the two are the same, that wherever fascism has gone there is darkness and brutality, death and destruction. There is no distinction."

Picasso shook his head as I spoke. "Yes," he said, "you are right, but I did not try consciously to show that in my painting. If you interpret it that way then you are correct, but still it wasn't my idea to present it that way."

"But," I insisted, "you do think about and feel deeply these things that are affecting the world. You recognize that what is in your subconscious is a result of your contact with life, and your thoughts and reactions to it. It couldn't be merely accidental that you used precisely these particular objects and presented them in a particular way. The political significance of these things is there whether you consciously thought of it or not."

"Yes," he answered, "what you say is very true, but I don't know why I used those particular objects. They don't represent anything in particular. The bull is a bull, the palette a palette and the lamp is a lamp. That's all. But there is definitely no political connection there for me. Darkness and brutality, yes, but not fascism."

He motioned to the color etching of the glass and the lemon. "There," he said, "is a glass and a lemon, its shapes and colors—reds, blues, yellows. Can you see any political significance in that?"

"Simply as objects," I said, "no."

"Well," he continued, "it's the same with the bull, the palette and lamp." He looked earnestly at me and went on, "If I were a chemist, Communist or fascist—if I obtain in my mixture a red liquid it doesn't mean that I am expressing Communist propaganda, does it? If I paint a hammer and sickle people may think it's a representation of Communism, but for me it's only a hammer and sickle. I just want to reproduce the objects for what they are and not for what they mean. If you give a meaning to certain things in my paintings it may be very true, but it was not my idea to give this meaning. What ideas and conclusions you have got I obtained too, but instinctively, unconsciously. I make the painting for the painting. I paint the objects for what they are. It's in my subconscious. When people look at it each person gets a different meaning from it, from what each sees in it. I don't think of trying to get any particular meaning across. There is no deliberate sense of propaganda in my painting."

"Except in the *Guernica*," I suggested.

"Yes," he replied, "except in the *Guernica*. In that there is a deliberate appeal to people, a deliberate sense of propaganda."

Simone Téry
Painting Is Not Done To Decorate Apartments—[1945]*

Spontaneous good humor characterizes this lively interview that comes to an unexpected climax when Picasso prepares a unique *written* statement about art and politics. Picasso is especially relaxed and open during this conversation with Simone Téry, evidently an intelligent and charming woman, and an experienced journalist who had witnessed the civil war in Spain, and clearly championed the Republican cause.[1]

While the written statement has been frequently reprinted,[2] the complete interview is translated and reproduced here for the first time, with an amusing illustration (fig. 146) and vivid description of the wartime studio where Picasso painted *Guernica*.

146.

"What's this, Picasso, you are in Paris? All the papers reported that you were at the front!"

"Yes," Picasso answered, "the newspapers made me an officer, but nobody said anything to me. Nobody knows anything about it at the War Ministry. All I know is that one day they asked me, 'Picasso, how would you like to go to the front as a war correspondent? You sure could paint some *Guernicas* out there! And you know, a war correspondent has officer rank.' Officer rank? I said, that's something!"

"You like that gold braid so much, Picasso?"

"It's not so much the braid," said Picasso modestly, "but you know, if I were an officer, I could get ahold of cigarettes. And perhaps they'd give me a bit of butter and some meat. And who knows, I might also be eligible for some coal."

*From "Picasso n'est pas officier dans l'armée française," *Les Lettres françaises*, 24 March 1945; trans., ECO. Is the title not a slightly malicious reference to Matisse's frequently decorative art?

1. Recorded in Téry's *Front de la liberté* (Paris, 1938) and the autobiographical novel *Où L'Aube se lève* (New York, 1945).

2. See Barr, pp. 247 and 267; French text on p. 269. Other translations of the written statement by Ashton, p. 149, and O'Brian, p. 376, have been partly followed and here are gratefully acknowledged.

This genius, this most famous and talked-about modern painter, this wild man, this *enfant terrible* of Montparnasse, didn't seem at all like the image I had formed of him. His powerful, swarthy, and deeply wrinkled face, brightened by fine white hair, radiates kindness, a sly serenity, even a sort of disturbing gentleness, which it would be naive to trust, no doubt.

"What do you mean, even you, a painter, can't get coal?"

"Don't you feel it?"

I felt it all too much. I had kept on my gloves, it was that cold in Picasso's studio—an enormous studio, like the loft of a country farm, with black beams under a whitewashed ceiling, but in the midst of old Paris. A long, emaciated dog, its ribs sticking out so that one can count them, is shivering with all its skinny body on the crumbling tile floor.[3] This dog's name is Kasbek, God knows why. Picasso explains that Kasbek is the name of the highest mountain in the Caucasus. Up on the walls, on the easels, Picasso's wartime paintings explode with funereal colors: grays, somber blues, black. A woman shaped like a mandolin is stretched out on a sofa, another bent like a stove pipe; cataclysmic quaking landscapes, of powerful construction, whose secret balance organizes their apparent disorder. This is certainly our Picasso as we've known him, emerging from war, invasion, terror, younger and more dynamic than ever.

"Tell me, Picasso, is that story true which is making the rounds all over the world? One day a Gestapo officer brandishing a reproduction of your *Guernica* asked you: 'You did that, didn't you?' And you are supposed to have answered: 'No, you did.' "

"Yes," Picasso laughs, "that's true, that's more or less true. Sometimes the *Boches* [Germans] would come to visit me, pretending to admire my paintings. I gave them postcards of my *Guernica* picture, saying: 'Take them along, souvenirs! Souvenirs!' "

"Some American newspapers have claimed that your joining the Communist Party was just a whim of yours, and that you've explained that art and politics have nothing in common." Picasso's good-natured face suddenly becomes serious.

"But I never said that! That's scandalous!"

" 'But do the Communists, my dear master,' a young American woman asked you maliciously, 'do the Communists understand your painting?' "

Picasso doesn't let himself get thrown so easily.

"There are some people who understand it, and some who don't. And there are some who understand English, and some who don't. There are some who understand Einstein, and some who don't. Wait a minute (this question is very important); I am going to give you a written statement so that nobody will have any doubts about this."

A few moments later, an excited Picasso comes back with two sheets of notebook paper on which he has scribbled in pencil. I decipher with some difficulty the aggressive phrases written in the purest Picasso style:

What do you think an artist is? An imbecile who has only eyes, if he is a painter, or ears if he is a musician, or a lyre in every chamber of his heart if he is a poet, or even, if he is a boxer, just his muscles? Far, far from it: at the same time, he is also a political being,

3. [Brassaï's photograph (plate 32) is a perfect illustration. See also p. 52, above.]

152

constantly aware of the heartbreaking, passionate, or delightful things that happen in the world, shaping himself completely in their image. How could it be possible to feel no interest in other people, and with a cool indifference[4] to detach yourself from the very life which they bring you so abundantly? No, painting is not done to decorate apartments. It is an instrument of war for attack and defense against the enemy.

"Now, is that clear, like that?" Picasso asks anxiously.

"It seems to me that it couldn't be more clear. If everybody doesn't understand your painting, surely the whole world will understand these words."

Picasso and Roland Dumas
The Future of Guernica—[1969 and 1977]*

Guernica was commissioned by the Spanish Republic in 1937, and Picasso maintained consistently that the painting, for years on extended loan to The Museum of Modern Art in New York, belonged ultimately to a democratic Spain. In October 1969, the Spanish Director-General of Fine Arts, Florentino Pérez Embid, startled a press luncheon in Paris by announcing that "the government of General Franco deems Madrid to be the place for *Guernica*, Picasso's masterpiece."[1] This comment was widely disseminated in Spain, as reprinted by Vicente Talón in *Arde Guernica*. When that book was reviewed in the ultra-right-wing journal, *El Alcázar*, Pérez Embid's comments appeared below a photograph of *Guernica* (surely an all-time first for the militarist organ):

> *Guernica* (given by Picasso to the Spanish people) is part of the cultural patrimony of this people and should be on exhibition in Spain as proof of the definitive end of the contrasts and differences aroused by the last civil conflict.[2]

Picasso sharply responded to these peace feelers of the Franco regime by instructing his lawyer, Roland Dumas, to formalize his wishes that *Guernica* remain in New York until it could find a permanent home in a democratic Spain, as discussed in the following press release. There was renewed interest in *Operación Retorno*[3] upon Picasso's death in April 1973, after Franco's death in November 1975, and especially in the months preceding the Spanish elections in June 1977—the reason for Dumas's detailed statement.

---

4. [Picasso's adjective, *ivoire*, means cool and hard, but also connotes "ivory-tower" remoteness.]

*Press release issued on 15 April 1977 by Picasso's lawyer, Roland Dumas, and made available by The Museum of Modern Art in New York. See John Newhouse, "An Air of Mystery," *The New Yorker*, 30 December 1985, pp. 33–57, for an informative and entertaining "profile" of this brilliant jurist and foreign minister in premier François Mitterand's Socialist government.

1. [*Le Monde*, 24 October 1969 (the eve of Picasso's birthday), p. 3, with a large headline: "*Guernica*" à Madrid? The Paris newspaper printed Picasso's reply through his lawyer with the caption: " 'Guernica' ne reviendra en Espagne qu'avec la République" (14 Nov. 1969, p. 2).]

2. [Quoted by Southworth, p. 280.]

3. [The Spanish epithet is a misnomer since *Guernica* was never actually in Spain (although one could argue that the Spanish Pavilion at the 1937 Paris exposition was the spiritual and artistic territory of Spain). See p. 126, and figs. 132 and 133.]

The status and fate of *Guernica*—the famous painting by Picasso of 1937 executed following the destruction of the small Basque village by Nazi planes—is the object of unfounded rumors and speculation.[4]

The commotion concerns, particularly, the sending of the masterpiece to Spain by The Museum of Modern Art in New York, where it has been on extended loan since September 1939 consistent with the wishes of Pablo Picasso.

Pressed by a request from the Spanish government for *Guernica*—which he deemed improper—Pablo Picasso charged me in 1969 with preparing documents describing his express wishes concerning the future of his picture.[5]

Pablo Picasso confirmed in writing what he had already on several occasions declared—notably to Mr. Barr, then Director of The Museum of Modern Art in New York, and to Mr. Rubin, Director of that museum's Department of Painting and Sculpture—namely that "*Guernica* and its preparatory studies belong to the Spanish Republic,"[6] but that the transfer to Spain could only be envisaged after the complete reestablishment of individual liberties in that country.

Pablo Picasso spoke of this decision on several occasions, both to his close friends and to the representatives of The Museum of Modern Art in New York, and to myself.

The fragility of the painting, he said, precludes any further travel after its installation in Madrid. Furthermore, he continued, a certain time should be allowed to pass to verify that once established, the democratic regime is no longer subject to a forcible coup which might reopen this question and that, finally, political relaxation should accompany a general détente.

4. [See Philip Nobile, "Skirmish over *Guernica*," *Harper's Magazine,* March 1977, pp. 21–22 (some errors), and Gerald Marzorati, " '*Guernica* will hang in the Prado as Picasso wished,' " *Art News,* May 1977, pp. 65–67 (the title quotes Dumas). Excellent subsequent summaries by James Markham, "A New Battle for *Guernica*," *The New York Times Magazine,* 26 November 1978, and Hilton Kramer, "When to Move Picasso's 'Guernica' from the Modern to the Prado," *The New York Times,* 16 July 1978 (sec. 2), revealing how the U.S. Congress was becoming involved. Section 605 of The Foreign Relations Authorization Act (PL 95–426, 7 Oct. 1978) eloquently describes *Guernica* as "a powerful and poignant symbol of the horror of war; this treasured painting, while universal in its significance, holds special meaning for the people of Spain by its representation of the tragic war which destroyed Spanish democracy." The law recognizes recent developments "toward the construction of a stable and lasting Spanish democracy," and supports *Guernica*'s transfer to Spain "at some point in the near future."]

5. [Picasso's formal understanding with The Museum of Modern Art, dated 14 November 1970, specified that:

> You have agreed to deliver the painting, studies and drawings to qualified representatives of the Spanish Government when civil liberties are established in Spain. You know that it has been my wish that this work and its studies return to the Spanish people.

Published in *La Odisea del "Guernica" de Picasso* (Barcelona, 1981, p. 221) by Rafael Fernández-Quintanilla, the career diplomat most involved in *Guernica*'s "return." The document also is reproduced in *Guernica-Legado,* p. 160.]

6. [In April 1971 Picasso wrote an emotional note (Fernández-Quintanilla, p. 222, and *Guernica-Legado,* p. 160):

> I confirm anew that since 1939 I have entrusted *Guernica* and the studies that accompany it to The Museum of Modern Art in New York for safe keeping and that they are intended for the government of the Spanish Republic.

Picasso's wording, "au governement de la République Espagnole," complicates the legal issue, since the democratic government of post-Franco Spain is a constitutional monarchy, not a republic. (Fernández-Quintanilla pointed out [p. 145] that this note was dated 14 April 1971, the 40th anniversary of the Spanish Republic's establishment in 1931.) Picasso also intended his sculptures for the Spanish Pavilion to revert to Spain (p. 72, above, and figs. 86 and 87), though they are not specifically cited in these two documents.]

All those who have heard directly from Picasso the instructions which he gave for *Guernica* are unanimous in believing that, while the wishes of the famous painter to see this prestigious work in Madrid were distinct and without ambiguity, he intended prudence in the realization of his decision.

He spoke to me numerous times about this anguishing subject. His preoccupation about *Guernica* took precedence over everything else. He furnished proof of this in agreeing to make arrangements in writing, which he had not done for any other problem touching on either his succession or his work. He did me the honor of confiding in me the responsibility of overseeing the execution of his wishes.

Admittedly, some progress has been realized in Spain. And a not-negligible evolution has occurred since the death of General Franco. But I cannot consider that this evolution has as yet terminated.

Neither have the conditions posed by Picasso himself touching on the security of the painting and the stability of a new and totally democratic regime been achieved.

The transfer of *Guernica*, finally, demands manifold technical precautions. These arrangements will require several months from the day when the decision of transfer shall be made.

For all these reasons and in accord with The Museum of Modern Art in New York which agrees to continue as "guardian," a mission which was initially confided to it by Picasso himself, *Guernica* shall stay in New York, to remain there until a new order is achieved in Spain.

Consequently, its transfer to the Prado in Madrid[7]—which is agreed upon in principle—cannot be realized for several years.

The present communication has been read to Mr. Rubin, Director of the Department of Painting and Sculpture of The Museum of Modern Art in New York, who has been good enough to agree to its terms.

7. [Other places have vied for the honor of receiving *Guernica:* The new Museum of Contemporary Art in Madrid, Barcelona with its fine Picasso museum, and the town of Guernica where a splendid museum was being planned specifically for the painting and related works (*L'Architecture d'aujourdui,* Oct. 1981, pp. xxv-vi); and *Architectural Design,* 52/5-6 (1982) pp. 74–75. Proud of his artistic heritage and his honorary directorship of the Prado during the civil war (p. 50, above), however, Picasso wanted *Guernica* to join the masterpieces of the Prado he most treasured: Velázquez's *Maids of Honor* and Goya's two great historical paintings, *The Second of May* and *The Third of May, 1808, in Madrid* (fig. 149). Since the main building is already overcrowded, the adjacent "little Prado" (fig. 138)—the Casón del Buen Retiro (appropriate name for the weary traveler's Spanish resting place)—was modernized to house *Guernica.*]

II.
THE SPANISH CIVIL WAR

Guernica would not exist without the Spanish Civil War. For a peacetime pavilion, Picasso would have painted a different canvas, a colorful decoration. Although it depicts neither air raid nor modern warfare, *Guernica* has immortalized the bombed city whose name it bears,[1] and it is admired as a great antiwar statement.

To see *Guernica* in its original context, therefore, we need to know something about the war and the bombing incident (summarized in the introduction, pp. 48–50 and 56–57). Primary sources collected in this section represent several viewpoints: historical facts are filtered through political sympathies. Picasso certainly read, in translation, the celebrated newspaper account by a British reporter passionately committed to the Spanish Republican cause.[2] He might also have seen quoted the eyewitness account by a Basque priest. The opposite side speaks through memoirs of Nazi pilots flying for General Franco, Nationalist messages denying or justifying the bombing, and captured telegrams from German diplomats worrying about international repercussions. In the last piece, a writer of postwar Madrid tries to sever *Guernica* from its civil war context and to restore it to the artistic heritage of Spain.

1. A Spaniard has argued that "the bombing of Guernica had a world-wide impact more because of the famous painting of Picasso than for the destructive effect of the bomb" (Gil Mugarza, *España en llamas, 1936* [Barcelona, 1968; an expensive book of civil war photographs], quoted by Southworth, p. 240. See also p. 57 and note 21.

2. The dilemma of an ideologically committed journalist (and how many reporters can remain uninvolved?), who must reconcile personal sympathies with objective professionalism, is explored by Phillip Knightley, *The First Casualty—From the Crimea to Vietnam: The War Correspondent as Hero, Propagandist, and Myth Maker* (New York, 1975); he includes Guernica and the civil war.

George L. Steer
The Tragedy of Guernica—[1937]*

The following report to *The Times* of London, also cabled to *The New York Times,* electrified the world and helped make the bombing of Guernica an international incident. Picasso surely read it in translation. Although several French papers reported the bombing,[1] Steer's was by far the most complete and stirring account; it was translated immediately and published in the April 29 edition of *L'Humanité* [fig. 78].

Steer's familiarity with Basque traditions, his passionate support of the Republican cause, and outrage over the bombing may have led him to exaggerate some details, to emphasize that Guernica was far behind the battle lines and not a military objective.[2] Certainly his vivid descriptions and convincing tone increased the emotional impact of his story. It has remained the most frequently cited account of the event.[3]

THE TRAGEDY OF GUERNICA
TOWN DESTROYED IN AIR ATTACK

EYE-WITNESS'S ACCOUNT

FROM OUR SPECIAL CORRESPONDENT
Bilbao, April 27

Guernica, the most ancient town of the Basques and the centre of their cultural tradition, was completely destroyed yesterday afternoon by insurgent air raiders. The bombardment of this open town far behind the lines occupied precisely three hours and a quarter, during which a powerful fleet of aeroplanes consisting of three German types, Junkers and Heinkel bombers, did not cease unloading on the town bombs

---

*Reprinted from *The Times* of London, 28 April 1937.

1. Southworth records early press coverage in his first chapter. Picasso would have seen the popular evening paper, *Paris-Soir,* and the pro-Communist *Ce Soir,* which carried reports by Noel Monks and Mathieu Corman; these eyewitness accounts also are included in Steer's pamphlet, *The Spanish War: Foreign Wings over the Basque Country* (London, 1937).

2. Hugh Thomas placed Guernica 30 kilometers from the front in his 1961 edition, but 10 miles (16 km) in the 1977 revision; the Nationalist telegram reduced the distance to 6 kilometers (p. 172, below). The closer to the front, the more Guernica could be considered a military target in the Nationalist drive to Bilbao.

3. In his first edition, Thomas closely followed Steer's account; see also Arnheim, p. 18, and Blunt, pp. 7–8. Steer expanded his material into *The Tree of Gernika* (London, 1938), still essential for Guernica studies, and fortunately excerpted in Sperber's 1974 anthology, *And I Remember Spain.* Spanish attempts to discredit him prove his effectiveness for the Republican cause (see the sharp attacks by Luis Bolín and Vicente Talón, pp. 169 and 171, below). Steer died a war correspondent's death in Burma (1909–1944).

weighing from 1,000 lb. downwards and, it is calculated, more than 3,000 two-pounder aluminium incendiary projectiles. The fighters, meanwhile, plunged low from above the centre of the town to machine-gun those of the civilian population who had taken refuge in the fields.

The whole town of Guernica was soon in flames except the historic Casa de Juntas with its rich archives of the Basque race, where the ancient Basque Parliament used to sit. The famous oak of Guernica, the dried old stump of 600 years and the young new shoots of this century, was also untouched.[4] Here the kings of Spain used to take the oath to respect the democratic rights (fueros) of Vizcaya and in return received a promise of allegiance as suzerains with the democratic title of Señor, not Rey [de] Vizcaya. The noble parish church of Santa Maria was also undamaged except for the beautiful chapter house, which was struck by an incendiary bomb.

At 2 a.m. to-day when I visited the town the whole of it was a horrible sight, flaming from end to end. The reflection of the flames could be seen in the clouds of smoke above the mountains from 10 miles away. Throughout the night houses were falling until the streets became long heaps of red impenetrable debris. Many of the civilian survivors took the long trek from Guernica to Bilbao in antique solid-wheeled Basque farmcarts drawn by oxen. Carts piled high with such household possessions as could be saved from the conflagration clogged the roads all night. Other survivors were evacuated in Government lorries, but many were forced to remain round the burning town lying on mattresses or looking for lost relatives and children, while units of the fire brigades and the Basque motorized police under the personal direction of the Minister of the Interior, Señor Monzon, and his wife continued rescue work till dawn.

Church Bell Alarm

In the form of its execution and the scale of the destruction it wrought, no less than in the selection of its objective, the raid on Guernica is unparalleled in military history. Guernica was not a military objective. A factory producing war materiel lay outside the town and was untouched. So were two barracks some distance from the town. The town lay far behind the lines. The object of the bombardment was seemingly the demoralization of the civil population and the destruction of the cradle of the Basque race. Every fact bears out this appreciation, beginning with the day when the deed was done.

Monday was the customary market day in Guernica for the country round. At 4:30 p.m., when the market was full and peasants were still coming in, the church bell rang the alarm for approaching aeroplanes, and the population sought refuge in cellars and in the dugouts prepared following the bombing of the civilian population of Durango on March 31, which opened General Mola's offensive in the north. The people are said to have shown a good spirit. A Catholic priest took charge and perfect order was maintained.

---

4. Sperber reprints a vivid description by an American visiting Guernica in February 1937: "In Bilbao, where we are staying, the war is a reality every minute of the day. . . . I have difficulty, here in this little country town, lying amid these gray and green Basque mountains, in believing there is a war." At the parliament building, he is shown "the carefully preserved trunk of the great oak," and the book of the Basque constitution, "hand-illumined in 1342, and the librarian told me one of the sentences of our constitution is from the ancient code" (pp. 171–72).

Five minutes later a single German bomber appeared, circled over the town at a low altitude, and then dropped six heavy bombs, apparently aiming for the station. The bombs with a shower of grenades fell on a former institute and on houses and streets surrounding it. The aeroplane then went away. In another five minutes came a second bomber, which threw the same number of bombs into the middle of the town. About a quarter of an hour later three Junkers arrived to continue the work of demolition, and thenceforward the bombing grew in intensity and was continuous, ceasing only with the approach of dusk at 7:45. The whole town of 7,000 inhabitants, plus 3,000 refugees, was slowly and systematically pounded to pieces. Over a radius of miles round a detail of the raiders' technique was to bomb separate *caseríos,* or farmhouses. In the night these burned like little candles in the hills. All the villages around were bombed with the same intensity as the town itself, and at Múgica, a little group of houses at the head of the Guernica inlet, the population was machine-gunned for 15 minutes.

Rhythm of Death

It is impossible to state yet the number of victims. In the Bilbao Press this morning they were reported as "fortunately small," but it is feared that this was an understatement in order not to alarm the large refugee population of Bilbao. In the hospital of Josefinas, which was one of the first places bombed, all the 42 wounded militiamen it sheltered were killed outright. In the street leading downhill from the Casa de Juntas I saw a place where 50 people, nearly all women and children, are said to have been trapped in an air raid refuge under a mass of burning wreckage. Many were killed in the fields, and altogether the deaths may run into hundreds. An elderly priest named Aronategui was killed by a bomb while rescuing children from a burning house.

The tactics of the bombers, which may be of interest to students of the new military science, were as follows:—First, small parties of aeroplanes threw heavy bombs and hand grenades all over the town, choosing area after area in orderly fashion. Next came fighting machines which swooped low to machine-gun those who ran in panic from the dugouts, some of which had already been penetrated by 1,000-lb. bombs, which make a hole 25 ft. deep. Many of these people were killed as they ran. A large herd of sheep being brought in to the market was also wiped out. The object of this move was apparently to drive the population underground again, for next as many as 12 bombers appeared at a time dropping heavy and incendiary bombs upon the ruins. The rhythm of this bombing of an open town was, therefore, a logical one: first, hand grenades and heavy bombs to stampede the population, then machine-gunning to drive them below, next heavy and incendiary bombs to wreck the houses and burn them on top of the victims.

The only counter-measures the Basques could employ, for they do not possess sufficient aeroplanes to face the insurgent fleet, were those provided by the heroism of the Basque clergy. These blessed and prayed for the kneeling crowds,—Socialists, Anarchists, and Communists, as well as the declared faithful in the crumbling dugouts.

When I entered Guernica after midnight houses were crashing on either side, and it was utterly impossible even for firemen to enter the centre of the town. The hospitals of Josefinas and Convento de Santa Clara were glowing heaps of embers, all the churches except that of Santa Maria were destroyed, and the few houses which still stood were doomed. When I revisited Guernica this afternoon most of the town was still burning and new fires had broken out. About 30 dead were laid out in a ruined hospital.

A Call to Basques

The effect here of the bombardment of Guernica, the Basques' holy city, has been profound and has led President Aguirre to issue the following statement in this morning's Basque Press:—

"The German airmen in the service of the Spanish rebels have bombarded Guernica, burning the historic town which is held in such veneration by all Basques. They have sought to wound us in the most sensitive of our patriotic sentiments, once more making it entirely clear what Euzkadis may expect of those who do not hesitate to destroy us down to the very sactuary which records the centuries of our liberty and our democracy.

"Before the outrage all we Basques must react with violence, swearing from the bottom of our hearts to defend the principles of our people with unheard-of stubbornness and heroism if the case requires it. We cannot hide the gravity of the moment; but victory can never be won by the invader if, raising our spirits to heights of strength and determination, we steel ourselves to his defeat.

"The enemy has advanced in many parts elsewhere to be driven out of them afterwards. I do not hesitate to affirm that here the same thing will happen. May to-day's outrage be one spur more to do it with all speed."

Alberto de Onaindía
Guernica Aflame—[1937]*

Low-flying planes pursued and machine-gunned a young Basque priest as he hid amidst trees on the outskirts of Guernica. He lived to tell of massive civilian casualties, of bomb craters, and a city aflame. Father Onaindía reported his experiences to the Basque President Aguirre in Bilbao, then went to Paris and gave extensive interviews, thus publicizing one of the horrifying eyewitness accounts of the Guernica incident.[1]

Late in the afternoon of April 26 I was going by car to rescue my mother and my sisters, then living in Marquina, a town about to fall into the hands of Franco. It was one of those magnificently clear days, the sky soft and serene. We reached the outskirts of Guernika just before five o'clock. The streets were busy with the traffic of market-day. Suddenly we heard the siren, and trembled. People were running about in all directions, abandoning everything they possessed, some hurrying into the shelters, others running into the hills. Soon an enemy airplane appeared over Guernika. A peasant was passing by. "It's nothing, only one of the 'white' ones," he said. "He'll drop a few bombs, and then he'll go away." The Basques had learned to distinguish between the twin-engined "whites" and the three-engined "blacks." The "white" airplane made a reconnaissance over the town, and when he was directly over the center he dropped three bombs. Immediately afterwards we saw a squadron of seven planes, followed a little later by six more, and this in turn by a third squadron of five

---

*"Guernika," from the excellent anthology of primary sources, Robert Payne, ed., *The Civil War in Spain, 1936–1939*, New York, 1962, pp. 195–97, by permission; Onaindía's account was reprinted from a pamphlet [Basque spelling, *Guernika*], published in Bilbao, 1937.

1. Father Onaindía was no ordinary parish priest. The 34-year-old Basque was canon of Valladolid Cathedral (north of Madrid) on leave from Catholic social work in Bilbao, where he became closely associated with President Aguirre. For extensive background material and international press coverage of Father Onaindía (and Nationalist attempts to discredit him, terming him a Communist and defrocked priest), see Southworth, pp. 138–54, and notes, pp. 449–56.

more. All of them were Junkers. Meanwhile Guernika was seized with a terrible panic.

I left the car by the side of the road and took refuge with five milicianos in a sewer.[2] The water came up to our ankles. From our hiding place we could see everything that happened without being seen. The airplanes came low, flying at two hundred meters. As soon as we could leave our shelter, we ran into the woods, hoping to put a safe distance between us and the enemy. But the airmen saw us and went after us. The leaves hid us. As they did not know exactly where we were, they aimed their machine-guns in the direction they thought we were traveling. We heard the bullets ripping through branches, and the sinister sound of splintering wood. The milicianos and I followed the flight patterns of the airplanes; and we made a crazy journey through the trees, trying to avoid them. Meanwhile women, children and old men were falling in heaps, like flies, and everywhere we saw lakes of blood.

I saw an old peasant standing alone in a field: a machine-gun bullet killed him. For more than an hour these eighteen planes, never more than a few hundred meters in altitude, dropped bomb after bomb on Guernika. The sound of the explosions and of the crumbling houses cannot be imagined. Always they traced on the air the same tragic flight pattern, as they flew over all the streets of Guernika. Bombs fell by thousands. Later we saw the bomb craters. Some were sixteen meters in diameter and eight meters deep.

The airplanes left around seven o'clock, and then there came another wave of them, this time flying at an immense altitude. They were dropping incendiary bombs on our martyred city. The new bombardment lasted thirty-five minutes, sufficient to transform the town into an enormous furnace. Even then I realized the terrible purpose of this new act of vandalism. They were dropping incendiary bombs to try to convince the world that the Basques had fired their own city.

The destruction of Guernika went on altogether for two hours and forty-five minutes. When the bombing was over, the people left their shelters. I saw no one crying. Stupor was written on all their faces. Eyes fixed on Guernika, we were completely incapable of believing what we saw.

Towards dusk we could see no more than five hundred meters. Everywhere there were flames and thick black smoke. Around me people were praying, and some stretched our their arms in the form of a cross, imploring mercy from Heaven.

Soon firemen arrived from Bilbao and started to work on some of the buildings which had not been bombed. We heard that the glow of the flames had been seen from Lequeitio, twenty-two kilometers away. Not even the people who went into the refuges were saved; nor the sick and wounded in the hospitals. Guernika had no anti-aircraft guns, no batteries of any kind; nor were there any machine-guns.

During the first hours of the night it was a most horrifying spectacle: men, women and children were wandering through the woods in search of their loved ones. In most cases they found only their bullet-riddled bodies.

The buildings near the Tree of Guernika, which stands on a small hill, were unharmed, but the City Hall with its valuable archives and documents was completely destroyed.

When it grew dark the flames of Guernika were reaching to the sky, and the clouds took on the color of blood, and our faces too shone with the color of blood.

2. [Possibly an awkward translation; in later memoirs, Father Onaindía described his shelter as a stone bridge over a river (Southworth, p. 139).]

Memoirs of the Condor Legion

Finally, in 1975, the West German Military Research Office published its study of Guernica, with contemporary diaries and postwar statements by retired officers. There is no startling new evidence, but the book confirms that elements of the Condor Legion and some Italian forces did indeed bomb Guernica. Poor visibility caused by smoke and dust from initial strikes made the bombadiers miss their military targets: access roads and the Rentería bridge (map, fig. 76). After that, they "felt little compunction about tossing their bombs right in the 'middle' [of town]."[1]

Especially interesting are Lieutenant Colonel von Richthofen's journals: they document how the Condor Legion, with extraordinary tactical autonomy, could dictate military decisions to their Spanish allies. Von Richthofen (cousin of the celebrated World War I ace) was the ambitious, efficient chief of staff, more crucial than his superior, General Sperrle, in planning such daily operations as the attack on Guernica. Also included are contradictory recollections of the very squadron commanders who led the air raid, with fascinating details: secrecy orders and clean-up operations to disguise the attack. The documents are translated here for the first time.[2]

Freiherr von Richthofen

Journal Entries—[1937]*

The Condor Legion's chief of staff is mysteriously brief about 26 April activities, which surely required extensive preparations. The following days show equally brief notations: "disturbing report that Guernica seems to be aflame" (27.4), and "confirmed report that Guernica is leveled to the ground" (28.4). The detailed summary of 30 April, reprinted below, followed his inspection trip. It was written later, during a two-month leave, when he was of course aware of the international uproar after the attack.[3]

1. Chillingly flippant in German: ". . . wenig Hemmungen hatten, einfach 'mitten hineinzuwerfen' * * *" From the introduction by the German captain who edited the collection, Hans A. Maier, *Guernica, 26.4.1937: Die deutsche Intervention in Spanien und der "Fall Guernica,"* (Freiburg im Breisgau, 1975), p. 66.

2. Some of this material reached the American and European public in a popular, dramatized version by Gordon Thomas and Max Morgan Witts, *Guernica: Crucible of World War II* (New York, 1975), with additional interviews of survivors and participants, and some 60 superb photographs. Their fictionalized format and imagined dialogues, and lack of documentary footnotes, unfortunately prevent the reader from distinguishing fact from fiction. Southworth criticized the quickly translated Spanish version, *El día en que murió Guernica* (Barcelona, 1976) as "highly censored" and "totally lacking in precision" (p. 495, note 2).

*Reprinted from Maier, ed., *Guernica, 26. 4. 1937*, pp. 103 and 109, by permission of author-editor and publisher. These valuable primary documents have not been exploited sufficiently: only a brief citation in Southworth, p. 495, and no references by Hugh Thomas (1977), who relies on the Thomas and Morgan Witts popularization. My translation was greatly facilitated by officers of the United States Air Force Detachment at Hancock Field, Syracuse, who helped me interpret technical terminology.

3. [Dr. Maier clarified the leave period as 11 May to 17 July 1937; he argues against von Richthofen's *intentionally* misrepresenting the Guernica incident (pp. 64–65, note 198). It is obvious, however, that the journal entries (especially 30 April) were composed with future readers in mind. Editorial changes also could have been made when the handwritten manuscript was typed in 1939.]

26. 4. 1937

Dispatch at once: A/88 and J/88 to chase up and down the roads in the Marquina-Guernica-Guerricaiz area. K/88 (after returning from Guerricaiz), VB/88 and the Italians to the roads and the bridge (including the suburb) immediately east of *Guernica*.[4] That's *got* to be closed off, if there's to be success against the enemy's personnel and materiel. Vigon[5] agrees to push his troops ahead so that all roads south of Guernica are blocked off. If that works, then we've got the enemy around Marquina in the bag.

30. 4. 1937

Guernica, a town of 5,000 inhabitants, literally leveled to the ground. Attack carried out with 250-kg and incendiary bombs—about one-third of the latter. When the first Junker squadron arrived, there was smoke already everywhere (from the VB [VB/88] which had attacked with 3 aircraft); nobody could identify the targets of roads, bridge, and suburb, and so they just dropped everything right into the center. The 250s toppled a number of houses and destroyed the water mains. The incendiaries now could spread and become effective. The materials of the houses: tile roofs, wooden porches, and half-timbering resulted in complete annihilation. Most inhabitants were away because of a holiday; a majority of the rest left town immediately at the beginning [of the bombardment]. A small number perished in shelters that were hit. Bomb craters can still be seen in the streets, simply terrific.—Town completely blocked off for at least 24 hours, perfect conditions for a great victory, if only the troops had followed through. Complete technical success of our 250s and EC.B.1.[6]

Otherwise, everything peaceful in Guernica. * * * sacred oak tree (newly planted oak, ancient trunk under glass) beneath which the kings for more than 1,000 years swore allegiance to the Constitution and laws of Viscaya.[7] Next to it, the church and parliament building. Nothing destroyed of this whole section on the edge of town. [See map, fig. 76.]

4. [Italics in the text. The designated units are: A/88—reconnaissance unit of the Condor Legion; J/88—fighter group, flying Heinkel 51s. K/88—main tactical bomber group flying Junker 52s and dropping conventional bombs. VB/88—special experimental bomber squadron [von Moreau, commander] flying new, faster Heinkel 111s, which dropped small incendiary bombs: one third incendiaries and two thirds 250-kilogram bombs.]

5. [Colonel Juan Vigón, Richthofen's Spanish counterpart: chief of staff to General Mola.]

6. ["and EC.B.1." handwritten addition. Refers to 1-kg incendiary bombs developed by I. G. Farben (summary of Maier's note). In other words, while criticizing Spanish troops, von Richthofen is pleased with the bombs' effectiveness; no complaints that military objectives—access roads, the bridge, or the railroad station—escaped demolition.]

7. [He has obviously read Steer's news report, p. 161, above! One final cryptic statement needs quoting, a personal letter, 25 May 1937, to an unidentified but personally close recipient: "All the excitement about German bombers is of course completely unjustified, since there are only Spanish units here! But as for Guernica, I probably behaved a bit like a lout!" (p. 112). In German—"wohl etwas rüpelhaft"—this is a ruthless understatement, more descriptive of a rowdy, uncouth country boy.]

Squadron Leader von Beust

Written Statements—[1955 and 1973]*

An attack that, for special propagandistic reasons, was discussed throughout the whole world at the time, will be noted here especially: the destruction of the town of Guernica on 25. 4. 37.[8] (The author of this statement personally participated in this mission as leader of the second attacking squadron.) The Reds at this time were streaming westward along the coastline towards the Iron Ring [fortifications encircling Bilbao] in order to take up new positions there. This retreat took a great number of units through Guernica, which was full of enemy troops, and south of town, across a small bridge.[9] This bridge was the assigned target, as well as the enemy troops very much concentrated there, as revealed by our reconnaissance. There were 3 attacking squadrons with 6 aircraft, flying some kilometers apart at approximately 3,500-meter altitude, approaching the target from the north—in other words, over the town.[10] So much dust and smoke developed after the first bombing run that all visibility was lost of the terrain, the target, and the town; thus the two following squadrons could only estimate where to drop their bombs. For that reason, and because of strong wind drift, the bulk of these bombs fell into the town. This error, due to purely technical reasons, was so skillfully exploited as propaganda by the opposition, that Franco feared political repercussions, and therefore the whole air attack was simply contested.

□ □ □

Already on the same day that the propaganda wave started and reconnaissance reports confirmed extensive destruction, we—the K/88 crew—were ordered not to talk about the attack and, if necessary, to deny it.[11]

---

*Appendix 15, pp. 156–57, in Maier, *Guernica*; typewritten statement of 1955 by Freiherr von Beust, with supplementary letter of 16 March 1973.

8. Corrected [in 1973] to 26. 4. 1937.

9. The Rentería bridge lies to the northwest of town. [This incorrect footnote by Maier further compounds the confusion, whereas on his map following p. 40, and on pp. 56 and 103, note 58, he correctly places the suburb Rentería and the bridge *northeast* of central Guernica; again, see fig. 76.]

10. [An approach of 3,500 meters (approximately 11,500 feet) or even 1,500 meters (just under 5,000 feet—von Knauer's estimate, below) is much too elevated for precision bombing of a small target, such as the bridge. U.S. Air Force officers considered 2,000 feet altitude appropriate for this purpose. For that matter, why did the Condor Legion not use their accurate Stuka dive bombers? Hugh Thomas wondered (*Spanish Civil War*, 1977 ed., p. 627).]

11. [Excerpted from the supplementary letter of 16 March 1973. Von Beust therein reiterated his previous views that the crew had not intended to destroy the town; he also volunteered the opinion that he doubted that "the Reds subsequently did more damage".]

Squadron Leader von Knauer

Written Statement—[1974]*

On 1. 5. 1937 I was sent in a passenger car (per order of Lieutenant Colonel von Richthofen, requested by General Sperrle) to Guernica, among other places, to ascertain conditions also in Guernica. Despite well dispatched bombing sequences, there was no lasting damage to the bridge, whereas the center of town was very much destroyed, especially the market place where there were still dead horses lying about. The effect of our 50-kilogram bombs could not possibly have been so powerful.[12] As I found out (in conversation with townspeople through my interpreter), the so-called Dynamiteros had had large storage depots of dynamite that were made to explode, either by our air attack or afterwards. And only thus could the great destruction be brought about and explained. I reported this in detail to Lt. Col. von Richthofen and also to my commanding officer, Major Fuchs.

1. The extensive destruction of Guernica can be explained through the dynamite storage depots.

2. Subsequent destruction by Red troops is unlikely, because of the rapid, panic-like retreat of the front lines.

3. Airdrop of 50-kilogram bombs, in closely spaced sequence.

4. The Moreau squadron did not attack Guernica on 26. 4. 1937.[13]

Contrary to all the reports in newspapers and books: K/88 attacked Guernica in V-formation, the squadrons following each other. Mine was the lead aircraft of the first squadron, with Major Fuchs aboard. The target was attacked in *one* assault with 50-kg bombs dropped in close sequence, from a height of 1,500 meters. Weather condition: blue sky; direction of assault: turning from the Bay of Biscay, from north to south. Probably because of northeast cross wind, the bombs were shifted in a westerly direction, so that the eastern edge of town was hit in part.

As I remember clearly, General Sperrle received an inquiry from Ambassador von Ribbentrop in London,[14] whether an international commission could go to Guernica to convince itself that German bombs could not possibly have caused this great destruction. The Condor Legion dispatched ordnance workers to Guernica to remove all remnants of tail fins, bomb duds, etc. Thereafter, Ambassador Ribbentrop was informed that a commission could go to Guernica at any time.

---

*Appendix 16, pp. 158–59, in Maier, *Guernica,* from a written statement of 6 January 1974. Von Knauer also refers to his logbook where he entered the military objective, the bridge, his altitude (1,500 meters), and the comment: good results *(Gute Wirkung)*—an odd evaluation if the bridge, which was not destroyed, was the main objective and not the entire town.]

12. [True enough—but von Knauer fails to report that the planes carried not only the 50-kg (110-lb) bombs, but especially the five-times-stronger 250-kg bombs, as stated in von Richthofen's journals.]

13. [An obvious attempt to deny the important role of von Moreau's experimental bomber squadron—the VB/88—whose *incendiary* bombs certainly were questionable ammunition against roads and a bridge of metal and concrete; cf. von Richthoften, p. 166, above.]

14. [See the cable messages, p. 171.]

German and Nationalist Telegrams—[1937]

While invading Nazi Germany in 1945, the United States Army discovered over 300 tons of diplomatic archives secreted away in the Harz mountains of Thuringia. These captured documents reveal that German diplomats worried about international reaction to the Guernica incident. They wanted to placate Great Britain; neither Germany nor Franco Spain would admit to the bombing, since both clearly benefited from the nonintervention policy of the Western democracies. Repeated German requests that Franco deny German involvement were ignored; instead, "the Reds" were blamed. Telegram 237 quotes the Franco press statement that remained the Spanish government position for some thirty years: Guernica was blown up by "the Reds"—the Basque Loyalists—preparing to evacuate the town from advancing Nationalist troops. Luis Bolín, Nationalist press and propaganda chief, probably devised this "explanation" of Guernica's destruction.[1]

Telegram to the German Embassy in Salamanca, Spain*

From Hans Georg von Mackensen, career diplomat and state secretary in the Foreign Ministry in Berlin during 1937–39.

No. 151   Berlin, 4 May 1937

In yesterday's debate in the British House of Commons on the incidents in Guernica, accusations against Germany were again made. Eden answered evasively, but ordered the British Ambassador and the Consul in Bilbao[2] to report and promised Commons a further answer before the Whitsuntide adjournment.

Our Ambassador in London[3] wires: "From various quarters the Embassy is

---

1. Bolín's memoir, *Spain—The Vital Years* (London, 1967) with an entire chapter and appendix about "The Guernica Myth," was discovered belatedly in America after Bolín's death (1897–1969). The controversy was kept alive throughout 1973, long after the wartime legend was no longer believed even in Franco Spain. (See Jeffrey Hart's endorsement of Bolín, "The Great Guernica Fraud, "*National Review,* 5 Jan. 1973, pp. 27–29; spirited debates in *NR,* 31 Aug. 73, pp. 936–42; Roger Williams's intelligent evaluation, "Report from Guernica: Was Picasso Duped?" *Saturday Review/World,* 20 Nov. 1973, pp. 10, 68–69; challenging letter, *SR/World,* 9 Feb. 1974, p. 5.)

*Reprinted from *Documents on German Foreign Policy, Series D, 1918–1945, volume III, The Spanish Civil War* (London, Paris, Washington, 1951), p. 270.

2. [In his expanded edition of *The Spanish Civil War* (1977), p. 986, Hugh Thomas appended the British Consul's letter to his Ambassador, Sir Henry Chilton:

On landing in Bermeo yesterday I was told about the destruction of Guernica. I went at once to have a look at the place and to my amazement found that the township normally of some five thousand inhabitants, since the September influx of refugees about ten thousand, was almost completely destroyed. Nine houses in ten are beyond reconstruction. Many were still burning and fresh fires were breaking out here and there, the result of incendiary bombs which owing to some fault had not exploded on impact the day before and were doing so, at the time of my visit, under falling beams and masonry. The casualties cannot be ascertained; probably never will, accurately. Some estimates put the figures at one thousand, others at three thousand.]

3. [Joachim von Ribbentrop (1893–1946) was German ambassador in London from 1936 to February 1938 when he was promoted to foreign minister in Berlin. Sir Anthony Eden spoke to the House of Commons as British foreign secretary.]

receiving communications making German fliers responsible for the bombardment of Guernica, in spite of our denials. In private conversations Franco's denial is still given prominence and is construed to mean that Franco indirectly admits the attack was made by German fliers. The debate in Commons could perhaps be taken as a basis for inducing Franco now to issue an energetic and sharp denial which would not be equivocally construed."

Please induce Franco to issue an immediate and energetic denial. Our press has rejected the false British reports, by using material meanwhile received which proves destruction of the city by the Bolshevists.

Mackensen

Telegram from the Ambassador in Spain to the Foreign Ministry, Berlin*

Sent by Wilhelm von Faupel, German chargé d'affaires after Berlin recognized the Nationalist insurgents in 1936; first German ambassador to Franco Spain since February 1937, in the Nationalist capital of Salamanca. (Madrid was still held by the Republican government.)

No. 237 of May 5   Salamanca, 5 May 1937

Answer to telegraphic instruction 151.

The denial agreed upon with Franco regarding Guernica has not been issued. On April 29 and April 30 the Nationalist Government's press bureau [issued] dispatches in the form of an article regarding the burning of Guernica.[4] These were also given to foreign press representatives. In the sharpest terms they reject as lies and slander the Basque Government's report regarding the alleged destruction of the city by German fliers. The interpretation that this denial indirectly admits a German plane attack is malicious and unsupported by the text of the denial. A translation of some of the important passages of the denial of April 29 follows:

"Guernica was destroyed with fire and gasoline. It was set afire and reduced to ruins by the Red hordes in the criminal service of Aguirre, the President of the Basque Republic. Aguirre planned the destruction of Guernica with the devilish intention of laying the blame before the enemy's door and producing a storm of indignation among the already conquered and demoralized Basques."

Faupel

---

*Documents, p. 281.

4. [Nationalist allegations that the Basques destroyed their own city were broadcast over Radio Nacional of Salamanca already on 27 April, at night, then disseminated to Nationalist papers, foreign reporters, and the pro-Nationalist French press agency Havas for distribution abroad. See Southworth, Guernica! for extraordinarily careful documentation of the event; his research (p. 33) confirms my deduction that Bolín himself fabricated this official "explanation".]

Telegram from the Ambassador in Great Britain to the Foreign Ministry, Berlin*

Von Ribbentrop's "urgent" cable is addressed to Hitler himself. The Spanish Republican government, reacting to Nationalist press allegations, had requested an international investigation and inspection of Guernica, which Franco troops had occupied on April 29th.

Urgent   London, 6 May
No. 261 of 6 May

For the Führer and Chancellor[5] and the Foreign Minister.

In yesterday's conversation with Eden regarding the Guernica incident, he declared that the British Government had not yet been able to form a final judgment regarding the matter, since reports thus far had been conflicting. * * *

During the conversation, Eden asked me casually whether Germany would agree to an international investigation of the incident. I stated that I wished to obtain the views of my Government on this point, and I request the earliest possible instructions. Possibly a proposal would have to be made by Belgium to extend the investigation to Red atrocities, more specifically to concrete instances of recent occurrence, if possible. In any case, I request such material at once. A note from the Red Spanish Government demanding an international investigation was received at the Foreign Office yesterday. It is to be expected that the Russians will bring up this demand in the committee as soon as possible.

Ribbentrop

A Nationalist Telegram to the Condor Legion**

Franco's General Headquarters was equally opposed to an objective, international investigation, and instead of providing the eagerly awaited denial of German responsibility, this telegram requested the Commander of the Condor Legion to confirm the bombing and to justify it as tactical support of Spanish "front-line units." A Spanish journalist, Vicente Talón, discovered this crucial message in the Spanish military history archives and published it in *Arde Guernica* (Madrid, 1970, 1973).[6]

---

*Documents, pp. 283–84.

5. [Hitler's reaction to this 6 May telegram are summarized in a Memorandum by Mackensen (*Documents,* p. 290): "that the investigation of a single military action was entirely outside the bounds of possibility and that such an investigation therefore had to be flatly rejected."]

**Reprinted from Southworth, *Guernica!* p. 301, by permission of the author and the University of California Press. Southworth underscores the importance of this telegram, "the only scrap of paper" documenting the close military cooperation between the Nazi Condor Legion and the Spanish Nationalists.

6. [Pages 112–13. *Arde Guernica* was an extraordinary book to have come out of Franco Spain, the first attempt to investigate the bombing, with some 70 sensational photographs of the destroyed city and personalities involved, and a chapter on Picasso's *Guernica* with excerpts of critical commentaries. Though Talón published the telegram, he maintained the myth—perhaps to placate Spanish censors— that German planes flew under direct orders from Berlin—thereby absolving the Nationalists of moral responsibility for the destruction of Guernica.]

I request Sander [General Sperrle] to inform Berlin that Guernica, a town of fewer than five thousand inhabitants, was six kilometers from the fighting line, is a highly important communications crossroad, has a factory for munitions, bombs and pistols; on the 26th it was a place for passage of units in flight and for the stationing of reserves. Front-line units requested directly to Aviation for the bombing of crossroads; this was carried out by the German and Italian [here Talón added a "sic"] airforce, and because of the lack of visibility, because of the smoke and clouds of dust, bombs from the planes hit the town.

Therefore, it is not possible to agree to the investigation; the Reds took advantage of the bombing to set fire to the town. The investigation constitutes a manoeuver of propaganda and an attack on the prestige of National Spain and nations friendly to it. The Red airforce constantly bombs important capitals far from the front, such as Saragossa, Valladolid, Córdoba, Melilla and other cities, leaving more than 300 dead and 600 wounded.

In no manner is it advisable to agree to [the investigation of] the matter of Guernica which has no real importance. Civilians assassinated by the Reds with the blessing of their government number more than 300,000, all known by diplomatic representatives of England, France and Russia.

Vicente Marrero
The Picture of All Bombed Cities—
[1951]*

While *Guernica* had become a world-renowned document of the Spanish Civil War, Picasso's painting was carefully ignored in Spain for some dozen years after the war had ended. The following excerpt comes from the first Picasso book published in Franco's capital in 1951.[1] Marrero concentrates on the most Spanish aspect of the artist's work, *Picasso and the Bull,* illustrating *Guernica, Minotauromachy,* and two apolitical scenes from *Dream and Lie of Franco* (tactfully omitting the title). By terming it "the picture of all bombed cities," he disassociated *Guernica* specifically from the Spanish Civil War, gave it a universal antiwar message, and thereby facilitated the Franco regime's campaign to have the painting "returned" to Spain (pp. 153–55, above).

In his great work *Guernica,* there are no ruins, no smashed houses or chimneys to remain standing in the rubble like giant's fingers pointing to the sky; the scanty flames in the picture are as small as the crest of a rooster. Within the space, which

---

*Reprinted from *Picasso and the Bull,* trans., Anthony Kerrigan (Chicago: Henry Regnery Co., 1956), pp. 75–77, by permission.

1. In Barcelona, however, two Picasso studies were published earlier: Cirici Pellicer's *Picasso antes de Picasso* (1946) and Gaya Nuño's small monograph, *Picasso* (1950). Only in the 1960s was *Guernica* occasionally reproduced in histories of the civil war or in cultural treaties (see Southworth, pp. 251–53).

could be an interior or could be *plein air,* there are only limbs and faces destroyed by fright and terror. The drama is an intimate one, so that only the faces betray its effects. In the midst of the humans are the horse and the bull. The horse is in the center of the canvas, its side transfixed by a lance, its mouth opened wide in a final cry, the tongue in the shape of a dagger. At its feet lies the rider, his sword broken. A figure who seems to have descended from heaven through a door suddenly thrust open pushes a lamp ahead of him. In the triangle of light which is formed from the two lower sides of the canvas up to the central height an anguished woman directs herself up to where the light begins, and in this illuminated area the central group of sufferers is structured. On the left, outside the area of light a threatening bull with curled tail dominates the entire composition; its snout seems to rest on the head of a desperate mother carrying the swaddling clothes of her dead child. At the other end, on the right, a man is caught in flames. All the mouths are open; the hands, where the lines of the tragedy are written, are also open. The black, white, grey, maroon[2] tones match the emotions of the drama. An electric bulb, the sun of disillusion, furnishes the rays of the only sun to shed light on these unfortunates. But a bird is flying, perhaps one raised by the very protest of the moribund horse, and it sings its song of life. The luminous triangle, too, despite the destruction, and the disarticulation of a composition reflecting bombardments and its effects, lends unity and force to the whole, as it tenses and sustains it. The bull triumphs over the work of desolation and chaos, wherein the cry of beings sacrificed to the cruelty of the world still rings out.

From this plastic composition it might be possible to make a meaningful juxtaposition by abstracting the fundamental themes: "the triangle," "transfixed by a lance," "the bird," "the victim," "the light from on high"; a dogmatic interpretation would be far-fetched, but still, there is at least a secularized Christian influence here. We can almost think of a Crucifixion, where the cross stands between the two thieves and the light of the sky forms a luminous triangle falling from the height. Rembrandt, perhaps?

The transcendent nature of this canvas has been obscured by a dismal political propaganda. And many people have chosen to see in it a work of propaganda, especially when it was first exposed to the French public in a pavillion facing the German representation in an exposition. The fact that Picasso identified his painting with the name of a city is a result of his profoundly realistic sense, which seeks always the concrete, the historic and still alive. Whatever political element there is in the painting is absorbed in the spiritual dimension, beyond all histrionics. The canvas, today more than ever, is no longer an illustration of one specific bombardment, but the picture of all bombed cities. It is the drama of thousands of European cities, impotent before brute force, before the bull of evil, whatever the flag it flies.

2. [Marrero obviously has not seen the original, nor has he carefully studied *Guernica* and its drawings, since he sees the woman with the lamp and the burning figure as men.]

III.
POETRY AND DRAMA

This part begins with the great lament by a Spaniard assassinated at the start of the civil war, and ends with the short play by a young Spaniard-in-exile from the Franco regime. Stephen Spender observed in his *Poems for Spain* that: "Poets and poetry have played a considerable part in the Spanish War, because to many people the struggle of the Republicans has seemed a struggle for the conditions without which the writing and reading of poetry are almost impossible in a modern society:

> To-morrow for the young poets exploding like bombs,
> The walks by the lake, the weeks of perfect communion . . .
> But to-day the struggle."[1]

Federico García Lorca
Lament for the Death of a Bullfighter—[1934]*

García Lorca's lament is the poetic equivalent of *Guernica*. They are blood relatives in color and imagery, in their persistent Spanish themes: "Oh white wall of Spain! Oh black bull of sorrow!" The first section's recurring refrain suggests the rhythmic drumbeat of a funeral procession. "Spain is the only country where death is a national spectacle," Lorca observed in 1933, "the only one where death sounds long trumpet blasts at the coming of spring" [to begin the bullfight].[1] The second section recalls the simple, passionate outcry of the Andalusian *canto hondo* ("deep song," like our blues that Lorca discovered and loved in New York in 1929–30).

As in *Guernica*, personal grief is transformed into universal statement. The final stanzas become a poignant memorial to the poet himself (1898–1936), assassinated at the start of the Spanish Civil War,[2] and a general lament for all young men wasted in that conflict, and indeed in all wars.

1. Spender and John Lehmann, eds. (London, 1939), preface, p. 7, quoting from the poem "Spain," by W. H. Auden.

*Reprinted from Federico García Lorca, *Lament for the Death of a Bullfighter and Other Poems* (Greenwood Press, Westport, Conn., 1977; from the 1937 Oxford University Press ed., A. L. Lloyd, trans.), pp. 3–19, by permission. Lorca completed the lament for his friend Ignacio in October–November 1934 (publ. 1935) during a particularly bloody prelude to the civil war, the uprisings of Asturian miners. Thus the poem's atmosphere of impending doom reaches beyond a purely personal response to a friend's violent death.

1. From "Play and Theory of the Duende," in Federico García Lorca, *Deep Song and Other Prose* ed. and trans. by Christopher Maurer (New York, 1980), p. 51; the volume also includes Lorca's essay on *canto hondo* (1922).

2. Though Lorca was apolitical, his writings and personality epitomized the free spirit of the Republic. His brother-in-law was Socialist mayor of Granada; both were among 572 "enemies of the new regime" executed by the Rebels. Ian Gibson in *The Death of Lorca* (London, Chicago, 1973) estimated that the total had risen to 4,000 by March 1939. For years, no one alluded to Lorca in Nationalist Spain and his burial site remained unmarked (*The New York Times*, 4 June 1976).

I

COGIDA[3] AND DEATH

At five in the afternoon.
It was exactly five in the afternoon.
A child carried a white sheet
at five in the afternoon.
A rush-basket of slaked lime
at five in the afternoon.
The rest was death and death alone
at five in the afternoon.
The wind bore away the cottonwool
at five in the afternoon.
And the oxide scattered crystal and nickel
at five in the afternoon.
Now the dove and the leopard are struggling
at five in the afternoon.
And a thigh with a desolate horn
at five in the afternoon.
The refrain of a song strikes up
at five in the afternoon.
Bell-jars of arsenic and steam
at five in the afternoon.
Groups of silence in the corners
at five in the afternoon.
And, all heart, the bull charges!
at five in the afternoon.
Just as the sweat of snow was coming
at five in the afternoon,
when the bullring was covered in iodine
at five in the afternoon,

death laid its eggs in his wound
at five in the afternoon.
At five in the afternoon.
At exactly five o'clock in the afternoon.

A coffin on wheels is his bed
at five in the afternoon.
Bones and flutes sound in his ears
at five in the afternoon.

3. *Cogida:* literally "the catching." The tossing of the bullfighter by the bull.

Already the bull is bellowing within his forehead
at *five in the afternoon.*
The room is iridescent with agony
at *five in the afternoon.*
Now from afar-off comes gangrene
at *five in the afternoon,*
a lily-trumpet through his green veins
at *five in the afternoon.*
His wounds blazed like suns
at *five in the afternoon,*
and the rabble shattered the windows
at *five in the afternoon.*
At five in the afternoon.
Ay, that terrible five o'clock in the afternoon.
It was five by all the clocks!
It was five in the shadow of the afternoon!

II

THE SPILLING OF THE BLOOD

   I do not want to see it!

   Tell the moon to rise,
   for I do not want to see the blood
   of Ignacio over the arena.

   I do not want to see it!

   The wide-open moon,
   horse of the quiet clouds,
   and the grey bullring of dream,
   with willows in the barreras.[4]
   I do not want to see it!
   May my memory be consumed by fire.
   Tell the jasmines
   with their minuscular whiteness!

   I do not want to see it!

4. *Barreras:* Wooden fence around the arena in which the bull is fought. The front row seats are also called "barreras."

The cow of the old world
passed her sad tongue
over a muzzle of bloodspots
spilt upon the sand,
and the bulls of Guisando,
half dead, half turned to stone,
bellowed like two centuries
weary of treading the earth.
No.
I do not want to see it!

Up the stairs went Ignacio
with all his death upon his shoulders.
He looked for daybreak,
but there was no daybreak.
He sought his dauntless profile,
and a dream misled him.
He sought his handsome body
and was faced with his unsealed blood.
Don't bid me to see it!
I do not want to feel the jet
each time slackening its force;
that jet that glistens on
the rows of seats, and pours
over the plush and leather
of the thirsty multitude.
Who calls to me that I should look?
Don't bid me to see it!

His eyes did not close
when he saw the horns near,
but the terrible mothers
lifted their heads.
And across the ranches
went a breath of secret voices
by which the herdsmen of the pallid mist
called to their heavenly bulls.

There was no prince in Seville
who could compare to him,
nor any sword like his sword
nor any heart so fervent.
Like a river of lions
his marvelous strength,
like a marble torso
his fine-drawn caution.
The air of an Andalusian Rome

gilded his head
on which his smile was a nard
of wit and intelligence.
What a great bullfighter in the ring!
What a splendid mountaineer in the mountains!
How gentle with the spikes of grain!
How firm with the spurs!
How delicate in the dew!
How dazzling in the festival!
How tremendous with the last
banderillas of darkness!

But now he sleeps endlessly.
Now mosses and grass
are opening with sure fingers
the flower of his skull.
And already his blood goes singing,
singing by the marshes and the meadows,
seeping in stiffened horns,
shuddering soullessly over the snow,
stumbling on its thousand little hoofs
like a great, obscure, sad tongue
till it forms a pool of agony
by the starry Guadalquivir.
Oh white wall of Spain!
Oh black bull of sorrow!
Oh stubborn blood of Ignacio!
Oh nightingale of his veins!
No.
I do not want to see it!
There is no chalice to contain it,
no swallows to drink it,
there is no frost of light to curdle it,
nor any song, nor flood of lilies,
there is no crystal to cover it with silver.
No.
I do not want to see it!!

III

BODY PRESENT

Stone is a forehead where dreams murmur,
there is no curving watercourse, nor frozen cypresses.
Stone is a shoulder to carry time
with its trees of tears and ribbons and planets.

I have seen the grey rains run towards the waves,
raising their gentle arms, pierced like a sieve,
that they may not be trapped by the rigid stone
that disperses their limbs, but absorbs not their blood.

For the stone traps seedlings and clouds,
skeletons of larks and wolves of darkness;
but gives neither sound, nor crystal, nor fire,
only bullrings, and bullrings and more bullrings, unwalled.

Now is Ignacio the high-born stretched on the stone.
Already he is finished; what is happening? Look at his face:
death has covered him with a pale sulphur,
and has set upon him the head of a sombre minotaur.

Now he is finished. The rain enters his mouth.
Like mad, his breath rushes from his staved-in chest,
and Love, drenched in tears of snow,
thaws upon the peaks of the cattle-lands.

What do they say? Here lies a stinking silence.
We have before us a laid-out body which is fading,
a bright form once with nightingales,
and we watch it filling with bottomless wounds.

Who wrinkles the shroud? What he says is not true!
Here nobody sings, nor weeps in the corners,
nor thrusts with spurs, nor terrifies the serpent.
Here I want only staring eyes
to see this body without hope of rest.

I want to see here men of hard voice,
those who break horses and who tame the rivers;
men of sonorous skeleton, and who sing
with a mouth full of sun and flints.

Here I would see them, before this stone,
before this body with its breaking reins,
I want them to show me how he may escape,
this captain bound in death.

I want them to teach me a lament like a river
with its gentle mists, and its depths of shade,
to bear the body of Ignacio away, that it may be lost
without hearing the double exhalation of the bulls.

That it may be lost in the round bullring of the moon
that simulates when young the immobility
of a suffering beast prepared for slaughter;
that it may lose itself in the night without a fish's song
among the white weeds of the clotted mist.

I do not want them to cover his face with shawls,
so that he may know the death that bears him off.
Look, Ignacio; you do not hear the wild hot bellow of
the bulls.
Sleep, fly far, rest: Even the sea must die!

IV

ABSENT SOUL

The bull does not know you, nor the fig tree,
nor horses, nor the ants in your own house.
The child does not know you, nor the afternoon,
for you are dead for ever.

The surface of the stone does not know you,
nor the black satin upon which you were destroyed.
You own dumb memory does not know you,
for you are dead for ever.

Autumn shall come with its little snails,
its grapes of mist and clustered mountains,
but none shall wish to look you in the eyes,
for you are dead for ever.

For you are dead for ever,
like all the dead of the whole earth,
like all the dead who are forgotten
in a pack of cringing dogs.

Nobody knows you. No. But I sing of you.
I sing for a later time of your profile and your grace,
the celebrated ripeness of your skill,
your appetite for death and the taste of his mouth,
and the sadness lying beneath your valiant joy.

We shall wait long for the birth, if birth there is,
of an Andalusian so bright, so rich in adventure.
I sing his elegance in words that tremble
and remember a sad wind through the olive-trees.

Picasso
Dream and Lie of Franco—[1937]*

If we study the prose poem "Sueño y Mentira de Franco" which Picasso composed with his etchings, we can see many correspondences between the vivid imagery of the poem and the drawings: "evil-omened polyps" or "cries of children cries of women" (see figs. 109 and 110, 147A and 147B).[1] "After all," Picasso told his biographer, "the arts are all the same; you can write a picture in words just as you can paint sensations in a poem."[2]

When Picasso's poems were first translated and published in 1935, the Surrealists greatly admired their stream-of-consciousness phrases, a "brilliant kaleidoscopic flow of images" that translate "into words his intimate visual life."[3] Even though she did not appreciate Picasso's poetry, Gertrude Stein perceived that "poetry for him was something to be made during rather bitter meditations, . . ."[4]—appropriate comments for the following selection.

fandango of shivering owls souse of swords of evil-omened polyps scouring brush of hairs from priests' tonsures standing naked in the middle of the frying pan—placed upon the ice cream cone of codfish fried in the scabs of his lead-ox heart—his mouth full of chinch-bug jelly of his words—sleighbells of the plate of snails braiding guts— little finger in erection neither grape nor fig—commedia dell'arte of poor weaving and dyeing of clouds—beauty creams from the garbage wagon—rape of maids in tears and in snivels—on his shoulder the shroud stuffed with sausages and mouths— rage distorting the outline of the shadow which flogs his teeth driven in the sand and the horse open wide to the sun which reads it to the flies that stitch to the knots of the net full of anchovies the sky-rocket of lilies—torch of lice where the dog is knot of rats and hiding-place of the palace of old rags—the banners which fry in the pan writhe in the black of the ink-sauce shed in the drops of blood which shoot him— the street rises to the clouds tied by its feet to the sea of wax which rots its entrails and the veil which covers it sings and dances wild with pain—the flight of fishing

---

*Reprinted from the English translation published in Barr, *Picasso,* p. 196, by permission.

1. A folder with a facsimile of Picasso's handwritten poem, French and English translations, and the two sheets of etched pictures, was sold for Spanish war relief at the Paris exposition in 1937 and abroad. See also p. 52, above, and part VIII.

2. Penrose (1958), p. 366.

3. Ibid., pp. 251–52. See also André Breton, *Cahiers d'Art* (special Picasso issue, 10, No. 7–10 [1935], pp. 185–91). For English translations of Picasso's poetry, see *Contemporary Poetry and Prose,* Aug.–Sept. 1936; *Poems: Pablo Picasso* (San Francisco, 1956); and *Picasso, Hunk of Skin* (San Francisco, 1968). Most biographers also include some examples (Penrose, Sabartés [1948], O'Brian, and *Picasso's Picassos,* 1981, pp. 99 and 101. For an early appreciation in English, see Clive Bell's 1936 essay reprinted in Schiff, pp. 86–87. José Ortega examined Picasso's writings in terms of *Guernica* and the civil war, in *Cuadernos Hispanoamericanos,* April 1979, pp. 158–72. Gasman exploited Picasso's writings most imaginatively in her dissertation and in "Picasso's 'Caseta,' His Memories, and His Poems," *Poetry East,* Spring–Summer 1984.

4. Stein, *Picasso: The Complete Writings* (Boston, 1985, Beacon paperback; first publ. 1938), pp. 82–83. In *Everybody's Autobiography* (New York, 1937) she addressed Picasso directly: 'it is all right you are doing this to get rid of everything that has been too much for you all right all right go on doing it but don't go on trying to make me tell you it is poetry" (p. 37).

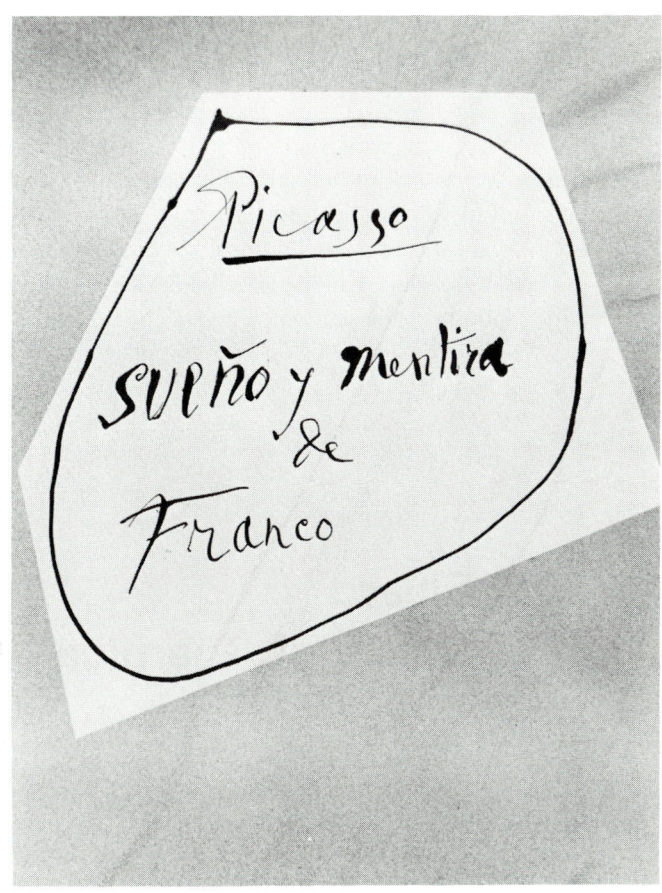

147A. Picasso. *Dream and Lie of Franco*, title page. Etching. (See Figs. 109 and 110.)

147B. Picasso. *Dream and Lie of Franco,* handwritten poem. Etching.

rods and the alhigui alhigui of the first-class burial of the moving van—the broken wings rolling upon the spider's web of dry bread and clear water of the paella of sugar and velvet which the lash paints upon his cheeks—the light covers its eyes before the mirror which apes it and the nougat bar of the flames bites its lips at the wound—cries of children cries of women cries of birds cries of flowers cries of timbers and of stones cries of bricks cries of furniture of beds of chairs of curtains of pots of cats and of papers cries of odors which claw at one another cries of smoke pricking the shoulder of the cries which stew in the cauldron and of the rain of birds which inundates the sea which gnaws the bone and breaks its teeth biting the cotton wool which the sun mops up from the plate which the purse and the pocket hide in the print which the foot leaves in the rock.

Paul Eluard
The Victory of Guernica—[1937]*

These verses were written while *Guernica* was being painted, testifying to the spiritual collaboration between poet and artist. (The poem was reproduced in large format and posted inside the Spanish pavilion; see Sert's recollections, p. 199, below.)

Paul Eluard (1895–1952), a lyrical poet unusually sensitive to the visual arts, was Picasso's special friend among the French Surrealists. They grew close after 1936, when Picasso illustrated Eluard's verses and the latter celebrated Picasso in prose and poetry; and they shared their anguish over the tragedy in Spain (p. 51, above).[1]

La Victoire de Guernica

1

Beau monde des masures
De la mine et des champs

2

Visages bons au feu visages bons au froid
Aux refus à la nuit aux injures aux coups

*Reprinted from Paul Eluard, *Oeuvres complètes* (Paris, Editions Gallimard, 1968), vol. I, p. 812, by permission of the publisher; English translation by Roland Penrose from *London Bulletin,* October 1938, pp. 7–8, by permission (reprinted also in Larrea, pp. 6–7).

1. From the poem and additional passages, Eluard wrote a film script for Alain Resnais's *Guernica,* primarily a black-and-white film collage of Picasso's works and news photographs; film script in Eluard, *Oeuvres complètes,* vol. II, p. 913; reprinted also in the periodical *Europe* (Paris, Dec. 1949 and again April/May, 1970).

3

Visages bons à tout
Voici le vide qui vous fixe
Votre mort va servir d'exemple

4

La mort cœur renversé

5

Ils vous ont fait payer le pain
Le ciel la terre l'eau le sommeil
Et la misère
De votre vie

6

Ils disaient désirer la bonne intelligence
Ils rationnaient les forts jugeaient les fous
Faisaient l'aumône partageaient un sou en deux
Ils saluaient les cadavres
Ils s'accablaient de politesses

7

Ils persévèrent ils exagèrent ils ne sont pas de notre monde

8

Les femmes les enfants ont le même trésor
De feuilles vertes de printemps et de lait pur
Et de durée
Dans leurs yeux purs

9

Les femmes et les enfants ont le même trésor
Dans les yeux
Les hommes se défendent comme ils peuvent

10

Les femmes les enfants ont les mêmes roses rouges
Dans les yeux
Chacun montre son sang

11

La peur et le courage de vivre et de mourir
La mort si difficile et si facile

12

Hommes pour qui ce trésor fut chanté
Hommes pour qui ce trésor fut gâché

13

Hommes réels pour qui le désespoir
Alimente le feu dévorant de l'espoir
Ouvrons ensemble le dernier bourgeon de l'avenir

14

Parias la mort la terre et la hideur
De nos ennemis ont la couleur
Monotone de notre nuit
Nous en aurous raison.

The Victory of Guernica

1

High life in hovels
In mines and in fields

2

Faces staunch in the fire staunch in the cold
Against denials the night insults blows

3

Faces always staunch
Here is the void staring at you
Your death shall be an example

4

Death heart overturned

5

They made you pay for bread
Sky earth water sleep
And the poverty
Of your life

6

They said they wanted agreement
They checked the strong sentenced the mad
Gave alms divided a farthing
They greeted every corpse
They overwhelmed each other with politeness

7

They insist they exaggerate they are not of our world

8

The women the children have the same treasure
Of green leaves of spring and of pure milk
And of endurance
In their pure eyes

9

The women the children have the same treasure
In their eyes
The men defend it as best they can

10

The women the children have the same red roses
In their eyes
All show their blood

11

The fear and the courage of living and of dying
Death so hard and so easy

12

Men for whom this treasure was extolled
Men for whom this treasure was spoiled

13

Real men for whom despair
Feeds the devouring fire of hope
Let us open together the last bud of the future

14

Pariahs
Death earth and the vileness of our enemies
Have the monotonous colour of our night
The day will be ours[2]

2. [For historic reasons, I have reprinted Penrose's nearly contemporaneous translation. In her illuminating study, *Poetry of the Spanish Civil War* (New York, 1975), Marilyn Rosenthal, however, provides her own fresh translations in the spirit of the 1960s and 70s: "We shall overcome"is Eluard's final line (p. 305).]

Ruthven Todd
Drawings for Guernica—[1938]*

The Scottish poet Ruthven Todd (1914–1978) typifies that generation of artists and poets who matured during the 1930s and responded passionately to the Spanish Civil War. The following lines capture his emotions upon seeing *Guernica* exhibited in London in 1938. While the verses describe images of the entire canvas, the title focuses on the related studies and drawings, which have impressed so many artists (cf. pp. 304 and 345).

For Pablo Picasso

The woman weeps forever as if her tears
Would wash away the blood and broken limbs
And the tortured horse whinnys and climbs
Iron hoof on broken beam towards electric stars.
Hands hold withered flowers, the broken sword
And the great arm reaches out with a lamp.
The frightened child in its mother's arms is limp,
Too terrified to listen to the comfortable word.

Still the great bull stands inside the shattered room,
Inside the world, and still the crouching mother runs
Feeling the child moving in her tightened womb,
Thinking of the small features and the forming bones.
Shut in forever by the grey wall the woman weeps
While the mad horse plunges up the useless slopes.

Fernando Arrabal
Guernica—[1959]**

Inspired by the right-hand section of Picasso's *Guernica*,[1] the Spanish playwright-in-exile imagined how the actual bombing might have affected an ordinary old couple: Fanchou and Lira try to make sense of the war, keeping up absurd and pathetic small talk while the old woman is trapped in the lavatory (fig. 148). Eventually both are buried under the debris. Arrabal's ending is typical of his black humor, yet the triumphant singing of the Basque national hymn to the sacred oak tree promises ultimate victory.

*From *London Bulletin* No. 8–9 (Jan.–Feb. 1939), p. 59. Todd is known for *Tracks in the Snow* (1946—essays on Blake, Fuseli, and John Martin), other studies of William Blake, and several volumes of poetry.

**Guernica*, pp. 9–10 and 26–27, from Fernando Arrabal, *Plays*, trans., Barbara Wright (London, 1967), by permission of the publishers, Calder and Boyars Ltd.

1. Arrabal's stage directions specifically citing Picasso's painting were deleted when the play was first published in Spain in 1959 with the transparent anagram title CIUGRENA.

Arrabal drew on his traumatic childhood for much of his art, which is regularly censored or attacked for its scatology, blasphemy, and surrealistic scenes of horror. Born 1932 in Spanish Morocco, he was raised in Nationalist Spain by his mother who collaborated with the very regime that had imprisoned his leftist-liberal father. Arrabal settled in Paris in 1955, but has frequently returned to post-Franco Spain where his work finally is being recognized: in January 1983 he received the prestigious Nadal Prize for his fiction.[2]

> *The sound of the boots of marching troops is heard for some ten seconds. Then the sound of an air raid: aeroplanes and exploding bombs. The curtain rises when the raid is over. The interior of a bombed house: crumbling walls, debris, stones.* FANCHOU *is in the house, near a table, in despair.*

FANCHOU: My precious, my lamb.
> *He searches a pile of rubble on his right, unsuccessfully.*
Where are you, my lamb?
> *He goes on searching.*

148. Stage design by Ruth Appelhof for 1979 production of Arrabal's *Guernica* at Cayuga Community College, Auburn, New York

2. In America he is best known for several plays, *The Architect and the Emperor* (1966, produced 1970 in Ontario); *And They Put Handcuffs on the Flowers* (staged 1972 in New York, derived from Arrabal's visit to Madrid where he was briefly imprisoned for "blasphemy and grave insults to the State"); and his frankly autobiographical film *Viva la Muerte* (released 1971). Another film he wrote and directed—*Guernica* (released 1976), a fantastic personal vision of the Basque war—is not related to the play excerpted here.

LIRA'S VOICE *[plaintively]:* Darling.

FANCHOU: Have you finished peeing?

LIRA'S VOICE: I can't get out. I'm stuck. Everything's collapsed.

> FANCHOU *climbs on to the table with some difficulty, trying to see* LIRA. *He raises himself on tiptoe. He sees her, and looks pleased.*

FANCHOU: Look at me.

> *He stands on tiptoe again.*

LIRA'S VOICE: Are you there?

FANCHOU: Go carefully, my precious.

LIRA'S VOICE: Ow, ouch.

> *She moans like a child.*

FANCHOU: Have you hurt yourself?

> *Pause.* FANCHOU *looks anxious.*

LIRA'S VOICE *[plaintively]:* Yes. All the stones fell on top of me.

FANCHOU: Try and stand up.

LIRA'S VOICE: There's no point, I won't be able to get out.

FANCHOU: Make an effort.

LIRA'S VOICE: Tell me you still love me.

FANCHOU: Of course, you know I do. *[Pause.]* You'll see, when you get out we'll do all sorts of lovely dirty things.

LIRA'S VOICE: Of course we will. *[Sounding pleased.]* You'll never change.

> *Sound of aeroplanes. Bombs start falling again for a few seconds. The raid stops.*

FANCHOU: Have any more stones fallen on you?

LIRA'S VOICE: No. Have they on you, my precious?

FANCHOU: No. Make an effort and get out of there.

LIRA'S VOICE: I can't. *[Pause.]* Look and see if they've hit the tree.

> FANCHOU *gets down off the table with difficulty. He goes over to the left. He has to clear a lot of rubble out of the way. Part of the window appears.* FANCHOU *looks out of it. He seems pleased. He comes back. He climbs on to the table again.*

FANCHOU: No, they haven't hit it, it's still there.[3]

* * *

LIRA'S VOICE: I can't move at all now. *[Plaintively.]* But when is this war going to be over?

FANCHOU: That's right, now her ladyship wants the war to be over when it suits *her* convenience.

LIRA'S VOICE *[whimpering]:* Can't they stop it?

FANCHOU: Of course they can't. The general said he wouldn't stop until he's occupied the whole country.

LIRA'S VOICE: All of it?

FANCHOU: Yes, of course, all of it.

LIRA'S VOICE: That's going a bit far.

---

3. [Consult the Index for the many references to this sacred oak tree.]

FANCHOU: Generals don't do things by halves: it's all or nothing.

LIRA'S VOICE: What about the people?

FANCHOU: The people don't know anything about making wars. And in any case, the general is getting an awful lot of help.

LIRA'S VOICE: Then it's not a game any more!

FANCHOU: You don't suppose the general cares, do you?

LIRA'S VOICE: I can't move at all, now. If any more stones start falling I shall be completely buried.

FANCHOU: What a bore. Don't worry. You'll see, the raids will soon be over.

LIRA'S VOICE: For good?

FANCHOU: For good.

LIRA'S VOICE: How d'you know?

FANCHOU [cut to the quick]: Do you doubt my word?

LIRA'S VOICE: No. [Skeptically.] Why d'you suppose I should doubt it?

 Three shells explode. A ghastly noise.

[Weeping bitterly.] Darling, I'm completely buried, come and rescue me.

FANCHOU: I'm coming this minute, my little lamb. You'll see, I'll get you out.

 FANCHOU goes over and climbs laboriously on to the debris. LIRA weeps.

LIRA'S VOICE: This time I really am going to die.

FANCHOU: Don't panic. I'm coming.

 FANCHOU moves laboriously over the debris. He reaches the place where LIRA is.

 My little lamb. Here I am. Give me your hand.

LIRA'S VOICE: Can't you see I'm covered in stones?

FANCHOU: I'll get you free this minute. You just wait, I'll get you out.

 Long raid. More stones fall. FANCHOU too is buried under the rubble.

 As the long raid is just coming to an end, the woman crosses from right to left. The little girl isn't with her this time. She is carrying a small coffin on her shoulder. She looks angry and helpless (see the Picasso painting). She disappears, left.

 In the background: the tree of liberty can be seen above the debris of the walls. The raid is over: there is now nothing but debris on the stage. Long silence.

 Two coloured balloons float gently upwards from the exact spot where FANCHOU and LIRA disappeared. Enter the OFFICER, who fires at them with his Lewis gun but doesn't hit them. The balloons disappear into the sky. The OFFICER fires again. From above, FANCHOU and LIRA can be heard laughing happily. The OFFICER is terrified, looks all round him, and goes out, right, quickly. Enter the WRITER. He gets up on to the table. He examines the place where FANCHOU and LIRA were. He looks pleased. He gets down from the table. He goes out, left, almost running, quite delighted, saying:

WRITER'S VOICE: I shall make an extraordinary novel out of all this. A magnificent novel! What a novel! . . .

His voice fades away in the distance. Pause. The sound of the boots of marching soldiers is heard close by. Further away, very softly, a group of men is singing 'Guernikako arbola.' The group gradually becomes more numerous and the voices gradually louder. Now a whole crowd is singing 'Guernikako arbola,' which finally completely drowns the sound of the boots, as the curtain falls.

IV.
GUERNICA IN EUROPE
1937–1938

I n this part, we follow *Guernica*'s experience in Paris and London, from the architect's reminiscences of how Picasso accepted the commission for the Spanish Pavilion in January 1937, to the painting's first exhibitions abroad, in October 1938. Also included are four very individual accounts of a visit to Picasso's studio, when *Guernica* was nearly completed, and a welcoming address to the construction workers when it was installed in the pavilion. They were shown how to appreciate the painting despite its modernist idiom, and this remains a recurring theme with early apologists: that *Guernica* can be meaningful to the proverbial "man [and woman] in the street." (See Ozenfant and Read in this section, McCausland and Soby in part V, and several debates in part VI.)

These are not objective accounts. Without exception, the writers were men totally committed to the Republican cause, deeply engaged in the struggle in Spain. The four Spaniards were refugees from their homeland, continuing the propaganda war in Paris. And they all knew Picasso, as did the Frenchmen who were some of Picasso's closest friends. The last selection are recollections of his long-time dealer, Kahnweiler, and even though written in the mid-1950s, they still convey the apocalyptic mood of human beings aware that the Spanish conflict prefigured a catastrophic world war. Accordingly, the Spanish Civil War was one of those dramatic incidents in history that captured the imagination; the warring sides appeared sharply defined in white and black, good and evil. For the liberal intellectuals around Picasso, Franco and his Fascist allies represented unmitigated evil, and *Guernica* became one of the weapons to combat that evil.[1]

1. Paul von Blum concludes that "The purpose of *Guernica* is frankly propagandistic," and that it is "a spectacular fusion of brilliant style with social content" (*The Art of Social Conscience*, New York, 1976, p. 92).

Josep Lluis Sert
The Architect Remembers—[1947]*

The architect of the Spanish Pavilion recaptures the informal atmosphere when Spanish Republican officials commissioned the painting, and recalls other important details about *Guernica,* its creation, installation, and import. Having fled his native Barcelona during the civil war, Sert designed and oversaw construction of the pavilion with his associate, Lluis Lacasa; he also organized changing exhibits and propaganda displays, and performed other information services for the Republican cause in Paris.

I just want to tell you a few facts about what happened in Paris at the time when Picasso was painting the *Guernica* for the Spanish Pavilion in the Paris World's Fair of 1937.

We had finished, together with my friend and colleague, Lluis Lacasa, the plans for the Pavilion in December 1936, and in January 1937, I went, together with Max Aub who was then the Cultural Delegate for the Spanish Embassy in Paris, and Louis Aragon, the poet, to see Picasso in the rue de la Boétie. We went to see him to ask him to paint a mural for the Spanish Pavilion, and we went to talk to him about his nomination as Director of the Prado Museum.

Picasso immediately answered us, showing us the plates he had just finished, which he called *Sueño y Mentira de Franco* [figs. 109, 110]. He showed us the plates, which were still unfinished, and he talked about these plates and explained what they signified, what symbols signified Franco and how the other symbols signified the people of Spain, or represented the people of Spain, and so forth.

Then, after that, he read the text of the *Sueño y Mentira de Franco,* and in reading the text of the *Sueño y Mentira de Franco,* I could foresee what Picasso was going to do when he painted *Guernica.* He read it with such extraordinary enthusiasm and force and violence that you could see that he would finally produce a picture of the type that he did.

Picasso did not go to work on the *Guernica* right away. He took months to begin it. I think he really started the *Guernica*—the sketches prove it—in the beginning of May, but we often talked about the picture. Picasso liked to talk about it, about what

---

*Reprinted with the kind permission of the late author (1902–1983) and The Museum of Modern Art from the typescript of the *Guernica* symposium held at the museum on 25 November 1947 (with minor corrections Sert made for this anthology); see also Sert's recollections in *Guernica–Legado,* pp. 24–30. (For further background, see pp. 51, 52, and 59, and the Bibliography.)

he was going to do, and one day, we gave him the measurements of the wall we had reserved for his picture and we discussed them. He said the picture was not going to be the whole length of the pavilion; the height was low and he wanted to have it in certain proportions. He promised to do the painting, but until the last moment we really doubted if he was going to do it at all. But Picasso always loved to keep his plans mysterious, the same as his pictures. He never liked to talk clearly of them.

Finally, we knew that he had begun the picture, he was working on it, and then, a few weeks after, I saw the picture in his studio, when he had some wallpaper on it. He had a stretch of wallpaper that he afterwards eliminated. In the book that has lately been published on *Guernica*,[1] and in *Cahiers d'Art* [1937] you can see the different phases. In several places, he had gone back to his old custom of the collage, of pasting wallpaper on certain parts of the picture.

He finally eliminated all those wallpaper fragments that he had pasted on the picture, and left the picture, as you well know, in black and white.

It was curious also that at the same time that Picasso was painting this picture— I don't know exactly what was the difference in time—Eluard was writing a poem called *La Victoire de Guernica* [pp. 186–89]. I think there is a lot of the poem in the picture and a lot of the picture in the poem. If you read the poem carefully, you will see how very parallel, how very close to the picture it is, and in the interpretations of the picture that are going to follow, I think it is very important to note that Eluard was writing this poem and that the poem was called *La Victoire de Guernica*, because many people take the picture as being simply a representation of the bombardment of Guernica. It is something more than that. In the picture, there is a lot of the victory of Guernica. There is a lot of the revenge of Guernica, a lot of what can happen afterwards as a result of the bombardment, as a result of this mass killing of people— such as, of course, was repeated in Rotterdam, in Warsaw, and all around Europe. The poem, therefore, is very close to the picture, so much so that when we had the Spanish Pavilion job, we reproduced the poem in the Basque Section, up in the Pavilion, and beside the poem of *La Victoire de Guernica*, there was a picture of Guernica burning and of the tree of Guernica, which represented to the Basques the symbol of liberty.

That tree of Guernica, of course, was burnt when the city was destroyed.[2] It was a very important thing for the Basques—not only that Guernica was destroyed and the people were killed, but because Guernica represented all their traditions. Guernica represented the most sacred hope of liberty that they had.

I want to be brief. Picasso continued his picture during May and June, and one day he brought it to the Pavilion. I think it was late June. I don't remember the date exactly. He brought it there. He was in love with his picture and he really considered it very important and part of himself. We once asked him when he was going to finish the *Guernica*, and he said, "I don't know when I will finish it. Maybe never. You had better come and take it whenever you need it."

But he brought the *Guernica* to the Pavilion. He put it on the concrete floor and put it on a stretcher on the wall. It was very curious to observe in the months that followed—and I lived there constantly—in reviewing the exhibits in the Pavilion, to

1. [A reference to Larrea's book, p. 280, below.]
2. [Miraculously, the oak tree survived (p. 161, above).]

see the reaction of the people. The people came there, they looked at this thing and they didn't understand it. The majority didn't understand what it meant. But they felt that there was something in it. They did not laugh at the *Guernica*. They just looked at it in silence. I watched them pass by. . . .

It is also important to note—and I would like to stress this—that it is now ten years since that happened. It was in 1937. For ten years, *Guernica* has not found a permanent wall. It has been traveling around the world, and it is now here in the Museum of Modern Art. Picasso said one day before us that the *Guernica* was for the Republican Government. He owns it now but he said, "the day the Republic is reestablished in Spain, I will give it to the Spanish government." So the final destination of the *Guernica* has to be some place in Madrid, some wall in Spain. For ten years now it has been traveling around the world. The best thing we can hope is that it will soon find a resting place.[3]

Visitors to the Studio, June 1937

Picasso always needed the companionship of friends and lovers to relax and to renew his energies for the intense hours of creative solitude. The *Guernica* period was no exception. He welcomed to his studio the stimulating visits of friends, and watched them react to the great work in progress. How fascinating to see the differences in these four eyewitness accounts!

The personal recollections of Juan Larrea (1895–1980), archivist and literary scholar working for Spanish Republican agencies in Paris, are darkened by his own experience in the civil war. Sharing a similar Spanish background, the Catholic poet José Bergamín (1897–1984) in 1971 wrote as passionately of Picasso's Spanish heritage as he had in 1937 (p. 211, below). The great English sculptor Henry Moore (1898–1986) recalls the event with much humor, relating the experience to his own work. Roland Penrose (1900–1984), art historian, Surrealist painter, and future biographer of Picasso, draws from his amusing recollections some persuasive arguments for *Guernica*'s universal meaning.

Individual temperaments and circumstances affected responses to *Guernica* in the studio, just as personal factors would color the reactions of every viewer in the years to come.

Juan Larrea
The Unveiling—[1970]*

The outbreak of the Spanish Civil War took me by surprise while I was in central France, and in spite of several attempts to settle in Paris, I was unable to do so until May 1937. From then on, I was in continuous contact with Picasso and witnessed the development of the several phases of *Guernica*. I also personally took charge of printing and distributing *Dream and Lie of Franco*.

---

3. [Sert died 1983 in Spain, after witnessing *Guernica*'s installation in Madrid—p. 134, above.]

*Unpublished letter to Ellen C. Oppler, 10 December 1970.

With regard to *Guernica*, I will relate an anecdote which could interest you—if you are not already familiar with it. It is common knowledge that during several days Picasso tried out covering some of the figures of his mural with patterned papers, such as decorative wallpaper, and also adding small colored paper strips to form a contrast with the monotonous severity of the black and white. During one of our visits we realized that most of the paper strips, which had been put on and torn off, had almost completely disappeared. Yet there still remained some toilet paper stuck to the hand of the same woman. Then one afternoon, toward the middle of June,[1] a group of us went to see the painting which was practically finished. We formed a line of some fifteen well-known persons in front of it and admired the monumental masterpiece which produced in me profound emotions. And then, when we were all more or less silent, Picasso stepped away from the group and, approaching the mural, tore off the remaining papers. (I think that the pink color of the dress of the woman who falls into the flames had been stuck back on.)[2] There were only the small pieces of red paper left. But moments later, Picasso repeated the maneuver: again he approached the mural and tore off the remaining paper strips and the last one to go was the one on the neck of the child. This evoked a spontaneous round of applause from those present and the applause was followed by warm congratulations. That is how *Guernica*—with its impressive austerity worthy of the Escorial monastery[3]—set off a wonderful hubbub. . . . If I am not mistaken, the mural received its name by *vox populi* [the voice of the people]. Paul Eluard, Christian Zervos, and other French personalities began to call it by this significant stark name inspired by that passionate temper of the times, a name that Picasso—sharing everyone's outrage—accepted as his own.

José Bergamín
Naked Poetic Truth—[1971]*

Guernica! What a monument of truthfulness and masterly skill! Those of us who watched it emerging step by step saw the struggle it cost the painter to press his poetry to the ultimate nakedness achieved in the mural. Our suggestions—such as they were—were inconsequential beside the sureness of the artist's instinct. But Picasso himself shrank from the terrible truth his hands revealed. He tried to hide it from the

1. [The "unveiling" probably took place earlier in June before state VII (fig. 52).]

2. [Larrea remembers correctly. In the photograph of state IV (fig. 37), a textured collage element is attached to the running figure at the right; this is removed in the photograph of state V (fig. 38), but reattached for state VI (fig. 45), which also includes the wallpaper "dress" for the grieving mother.]

3. [The Escorial was the royal residence and monastery north of Madrid built for Philip II in the late 16th century. The pure geometric forms of its architecture, and the restrained colors of gray granite stone, whitewashed walls, and dark wood accents give it a stark beauty particularly appealing to modern sensibility.]

*From Bergamín's introduction to Klaus Gallwitz, *Picasso at 90: The Late Work* (New York, 1971), p. 9, by permission.

eye, to clothe it with cutouts of colored paper. "What do you think?" he would ask us. Wordlessly we said no. The pure white, the gray, and the black of *Guernica* answered for us. Little by little the experiment was reduced to one tiny scrap of paper, a red tear of blood. Picasso moved it about against his figures' eyes. Obstinately, and with a hint of childish mischief, he refused to relinquish it entirely. Finally the tear disappeared. And *Guernica*—white, gray, and black—remains for all time an undying testimony of art. Here the painter has professed his purest, most brutally naked, most poetic truth. This is what sets *Guernica* apart from the fiery brilliance of Picasso's other pictures. This shockingly naked thing haunts us with the disturbing question of its anxiety.

Henry Moore
With Picasso—[1961]*

Did you get to Spain during the civil war?

No. A whole party of us were going to go—Auden and Spender and Blackett and Bernal[1] and people like that, and Alexander Calder[2] wanted to come along, too—but we weren't allowed to, at the last moment.

Most artists were of the same mind about Spain—I remember that when Irina[3] and I were in Paris in the summer of 1937 Picasso invited a whole lot of us to go along to his studio and see how his *Guernica* was getting on. There was a big lunch, with Giacometti, Max Ernst, Paul Eluard, André Breton, and Irina and me, and it was all tremendously lively and exciting and we all trooped off to the studio, and I think even Picasso was excited by our visit.

But I remember him lightening the whole mood of the thing, as he loved to do. *Guernica* was still a long way from being finished. It was like a cartoon just laid in in black and grey, and he could have coloured it as he coloured the sketches. Anyway, you know the woman who comes running out of the little cabin on the right with one hand held in front of her? Well, Picasso told us that there was something missing there, and he went and fetched a roll of paper and stuck it in the woman's hand, as much as to say that she'd been caught in the bathroom when the bombs came. That was just like him, of course—to be tremendously moved about Spain and yet turn it aside with a joke.[4]

---

*From Vera and John Russell, the *Sunday Times* of London, 17 December 1961, p. 18, by kind permission of John Russell.

1. [The poets W. H. Auden and Stephen Spender (p. 216), and the scientists J. D. Bernal (Marxist don at Cambridge University) and probably P. M. S. Blackett, physicist concerned with the far-reaching consequences of atomic energy and 1948 winner of the Nobel Prize in Physics.]

2. [The American sculptor who designed the Mercury Fountain in the Spanish Pavilion (fig. 89 and p. 72, above).]

3. [Henry Moore's wife, Irina.]

4. [This part concludes with a discussion of Henry Moore's shelter drawings as his "counterpart of *Guernica*," in that they "did seem to get through to a much larger public" than Moore had reached before.]

Roland Penrose
The Universality of Meaning—[1959]*

During the weeks in which the great painting evolved through such startling changes, Picasso at times reverted to his former practice of pinning pieces of patterned wallpaper to the canvas so as to introduce colour and the presence of another kind of reality. When visitors arrived he discussed with them the movements of the figures as though the painting were alive. Once when the picture was nearly finished I called with Henry Moore. The discussion between us turned on the old problem of how to link reality with the fiction of painting. Picasso silently disappeared and returned with a long piece of toilet paper, which he pinned to the hand of the woman on the right of the composition, who runs into the scene terrified and yet curious to know what is happening. As though she had been disturbed at a critical moment her bottom is bare and her alarm too great to notice it. "There," said Picasso, "that leaves no doubt about the commonest and most primitive effect of fear."

It is the simplicity of *Guernica* that makes it a picture which can be readily understood. The forms are divested of all complications which would distract from their meaning. The flames that rise from the burning house and flicker on the dress of the falling woman are described by signs as unmistakable as those used by primitive artists. The nail-studded hoof, the hand with deeply furrowed palm, and the sun illuminated with an electric light bulb, are drawn with a childlike simplicity, startling in its directness. In this canvas Picasso had rediscovered a candour of expression which had been lost, or overlaid for centuries with the refinements of artistic skill. He had proved such excellencies to be unnecessary, even a hindrance to an understanding of reality. * * *

Guernica has been compared with other great works such as *The Massacre at Chios* by Delacroix, Géricault's *Raft of the Medusa* and Goya's *Madrid 3 May*. In the scale of its monumental appeal it has much in common with these paintings, but whereas they all used the recognized idiom of their time to portray catastrophes that had occurred, in *Guernica* Picasso found a more universal means of conveying the emotion centered round a given event, and in consequence arrived at a timeless and transcendental image. In addition, the symbolic use of the familiar and humble enabled him to present disaster in an emotional way without overstatement. It is not the horror of an actual occurrence with which we are presented; it is a universal tragedy made vivid to us by the myth he has reinvented and the revolutionary directness with which it is presented. The power of *Guernica* will grow.

---

*From Roland Penrose, *Picasso: His Life and Work* (New York, 1958), pp. 275 and 277, by permission of Sir Roland.

[Max Aub]
Welcome to the Pavilion—[1937 and 1967]*

Construction workers completing the Spanish Pavilion in July 1937 heard the following address in French. The speaker[1] fervently underlined the universal meaning of *Guernica,* and with simple, effective descriptions made its imagery accessible to the workers.

I reproduce part of this text, which came into my hands in an unlikely manner, because, undoubtedly, it is the first that speaks of Picasso's *Guernica* with which I had so much to do and which I have seen so much. Someday I hope to see it in the Prado, where it should be, along with *Las Meninas* [of Velázquez]. * * * It seems almost impossible in the struggle that we are conducting, that the Spanish Republic has been able to construct this building. There is in it, as in everything of ours, something of a miracle. I am not speaking of the construction itself, the result of the work of our architects Lacasa and Sert, and of yourselves. Man has invented work and it in turn has shaped us. The rest is paralysis, putrefaction, and death.

At the entrance, on the right Picasso's great painting leaps into view. It will be spoken of for a long time. Picasso has represented here the tragedy of Guernica. It is possible that this art be accused of being too abstract or difficult for a pavilion like ours which seeks to be above all, and before everything else, popular manifestation. This is not the moment to justify ourselves, but I am certain that with a little good will, everybody will perceive the rage, the desperation, and the terrible protest that this canvas signifies. Our time is that of realism, but each country perceives the real in a certain way. Spanish realism does not represent only the real but also the unreal because, for Spain in general, it has always been impossible to separate what exists from what is imagined. This sum total forms the profound reality of its art. That is why Goya and Picasso are realist painters even if they appear to other people like extravagant personalities of that "unknown people"—as President Azana said recently—"a terrible people, the Spanish people, terrible principally to themselves because it is the one people of Europe capable of pricking itself with its own sting." How terrible is this picture by Pablo Ruiz Picasso, painter of Málaga.

Look at this painting attentively, profoundly; let us not be intimidated by its

---

*From the essays by Max Aub (1902–1972), *Hablo Como Hombre* (Mexico, 1967), pp. 13–16; English translation adapted from Catherine B. Freedberg (with Raphael Crespo), who generously made it available from her Ph.D. dissertation.

1. As Deputy Commissioner of the Spanish Pavilion, Max Aub (born in Paris of French and German parents who emigrated to Spain) would have been the most likely Spaniard to speak fluently in French. Nevertheless, with his introductory words he mystified the origins of this talk. Despite her interviews with Sert, Freedberg was unable to confirm Aub's authorship, although she also considers it probable. Otherwise, why would Aub have included it among his own essays?

difficult appearance and extreme colors. Look, workers, at this figure on the right; this falling woman, desperate. The genius of the painter in order to give the sensation of ruin and emptiness, has rent her with greys, has shortened her, summarily, in order to give that horrible appearance of falling. Everything in this picture seeks to express, by means of colors and lines, more than has been said by similar means. And in order to accentuate this fury of man, of the painter, against destruction, Picasso has imprisoned in a room a neighing horse which kicks the body of a militiaman; a woman constructed of just a head and hands, leans out with a light, in a futile but superhuman effort, while her body remains in the window and she herself becomes a torch. See, further to the left, that furious bull and that woman with her dead son on her knees. Forming the base of the painting, the assassinated militiaman brandishes in his fist a sword now useless. And in order to express all his feelings, Picasso needs to show both eyes of characters, even when in profile. To those who protest saying that things are not thus, one must answer asking if they do not have two eyes to see the terrible reality of Spain. If the picture by Picasso has any defect it is that it is too real, too terribly true, atrociously true.

I would wish to make you understand, with this single example, the effort of those who collaborated on this undertaking: the sculptor Alberto, with his magnificent cry of hope that rises at the entrance of the pavilion [fig. 83]; Joan Miró with his great, extraordinary, and splendid picture [fig. 93B].

When they say that these artists work only for a few, tell them that it is not true. That they are Spaniards who express the reality of Spain in their own way and manner. * * *

The Spanish Pavilion is honored to have as its first public those who built it, and hopes that your sacrifice and work will not have been in vain, and that the visitors to the exposition will understand our truth. I hope that when it closes its doors, we shall destroy this building with the joy afforded by a decisive victory over Fascism.

The Guernica Volume
of Cahiers D'Art, 1937

Guernica and related topics dominated *Cahiers d'Art* during 1937. This influential periodical sought to re-create the emotionally charged atmosphere of the Picasso circle for its European readers, and even across the Atlantic where Americans eagerly studied the magazine for the latest news from Paris. The spring issue already had reproduced several states of *Dream and Lie of Franco* (figs. 109–110), Eluard's poem (pp. 186–89), and José Bergamín's article linking Picasso to Goya: "Our current war of independence will give Picasso conscious fulfillment for his pictorial, poetic, and creative genius, as the earlier one had given Goya."[1]

The historic summer issue devoted to *Guernica* fulfilled Bergamín's prophesy. Picasso's admirers, actively supporting the Spanish Republican cause, in their essays "waxed positively poetic over *Guernica* in phrases mixed with outrage and compassion."[2] Superb reproductions of Picasso's preparatory studies and Dora Maar's photographs of the several states of the painting-in-progress made this a unique achievement in magazine publishing that enabled the reading public to witness the very creation of *Guernica*.

Christian Zervos
The Story of a Painting*

Zervos, founder and managing editor of the magazine since 1926, contributed the lead article. It is a passionate tribute to Picasso's newly demonstrated political engagement, with dramatic references to the Spanish Civil War. Included are perceptive observations about the painting, its exterior/interior spaces, subdued color scheme, and the meaning of the bull. In 1937, Zervos (as did Leiris) saw this Spanish icon as "full of promise," whereas the realities of Franco's victory later made him omit all references to the bull.[3]

Guernica, Picasso's painting installed in the entrance hall of the Spanish Pavilion at the Paris Exposition, is undoubtedly the artist's most humane, most stirring work, engaging his most passionate feelings. That explains the poignant quality of these images immersed in the emotional current of their birth.

---

1. Bergamín, "Francisco Goya: Tout et rien de la peinture," *Cahiers d'Art* 12, no. 1–3, p. 6.

2. Lipton, *Picasso Criticism*, p. 272.

*"Histoire d'un tableau de Picasso," *Cahiers d'Art* 12, no. 4–5, 1937, pp. 105, 106, 108, 110–11 by permission [trans. ECO]. See also Lipton's astute evaluation of Zervos as a critic over the decades (pp. 148 ff., 191–94, 247ff.); I have occasionally followed her translation. I am also indebted in part to P. S. Falla's wording for selections in McCully, *A Picasso Anthology*; about half of the Zervos excerpt (pp. 202–6) coincides with mine.

3. When he adapted this essay for the preface of his Picasso oeuvre catalogue (vol. IX for 1937, publ. in 1958). Zervos's continuing political role during the Nazi occupation of Paris, the clandestine Resistance work of his publishing house, is noted by Herbert R. Lottman, *The Left Bank: Writers, Artists, and Politics from the Popular Front to the Cold War* (Boston, 1982), pp. 186 and 199.

Picasso had wondered for a long time whether he would turn his attention to the events in Spain, whether he should devote himself to them intensely, become intimately involved—or else ignore them as much as possible, considering their uncertainties. For a long time he fought his own feelings, even the most pressing demands of his mind; for a long time he had to guard against his heart, in order to preserve what is unique in man, and to avoid the snares of passion.

At almost every stage of Picasso's life, the impulse that pushes him towards compassion also contains a capacity for disengagement. As soon as he feels the increasing emotional implications of the event, he becomes impatient, which even makes him react violently.

* * *

Only when Picasso became fully aware of the Spanish conflict and of where it was going did he allow himself to paint it with passion. Without throwing himself directly into the fight, he nevertheless linked his innermost destiny to that of men aspiring to clear for themselves a path to the future.

He painted it under the sign of anger. It is the reaction of the creative man confronting a vague, aberrant force totally committed to stopping the progress of new tendencies and insuring its rule of disaster; it is the violent reaction of a man when events make him suspect some scheme that undermines and questions the very order of humanity, that tests the essential qualities of the human mind in the vilest manner, and extinguishes the last hopes of civilization.

When this anger arises in man, his inner world must necessarily make room for his outer one; as a result, the power of his mind is enhanced by the tension around it. That accounts for the fact that all Spanish poets attacked those very institutions which represented hatred of true creativity and that all parasites of arts and letters sought refuge in ignominious neutrality.

* * *

In *Guernica*, expressed in the most striking manner, is a world of despair, where death is everywhere; everywhere is crime, chaos, and desolation; disaster more violent than lightning, flood, and hurricane, for everything there is hostile, uncontrollable, beyond understanding, whence rise the heart-rendering cries of beings dying because of men's cruelty.

From Picasso's paintbrush explode phantoms of distress, anguish, terror, insurmountable pain, massacres, and finally peace found in death. And above so much sadness, the bird lifts up its song of life, and the bull—like the winged, mythological creatures of antiquity—contemplates man's work of destruction. What throbbing life full of promise, beside the most desolate vision. A sense of permanence, of imperishable force emanates from him. His serene look convinces us that nothing essential is ever lost, that one will always find him again amidst the ruins, after small particles have disappeared with wear and tear and catastrophes; that one can strip bodies of their flesh without stopping the youthful vigor of a people from realizing its full destiny.

The artist's denunciations—transformed here into visible sensations, I would even say in looking at certain figures, into audible sensations—create extreme tension, arouse a flood of emotions that reach the depth of human grief. The spectators whose attention thus is drawn to an emotional truth don't realize anymore that it is a pictorial phenomenon that disturbs, overwhelms, and revolts them. Transformed into expressive value, the painting releases a strong instinctive reaction, controlled and condensed into a kind of automatism.[4] The marks which cover the surface are energetic; they force us to live the times that, by numerous subterfuges, we work hard to escape. In experiencing these times we become more sensitive to evil-doings and allow a gnawing obsession to win, which succeeds in awakening conscience.

One can therefore assert that this work will forever enter our hearts, will inspire, stir up feelings, and arouse convictions that there are greater things than seeming reality and that to participate in their grandeur is to rise again somewhat in dignity.

* * *

Picasso changed the scene of action and narrowed its space at the same time that he went beyond esthetic sensation in order to represent this great and humble people whose suffering, sacrifices, and hopes give life its sanctity. In the first states of the painting, the drama unfolded outdoors. But the atmosphere of an interior is more suited to dream, ever present in this work. Is it not much more effective that this tragedy be developed and resolved on the narrow stage of a humble interior, which thus becomes an altar of sacrifice and purification with spiritual qualities?

The relentless emotions of the dramatic event, moreover, required strict correspondence of color scheme, imposing severe moderation and austerity. Lack of color helped the figures achieve their full emotional effect. Expression and color are indeed closely related; whites, blacks, and grays only can express Sorrow, stripped bare, like all great abstractions. One could not emphasize better the extraordinary tension of these figures or find more appropriate accessory to their heroic mourning garb. When the artist began the picture, he had not completely decided on the tonalities that he would use ultimately. The three colors imposed themselves on his paintbrush as the drama took hold of his imagination. One should note that while he was working, the artist tried to test himself, to prove that he was not just following a sentimental impulse, but that he had truly obeyed his deepest instinct. Accordingly, he had introduced patches of vibrant color, with wallpaper; but these experiments, visible in certain states reproduced here [figs. 37 and 45], were always rejected and the colors were finally kept to the sober range of white, black, and gray, heightened in places by little black dots which increased their resonance.

This reductiveness at first may disconcert eyes accustomed to bright color, but if they look attentively they will perceive the marvelous way Picasso uses the most somber shades. He extracts from them an infinite network of relationships. Skillfully, vigorously, with carefully measured chords, he attacks our vision. The harmony of these silent colors, emerging from a rhythmic ensemble that is complex in its interaction, but clear in effect, is not resolved in a final chord but, on the contrary, in dissonance—appropriate to the figures, emphasizing their desperate condition.

What is especially impressive about this painting is how the artist played with dissonance. Picasso heightened his capacity to violate, to control our synesthetic reaction by means of simplified forms, abbreviated drawing, with evocative marks and figuration, not as in reality, but by the shock they produce (eyes shaped like flowers, as though scratched with nails; or tears marked with sharp strokes that grip and torture you). These visionary forms are more powerfully evocative than shapes drawn with every realistic detail; they challenge people to understand their actions

4. [This is the first of two evident references linking Picasso to Surrealism: cf. Lipton's brief comment, p. 274.]

and to see them as they really are. As with instruments of witchcraft, they spread malignant germs against the leaders whom Picasso has condemned to death.

A man's ability to extend his strength as far as he wants, to master powers of incalculable range that he can mobilize at will, and to translate these powers into flaming symbols—that is not associated with a normal state but emanates absolutely from his supernatural gifts.[5] This explains Picasso's demonic aspect and the grandeur of his work.

Jean Cassou
Picasso Witness*

Jean Cassou, friend of Zervos and frequent critic for *Cahiers d'Art,* contributed an inspired, evocative "mood piece" to the *Guernica* issue.[6] Born 1897 in Spain, he was directly involved in the civil war and courageously joined resistance fighters in Spain and during the Nazi occupation of France.

Goya is brought back to life as Picasso; but at the same time, Picasso has been reborn as Picasso. It had been the immense ambition of this genius to keep himself forever apart, denying his own being, making himself live and carry on outside his own realm—like a ghost frenzied to see his vacant home, his lost body. The home has been found again, both body and soul; everything that calls itself Goya, that calls itself Spain has been reintegrated. Picasso has been reunited with his homeland. Also, his people have restored Picasso to life. Everything comes together again in one thing unchanged throughout time. The same stock, the same passion from which death can take nothing, presents the very same appearance under the guise of many faces, many dates, many places. Sometimes, when we remember having seen this thing at the Prado, we call it Goya. When we encounter it on the walls of this poor, genuine, and tragic Spanish Pavilion of 1937, we remember the most glorious contemporary painter, and we call it Picasso. When we read about it in the newspapers and when we think of a bloody land, we call it Spain. Always the same destruction is constantly renewed. It is the ruin of San Antonio de la Florida and it is Guernica. These names—and what names, the most impassioned in the world!—mark this painting, which until now resisted meaning. Now, it overflows with fullness and total presence, with sight and sound. It expresses our most private tragedy, which we all share most deeply. Genius has spoken.

5. [Many of Zervos's readers would make the association between *surnaturel* and related meanings: surreal and subconscious, see note 4, p. 208.]

*Cassou, "Le Témoignage de Picasso," *Cahiers d'Art* 12, no. 4–5, p. 112 [trans. ECO].

6. Lipton, p. 274. After his early reviews of 1926 and 1927, Cassou published a book on Picasso in 1937 (rev. ed., 1946),; he directed the Musée National de l'Art Moderne in Paris from 1946 to 1965. For his work during the Resistance, see *The Left Bank,* pp. 203–4.

Michel Leiris
Death Notice*

The distinguished ethnographer and Surrealist poet close to Picasso avoids those generalizations about Spain that characterize the other essays. Instead, he offers a highly personal, sensitive response to the painting itself—a lyrical equivalent full of memorable visual imagery.

The world transformed into a furnished room—where, gesturing wildly, we all wait for death. The sun reduced to the shape of an electric bulb glaring in mean intimacy within an inch of our heads, the terrors of the horse writhing like Pegasus suddenly caught in some dreadful cut-throat place, the bull—the only victorious one—eternally thrusting up his horns, the convulsed human beings, the hard table, the bird shrieking itself hoarse: it is useless to seek words to describe this epitome of our black-and-white catastrophe, this life which we lead like chess pieces that might feel, like so many thrusts of the knife, all the hostile moves among them, according to the whims of the players but are unable to have their agony modify in any way the rules of a brutal geometric game.

To take up a pen, line up words as if they could add anything to Picasso's *Guernica*, is the most useless of undertakings. In the black-and-white rectangle of ancient tragedy, Picasso sends us our death notice: everything we love is going to die, and that is why right now it is important that everything we love be summed up into something unforgettably beautiful, like the shedding of so many tears of farewell.

Just as the wail of the "canto hondo" first must rise up in the singer's throat for its everyday torment to glow nacreous and iridescent, the black-and-white exhalations of a dying world that the most frightful meteoric events—sharp knives of our passion—soon will pierce to the bone, in Picasso's hands become crystallized and sparkle like diamonds.

*Leiris, "Faire-part," *Cahiers d'Art* 12, no. 4–5, p. 128; the poetic imagery freely translated by ECO. Leiris (b. 1901) continued writing criticism about Picasso, e.g., "The Artist and his Model" in *Picasso in Retrospect,* pp. 243–62. During the Nazi occupation of Paris, his wife (Kahnweiler's sister-in-law) managed the Jewish dealer's art gallery.

José Bergamín
Picasso Enraged*

The Spanish poet, critic, and philosopher, one of the exiles in Paris, drew this "pen portrait of Pablo Picasso, a work of friendship."[7] Writing with passionate conviction and lyrical phrases about their common cultural heritage and Picasso's place in Spanish tradition, Bergamín (much like Zervos) needed to conclude in a hopeful vein. Instead of ending with the bombing of Guernica, symbol of destruction, he cites "the miracle of Madrid," the capital that endured shelling for weeks and triumphantly resisted capture by Franco forces in November 1936 (p. 50, above).

> "Is this fury then so great?"
> (Lope de Vega)

So great was this Spanish fury and is still so great, that it stabs us in the eye with its evidence, its clear and simple manifestation in a stirring painting. This dramatic, vital axiom, this tragic evidence bears the name, Madrid 1808, and Madrid 1936.[8] It is called Goya and it is called Picasso.

149. Francisco Goya. *The Third of May, 1808, in Madrid*. 1814–15. Oil on canvas, 8'9" x 13'4" (2.66 x 3.45 m). The Prado, Madrid

*Bergamín, "Le Mystère tremble: Picasso furioso," *Cahiers d'Art* 12, no. 4–5, pp. 135, 138, 139 trans. ECO. Written in Spanish, translated into French by Cassou, whose essay makes an interesting comparison with this excerpt. Another, partly different, selection is in McCully, *Picasso Anthology* (pp. 206–8).

7 Bergamín's own phrases in his preface to Gallwitz, *Picasso at 90*, p. 12.

8. [Goya commemorated the bloody uprisings against Napoleonic occupation in two vast canvases, *The Second of May, 1808, in Madrid*, and *The Third of May, 1808, in Madrid* (fig. 149) in the Prado. Similarly, "Madrid 1936" marks the defense of Madrid in November 1936 as a major victory for the Republic.]

In linking these two names, no formal relationship is intended. Between these two styles of painting there is no similar motif or direct esthetic, pictorial equivalence. If we mention them together now, it is because their work reflects the same original shock. Because the same anger arises in them, the same furious will to be, that is purely Spanish and of the people.

It is not painting, but history, repeated on these canvases.

The Disasters of War, by Goya and Picasso,[9] do not present the same point of view, but they both express the courage of the Spanish people that inspired them. The same kind of understanding, which prefers painting to history: "because it delivers everything at once." The kind, as we say in Spain, that "enters the eyes."

The Spanish fury that this painting expresses is so great that in entering our eyes it sweeps us away in stormy rapture. With our eyes we have to follow these images to their extreme view of terror. Decanting, purifying, powerful cleansing of the spirit. One cannot think or feel confused before this violently pure and lucid canvas painting by Pablo Picasso. Guernica? It means Madrid; it means Spain and the wrath of the Spanish people.

* * *

This admirable canvas tells us the simplest thing with obvious clarity: it simply says to us: yes and no. It tells us the truth. Doubt is no longer possible; it leaves no room for doubt. It puts everything so well, fully in its place, so completely, that everything becomes clearly, thoroughly, a yes or a no. It is what it is, and not what it would seem to be; it is even that if it were to appear not to be. Realism and classicism shake hands in this powerful painting. We might even say that they raise their clenched fists.[10] The plain truths revealed here are like raised fists and with what pure, powerful, vivid, real, and just clarity! * * *

It is a painting wherein thought bursts like a rocket, an explosion. And its extreme character—its perfection, its accuracy—is such that fury and enthusiasm, things that usually follow each other, here are brought together in the same space, become simultaneous, identified with each other. How, we wonder, can this terrifying beauty, made of motion, of dramatic dynamism, express itself so clearly, with such serene and certain appearances? How can wrath shatter into surfaces of such bright, pure quality, so rhythmic and well balanced? Both waterfall and dormant pool of water.

Because this fully humane painting contains the reality which it expresses: Spanish fury. It contains, limits, determines, expresses it.

What is its reality, if not that?

The trembling of the mystery of its creation, yet seeming motionless like the stars.

Picasso paints veraciously, he paints the truth. Real things, obvious things, the way they are. The truth about things. That's why this painting is not only true as painting, it is true as history: truer than history.

May the pictorial miracle happen and create speech, poetry. * * *

9. [Bergamín is relating Picasso's *Guernica* and its studies to Goya's etching cycle, *The Disasters of War* (figs. 150A and 150B). He had suggested the Goyesque title for *Sueño y Mentira de Franco*, which recalls "el sueño de la razon produce monstruos" ("The Sleep of Reason Produces Monsters") from Goya's *Los Caprichos* (1799).]

10. [A reference to the *Guernica* study of 9 May and the first photograph of the canvas (figs. 15 and 18).]

150A. Francisco Goya. *Wreckage of War,* plate 30 from *Disasters of War,* c. 1810. Etching and aquatint, 5½ x 6⅝″ (14 x 17 cm). The Metropolitan Museum of Art, New York (Harris Brisbane Dick Fund, 1932)

150B. Francisco Goya. *Truth Is Dead,* plate 79 from *Disasters of War,* c. 1820. Etching and aquatint, 6¾ x 8¾″ (17.5 x 21.5 cm). The Metropolitan Museum of Art, New York (Rogers Fund, 1922)

The people whom this poetry and this painting show as if predicting their history, are a positive, genuine people, whole and unique. And alone, entirely alone in their truth. A people who live and die truthfully, completely.

That is why I would prefer that this extreme work of Picasso's—where the yes and the no of life, in all their truth and justice, reveal themselves to us to the point of exhaustion, of death—should bear the name of what it is historically, despite appearances, in its reality and not its representation: the miracle of Madrid. Seen and not seen. Mystery triumphant. Trembling mystery alive with the fury of the Spanish people, seized like flames in shadow. For light appears amidst darkness in this truly immortal painting.

Amadée Ozenfant
A Visitor's Journal—[1937]*

The painter Ozenfant adopted a casual, colloquial manner for his reactions to the various pavilions at the exposition. Here he defends *Guernica* against left-wing attacks, illustrating how it could reach ordinary people.[11]

Sunday. I am writing at a little table in the Catalan café of the Spanish Pavilion. Sorrowful. The exhibition of Spanish sorrow. Beneath a poignant photograph of orphans one reads: "Their parents were all they had had in the world . . . and suffering has made their expression as profound as that of grown men."

The huge *Guernica* by the great Spanish painter is before me.

This man is always ahead. We have known times when facility was all the rage; thereby everything was diminished. Our own period is grandiose, dramatic, dangerous: *Guernica* is worthy of that. Worthy without putting on a carnival show, without double-entendres or word games understood only by the select few. Without concessions to the dangerous tendency of leftist groups who too often value only "subject matter," and who support platitudes provided they have "the right ideas." They frequently ignore, or underestimate, values of poetry and visual music; favoring the dullest scene, they overlook the powerful social impact, always revolutionary in a way, of intensely beautiful things. Incompetent people of this kind are dangerous, like the iconoclast for whom two wooden boards nailed together to form a cross has greater value than the most moving Christ figure. Thus they deny the evidence that

---

*Ozenfant, "Notes d'un touriste à l'exposition," *Cahiers d'Art* 12, 8–10, p. 247; this fall–winter 1937 issue followed the *Guernica* number and covered the exposition as a whole, with excellent illustrations of various pavilions.

11. Ozenfant (1886–1966) with the architect Le Corbusier had developed Purism as a variant of Cubism and previously had attacked Picasso's painting as being too personal, not enough expressive of the modern machine age. See his theoretical writings in *L'Esprit nouveau* (1920–25) summarized also in *Art* (1928), translated in 1931 as *Foundations of Modern Art*.

religious faith is aroused more by the cathedral of Notre-Dame or Chartres than by a similar church that's miserable architecture. Now, what is so special about a beautiful work, if not the power of certain forms to affect our senses, and then to sway our intellectual and moral convictions?

Guernica makes one *feel* the frightful drama of a great people abandoned to medieval tyrants, and makes one *think* about that drama. The master has used only those means that properly belong to the visual arts, and yet he has made the whole world understand the immense Spanish tragedy—if people have the eyes to see. Here's proof:

Some lady[12] goes past my table, she's come down from the second floor where there are exhibitions of Spanish war photographs: one sees children massacred by Christians and Franco's Moors. The woman says to her daughter:

> "That's all terrifying! It sends shivers down my spine as if I had a spider running down my neck." She looks at *Guernica* and says to her child: "I don't understand what is going on there, but it makes me feel awful. It's strange, it really makes me feel as if I were being chopped to pieces. Come on, let's go. War is a terrible thing! Poor Spain!"

And dragging her kid by the hand, she goes off, uncertain, into the crowd.

Guernica in London, 1938

These two essays were published in October 1938, when *Guernica* and its studies were first exhibited in London to raise funds for Spanish refugee relief. Though less feverish than the French writings, they are as eloquent, and are among the most effective and enduring of the *Guernica* commentaries.[1] Stephen Spender had been in Spain for the International Writers' Congress in Madrid, had written poignant reportage and poetry about aspects of the war he had witnessed, and with vivid imagery now recorded a poet's intense, personal response to *Guernica*. Born in 1909, Spender typifies that generation of British poets and intellectuals who saw in the Spanish Civil War ideals worth dying for, as many indeed did.[2] Slightly older, Herbert Read (1893–1968) was no less fervent in his support of the Republican cause; his broad humanist vision and gift with words infuse the short essay with remarkable power.

12. [The French, "une petite bourgeoise," difficult to translate, connotes a well-dressed, somewhat frivolous young woman whose main concern certainly would not be the Spanish Civil War.]

1. Included in several anthologies: Spender in Sperber's, which also reproduces two examples of his reportage and three poems; Read in the collections by Schiff and McCully.

2. *Journey to the Frontier* by Peter Stansky and William Abrahams (New York, 1966) is an outstanding biography of two talented young poets who died in the war: Julian Bell (1908–1937), son of the art critic Clive Bell and the painter Vanessa Bell, and John Cornford (1915–1936), son of the classicist F. M. Cornford and the poet Frances Cornford.

Stephen Spender
Picasso's Guernica at the
New Burlington Gallery*

Guernica affects one as an explosion, partly no doubt because it is a picture of an explosion. If one attempts to criticize it, one attempts to relate it to the past. So long as a work of art has this explosive quality of newness it is impossible to relate it to the past. People who say that it is *excentric*,[1] or that it falls between two stools, or that it is too horrible, and so on, are only making the gasping noises they might make if they were blown off their feet by a high-explosive bomb. All I can try to do is to report as faithfully as possible the effect that this very large and very dynamic picture makes on me.

In the first place, it is certainly not realistic in the sense that Goya's etchings of another tragedy in Spain are realistic. *Guernica* is in no sense reportage; it is not a picture of some horror which Picasso has seen and been through himself. It is the picture of a horror reported in the newspapers, of which he has read accounts and perhaps seen photographs.

This kind of second-hand experience, from the newspapers, the news-reel, the wireless, is one of the dominating realities of our time. The many people who are not in direct contact with the disasters falling on civilization live in a waking night-mare of second-hand experiences which in a way are more terrible than real experiences because the person overtaken by a disaster has at least a more limited vision than the camera's wide, cold, recording eye, and at least has no opportunity to imagine horrors worse than what he is seeing and experiencing. The flickering black, white and grey lights of Picasso's picture suggest a moving picture stretched across an elongated screen; the flatness of the shapes again suggests the photographic image, even the reported paper words. The centre of this picture is like a painting of a *collage* in which strips of newspaper have been pasted across the canvas.

The actual figures on the canvas, the balloon-like floating head of a screaming woman; the figure throwing arms up in despair; the woman running forwards, and leaving behind one reluctant, painful, enormous, clumsy leg; the terror of a horse with open mouth and skin drawn back over the teeth; the hand clutching a lamp and the electric lamp glowing so that it shows the wires, as though at any moment the precious light may go out; the groaning bull, the woman clutching her child, a complex of clustered fingers like over-ripe fruit; all this builds up a picture of horror, but to me there is grandeur in the severed arm of a hero lying in the foreground, clutching the noble, broken, ineffective sword with which he has tried to ward off the horrors of mechanical destruction; and there is pity in the leaves of the little plant growing just above this hand.

*From *New Statesman and Nation* (London), 15 October 1938, pp. 567–68, by permission of the author.

1. [Spender is referring to André Gide's unusual criticism in *Verve*, December 1937, p. 9, which termed *Guernica* "one of the least centralized of Picasso's composition . . . one of the most excentric . . ."]

Picasso uses every device of expressionism, abstractionism and effects learnt from *collage,* to build up the horror of *Guernica.* Diagonal lines of light and shade in the background, suggest searchlights and confusion, and the violent contrasts of the faces revealed in a very white light suggest the despair of light and darkness in air raids; despair of the darkness because it is too complete and you are lost; despair of the light because it is too complete and you are revealed to the enemy raiders.

The impression made on me by this picture is one that I might equally get from a great masterpiece, or some very vivid experience. That, of course, does not mean that it is a masterpiece. I shall be content to wait some years before knowing that. But it is certainly worth seeing. And if you don't like, or resist, or are overwhelmed by explosions, there are the sixty-seven studies for *Guernica,* some of them quite unlike anything in the picture itself, which are certainly amongst the most beautiful and profound drawings Picasso has ever made [cf. pp. 304 and 345, below.]

Herbert Read
Guernica: A Modern Calvary*

Art long ago ceased to be monumental. To be monumental, as the art of Michelangelo or Rubens was monumental, the age must have a sense of glory. The artist must have some faith in his fellowmen, and some confidence in the civilization to which he belongs. Such an attitude is not possible in the modern world—at least, not in our Western European world. We have lived through the greatest war in history, but we find it celebrated in thousands of mean, false and essentially unheroic monuments. Ten million men killed, but no breath of inspiration from their dead bodies. Just a scramble for contracts and fees, and an unconcealed desire to make the most utilitarian use of the fruits of heroism.

Monumental art is inspired by creative actions. It may be that sometimes the artist is deceived, but he shares his illusion with his age. He lives in a state of faith, of creative and optimistic faith. But in our age even an illusion is not tenable. When it is given out that a great Christian hero is leading a new crusade for the faith, even his followers are not deceived. A Christian crusade is not fought with the aid of infidel Moors, nor with fascist bombs and tanks. And when a Republic announces that it is fighting to defend liberty and equality, we are compelled to doubt whether these values will survive the autocratic methods adopted to establish them. The artist, at the lowest level of prestige and authority he has ever reached in the history of civilization, is compelled to doubt those who despise him.

The only logical monument would be some sort of negative monument. A monument to disillusion, to despair, to destruction. It was inevitable that the greatest artist

---

*From *London Bulletin* VI (October 1938), p. 6, reprinted by permission of Benedict Read and David Higham Associates, Ltd. When Herbert Read wrote this essay, he was editor of *Burlington Magazine,* had taught art history at several universities, and published collections of poetry, literary criticism, and art history (*Surrealism, Art and Society*).

of our time should be driven to this conclusion. Frustrated in his creative affirmations, limited in scope and scale by the timidities and customs of the age, he can at best make a monument to the vast forces of evil which seek to control our lives: a monument of protestation. When those forces invade his native land, and destroy with calculated brutality a shrine peculiarly invested with the sense of glory, then the impulse to protest takes on a monumental grandeur. Picasso's great fresco is a monument to destruction, a cry of outrage and horror amplified by the spirit of genius.

It has been said that this painting is obscure—that it cannot appeal to the soldier of the republic, to the man in the street,[1] to the communist in his cell; but actually its elements are clear and openly symbolical. The light of day and night reveals a scene of horror and destruction: the eviscerated horse, the writhing bodies of men and women, betray the passage of the infuriated bull, who turns triumphantly in the background, tense with lust and stupid power; whilst from the window Truth, whose features are the tragic mask in all its classical purity, extends her lamp over the carnage. The great canvas is flooded with pity and terror, but over it all is imposed that nameless grace which arises from their cathartic equilibrium.

Not only Guernica, but Spain; not only Spain, but Europe, is symbolized in this allegory. It is the modern Calvary, the agony in the bomb-shattered ruins of human tenderness and faith. It is a religious picture, painted, not with the same kind, but with the same degree of fervor that inspired Grünewald and the Master of the Avignon Pietà, Van Eyck and Bellini. It is not sufficient to compare the Picasso of this painting with the Goya of the *Desastres*. Goya, too, was a great artist, and a great humanist; but his reactions were individualistic—his instruments irony, satire, ridicule. Picasso is more universal: his symbols are banal, like the symbols of Homer, Dante, Cervantes. For it is only when the widest commonplace is infused with intensest passion that a great work of art, transcending all schools and categories, is born; and being born, lives immortally.

---

1. [Read is referring to lively debates in the London *Spectator* where its Marxist art critic, Anthony Blunt, attacked the *Dream and Lie of Franco* as ineffectual. Though Picasso registers "genuine, but useless horror," Blunt claimed that his symbolism "cannot reach more than the limited coterie of aesthetes" ("Picasso Unfrocked," *Spectator*, 8 Oct. 1937—representing a typical Marxist / Leninist position, as explored in part VI). Among spirited letters to the editor was Herbert Read's description of *Guernica*, which he had recently seen in Paris:

> This painting is virtually in the marketplace, where Mr Blunt wishes to see all art, and hundreds of thousands of people have seen it and, as I can testify from personal observation, accepted it with the respect and wonder which all great works of art inspire (letter of 15 Oct. 1937).

Discussions continued on 22 and 29 Oct., and 5 Nov. 1937.]

Daniel-Henry Kahnweiler
Guernica: Massacre of the Innocents—
[1956]*

These are recollections by Picasso's oldest friend in Paris and art dealer since around 1908.[1] Kahnweiler's passionate observations about war and peace draw on personal experiences: after World War I, the French government confiscated and sold his paintings as enemy property; in 1940, as a Jew and former German, he had to flee and hide from the Nazis occupying Paris.[2]

Picasso's first studies for his big picture date from the first of May. The Spanish Republican Government, as of January 1937, had commissioned from him a large mural for its pavilion at the Universal Exposition which would open later that year in Paris. Picasso had agreed, but had not yet done anything about it. Under the impact of emotional shock he now set to work. The studio in the *rue des Grands-Augustins* [cf. p. 52, above] was not big enough: the huge stretcher had to be placed at an angle. The composition underwent numerous changes in its development. Thus the head of the bull, initially turned to the right, now looks toward the left; the dead warrior, whose head was at first in the middle, his feet towards the left, has been reversed. The little flower (Hope?) appeared only at the end, clutched in the fist with the broken sword.[3]

These are examples of Picasso's extraordinary ability to live in the present moment, to forget the past, and not to bother with the future, which gives all of his work the quality of continuous creation. I have quoted already elsewhere his saying to me long ago: "In the beginning you have to have an idea, but only a vague idea." He defended his freedom all the time. Any number of pictures could be found, painted over, beneath the definitive version of many a work. In the case of *Guernica*, we at least have a series of photographs of the various states.

Much has been written about this picture, one of the most stirring art works of all times. *Guernica* is the dazzling proof that people are mistaken who speak of Picasso and his friends as "formalists"—artists preoccupied only with formal problems. Just as people deceive themselves who see only dry mathematical exercises in the music of Arnold Schoenberg, Alban Berg, Anton Webern.

---

*Excerpted with the kind permission of the late author (1884–1979), from his introduction to the exhibition catalogues, *Guernica* (Stockholm, 1956) and *Picasso: Guernica* (Brussels and Amsterdam, 1956) [trans. from German by ECO].

1. Leaving his German banking background, he discovered modern art for himself in Paris and in 1907 opened a small gallery where he showed and occasionally sold the latest paintings by Derain and Vlaminck, Picasso and Braque, Gris and Léger. See *My Galleries and Painters* [1961, 1971] and his early defense of the new style, *The Rise of Cubism* [1949, first publ. 1920], also his excellent monograph, *Juan Gris* [1947].

2. His art gallery was continued by his sister-in-law; the Galerie Louise Leiris still represents the Picasso Estate in Paris.

3. [Figs. 15 and 18; figs. 18 and 28; and fig. 52].

A *Survivor of Warsaw* by Schoenberg—like *Guernica*—is the violent protest against brutality, of a deeply perturbed man who wants to share his indignation and grief. Art, for Picasso, for Schoenberg, has never been an end in itself, but rather a way to communicate with others. Historical circumstances determined that the formulas which these two artists had at their disposal were no longer adequate for transmitting their message. They had to invent a new grammar and a new syntax—not at all just as a game, or desire for formal perfection—but purely to be able to express themselves. Picasso has always talked about himself in his art: his joy and his pain. His work is entirely autobiographical. His case is not unique today. I don't think I am mistaken in asserting that our age has turned many worthy creative minds toward confessional forms of literature. Picasso's life is inscribed in his work. * * * At the time of the military uprising, he joined the side of the Republic, resolutely declaring his loyalty. I remember his happiness at the—ephemeral—victory at Teruel, his sadness when he saw the defenses of the Republic, abandoned by the Western powers, stave in bit by bit, before Franco, supported by Hitler and Mussolini. Actually, Picasso thinks about world events to the extent that they are human concerns. I believe I have already described him as the most human of men. It is as a human being that he reacts to events. What he experienced with the massacre of the innocents of *Guernica* was immense pity, which extends even to the inanimate object. It is suffering which moves him deeply:

> . . . cries of children cries of women cries of birds cries of flowers cries of timbers and of stones cries of bricks cries of furniture of beds of chairs of curtains of pots. . . .

One reads this heartrending lament in his text for *Dream and Lie of Franco* [pp. 184, 186] but in these few lines has Picasso not given the most faithful description of his great painting? What had already affected the young Picasso long ago was the Lumpen-proletariat of Barcelona, with its beggars, blind people, cripples, and prostitutes. "The Disasters of War,"[4] for him is the suffering of all creatures. *Guernica* does not exalt the combatants, but weeps for the victims: the dead, the dying, and the distressed survivors who mourn their families. Only the bull stands erect, indomitable. His meaning has been much discussed; but his presence, his beautiful anthropomorphic head, appearing in the studies leaves no doubt: he is the invincible Spanish people. What remains is hope.

> Real men for whom despair
> Feeds the devouring fire of hope

wrote Paul Eluard, Picasso's friend, in his admirable poem, "The Victory of Guernica,"[5] at the same moment.

The real significance of Picasso's great painting, however, far surpasses the incident in the Spanish Civil War which gave rise to it—just as this particular bombing preceded so many others, infinitely more horrible. Picasso will never cease standing up against vile brutality, convinced that sooner or later—to cite Eluard once more: "The day will be ours."

4. [Reference to Goya's etching cycle protesting the Napoleonic invasion of Spain; figs. 150A and 150B.]

5. [For Eluard's poem, see pp. 186–89. When Kahnweiler reprinted this *Guernica* essay in *Confessions esthétiques* (Paris, 1963), p. 132, he began by quoting the first eight lines of "La Victoire de Guernica." See Sert's similar emphasis on Eluard's contemporaneous poem (p. 199, above).]

V.
GUERNICA IN AMERICA
1939–1974

In 1937, American critics mentioned *Guernica* only briefly, in reports of the Paris exposition. *Life* magazine reproduced the first photograph of *Guernica* in July 1937 for its mass-circulation American readership, with somewhat flippant comments.[1] Reprinted here is Emily Genauer's lively report for her New York daily, featuring a *Guernica* reproduction and Picasso's alleged political statement, best known through Elizabeth McCausland's version in the *Springfield Republican*. A less familiar McCausland review is included instead.

Only after May 1939 did American critics focus on *Guernica*, when it arrived in New York and traveled throughout the country, raising funds for Spanish refugee relief. Henry McBride opened *Guernica*'s American tour with a persuasive and widely quoted essay. *Art News* carried the best review in an art magazine. The important Picasso retrospective at The Museum of Modern Art, which traveled to several museums during 1939–1941 (see Chronology), included *Guernica* and triggered sharp debates, such as the *Parnassus* items. The abstract painter Ad Reinhardt in 1947 created a didactic newspaper feature that is still a remarkably good introduction to *Guernica*.

Marxism so dominates criticism during the 1940s that it merits separate study, in part VI. One cannot generalize so readily about later evaluations, although a formalist viewpoint prevails among artists and critics close to the studios; these diverse formal and iconographic studies are reprinted in parts VII and VIII.

No survey of *Guernica*'s experiences in this country would be complete without a section on its vital role during a war that recalls the Spanish Civil War in its divisiveness. During the Vietnam conflict, *Guernica* was rediscovered politically, and celebrated as a universal antiwar statement.

---

1. 26 July 1937 issue, p. 64:

The dislocated bull at left, possibly symbolizing the Rebels, really means that Picasso has lately specialized in bullfights. The head coming down the stairs is adding a kerosene lamp to the electric lighting. The broken sword of Guernica is obvious symbolism. The creature running at lower right suggests the work of James Thurber of the *New Yorker*.

Years later, however, *Life* compensated for this cavalier treatment with a special *Guernica* article in its superb double issue on Picasso, 27 December 1968, pp. 86–94B.

First Reviews, 1937–1940

Emily Genauer
Picasso's Mural Draws Throng: Painter Says Work Defends Loyalists—[1937]*

The New York World Telegram carried the first vivid description and large reproduction of *Guernica* in an American newspaper, with a 4-column caption: "Picasso's Panel of War that Excited Paris." Of greatest interest is Genauer's lengthy quotation from the famous political statement attributed to Picasso, best known and frequently reprinted from the version published by McCausland (whose *Guernica* criticism appears below).[1] The political text, however, must have been written in part or entirely *for* Picasso. Although it undoubtedly expressed his sentiments in 1937, its rhetoric does not consistently reflect the typical cadences of Picasso's natural speech.[2]

Spain, of all the countries exhibiting in the Paris International Exposition of Arts and Techniques, turns out to have the most sensational pavilion. And for a very simple reason. Other nations spent fortunes on mechanical and electrical displays, dramatic posters, on comprehensive exhibits of handicrafts, industry and agriculture. Spain

*The New York World Telegram, 21 August 1937, by permission of Emily Genauer, who emphasized that she filed the story immediately after the press reception and inauguration of the Spanish Pavilion in mid-July (telephone interview, April 1971). A fine biographical essay about Ms. Genauer is included by Judy Collischan Van Wagner, in *Women Shaping Art: Profiles of Power* (New York, 1984), pp. 13–26.

1. McCausland's Sunday feature, 18 July 1937, for the *Springfield Republican* carried the text, reprinted by Barr, *Picasso*, pp. 202 and 264, from which it has been widely reproduced as an authentic Picasso statement (Ashton, pp. 143–44, for example).

This political statement had been prepared earlier, in May–June, and evidently handed out again to American journalists in Paris. Picasso reportedly told the left-wing American Artists Congress in New York: "In the panel *on which I am working*, which I shall call *Guernica*, and in all my recent works of art, I clearly expressed * * * [my italics; see note 4]. This was first recorded on 6 July 1937 in the American Communist organ, *The Daily Worker*, as Picasso's message to his "friends in America," transmitted through the North American Committee To Aid Spanish Democracy. Briefer quotations also appeared in the Communist cultural magazine, *New Masses* (art review, July 13). Two magazines closely aligned with the American Artists Congress later carried the text: *The American Artist* in its summer issue and *Art Front* of the Artists' Union, in October (with enthusiastic endorsements by Stuart Davis, Rockwell Kent, and other artists).

2. [See Picasso's own statements in parts I and VI.]

just happens to have been the birthplace of Picasso, certainly among the greatest living painters in the world, and considered by many savants to be the first among them all.

So Picasso, who has lived in Paris for more than thirty years, was commissioned to do for a long wall on the main floor, a tremendous mural, about 25 by 45 feet,[3] with the Spanish Civil War as its theme. And because it is by Picasso, and because it is in his typical abstract manner and therefore incomprehensible to most people who see it, the pavilion turns out to be one of the most crowded and provocative in the whole shebang.

The specific subject of this panorama of weird forms developed in somber grays, black and white, is the tragedy of Guernica. One can distinguish the head of a bull, dying horses and people imploring aid.

A cocktail party was given to celebrate the opening of the pavilion, and Picasso himself was there. The panel itself must definitely quash widely circulated reports that the great painter has favored the cause of the Spanish Fascists. But Picasso made his stand even clearer.

"The Spanish struggle is the fight of reaction against the people, against freedom," he said. "My whole life as an artist has been nothing more that a continuous struggle against reaction and the death of art. How could anybody think for a moment that I could be in agreement with reaction and death, against the people, against freedom?[4] In the panel I clearly express my abhorence of the military caste which has sunk Spain in an ocean of pain and death.

"In the whole world, the purest representatives of universal culture join with the Spanish people. In Valencia I investigated the state of pictures saved from the Prado[5] and the world should know that the Spanish people have saved Spanish art. Many of the best works will shortly come to Paris and the whole world will see who saves culture and who destroys it.

"As to the future of Spanish art, this much I may say to my friends in America. The contribution of the people's struggle will be enormous. No one can deny the vitality and the youth which the struggle will bring to Spanish art. Something new and strong which the consciousness of this magnificent epic will sow in the soul of Spanish artists will undoubtedly appear in their works. This contribution of the purest values to art will be one of the greatest conquests of the Spanish people."

3. [In her enthusiasm, Genauer nearly doubled *Guernica*'s dimensions of 11'6" x 25'6".]

4. [Here the Genauer text omits some sentences referring to Picasso's directorship of the Prado Museum and to "the panel on which I am working, which I shall call *Guernica*." See Failing's essay, p. 341, above, for additional quotations from the McCausland version.]

5. [Not quite, but it makes a good story! It was Christian Zervos who inspected the treasures of the Prado sent to Valencia for safekeeping; see p. 50, above.]

Elizabeth McCausland
Guernica, Picasso's Great Mural, Shown—[1939]*

McCausland's art reviews of the 1930s demonstrate her early recognition of Picasso and fervent support of the Spanish Republican cause. An art critic with a strong social conscience and political astuteness, she used *Guernica* to wake up her readers to political realities as she saw them. She began her review of *Guernica* in New York by quoting Steer's account of the bombing (pp. 160–63) and concluded with Picasso's text for the *Dream and Lie of Franco* (pp. 184, 186), probably its first appearance in English, in an American newspaper. Explaining that *Guernica* was being shown for the benefit of the Spanish Refugee Relief Campaign, with 50 cents admission charge, she emphasized: "It is a half dollar well spent; for it symbolizes the passage from isolation to social identification of the most gifted painter of our era."

Picasso has been the most versatile and prolific of the inventors of the 20th century. In his "blue" and "rose" periods he painted some of the most beautiful and sensitive canvases of our time. In his cubist, neoclassic and psychological[1] periods, he pushed experimentation to ever farther horizons. Where he was going was not always clear; nor could the painter perhaps have given an answer to the question. He was a creator in search of his soul, we may say.

Now he has found his soul not in the studio, not in the laboratory of plastic research, but in his union with the people of his native land, Spain.[2] In the painting, *Guernica,* he functioned not only as a son of Spain but as a citizen of the democratic world. And how did he function in this new unusual capacity? By bringing to it the cumulative experience of the previous 40 years' experiments.

The result is a canvas of amazing plastic complexity, imbued with esthetic ideas and concepts from cubism, abstractionism, neoclassicism and the psychological period. But all these attributes are only means to an end. Picasso has used the skill and dexterity of his method to convey a message. He wants to speak to all those who see his work. And what does he want to say?

He wants to cry out in horror and anguish against the invasion and destruction of the Spain of his love. He wants to protest with his art against the betrayal accomplished by Franco and his fascist allies. He wants to awake in the breasts of all who see *Guernica* an inner and emotional understanding of the fate of Spain. He wants simple and well-meaning citizens everywhere to live through the tragedy of bombardment, physical mutilation and death, so that they in turn will raise their voices in a passionate cry for justice and peace.

---

*Excerpting a 21 May 1939 article for the *Springfield Republican* from McCausland's *Picasso* booklet, by permission of the publisher, ACA Gallery, NYC. A graduate of Smith College, McCausland was art critic of the nearby *Springfield Republican* from 1923 to 1935, and thereafter became its art correspondent in New York. She also taught at several colleges, organized many art exhibitions, and wrote about American artists until her death in 1965.

1. [Meaning, Surrealist.]

2. [An interesting parallel with Cassou's essay (p. 209), which McCausland could have read, and with John Berger's conclusions written much later (p. 271).]

Henry McBride
Picasso's Guernica Here—[1939]*

Welcoming *Guernica* to New York in 1939, McBride wrote a balanced and effective essay for his newspaper readership. He clearly and sympathetically discussed the painting's political origins, symbolism, and modernist style. This *Guernica* essay, by perhaps the most respected American art critic at a daily paper, reached a nationwide audience when *Art Digest* quoted his review with the editorializing caption: "Picasso's *Guernica* Misses the Masses, but Wins the Art Critics" (15 May 1939).

What from any point of view, is the most remarkable painting to be produced in this area—the already famous "Guernica" by Picasso—has arrived in this country and is being shown in the Valentine Galleries for the benefit of the Spanish refugees campaign. This is the most sensational event in a season that has not been too prodigal with excitements, and to see it is an obligatory experience.

It was painted two years ago as a decoration for the Spanish Pavilion in the Paris World's Fair and it was instantly recognized by most connoisseurs as an extraordinary achievement and destined without doubt to be regarded as Picasso's masterpiece. Certainly it is the most stunning attack that has yet been made upon the eyes and nerves of the art-loving portion of the public.

It will be much talked about and long talked about. Years after the present war fevers shall have been replaced by some other kinds of fevers—for in the long history of the world there never has been a time when human beings have not itched with unholy desires of some sort, and so it seems likely that we shall continue to be the bad numeros that we have always been—years hence, I repeat, when we shall be able to look on this present period with detachment, just because we shall then be immersed in some other kind of deviltry, we shall regard this "Guernica" as the most concrete and powerful statement of the hatreds generated by these political wars of the present.

It is full of war passion. It was begot out of the rage felt by the artist when he learned of the destruction in the late war of the old Basque town of Guernica. You don't have to be especially susceptible to cubism to understand it. It is only too plain. Death and destruction are furiously indicated and the gestures of the victims have a largeness and a ferocity unequaled in art since medieval times.

This sounds like propaganda and in fact the picture was intended to be such, but it ended in being something vastly more important—a work of art. Picasso is an ardent communist and in painting "Guernica" he was attacking Franco with might and main, but the futility of propaganda in the hands of an artist is once more illustrated for always in the case of the good artist the genius of the painter takes charge

*Reprinted from *The New York Sun*, 6 May 1939; included also in *The Flow of Art: Essays and Criticism of Henry McBride* (Daniel Cotton Rich, ed., New York, 1975), pp. 367–69. McBride (1867–1962) was an early friend of Gertrude Stein's in Paris, where he met Picasso briefly in 1914. Writing for *The Sun* ever since his review of the Armory Show in 1913, he continued as an informative and entertaining spokesman for modernism well into his 80s, when he joined *Art News* in 1950.

of the situation and the politician in him disappears in the effort to turn out a good picture. People who see the picture in this country and who respond to its horror will see it simply as an argument against war in general. Picasso aimed it at one set of disputants but it puts the curse upon all disputants. Death is very similar on both sides of the battle lines.

Technically the work is overwhelmingly clever. It is twenty-eight feet in width and the great reduction necessary in the photo reproductions destroys the surface variety that the picture has, though it does give an idea of the massive composition founded on a great triangle, with the lighted lamp at the apex of it, and not by accident, for nothing in the picture is an accident. With this vast mural are shown some of the many preparatory studies for it, all of them in bold, unerring lines that are amazing in force. Picasso is continually inventing. Apparently for every new set of emotions that creeps into his life he has to have a new set of symbols, and so we behold him prodigal, on the present occasion, with a group of revolutionary forms that no one on earth but he could have achieved, and all of them have a compelling authority that demands their acceptance into the new language that all the lesser artists will shortly be using.

For reasons of his own, Picasso did this picture in black and white. He can be a great colorist when he chooses to be and there seemed no special necessity to abstain from color in the Spanish Pavillion—but, of course, he had his reasons. Even in the black and white artists will still find color, however, for there is an emphatic and lyrical play of values against values that runs all through the piece. It actually looks richer and more eloquent as it hangs now in the Valentine Gallery than it did in Paris, for the light that falls upon it is eminently becoming and emphasizes the unity of the design and its tremendous and dramatic thrust.

"Guernica" has already been exhibited in London and will doubtless be shown in some of our other cities before seeking permanent asylum in some museum. It had been supposed all along, by the prophets, that it would be the star item in the opening exhibition of the Museum of Modern Art,[1] which is scheduled for next week, but the express stipulation of the artist that it should be shown for the benefit of political refugees prevented this arrangement.

---

1. [Founded in 1929, the museum in 1939 celebrated its permanent new home on 53 Street with a brilliant installation of its collection. Chipp has included entertaining details in his account of *Guernica's* arrival in New York (*Art News*, May 1980, pp. 108–10).]

Doris Brian
A Picasso Premiere: Guernica and Studies in Benefit Exhibition—[1939]*

In contrast to the provincialism of *Art Digest,* the *Art News* critic understood Picasso's formal language and discovered *Guernica*'s art-historical roots. Doris Brian commented intelligently about Picasso's neutral color scheme and discussed the relationship between *Minotauromachy* and *Guernica*—possibly the first time in print.

A few days after the event, Picasso, in a spurt of feverish activity, started a series of fervid drawings and paintings which were crystalized in the mural, *Guernica,* commemorating the air raid on the Basque town. Originally placed in the Spanish Pavilion at the Paris World's Fair of 1937, the painting, together with a representative assortment of the dozens of studies, is now shown at the Valentine Gallery for the benefit of the Spanish Refugee Relief Campaign.

As a monument to the disaster at Guernica its significance is limited because of the relative smallness of a public able to comprehend its obtuse language; as a monument to Picasso, its possibilities are tremendous. Analogies to Goya have been drawn, and surely they hold water. In a great many ways, however, it is the spiritual successor of Géricault's *Raft of the Medusa* and the Delacroix *Massacre of Scio*—both in the Louvre. It is as expressive of the most advanced aspects of contemporary art as those works were of the nascent Romanticism of their era.

Emerging from a two year lull in artistic activity, Picasso unexpectedly espoused a cause with amazing vehemence and produced a masterpiece. Stylistically, it of course has ties with the rounded shapes and complicated points of view which the artist had been employing since 1927. In subject matter and in composition it seems to spring somehow from the much more naturalistic etching of 1935, *Minotauromachy,* an impression of which is now on view at the Museum of Modern Art. In spirit it is an outgrowth of the same forces which prompted the bitter etchings, *Songe et Mensonge de Franco,* a few months earlier.

From these foundations, and from the infinitely more violent studies, grew the final recitation of the horror of the human and animal victims of a bombing. Disciplined and carefully organized despite the apparent confusion, the figures were changed and turned about even after the painting was commenced. Fitted into a complicated triangular design, each element has a formal and psychological relationship to the whole. It is fortunate that the color schemes were abandoned in favor of black, white and grey relieved by textural indications, for the composition, characterized by power of design and emotional impact, could probably not have withstood the added weight of the brilliant tonality which has become Picasso's recent idiom.

* *Art News,* 20 May 1939, p. 12, by permission; Doris Brian was an associate editor of the magazine.

James Thrall Soby
Picasso: A Critical Estimate—[1939]*

James Thrall Soby (1906–1979) energetically praised *Guernica* in reviewing the great retrospective at The Museum of Modern Art, "Picasso: Forty Years of His Art." He had seen *Guernica* at the Paris Exposition, and had championed recent styles such as Surrealism in his book, *After Picasso* (New York, 1935).

Finally there is *Guernica*. The vast mural is presented in more spacious quarters than have been provided for many other pictures in the exhibition. It is, in the opinion of the writer, the most forceful achievement of art in our century. The mural is accompanied by a large number of preliminary sketches which Picasso made in the frantic month before *Guernica* took final form. A curious thing about the mural itself is that, though organized on an abstract formula, it supplies and evokes a far more complete sense of the horror, the fury and even the locale of the war than does Delacroix's representational stage-piece on the Greek War for Independence, the *Massacre of Scio*. *Guernica* is not, however, something to be discussed in a paragraph; it is an accomplishment to be seen as often as anyone can visit the exhibition, which should at all costs be very often indeed.

Virginia Whitehill
On Public Taste and Picasso—[1940]*

An art educator and contributing editor to *Parnassus* quickly counterattacked. Virginia Whitehill claimed that "for the average gallery-goer, *Guernica* must remain unpleasantly incomprehensible." As an example of art for the people, she praised the paintings by Luis Quintanilla, then on exhibition in a New York gallery (fig. 151) and p. 232, below.

It did not require the mammoth Picasso exhibition at the Museum of Modern Art for final confirmation of the fact that the great painter of 1905 is today only an important figure in an unimportant movement. * * *

*Reprinted from Soby's thoughtful five-page review in *Parnassus* 11 (Dec. 1939), p. 9, by permission. *Parnassus* was one of the official publications of the College Art Association until the *College Art Journal* replaced it in 1941. For other reviews of this first Picasso retrospective, see the Kibbey bibliography, item 488.

*From the editorial, *Parnassus* 12 (Jan. 1940), p. 12, by permission of CAA.

Arranged chronologically, the catalogue brilliantly annotated by Alfred H. Barr Jr., it carried the story from the incredible Roses of 1898 to the equally incredible Guernica of 1937. The latter, which together with the preliminary sketches was handsomely housed in a spacious gallery of its own, received reverent consideration from the Faithful and the voices which dared suggest that the emperor had no clothes were faint and few. That Guernica is considered great by some of the most intelligent and open-minded of Picasso's admires is without doubt. James Thrall Soby, in reviewing the exhibition in the December issue of Parnassus, states that the mural is "in his opinion the most forceful achievement of art in our century," and this estimate would receive confirmation from any serious Picasso students.

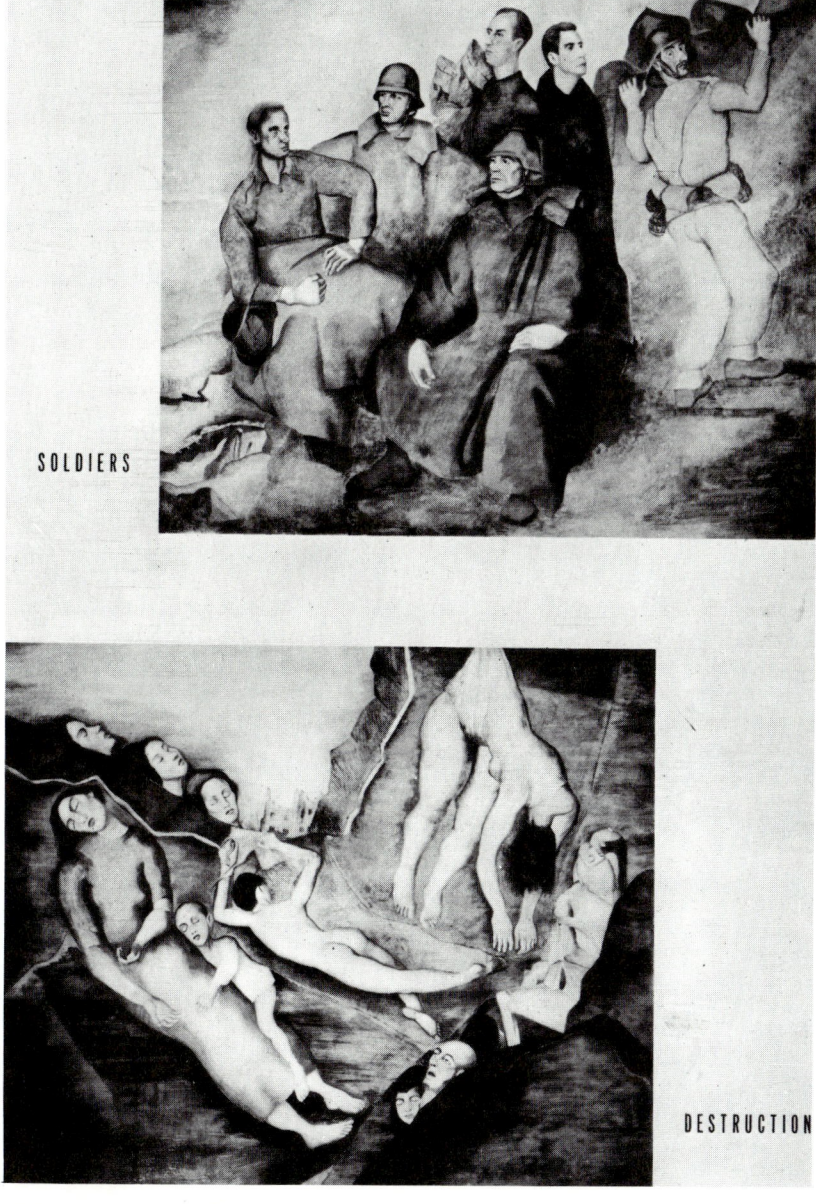

151. Luis Quintanilla. *Soldiers* and *Destruction,* paintings for the Spanish Pavilion, The World's Fair, New York, 1939–40. Present whereabouts unknown. Courtesy Frick Reference Library

For the average gallery-goer Guernica must remain unpleasantly incomprehensible, and the purpose of the present editorial is merely to deplore the dishonesty of the American art public when confronted with work which it can neither understand nor appreciate but which it feels nevertheless obligated to accept. Surrealism, whatever its claims, is fare for the few. In these days of dictatorships, when democratic freedom of thought and expression is the nation's sweetest possession, it seems a pity that the tremendous influence wielded by the Museum of Modern Art should impose, through no fault of its own, an intimidating effect upon the average gallery-goer. The reason for this, may in part be due to the actual, physical impressiveness of the institution and the authoritative presentation of such exhibitions as the Picasso, which by their very size and thoroughness discourage dissenting opinions. But even more is it due to the reluctance of the majority to say what they don't like if this dislike happens to be currently deprecated by those in the know. Nevertheless I would hazard a guess that in any safe and secret ballot on the relative merits of Guernica and the war documents of Luis Quintanilla the election would light upon the latter, for it is in his simple, factual frescoes and sincerely felt, sensitive drawings rather than in the obscure symbolism of Picasso's vast mural, that the face of the Spanish War is shown to humanity.

Ad Reinhardt
How To Look at a Mural:
Guernica—[1947]*

This was Reinhardt's last contribution to *P.M.*, "the anti-fascist, anti-anticommunist New York tabloid [that] was founded by multi-millionaire Marshall Field to add a fresh voice to a national press that was almost wholly conservative, isolationist, anti-labor, anti-civil-rights, anti-Russia, . . ." according to his friend Thomas Hess.[1] Reinhardt's Sunday feature had appeared almost fortnightly, beginning on 27 January 1946 with "How To Look at a Cubist Painting" (fig. 152A), to the delight of the artist's friends, abstract painters and intellectuals. They could appreciate his Joycean puns, witty spoofs of art textbooks, satire of the New York art scene, and adaptations of Max Ernst's Dadaist montages combined with comic strips—while his less sophisticated readers enjoyed them at instructive face value. Hence Reinhardt could gleefully reproduce (in the 8 Sept. 1946 cartoon) this letter from Sinclair Lewis, prize-winning author of *Main Street* and *Babbitt*:

> Let me congratulate you on your *P.M.* series on modern art, which incredibly manages to be equally informative and amusing. Most advocates of modern art have so unpleasant and high-nosed an attitude toward untutored laymen like myself that they rouse only irritation, but your missionary zeal is so tempered with good nature and humanness that it is a delight.

*Reprinted from *The Art Comics and Satires of Ad Reinhardt*, Thomas B. Hess, ed., Kunsthalle Düsseldorf and Marlborough Rome, 1975 (facsimile reproductions with introductory essay by Hess); by permission of Reinhardt's heirs.

1. Introduction, p. 25; the editor of *Art News* also recalled their 15-year friendship (p. 5).

Unlike Reinhardt's zany satire in previous features, the *Guernica* page (fig. 152B) was "serious" and quite "appropriate to *P.M.*'s editorial slant. Possibly he was having difficulties with his employers, and this eloquent analysis of *Guernica* was meant to ease their minds without compromising his position."[2]

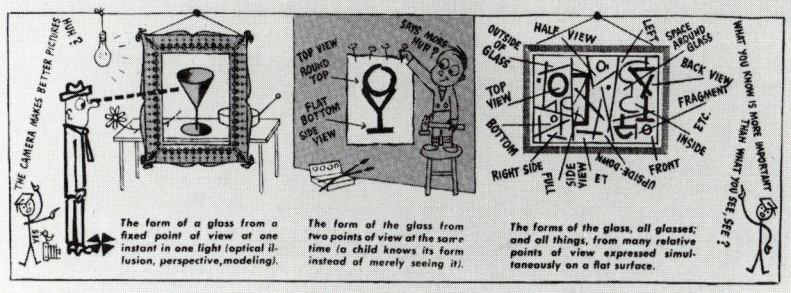

152A. Ad Reinhardt. *How To Look at a Cubist Painting*. Drawing for Sunday feature, *P.M.*, 27 January 1946

2. Ibid., p. 39. This final contribution appeared on 5 January 1947, after Reinhardt had just been fired from *P.M.*, probably more for his activism in the American Newspaper Guild's labor dispute with the paper than for blithely ignoring editorial preference for social realist art. See Lucy R. Lippard, *Ad Reinhardt* (New York, 1981), p. 132, note 16; also the excellent Chronology (pp. 198–200) detailing Reinhardt's amazingly diverse intellectual interests and studies in art history.

233

HOW TO LOOK AT A MURAL

Some words about the Picasso "Guernica" mural by Ad Reinhardt*

Almost ten years ago, a small, quiet ancient holy Basque town, full of refugees, became the target for the first "total" air-raid. It was wiped out in three and a half hours. Two days later the most famous living artist, the freest and most prolific painter of all time, started a mural that was to become the greatest anti-fascist work-of-art and the most impressive and monumental painting of the twentieth-century. The mural (12 × 26 feet) represented the Spanish Loyalist Government at the Paris World's Fair (1937), later toured London and America's seven largest cities, was seen by over a million people, raised over $10,000 here to save many Spanish lives, and may be seen now at the Museum of Modern Art.

The mural is not a picture-copy-imitation of a real scene you might see, or a simple poster or banal political-cartoon which you can easily understand (and forget) in a few minutes, but a design that diagrams our whole present dark age. It is a painting of pain and suffering. It symbolizes human destruction, cruelty and waste, not in a local spot but all over our one-world. It challenges our (yours, too) basic ways of living, thinking and looking.

A story tells how a Nazi official who, looking at a photograph of this mural, remarked to Picasso, "So it was you who did this," received the answer, "No, you did."

The bull, bristling, brute-stupidity (Franco-Fascism), a moment of pause, retreat, a preparation for another attack, a defiant, erect tail, alert, sharp ears, staring eyes that see without looking, a creature without mind or human heart . . .

A mother, anguished, a fierce cry to the skies, a pointed, paralyzed tongue, eyes and nostrils that become teardrops, a desperate pull up, a drag down, a lifeless child, limp as a rag-doll, lips sealed in innocence . . .

The mural is an allegory. A pointing out of its symbolic-meanings will not explain its art-meanings (a last recombination of cubist and expressionist-surrealist-illustration, the end of a fine-art-picture-tradition). Here are, for what they are worth, some long labels. You see what you know and you don't look for what you don't want to see.

The design (photo-montage—like) is set in a self-limited stage-world, an interior-exterior, an inside-room and an outside-town-square simultaneously. The color is black, white, pale and dark gray. (The dead have no color.)

A horse, dying, on one knee, (Spain), disemboweled, a stab in the back from above, a rigid tongue and raging throat, a twisted body, a newspaper-texture (cubist-pasted-paper) (headlines) . . .

A sun (source of life), a radiant eye of the dark night, an electric-artificial-light-bulb (man's fateful discovery), all-seeing-God's-eye-witness.

A face aghast, a classic profile, a flying-thrust out of a window (like a fusion of fast photographic images), a terrified hold on breasts, an oil lamp (Truth) lights the tragedy.

A building aflame, an open-window, a falling, shrieking woman on fire, a half-opened door . . .

A hand, helpless, clumsy, chopped-off, scattered, divided fingers, stuck out like sore thumbs in all directions, a palm with crossed fatal life-lines . . .

A woman, dazed, fascinated, a looking-up-lunge, nipples bolted on breasts, imprisoning maternity, futile appealing hands, a painful dragging of torn, broken feet . . .

A man, decapitated, the bust of a smashed statue (the young Republic), eyes that cannot see straight, and roll in reflex-action, a look down into a hollow, open mouth with no sound, a look up under a nose (a circulating viewpoint from where you look), a cold, iron horse-shoe (good luck) turned as if seen from below, warns and threatens the onlooker (you) . . .

*The two most recent books on the artist are Alfred H. Barr's "Picasso, Fifty Years of His Art" (Museum of Modern Art) and Harriet and Sidney Janis's "Picasso, the Recent Years, 1939–1946" (Doubleday & Co.)

An arm, dismembered, mutilated, a clenched fist, a frozen grip of death, a broken sword, a hopeless defense gesture against a surprise attack, a young flower-blossom (renewal of life, hope) ". . . the last bud of the future"—Eluard.

"No, painting is not done to decorate apartments. It is an instrument of war" . . . against "brutality and darkness"—Picasso.

HOW TO LOOK at a mural

Some words about the Picasso "Guernica" mural by Ad Reinhardt ✱

Almost ten years ago, a small, quiet ancient holy Basque town, full of refugees, became the target for the first "total" air-raid. It was wiped out in three and a half hours. Two days later the most famous living artist, the freest and most prolific painter of all time, started a mural that was to become the greatest anti-fascist work-of-art and the most impressive and monumental painting of the twentieth-century. The mural (12 x 26 feet) represented the Spanish Loyalist Government at the Paris World's Fair (1937), later toured London and America's seven largest cities, was seen by over a million people, raised over $10,000 here to save many Spanish lives, and may be seen now at the Museum of Modern Art.

The mural is not a picture-copy-imitation of a real scene you might see, or a simple poster or banal political-cartoon which you can easily understand (and forget) in a few minutes, but a design that diagrams our whole present dark age. It is a painting of pain and suffering. It symbolizes human destruction, cruelty and waste, not in a local spot but all over our one-world. It challenges our (yours, too) basic ways of living, thinking and looking.

A story tells how a Nazi official who, looking at a photograph of this mural, remarked to Picasso, "So it was you who did this," received the answer, "No, you did."

The mural is an allegory. A pointing out of its symbolic-meanings will not explain its art-meanings (a last recombination of cubist and expressionist-surrealist-illustration, the end of a fine-art-picture-tradition). Here are, for what they are worth, some long labels. You see what you know and you don't look for what you don't want to see.

The design (photo-montage-like) is set in a self-limited stage-world, an interior-exterior, an inside-room and on an outside-town-square simultaneously. The color is black, white, pale and dark gray. (The dead have no color).

The bull, bristling, brute-stupidity (Franco-Fascism), a moment of pause, retreat, a preparation for another attack, a defiant, erect tail, alert, sharp ears, staring eyes that see without looking, a creature without mind or human heart . . .

A horse, dying, on one knee, (Spain), disemboweled, a stab in the back from above, a rigid tongue and raging throat, a twisted body, a newspaper-texture (cubist-pasted-paper) (headlines) . . .

A face aghast, a classic profile, a flying-thrust out of a window (like a fusion of fast photographic images), a terrified hold on breasts, an oil lamp (Truth) lights the tragedy.

A mother, anguished, a fierce cry to the skies, a pointed, paralyzed tongue, eyes and nostrils that become teardrops, a desperate pull up, a drag down, a lifeless child, limp as a rag-doll, lips sealed in innocence . . .

A sun (source of life), a radiant eye of the dark night, an electric-artificial-light-bulb (man's fateful discovery), all-seeing-God's-eye-witness.

A building aflame, an open-window, a falling, shrieking woman on fire, a half-opened door . . .

"No, painting is not done to decorate apartments. It is an instrument of war" . . . against "brutality and darkness"—Picasso

A hand, helpless, clumsy, chopped-off, scattered, divided fingers, stuck out like sore thumbs in all directions, a palm with crossed fatal life-lines . . .

A man, decapitated, the bust of a smashed statue (the young Republic), eyes that cannot see straight, and roll in reflex-action, a look down into a hollow, open mouth with no sound, a look up under a nose (a circulating viewpoint from where you look), a cold, iron horse-shoe (good luck) turned as if seen from below, warns and threatens the onlooker (you) . . .

A woman, dazed, fascinated, a looking-up-lunge, nipples bolted on breasts imprisoning maternity, futile appealing hands, a painful dragging of torn, broken feet . . .

✱ The two most recent books on the artist are Alfred H. Barr's "Picasso, Fifty Years of His Art" (Museum of Modern Art) and Harriet and Sidney Janis's "Picasso, the Recent Years, 1939-1946" (Doubleday & Co.)

An arm, dismembered, mutilated, a clenched fist, a frozen grip of death, a broken sword, a hopeless defense gesture against a surprise attack, a young flower-blossom (renewal of life, hope) " . . . the last bud of the future"—Eluard.

152B. Ad Reinhardt. *How To Look at a Mural* [*Guernica*]. Drawing for Sunday feature, *P.M.*, 5 January 1947

Guernica and Anti-Vietnam Protests in the 1960s and 1970s

Protests in America against the war in Vietnam used *Guernica* as a peace symbol; posters with the fallen warrior (figs. 128A and 128B) appeared in marches against U.S. military involvement in Southeast Asia. In 1967, some 400 artists and writers petitioned Picasso: "Please let the spirit of your painting be reasserted and its message once again felt, by withdrawing your painting from the United States for the duration of the war." Picasso did not reply, but Kahnweiler cited the artist's 1956 comment: "It will do the most good in America."

A similar demand was sent to Picasso in 1970, reprinted below. Responding to this appeal, Professor Meyer Schapiro argued eloquently against this particular protest. Another document celebrates a notorious 1974 incident when a young Iranian artist, Toni Shafrazi, sprayed *Guernica* with the words, "Kill Lies All" (fig. 156). The concluding item illustrates how grade-school children saw *Guernica* in appealingly personal ways, relating the painting to the war in Vietnam and to the racial strife of this turbulent decade.

Jeanne Siegel and Artists Discuss: How Effective Is Social Protest Art?— [1967]*

In mid-1967, following intense anti-Vietnam protests, several participants in Angry Arts Against the War in Vietnam[1] discussed the effectiveness of protest art and quickly focused on *Guernica*. Their spirited arguments inevitably reflect their painting styles that ranged from the somber, nearly monochrome abstractions of Ad Reinhardt (1913–August 1967) and the geometric speedway image of Allen d'Arcangelo (b. 1930), to the controversial constructions by 29-year-old Marc Morrel.[2] Leon Golub, then painting tortured, battling figures in response to reports of Vietnam atrocities, was *Guernica*'s strongest champion.[3]

REINHARDT: For over thirty years I was never sure about what protest art did exactly. I know that at one point I thought that perhaps murals or public statements, signs and parades, political cartoons in newspapers, and now things that happen on TV—

---

*Published by permission of Jeanne Siegel, the art historian-critic who organized the artists' symposium aired over WBAI radio, New York; a slightly edited version is included in her collected essays, *Artworks: Discourse on the 60s and 70s* (Ann Arbor: UMI Research Press, 1985), pp. 101–19.

1. Protest activities had included the petition to Picasso; a concert, poetry reading, and film collage; a fund-raising portfolio of prints and poems; and a 10-foot high, 120-foot long Collage of Indignation, 150 artists collaborating, shown at Loeb Student Center, New York University.

2. His construction incorporating the American flag was removed from Loeb Center; his dealer was convicted for exhibiting Morrel's work, considered to be "defacing and mutilating" the flag.

3. Born 1922, Golub recalls that *Guernica* made a lasting impression on him when he saw it in 1939 as a young student beginning art-history courses at the University of Chicago [1971 interview with ECO]. See also Donald Kuspit, *Leon Golub: Existential/Activist Painter* (New Brunswick: Rutgers University Press, 1985), pp. 13, 45, 62, 69 (note 31), and Chronology, p. 199.

the publicity might do something [see fig. 152B]. I'm not so sure, just from a social and political point of view what protest images do, and I suppose I would raise a question. I suppose this is an advertising or communications problem. In no case in recent decades has the statement of protest art had anything to do with the statement in the fine arts.

SIEGEL: Would this apply to Picasso's *Guernica*?

GOLUB: You know we wrote a letter which about a thousand or so artists signed to request that Picasso pull *Guernica* out of the Modern Museum as a protest against the war in Vietnam.[4] This would make the painting work again like it once worked.

REINHARDT: I talked to Barney Newman about it. He thought it was a ridiculous request that we should ask him to remove it.

D'ARCANGELO: First of all you put the museum on the spot and I don't think that should be.

GOLUB: It happens to be the temporary possessor of this object. This object was made for a very specific purpose. It was made to dramatize Picasso's anger and denunciation of Fascism, of great countries attacking small countries or attacking villages. Since then this particular painting has become an object of holy veneration and it's become a mystical thing but it's lost its effectiveness. People come and look at it and they don't even know what they're looking at in a certain sense.

REINHARDT: It might have a symbolic value, but actually it's just a cubist-surrealist painting of some kind.

GOLUB: It's a war painting.

REINHARDT: I wouldn't agree with you. It doesn't tell you anything about the Spanish war and it doesn't say anything about war. Picasso himself just committed himself about something like darkness and brutality. Actually I'm against interpretation anyway but the most interesting or at least the most relevant interpretation seems to be the psychoanalytic one in which Picasso reveals himself to be an open book.

GOLUB: Now, you're dealing with certain universal symbols. You're dealing, for example, with the bull which comes down all the way from Crete. It's a Spanish symbol. Also, these things appear in Spanish apocalyptic art of the 10th century. There are manuscripts which relate to this kind of thing [fig. 106].[5] When you see a horse that's disemboweled, you recognize it as a disemboweled horse. When you see a mother holding a dead child which appears in that thing you recognize it as a mother holding a dead child.

REINHARDT: They're like cartoons.

GOLUB: You may call them cartoons but the point is they have rhetorical purpose.

REINHARDT: They have no effectiveness at all.

GOLUB: They have a tremendous effectiveness on me even today.

REINHARDT: That Spanish war was lost.

GOLUB: Well, paintings don't change wars. They show feelings about wars.

REINHARDT: It didn't explain about Spain to anyone.

SIEGEL: Even though the painting itself perhaps doesn't explain it, there is a story that always accompanies the painting that tells its history.

4. [See a similar petition of March 1970, pp. 239–40.]
5. [Golub in 1958 wrote an unpublished paper on *Guernica* and the Apocalypse of Saint-Sever.]

MORREL: When classes are taken around I've heard the speeches that go along with it and they're very powerful and perhaps explain the painting better than what Picasso was actually trying to do or say.

GOLUB: He knew what he was saying. He was in full command all the time.

REINHARDT: Picasso is in full command. Nobody is raising a question there. It's a question of what he was trying to do and what he did do and what did happen.

* * *

D'ARCANGELO: I think the sense of the discussion involves the communication of anger or the communication at least of feelings about a particular political situation which is quite a different thing. In the sense of the esthetic dialogue that an artist is involved in, he's involved in that all the time. And the work may be contrary to an esthetic position or not. I mean, that's something that's going on.

REINHARDT: Remember Jasper Johns' flags. Now, there was something comic and satirical about that when it was first shown. I don't know whether it was camp or what but it was something and the New York World's Fair used it and they played *America the Beautiful* with it, and they showed it as a straight painting of a man who painted the flag and they used it in the most patriotic way, jingoistically. Now what the artists had in mind and what actually happened—the problem is what do these images do?

GOLUB: Let's say that in these flags there is a certain element of satire, of irony, of disengagement, you know, even of nostalgia on the part of this art. But the threats that are involved in Jasper Johns' flag are minimal. That's why they can be used in a World's Fair and everything else. Now the threats that are implied by the nature of the *Guernica* are of a totally different order of things. This does not take away from the nature of what Jasper Johns is saying but when you make a reference from the *Guernica* to Jasper Johns in terms of the social action of a painter, I just want to say that in the *Guernica* itself there are the kinds of things which would make it a very unlikely object to be shown in Spain today. And the fact is that the Spanish know this, because, someone told me the other night, apparently some several thousand Spanish college students had what must have been a near riot, demanding that the *Guernica* be brought into Spain. In other words, they are demanding through that painting—they know what that painting means, you see and they're demanding that that painting again engage itself in this way.[6] This doesn't take away from what other artists are doing with it but there's a special quality to this.

D'ARCANGELO: But I think what's happened with *Guernica* is that it's acquired the properties of a holy relic and it's functioning more that way than it is in terms of its immediate impact as a political statement. I think it's more the historicity of the painting that's involved now than the actual thing itself because I agree with Ad that when you look at it you don't see a particular comment about fascism and you don't see anything there; there's no response in terms of Spain unless you read the little thing that goes alongside it. What you do deal with is human suffering.

* * *

6. [A decade later, *Guernica* in replica commemorated the 40th anniversary of the bombing: Fig. 153.]

153. Replica of *Guernica* to commemorate the fortieth anniversary of the bombing in the town of Guernica, Spain. April 1977. UPI Photo

Art Workers Coalition
Artists and Writers Protest to Picasso—[1970]*

FOR IMMEDIATE RELEASE   13 March 1970

LETTERS TO PICASSO REQUEST REMOVAL OF *GUERNICA* AS WAR PROTEST

A package containing 265 signed letters to Pablo Picasso, requesting that he remove *Guernica* from the Museum of Modern Art in New York, was mailed to his home in the south of France on March 13. This open letter, which has been signed by many leading American artists and writers, states that in view of the Songmy massacre[1] this nation and this museum no longer have the right to hold for safekeeping this monumental cry against the slaughter of innocents.

The petition for support of this request to Picasso is also circulating among artists and writers in France, Spain and other countries.

*Made available by Rudolf Baranik, signing for the Artists and Writers Protest Against the War in Vietnam.

1. [American correspondents reported that U.S. Infantry in March 1968 had shot hundreds of civilians, dynamited and burned the South Vietnamese hamlet Mylai near the village of Songmy; Lt. William Calley was court-martialed for executing 109 villagers (*Life* magazine, 5 Dec. 1969, and *Harper's* magazine, Mar. 1970).]

The open letter, which was initiated by Art Workers Coalition and Artists and Writers Protest, reads:

Dear Pablo Picasso,

When the Franco government of Spain recently invited you to return and to bring *Guernica* to Madrid, you said no: only when Spain is again a democratic republic will *Guernica* hang in the Prado.[2]

American artists have always been proud of the fact that your great painting, an outcry against injustice, hangs in our leading museum, in temporary refuge on the way to your freed homeland.

But things have changed. What the U. S. Government is doing in Vietnam far exceeds Guernica, Oradour and Lidice.[3] The continuous housing of *Guernica* in The Museum of Modern Art, New York, implies that our establishment has the moral right to be indignant about the crimes of others—and ignore our own crimes.

American artists want to raise their voices against the hundreds of Guernicas and Oradours which are taking place in Vietnam. We cannot remain silent in the face of Mylai. [See figs. 154 and 155.]

We are asking your help. Tell the directors and trustees of The Museum of Modern Art in New York that *Guernica* cannot remain on public view there as long as American troops are committing genocide in Vietnam. Renew the outcry of *Guernica* by telling those who remain silent in the face of Mylai that you remove from them the moral trust as guardians of your painting.

American artists and art students will miss *Guernica* but will also know that by removing it you are bringing back to life the message you gave three decades ago.

2. [See pp. 153–55.]

3. [Lidice was razed in 1942, its Czech inhabitants shot or deported, in reprisal for the assassination of Reinhardt Heydrich, SS chief and governor in Bohemia. Similarly, the Nazi SS in 1944 executed hundreds of French civilians in Oradour near Limoges.]

155. Art Workers Coalition Protest, with their Mylai Massacre poster, ''. . . And Babies'' (Poppy Johnson, Jan Hendricks, Kevin Quinn). 8 January 1970. Photo by Jan van Raay

154. Protesting the Mylai Massacre. Members of the Guerilla Art Action Group of the Art Workers Coalition hold a memorial service for all children killed by war (Reverend Stephen Garmey, artist Joyce Kozloff, and her son Nicholas). 3 January 1970. Photo by Jan van Raay

Meyer Schapiro
Letter to the Art Workers Coalition—
[1970]*

Dear Friends,   27 February 1970

I do not agree that "the continuous housing of *Guernica* in The Museum of Modern Art implies that our establishment has the moral right to be indignant about the crimes of others—and ignore our own crimes." This statement seems to me unwarranted and even nonsensical. In hanging *Guernica* the Museum no more protests against the crime of Guernica than the Metropolitan Museum protests against the crucifixion of Christ in hanging a painting of that subject. Is Franco's eagerness to hang *Guernica* in the Prado[1] a protest against the bombing? To ask Picasso to withdraw his painting from the Museum because of the massacre at Mylai is to charge the Museum with moral complicity in the crimes of the military. This I cannot do. Though I share your feelings about the government's whole action in Vietnam, I will not sign your letter to Picasso.

Please allow me to comment further. As an argument for removing his *Guernica* from the Museum, you remind Picasso that he has refused the invitation from Franco to return to Spain and to bring *Guernica* to hang in the Prado; he said that he would do so "only when Spain is again a democratic republic." On this point, two remarks: The Museum is not like the Prado an institution of a dictatorship; the United States is a democratic republic as much as was Spain in the years before the Franco regime. The public protests against the Vietnam war, the open discussion of the issues, and the election to Congress of representatives who oppose our part in the war, show that the United States is a democratic republic, however ignorant and immoral may be the views of the majority that support the policy of our government in Vietnam. The role of the United States during the Spanish Civil War, when our government imposed an embargo on trade with the Spanish republic, was hardly a moral one; would it have justified asking Picasso in 1939 not to entrust his *Guernica* to The Museum of Modern Art? A democratic republic is capable of great evils like a dictatorial state. But unlike the latter it has a free press and free elections through which individuals and organized groups may criticize, resist and act to change what they believe is wrong.

---

*Letter published by permission of the author. This distinguished art historian and professor at Columbia University was an influential Marxist critic during the 1930s and 1940s; he had signed the 1967 petition but considered the 1970 protest illogical. He is the author of monographs on van Gogh, Cézanne, and several volumes of his collected writings, such as his essays on modern art published in 1978.

1. [See pp. 153–55.]

By all means ask Picasso to voice his protest against the war in Vietnam; but do not urge him to remove his picture from the Museum as a sign that he condemns the hypocrisy of "our establishment" which fails to protest with you. That is a piece of self-righteous moralism that the community of protesting artists would find it hard to live up to in their own daily collaboration with museums, schools, galleries and collectors.

Sincerely,
Meyer Schapiro

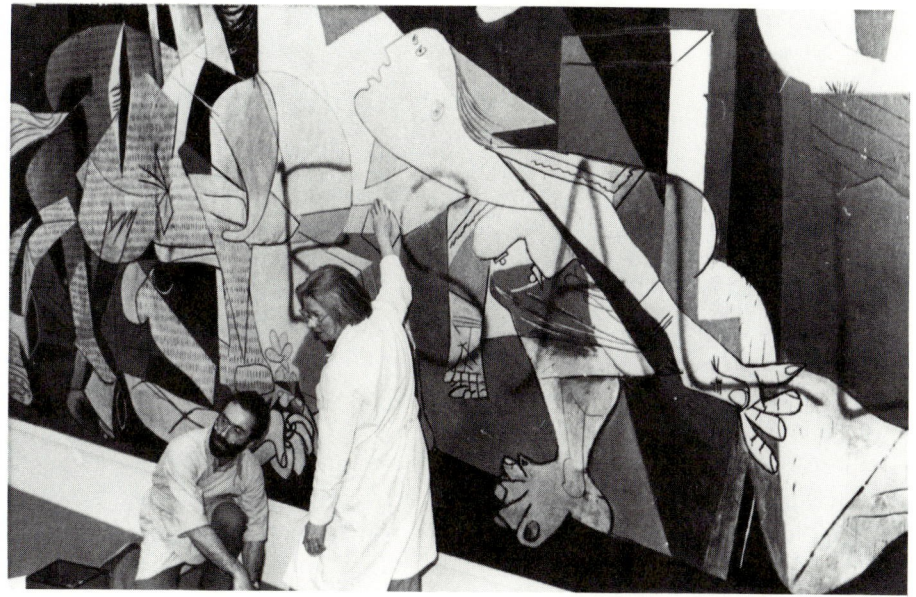

156. *Guernica* sprayed with red paint. 28 February 1974. Members of the Conservation Department, The Museum of Modern Art, New York, cleaning up. AP Wirephoto

Guerrilla Art Action Group
Guernica/Mylai—[1974]*

To: Richard Oldenburg, Director   28 February 1974
       The Museum of Modern Art
       11 West 53 Street
       New York City

And to: The District Attorney
          Manhattan Office
          New York City

Toni Shafrazi has now joined Picasso in a collaborative work called GUER-NICA/MYLAI—each artist in his own way expressing his own anger and disgust of a genocidal action by governments against an innocent people: PICASSO, of the saturation bombing by Nazi planes of the tiny town of Guernica, SHAFRAZI, of the mass murder by the U.S. troops of men, women, children and babies in the hamlet of Mylai.

It is a compounding of the U.S. Government crime that MOMA should have arrested Shafrazi and erased his work of art [fig. 156].[1]

We as artists and as individuals, who also denounce the U.S. Government whitewash and cover up of Mylai, demand the immediate release of Shafrazi and the dropping of all charges against him.

Toni Shafrazi's art action is, as was Picasso's originally, a profound, tormented, humanistic expression against the callousness barbarity of a nation.

Jon Hendricks   *Jean Toche*

*Made available by Jean Toche, conceptual artist and leader of the Guerilla Art Action Group. He suffered the same fate as Shafrazi after distributing a second statement applauding the Iranian artist for having "freed *Guernica* from the chains of property, and returned it to its revolutionary nature," and for urging the "kidnapping" of all museum officials and benefactors. Thomas Hoving, Director of the Metropolitan Museum, did not interpret this as a symbolic action, was not amused, and notified the F.B.I.! Shafrazi and Toche later were released on bail, were tried and received suspended sentences. Shafrazi now runs a successful art gallery in Soho, New York City.]

1. [Protected by a heavy coat of varnish, *Guernica* was immediately cleaned of Shafrazi's red spray paint.]

Let the Children Speak—[1970]*

When *Guernica* toured the United States in 1940–1941, a nationally known painter and educator characterized the mural as "a purely decorative black and white composition of moderate originality and inventiveness," whose paint quality "does not excel the application of an average house painter." More startling, Frederic Taubes asked: "Can there be any doubt that the 'pathetic symbol,' if entitled *Ballet Russe de Monte Carlo* (instead of *Guernica*) would have evoked from the connoisseur a feeling of joy and exhilaration . . .?"[1] (He later refined his claim, that *Guernica*'s images might suggest *The Bull in a China Shop*, "a scene from the Ballet Russe de Monte Carlo, or some such gay affair.")[2]

In 1970 I decided to test Taubes's peculiar assertions by showing a reproduction of *Guernica* to a class of fifth-graders not familiar with the painting. They were asked to fill out a questionnaire and also to draw their reactions. Most of the children (28 out of 44) recognized scenes of killing and fighting; others emphasized rioting, screaming, and suffering. The children dramatically related *Guernica* to their own experiences: television coverage of racial riots and the war in Vietnam. Their imaginative and spontaneous responses refute Taubes's ideas, and demonstrate *Guernica*'s impact, even in reproduction. A selection is reprinted here.

Question: What do you think is happening in the picture?

> It's at night and it's all kinds of scary things in it and people are killing.
> People and animals are being killed by the dragon.
> I think it looks like there was a massacre of killings at a ranch.
> It looks like one of those knock-down, drag-out fights.
> It's a war taking place and people are killing and fight each other.
> It looks like a man just got back from war and all the people think he and his horse are hurt.
> It's a place where nobody can or wants to do anything.
> It looks like the world is coming to an end.[3]
> Life at its worst aspect.

Question: Why do you think the artist used only black and white for this painting? [Most of the children assumed that the artist knew exactly what he was doing, either for formal or expressive reasons. They were especially sensitive to the latter.]

---

*I am indebted to Kenneth Marion, graduate student in my Picasso seminar, for conducting this experiment in 1970. Enrolled in the Maxwell School of Citizenship and Public Affairs, Syracuse University, Mr. Marion had previously taught these same children at their progressive, integrated city school; hence they were comfortable with this assignment.

1. Taubes, "The Critic's Mystification," *Pacific Art Review* II (1942), pp. 4–6, replying to Harriet and Sidney Janis, "Picasso's Guernica—A Film Analysis," *Pacific Art Review* I (1941), pp. 14–23. Taubes (1900–1981) is best known as contributor to *American Artist* magazine and author of popular handbooks, such as *The Painter's Dictionary of Materials and Methods* (1971).

2. Taubes, *Modern Art—Sweet or Sour* (New York, 1958), p. 101.

3. This boy previously had seen a reproduction.

Because black and white is best for this painting.

To make it look like a photograph.

Because black and white makes it look abstract, and besides it doesn't need color.

The black as background makes white stand out.

To express more clearly what he's trying to show.

Maybe that's the way he felt.

Black and white are the end of all colors.[4]

Because it doesn't look happy. It looks sad.

It [use of colors] would make the situation look brighter and it isn't.

He used black and white to bring out the meaning of the painting such as dead people and fierce animals.

Like to show black and white hating each other and like a war in battle.[5]

Black and white trying to show the racial problem and trying to keep the picture plain like life.[6]

Question: Do you like this painting? Why? Or why not? [Only six children disliked the painting, because it looks "mixed-up" or "weird," or had no color; three disliked the subject matter: "too much unpleasantness." Another five were less than enthusiastic: "It's OK" and "Yes and no," and "I like it some and it's OK, because it expresses your own feeling."]

Yes, because it's different.

Yes, it's strange. You don't see many things like that.

Yes, it makes you think about it hard.

I like it because to understand this picture you have to study and look at it closely and I like things like that.

Yes, because it is very artistic. You really have to have a mind to think up something like that.

Yes, it gives the artist's opinion about death.

Yes, because he shows how blacks and whites hates each other and maybe if people see it the way I do they may understand.[7]

Yes, because it show his true feelings.

Yes, because it is very describing of what it is to me.

Yes, it has a lot of meaning to me. I don't know why but it just does.[8]

4. This is the same boy as for note 3.
5. The same girl as for note 7.
6. The same boy as for note 8.
7. The same girl as for note 5.
8. The same boy as for note 6.

VI.
MARXIST–STALINIST
DEBATES

Politics have swayed *Guernica*'s viewers ever since it was exhibited in the Spanish Republican Pavilion at the height of the civil war in 1937. Specifically Marxist attitudes inform many early reactions, such as the welcoming address to the building's construction workers (pp. 204–5), or the commentaries emphasizing that "the common man" *was* moved by *Guernica* despite its modernist style (Ozenfant writing in France, Read in England, or McCausland in America, pp. 215, 218, 226).

Marx and Engels considered the artist completely a product of his time and place who expressed social and universal truths in his work. They allowed for stylistic freedom; accordingly, the first five or six years of the Russian revolution produced a dazzling burst of creativity and experimentation in the arts.[1] Lenin, however, disliked abstract art and believed—with some justification—that since he could not understand it, neither could the masses.[2] He declared: "Art belongs to the people. With its deepest roots it should penetrate into the very thick of the toiling masses. It should be understood by these masses and loved by them."[3] By the later 1920s, the doctrine of socialist realism was severely restricting artistic freedom. Furthermore, Lenin and Stalin, his far more rigid successor, decreed that "art must intentionally serve as a weapon for social propaganda in the class struggle."[4] Picasso—who proudly treasured his personal and artistic freedom—was bound to be in trouble.

This part begins with Picasso's statement upon joining the French Communist Party in 1944, followed by two selections from American sources: a

---

1. See the basic survey, Camilla Gray, *The Great Experiment: Russian Art, 1863–1922* (New York, 1962, 1970) and the exhibition catalogue, *The Avant-Garde in Russia: 1910–1930* (Los Angeles, 1980), with fascinating illustrations, important essays, and bibliography. For a general overview, see Donald D. Egbert, *Social Radicalism and the Arts: Western Europe* (New York, 1970), especially chs. 1 and 2; also his paperback, *Socialism and American Art* (Princeton, 1967). An essential anthology is Maynard Solomon's *Marxism and Art: Essays Classic and Contemporary* (New York, 1979).

2. Egbert, *Social Radicalism*, p. 293. Lenin admitted to the German Communist and feminist Klara Zetkin: "I cannot value the works of expressionism, futurism, cubism, and other isms as the highest expressions of artistic genius. I don't understand them. They give me no pleasure." From *Reminiscenses of Lenin* (New York, 1934), pp. 12–13.

3. From John E. Bowlt's superb anthology, *Russian Art of the Avant-Garde: Theory and Criticism, 1902–1934* (New York, 1976), p. 271, reprinting a 1928 Declaration of the Association of Artists of the Revolution.

4. Egbert, *Social Radicalism*, p. 82.

1941 attack on *Guernica,* and a lively debate in the Communist weekly, *New Masses.* The Soviet critic Vladimir Kemenov exemplifies the orthodox Stalinist viewpoint. Two examples from the most liberal wing of the Marxist–Stalinist continuum conclude the selections: Max Raphael and John Berger, whose background in art history and sensitive eye for painting, in each case, temper their Marxist ideology.

Picasso
Why I Became a Communist—[1944]*

On the eve of his 63rd birthday, Picasso explained to the *New Masses* why he joined the French Communist Party. The American Communist weekly somewhat edited and shortened the message transmitted by a French journalist and published in *L'Humanité;* this fuller version is translated below.[1] Picasso's statement is a curious blend of typically personal and creditable phrases with proper political expressions, perhaps helped along by the interviewer. Nevertheless, the sentiments undoubtedly were Picasso's in 1944, soon after the liberation of Paris.

Thereafter, he dutifully played the Party game. Though he feared air travel, he participated in four international peace congresses, released his pigeon lithographs for "peace dove" posters,[2] and received the Lenin Peace Prize in 1950 and again in 1962. As anti-American gestures, he painted *Massacre in Korea* in 1951, and the two huge panels, *War* and *Peace,* for the Temple of Peace at Vallauris.[3] Meanwhile, the Soviets more than ever criticized Picasso's art according to socialist-realist doctrines (p. 260). These public attacks culminated in the tragicomic affair of the Stalin portrait in 1953. Invited to join tributes to the deceased Soviet leader in *Les Lettres françaises,* Picasso sent an idealized, obviously well-intentioned drawing of a youthful Stalin; it was rudely criticized by Soviet diplomats and French Communist spokesmen. Picasso's comment: "When you send a funeral wreath, the family customarily doesn't criticize your choice of flowers."[4]

*Translated from the complete French text of Pol Gaillard's interview, *L'Humanité,* 29–30 October 1944, reprinted in Barr, pp. 267–68. Cf. *New Masses,* 24 October 1944, p. 11, shortened text. My translation also is indebted to English versions published by Cabanne, p. 366, and O'Brian, pp. 373–74.

1. Picasso's joining the Communist Party had made front-page news in *L'Humanité,* 5 October 1944. Fearing negative repercussions among Picasso's American friends and art collectors, Kahnweiler reportedly arranged for this message to America (Cabanne, p. 366). See also Jean Sutherland Boggs, "Picasso and Communism," *Arts Canada,* September/October 1980, pp. 31–36.

2. Picasso flew to Wrocław, Poland, for his first peace congress in August 1948 (Gilot, pp. 215–17). For the second congress in Paris, April 1949, Picasso's lithograph of a white pigeon—a gift from Matisse—was transformed into the famous peace dove (Bloch 583, 9 Jan. 1949; Wertenbaker reproduces the actual poster, p. 150). A dove in flight (Bloch 679, 9 July 1950) became the poster for the peace congress in Sheffield, England, in November 1950, when Picasso spoke the memorable words: "I stand for life against death; I stand for peace against war." See Penrose, p. 328; he also documents Picasso's trip to Rome in [November?] 1951 for his last international peace meeting (pp. 329–30), which is frequently omitted from Picasso chronologies.

3. See Claude Roy, *La Guerre et la Paix* (Paris, 1954), and Leymarie, pp. 115 and 142–43, for illustrations. The two huge panels, *War* and *Peace,* were completed in late 1952, sent to the Milan retrospective in 1953, and then installed in 1954 in the deconsecrated chapel for which they were designed; Picasso in 1958 added the semicircular apse panel with its joyous sun motif. Kirsten Hoving Keen has analyzed Picasso's compliance with Communist expectations of anti-American imagery: "Picasso's communist interlude: the murals of 'War' and 'Peace,' " *Burlington Magazine,* July 1980, pp. 464–70.

4. A good summary of Picasso's stormy relationship with the Communists is in *The New York Times,* 1 May 1962, p. 11, when he received the Lenin Peace Prize for the second time. The original *Times* story (20 March 1953) is quoted by Egbert, p. 349; See *Picasso 1980,* p. 284, for illustration.

I would much rather answer you with a picture; I am no writer, but since it is not very easy to send my colors by cable, I will try to tell you in words.

My joining the Communist Party is the logical outcome of my whole life, of all my work. For I am proud to state, I have never considered painting an art simply of pleasure, of diversion. I have wanted with line and color—since those were my weapons—to gain more and more deeply a knowledge of the world and of mankind, so that that knowledge would liberate all of us increasingly every day. I was trying to say, in my own fashion, what I consider to be the truest, the most just, the best; and that was, quite naturally, also the most beautiful—something the great artists know very well.

Yes, I do feel that I have always done battle with my painting, truly as a revolutionary. But I have now come to understand that even that is not enough: these terrible years of oppression have shown me that I must fight not only with my art but with my whole being.

And so I approached the Communist Party without the slightest hesitation, because actually I had always been there. Aragon, Eluard, Cassou, Fougeron,[5] all my friends know that very well; it was some sort of "innocence" which kept me from joining officially: I believed that my work, the fact that my heart belonged, were enough; it was already my Party. Is it not the Communist Party that works hardest to understand and to construct the world, to help people of today and of tomorrow to become more sane, freer, happier? Was it not the Communists who were the bravest in France, as well as in the USSR or in my own Spain? How could I have hesitated? Because I was afraid of making a commitment? But I have never felt more free, more completely myself. And I also was so eager to find a country of my own again: I have always been an exile, and now I am one no longer. While I am waiting for the time when Spain can finally welcome me back, the French Communist Party has opened its arms to me. There I have found all those whom I respect the most, the greatest scientists, the greatest poets, and all those beautiful faces of the Paris insurgents which I saw during those days in August.[6] I am again among my brothers.

5. [The most obvious instance of editing. The first three Communist writers (Aragon had rejoined in 1931, Eluard in 1942), who undoubtedly persuaded Picasso to join the Party, were indeed his friends; but the socialist-realist painter André Fougeron certainly was not. Picasso wholeheartedly disliked his work and resented his semiofficial position with the Communists (Gilot, pp. 303–4; Egbert, 1970, p. 335, for illustration). Similarly, the *New Masses* version inserted the names of Paul Langevin and Joliot-Curie (incorrectly using Frederick instead of the French Frédéric) in the final paragraph to illustrate "the greatest scientists"—hardly close friends, but scientists Picasso met through the Communist peace movement.]

6. [A reference to the liberation of Paris in August 1944; in paragraph 3, the phrase: "these terrible years of oppression" refers to the Nazi occupation of Paris.]

Vernon Clark
Picasso and Social Protest—[1941]*

This article from an American Marxist quarterly is early and influential criticism of Picasso for using a modernist style to convey *Guernica*'s political message. Clark's Marxist orientation was a common viewpoint during the 1930s and 1940s, but he soon abandoned it.[1]

> We are the hollow men
> We are the stuffed men
> Leaning together
>
> *T. S. Eliot*

On April 28, 1937,[2] General Franco's German allies appeared in their Junkers over the Basque town of Guernica and in short order reduced the ancient shrine to a shambles. "Immediately," Mr. Barr of the Museum of Modern Art tells us, "[Picasso] prepared an artist's revenge." And, indeed, "artist's revenge" puts the matter well, since I believe we will find that the protest is more esthetic than practical.

The *Guernica* mural allows no simple analysis. Had this painting been presented to us as have the cubist creations of the past our problem would have been less involved. We might have applied the rules given us by the abstractionists and their critics, analyzed the weights and tensions, classified the distortions and allusions, and called the matter done. But Picasso has complicated our task. He requires us, by virtue of his captioning, to consider the mural not only as an abstraction but as an excursion into social protest as well.

Since Picasso's orientation toward the social scene is not made clear either by this work or by his past performances (excepting perhaps the vague humanitarianism of the "Blue" and "Harlequin" period), we are obliged to do more than form an esthetic judgment. It is here that the great difficulties arise.

I do not remember ever standing before another cubist painting and feeling any particular concern about the relation between the subject matter and the means used to express it. After all, the amount of emotional involvement to be felt before an *Absinthe Drinker* or a *Still Life with Mandolin* is decidedly limited, and one is usually relieved beforehand of the need to react in purely human terms to subjects and situations so remote from our experience. But what are we to say when Picasso chooses for his subject an event as compelling as the destruction of Guernica?

---

*"The *Guernica* Mural—Picasso and Social Protest," *Science and Society*, winter 1941, pp. 72–78, reprinted by permission of the author's widow who kindly provided biographical information. Despite the importance of this early article, very little has been known about the author. (Schiff termed him "the great unknown" of his anthology [p. 177] and was unable to trace him through the current editors of *Science and Society*.)

Clark (1911–1967) was a graduate assistant in art education at Teachers College of Columbia University when he wrote this essay. During and after the war he studied psychology, trained in psychiatric social work at the Veterans Administration, and practiced psychotherapy in Chicago until his death.

1. Cf. Seckler's debate with Picasso, pp. 146–51; indeed the two young men were friends and had been discussing *Guernica* in New York.

2. [A common error derived from Barr's phrase, "On April 28, 1937, the Basque town of Guernica *was reported* destroyed" (*Picasso: Forty Years of his Art*, 1939, p. 174); my italics—see Chronology.]

For the first time in the history of cubism it is the spectator and not the picture that speaks first. Our critical approach undergoes a complete change. The very news that the mural has been painted, let alone the experience of seeing the work itself, is enough to flood our minds with the most passionate questionings. Is there to be found here a forceful condemnation of fascist brutality? Does the treatment as a whole reveal confidence in the justice and ultimate victory of the cause the artist has undertaken to support? Or is this merely the self pitying wail of a bourgeois Brahmin who sees in the ruin of Spain a threat to his own cozily introspective life? These questions which arise so insistently are bound to color our estimation of the work.

We are immediately struck, when we examine the *Guernica,* by the strange lack of relationship between the subject and the method of presenting it. This, of course, represents nothing new in Picasso's career; such a lack of harmony between technique and content appears consistently throughout his painting. The artist has apparently set a limit upon his feelings and upon the intensity of his expression beyond which he has arbitrarily forbidden himself to go. Whenever the emotional content of a subject tends to get beyond these self-imposed limitations it is immediately checked by a muted method that expresses itself in restrained color, static compositions, and less compelling forms. The "Blue" and "Harlequin" periods, of which the major motifs are types of human suffering, show all these characteristics at once; we recall the quietest of quiet compositions and a color range that departs almost hesitantly from the neutrals. Conversely, it is in the Still Life studies (1924–26 [e.g., fig. 105]), where the subject matter is without any appeal in its own right, that the dazzling coloristic and formal virtuosity of the artist finds full play.

By such means as these Picasso has long managed to maintain a paint-and-canvas sovereignty unequaled in its way in the history of art; has built up a controlled range of sensations which can be manipulated as easily as a new-type oil burner. I do not mean to imply that the work of Picasso is inexpressive of many aspects of modern life. We hardly need develop here how such a need for sovereignty, especially of the studio variety, grows naturally out of the insecurity the artist feels in the face of the incongruities he sees and under which he suffers in present-day society.

And what of *Guernica?* Hailed by most critics as independent of all previous periods, this work seems to me the culmination *ad absurdum* of all the trends, artistic and psychological, that the artist has developed in the past. Here the whole principle of muted and controlled emotion is brought out in unusually sharp relief, but with a difference. In this case the subject matter is so extraordinarily powerful in its own right that it will not stay in place; will not respond so easily to the controlling devices that are adequate with less compelling themes. Hence Picasso has needed to resort to the most drastic muting methods, the most remote allusions, the most involved de-emotionalizing mechanics to attain that balance and tranquillity on which he believes the esthetic sovereignty of the artist depends. If we keep this process in mind it will help us understand more easily many of the peculiarities of the *Guernica.*

Many critics have treated the structure and composition, the thrusts and movements of this work as inherently expressive of protest against the horror of war. I can hardly account for such an attitude toward a work which, whatever may be said of its abstract merits, is certainly most perfunctory in solving the problem of the relation of the composition to the essential message of the picture. Let us consider the barest and most essential elements of the composition. The central pyramidal construction emerges at once, flanked on either side by forms which, although diverse within themselves, are, as far as weight is concerned, as near to symmetry as anything in cubist painting. This produces an underlying structural quietness that seems far removed from the realities of the Spanish war. Of course there is no indication here of any lack of penetration on the part of the artist. It is, rather, only one illustration of his resolve to maintain a firm hold over his subject—in this case by the use of a composition that is basically quiet.

An analysis of the curved- and straight-line content of the painting will show that the same principle holds. It is at once apparent that these two elements are almost entirely equal; in no case is there any dramatic emergence of one at the expense of the other. Wherever a strong opposition occurs it is always muted by an adroit flowing together of the main curves or a transitional, fanlike arrangement that blunts the oppositional impact of the straight lines.

Significantly, all this happens within the composition without a great deal of connection with the dramatic emphasis of the subject matter. For example, were we to make a graph of the main lines and movements and then place within it a series of colored spots to indicate the placing of the representational elements, i.e., agonized human beings, animals, etc., we would find that they occur well out of the range of the structural crises. Curiously, it is possible to construct a graph of the structure without showing the representational elements, or to make one of the representational elements without showing the structure. It is interesting to compare this method with such works as Goya's *Horrors of War* etchings [*Disasters of War*, figs. 150A and 150B] where representation and structure are inseparably related—so entirely integrated that such an analytical dissection as this is quite unthinkable. But in the *Guernica* whatever specific feelings we get about the horror of war, even in the abstract sense, must be got from the details (pointed tongues, evidences of dismemberment, etc.) and with little help from the main drives of the canvas.

Again, the color, or rather the lack of it, supports this theory of dissociation. At the end of a tradition that has regarded color as the most forceful vehicle of emotional expression, Picasso has chosen to discard this vital element entirely; has confined himself to the most limited range of relationships imaginable. That these harmonies of black, white, and the warm and cool grays are worked out with infinite finesse is beyond question. The astonishing thing is that the spectator must combine such a subtle and delicate esthetic experience with subject matter second to none for strong emotional impact. It is true, of course, that black and white contrasts can be used as forcefully as any conceivable arrangement of color, but what is important here is that the major contrasts once again occur, not in relation to the subject matter, but to the abstract structure. Only in cases where the pictorial elements are well out of the dramatic center of the work do they receive full support from strong black and white contrasts. Again, in the central areas the passages which are psychologically compelling are subdued by such subtle gradation through the grays that in most cases the forms emerge with nothing stronger than line to define them and are incapable of competing with the purely formal aspects of the work. The spectator must become two persons, one who examines and enjoys the abstract-esthetic qualities of the mural, and the other who hunts and picks among the details in search of symbols that refer to the destruction of Guernica.

But there is another important element that demands our attention. The dissociation of the subject matter and the method of expression has vital and curious implications—hints that the protest of this artist may not be so clearly directed against the destruction of Guernica as we are led to believe. At any rate it lacks the direct drive and unity of purpose to be found in a similar subject treated by Goya. Yet the artist must feel strongly, must feel a deep resentment or fear—else the mural never would have been painted.

The underlying motive becomes more clear if we examine carefully the type and implication of the symbols used. At first glance the symbolism seems basically the same as in earlier work; Picasso alludes to the remote and romantic as he always has in the past. But the strangeness in this case springs from the use of such archaic symbols as classical profiles, swords, oil lamps, etc. to express the social struggle as we know it today. These symbols seem far removed indeed from the problems of our time, and their remoteness is emphasized by the fact that the whole drama of the picture takes place not only in an exceptionally shallow space, but in an interior space as well. It is as though the artist has sought to blunt the impact of an event he fears by removing it from the real world into the easily controlled area of a stage. The two allusions to artificial light seem to confirm this.

Aside from these, we note the use of the symbolism of the bull ring. If we are to trust Ernest Hemingway for the esthetic meaning of the bullfight, the manner in which these symbols are used becomes more than revealing. To the Spaniard the bullfight is a drama in which the animal stupidity and brute force of the bull are overcome by the intelligence and human art of the *toreros*. Now there is nothing surprising in the fact that Picasso has used the bull as a symbol of Franco and fascist brutality.[3] But it is surprising that the bull, villain of the piece, is the only figure in the mural that has any dignity—the only figure whose strength is solidly grounded, both in abstract structure and pictorial detail, and in which these two elements are united toward a single end. The exaggerated testicles, the defiantly erect tail, show clearly that the artist has been at great pains to build up the dominance of this symbol of fascist victory. Although the bull is certainly not put forward to persuade us or to win our admiration, we can sense here more than a hint of resignation before an enemy both successful and strong.

Nevertheless, one is obliged to resist even an overwhelming enemy. But where shall the artist turn for allies? To a cause represented by a bemattressed, disemboweled horse? In the bull ring, we remember, the horse is the comic relief, the symbol of the decrepit, the broken down, the ridiculously outworn. Yet it is with such symbols as this that Picasso identifies the things that died at Guernica—with such symbols as a warrior whose decapitation reveals the hollow body of a mannequin. This theme is borne out by all the scarecrow figures that occur throughout the mural. We see eyes placed awry in the heads of the figures; we see stuffed and clumsy hands, each finger of which has its own direction. These are eyes incapable of seeing rationally. These are hands incapable of grasping firmly the weapons of defense. I understand that the delusion of the mutilation or displacement of the essential organs and members of the body is a well-defined characteristic of certain types of mental illness, as Dr. Paul Schilder has pointed out in his book, *The Image and Appearance*

3. The bull has long been associated with the death-and-resurrection motif in religion, as, for example, in the mysteries of Dionysus of ancient times. It is therefore suggested that Picasso has used this symbol to allude to the resurrection of the Spanish people and not as an emblem of fascist brutality at all. Without going into the problem at any length, I should like to point out that there seems little reason or justification in divorcing the bull from the context in which Picasso has consistently placed it (i.e., the bullfight), not only in the *Guernica*, but in the *Dream and Lie of Franco, Minotauromachy*, as well as numerous other works. Nor must we overlook the fact that in one of the *Guernica* sketches the bull actually appears with the face and characteristic military cap of General Franco himself. [Unfortunately, Clark does not illustrate this last point.]

of the Human Body. In such cases the sufferer experiences horrible sensations of inadequacy and helplessness and imagines that the simplest functions are beyond his control. It is important to note that these delusions arise from the *inner* instability of the victim and do not refer to any objective reality of oppression or persecution. Yet it is in such terms that Picasso has drawn his picture of the Spanish people. And it seems to me rather obvious that the quality of their three-year struggle against fascist invasion can hardly suggest any such inner instability or lack of unified purpose on the part of the Loyalists, except to those who are without secure faith in the justice and victory of the cause they defended.

The similarity of Picasso's symbols and the symbols used by T. S. Eliot, that prince of disillusionment, begins to emerge more clearly. These are indeed the hollow men, the stuffed men with whom the artist must identify himself and whom he must at the same time strive to reject. Nor does the analogy end here. The network of lines that enmesh the whole mural, the toying with the crossed life lines in the hands of all the figures, becomes the inexorable web of destiny. As Eliot has read his own fate and the fate of his world in the medieval Tarot pack, so Picasso has resorted to the lore of the palmist for a comparable symbol.[4]

Picasso's disillusionment is not mocking and impertinent as is Eliot's. Eliot wrote in this vein during less trying years when cynicism could be cultivated with fair comfort in the university and the café. But the *Guernica* was painted face to face with a struggle that has become an uncomfortable reality of bombs and bullets; barbarian reaction has come to threaten even one's right to be disillusioned. "I do a picture," says Picasso, "—then I destroy it."[5] There is little wonder that he finds cause to protest when this latter office falls into ruder and more practiced hands.

In the *Guernica* it would seem that what Picasso mourns is not so much the ruin of a Basque town as the destruction of his own studio. And by the destruction of his studio I mean the passing of that complex, introspective world where the sovereignty of the artist, at least on canvas, has found during the last half century so convincing a semblance of reality. The mural is the meeting place for all the many ends of Picasso's eclecticism. Cubism, analytical and synthetic, and the nostalgic allusions of the classical period are brought together as though for a last and forceful statement, and in a context plainer than anything we have seen before. Picasso has revealed himself as the painter laureate of the Wastelanders—of those who see with amazing penetration into the cruelty and contradictions of modern society, yet are unable to ally themselves with any of the forces that are deciding the issues of the day. He has preferred to vacillate at a time when vacillation is both dangerous and expensive.

Although the *Guernica* mural has shown us that Picasso remains the unchallenged master of abstract art, we see at the same time that cubism cannot be made to bear the weight of social meaning. The Ivory Tower, embattled at last, watches with just apprehension the advance of its dual enemies. Fascism comes down over the mountains—the people march up from the plains. The half-world may well tremble. Once again we turn to Eliot for a terse statement,

> I have seen the moment of my greatness flicker
> I have seen the Eternal Footman hold my coat—and snicker
> and in short, I was afraid.

4. [For a palmist's comments, see pp. 93–94, above.]
5. [From the 1935 interview, p. 142, above.]

New Masses
A Reader Symposium—[1945]*

The editors of the Communist weekly *New Masses* in mid-May 1945 reported that their publication of Seckler's interview with Picasso (pp. 145–51) "proved how live an issue art is by drawing the largest readers' mail we have received on any matter in recent months."

The following sampling reveals an amazing range of attitudes toward Picasso among American Communists and leftists. Rockwell Kent (1882–1971), realist painter, illustrator, and supporter of Communist causes, began the debate with a simple-minded call for a people's art; a rigidly Party-line rejection of *Guernica* followed. More interesting, however, are letters opposing Rockwell Kent's narrow definition of art for the people: several readers added comments that might have surprised orthodox Marxists–Stalinists.

Rockwell Kent: "That Ivory Tower," 3 April 1945

If we ever get to have a people's art, it will be an art that people can understand. The people have got to help the artists by telling them honestly whether or not they do understand.

Let me, as one of the people, start this by honestly saying, apropos of the article on Picasso (*New Masses*, March 13) by Pfc. Jerome Seckler, that I don't understand Picasso. Let me, all for the sake of honesty, go a little farther, say that such pictures as are shown with that article strike me as just plain silly, that, as they appear there, they haven't a single redeeming feature. * * *

Rockwell Kent, 15 May 1945

* * * I have written of Picasso not as an artist specially concerned with the problems of esthetics, but as a citizen respectful of people. * * *

That Picasso has become a Communist is to his everlasting honor. It is evidence of his good heart. Of his understanding of Marxism one may have some doubt.

A Reader from New York City, 15 May 1945

* * * Then *Guernica!* Here Picasso found a positive reason for his art. *Guernica* was his first positive identification with the force of progress—the group as against the individual. The importance of *Guernica* was just that. * * *

*Reprinted from *New Masses:* "That Ivory Tower," 3 April 1945, p. 17; "Rockwell Kent and Picasso," 17 April 1945, p. 17; "Understanding Picasso—A Reader Symposium," 15 May 1945, pp. 26–27.

Guernica failed! One hears so much dribble about the tremendous emotional impact of the work. I am not here discussing the pyrotechnics of the work; only how far it succeeded in saying what the artist set out to say. One Goya etching from the "Disasters of War" said more for his day and speaks with burning tongue even in our own times. Picasso had gone so far along the path of violent romantic brutalism that no matter how great his desire to identify himself with the large group, he could not readjust so rapidly. The attempt was a failure—but a glorious one! Glorious, because a great artist identified himself with the forces of progress. * * *

Picasso's great courage maintained itself under Nazi oppression. Then at liberation, the natural fulfillment of his striving for order after all the orgy of destruction, and his identification with the Communist Party of France. This should now be followed by a new period of enlarged humanism, greater realism and more clarity and hope.

A Reader from New York City, 17 April 1945

Picasso has proved by many acts that he is a Communist. His canvases have opened up new fields of esthetic exploration for a whole generation of painters. His position as one of the greatest painters in the long history of art is hardly open to question whether one uses as a yardstick quantity of production, or financial success, or originality, or technical facility, or range and variety of expression, or emotional intensity, or direct influence on other artists. Picasso argues that since he is a painter and since he is a Communist, he is a Communist painter. There is no evidence that Picasso is suffering from a split personality. I think his argument is quite cogent. I think we should revise our preconceived prejudice as to what kind of pictures a Communist painter will paint. Maybe Picasso has been painting them.

A Reader from Hollywood, California, 15 May 1945

* * * The point is that we have to stop approaching all art with the question what does this represent? Picasso frankly and admittedly is preoccupied with the *way of seeing*, with the method of translating what is, as he sees it. * * * His great contribution, as I see it, is that he has taught us awareness of the different ways of seeing and has freed art and artists from the formal adherence to the conventional method of translating reality into a two-dimensional picture. His certainly will not be the last word. Nor is he necessarily right or wrong. But he has enriched his craft the same way the jazz musician has enriched music—by making his instrument sing in new ways.

I have observed that children respond easily and positively to abstract art. I think this is due to their lack of inhibition and formal training and to their willingness to let their imagination run freely and joyfully. [See pp. 244–46.]

A Reader from Berkeley, California, 15 May 1945

Rockwell Kent seems to forget that the painter has the function not only of satisfying a current level of popular taste but also of raising that level of taste. In this respect he has an active, as opposed to a purely passive, role to play—a role which is comparable to that of the Communists in politics. The Communists would never think of adulterating their program in order to make it more palatable to the prejudices of broad sections of the people. Rather, they seek to raise the political understanding of the people to the level of Marxist doctrine. With Picasso it is a question of helping people to understand his art, not of expecting him to reduce it to their level of understanding.

Vladimir Kemenov
Soviet Denunciation—[1947]*

The following attack in an English-language Soviet propaganda magazine typifies the most rigid official Soviet attitude toward Picasso. Published in late 1947,[1] and thus despite Picasso's membership in the French Communist Party, it followed a *Pravda* editorial denouncing the "bourgeois decaying art" of Matisse and Picasso. The latter did not comment publicly, but reportedly told a non-Communist friend: "I don't try to advise the Soviets on economics, why should they try to tell me how to paint?"[2]

Picasso's Communist reputation was quickly rehabilitated after Stalin's death, however. His Italian retrospective in May 1953 was highly praised,[3] and a massive showing of his art— some 90 works in various mediums—was held for the first time in Moscow and Leningrad to celebrate his 75th birthday.[4] Finally, in May 1962, Picasso received the Lenin Peace Prize, not specifically for his art but "in recognition of outstanding services in the struggle for maintenance and strengthening of peace."[5]

---

*Reprinted from "Aspects of Two Cultures," *VOKS Bulletin*, No. 52, 1947, pp. 29–30, published by the USSR Society for Cultural Relations with Foreign Countries. Kemenov was editor in chief, a specialist on socialist realism, and director of the Tretiakov Gallery of Russian Art in Moscow.

1. The editorial marked the beginning of Andrei Zhdanov's hard-line control and purges of Soviet artists and intellectuals and the formation of the Comintern in September 1947.

2. Janet Flanner, *Men and Monuments* (New York, 1957), p. 200; her version of the Kemenov attack (p. 199) has been frequently quoted.

3. Ilya Ehrenburg, Picasso's old-time friend from prewar Paris, eulogized him in the Italian Communist organ, *L'Unità*.

4. Picasso's telegram to Soviet artists and "A Visit to Picasso" were published in the Soviet propaganda magazine, *Culture and Life* (vol. I, 1957, pp. 21 and 26–28).

5. *The New York Times*, 1 May 1962, p. 10, quoting the Soviet News Agency Tass; see p. 11, for art critic John Canaday's summary of Picasso's changing fortunes with the Soviets.

Even those formalists, who, like Picasso, have repeatedly professed sympathy for the struggle of democracy against fascism show a marked unwillingness to apply the progressive aspects of their world outlook to their artistic practice. A yawning chasm still exists in their work to this day, resulting not merely in the failure of these artists to advance the struggle of their peoples against fascism and reaction by their creative efforts, but also, objectively, in their furthering (through their art) the very aims of the bourgeois reaction against which they vehemently protest in their political utterances and declarations.

By proclaiming "art for art's sake," void of all contact with the struggle, aspirations, and interests of the wide masses, by cultivating individualism, the formalists are affirming the very thing the reactionaries want them to. They are playing into the hands of the decadent bougeoisie who in their efforts to preserve their domination look with hatred upon the development of the consciousness of the masses, upon the growth of their sense of human dignity and their feeling of solidarity, upon any rousing of their activity through the means of realistic art rich in ideological content.

It is frequently said that in his pathological work Picasso had deliberately created an ugly and repellent image of contemporary capitalist reality in order to rouse the spectator's hatred for it—that Picasso is the artist of "Spanish democracy."

This, obviously, is not true. Although Picasso's early works of his "blue" period still retain some connection with Spanish painting, when he turned to Cubism his art became absolutely abstract. He then renounced all the traditions of realistic art, Spanish included, and followed the line of cosmopolitanism, of empty, ugly, geometric forms, which are as alien to Spanish as to any other democracy. When Picasso wanted to portray the suffering of the Spanish people in the war against Italian and German Fascism, he painted his *Guernica*—but here, too, instead of heroic Spanish Republicans, he showed us the same wretched, pathological and deformed types as in his other paintings. No, it is not in order to expose the contradictions of reality nor to arouse hatred for the forces of reaction that Picasso creates his morbid, revolting pictures. His is an aesthetic apologetics for capitalism; he is convinced of the artistic value of the nightmares called into being by the disintegration of the social psyche of the capitalist class.

Max Raphael
Discord between Form
and Content—[c. 1947 and 1968]*

The distinguished German-born writer Max Raphael (1889–1952) examined *Guernica* from esthetic, philosophical, and Marxist viewpoints and judged it a tragic failure: "Picasso, the greatest artist of our time, was unequal to the challenge of his age, belonging as he did to a class and intellectual elite which had outlived their usefulness." The following extracts include Raphael's discussion of allegorical meanings and his Marxist conclusion.

Raphael's erudite and Germanic language is occasionally difficult to penetrate, especially in translation, and his Marxist arguments may become irritating, but persistent readers will be rewarded for their intellectual efforts. They will share the insights of a man gifted with an unusually keen eye for artistic form, and join a brilliant mind at work.

Whether symbol, allegory, or metaphor,[1] all must remain a very low sort of mystification as long as they do not either derive from the life of the society that believes in them and whose artists share this belief, or else represent a cultural tradition so that an artist who employs them can appeal to a certain class and expect to be understood. Now, even the latter alternative is scarcely applicable here. The horse is commonly regarded as a noble, spirited animal, man's companion in some of his most dangerous undertakings; in earlier epochs, when man had not yet learned to ride, he believed that the horse carried the powers of the dead to the fields of the ancestors. Even in the bullfight the part played by the horse has only recently taken on a meaner character. Picasso's personal allegory and personal magic may of course owe something to it. But the important consideration here is not only the fact that individual allegories, perhaps valid in easel paintings for aesthetes, are out of place in a historical painting intended to influence the masses. Even if Picasso had resorted to the long-forgotten banderole,[2] the fact would remain that individual allegories can appear only when form is divorced from content and some substitute for their missing unity must be found—i.e., on the borderline between art and literature. Were

*Reprinted from chapter V, *The Demands of Art,* trans. Norbert Guterman, Bollingen Series LXXVII (Princeton, 1968), pp. 153–57, 174–75, and the conclusion, pp. 177–79, by permission of Princeton University Press. (The German title, *Wie ein Kunstwerk gesehen sein will,* is translated literally: "How a work of art wants to be seen," or "demands to be seen.") This *Guernica* chapter was written around 1947, evidently stimulated by Larrea's work (pp. 280–85), and quite possibly by Vernon Clark's essay as well (pp. 252–56). It was Raphael's third Picasso work. Having studied art history, philosophy, and political economy with some of the best minds of Europe (Heinrich Wölfflin, Georg Simmel, Henri Bergson), the 24-year-old scholar first tackled Picasso after a Paris encounter: *Von Monet zu Picasso* (1913). He later returned to France to escape the Nazis and wrote *Proudhon, Marx, Picasso* (Paris, 1933; New York, 1979; see also Lipton's analysis with generous quotations, pp. 312–20). He saw *Guernica* in Paris in 1937 and rediscovered it in 1941 when he emigrated to America.

1. [In the preceding pages, Raphael had summarized and demolished the various interpretations of Picasso's symbolism by Herbert Read, Christian Zervos, Vernon Clark, and especially Juan Larrea.]

2. [*Banderole*: a painted or carved ribbon-like scroll with an inscription or device—hence, an explanation.]

Picasso to provide an allegorical key to *Guernica,* it would still be true that what he produced is ineffectual as propaganda and dubious as a work of art.

Nonetheless, one is reluctant to accept the extreme diversity of the existing interpretations as final. In point of fact the diversity may be legitimate, provided that some common principle of analogy runs through all interpretations. We have no choice but to study form and content separately, to find out whether—if not unity, congruence, or coincidence—at least some approximation, parallelism, or correspondence obtains between them. For only in this way can we ascertain the method by which *Guernica* was created, and the reason for Picasso's choice of it. * * *

We have already noted that, contrary to our reading habits, *Guernica* starts at the right. There we find the woman who is on fire, wildly extending her arms while the rest of her body seems to be sinking into a funnel-shaped form. The fire could only have been produced by the bombing; Picasso follows history here, showing the effect of the bombing and assuming that the viewer will know what caused the fire. But the painter also shows the burning woman as an emotion which reaches its highest point through pain, its boiling point, as it were: the affect of completely helpless panic in the face of unexpected death, as sudden as it is certain.

At the left the counterpart of this panic terror is a kind of imperturbability. Here too we have the panic scream, a mother in despair over her dead child; but above her is the stoic ataraxia[3] of the bull, whose head is turned around—the posture is known to us from paleolithic art, where the bull's head is given in profile, the horns in frontal view. The animal's open mouth is just above the mother's. Even were the tongues not stressed, we would suspect that some oral transfer of energies is taking place here. The bull, the active male standing over the receptive woman, is here an agent of fecundation of which the mother, in an agony of sorrow, is yet unaware. The suggestion is that of new life succeeding destruction. The bull as a metaphor of male strength is so ancient in human history that the image may be regarded as part of our cultural heritage. It may denote here the sexual energy of the Spanish people or simply that of life in general.

When we turn from the nonallegorical scene of helpless panic at the right, and the allegorical image of ataraxia at the left, to the large middle portion of the painting, what do we find? Surely we must here recognize the dying horse and the dying man beneath. How have these deaths come about? Was the man riding the horse and were both killed together by the same external cause? Or was there some sort of struggle between man and horse in which each mortally wounded the other? Or were they both struck down by the external cause while they were struggling? What suggests the struggle is the spearlike weapon that pierces the horse and a small wound which may have been a blow from the sword. What suggests an external cause of death is the third and largest wound in the shape of an up-ended lozenge. This last possibility seems the most plausible. In this case the warrior would stand for a soldier of Republican Spain and the horse would stand for Franco or Fascist Spain. Such an interpretation gains support from a sketch by Picasso showing Pegasus emerging from the horse's wound; thus the horse would be equated with Medusa, and would become a symbol of Franco. This is an odd mixture of the representational and the allegorical. The forces of the Spanish Civil War are present—but it is not their struggle with each other that is portrayed; rather, we see them overwhelmed by external

---

3. [*Ataraxia:* Greek for calm, denotes intellectual detachment, imperturbability.]

forces and struggling against death. It is possible that the horse is uttering a curse (depicted in a form which appears as a weapon on the ceiling of Altamira[4]) and that the soldier senses the bull's magical transfer of power to the woman. If so, the form above the horse's head would have to be an allegory of the Nazi bomb, for all that an electric light bulb was drawn inside it at the last minute; the form itself seems to reproduce the Greek symbol of lightning. It is interesting to note that the large central area is the most ambiguous part of the painting, a fact all the more significant in that it depicts a struggle. If we disregard the objects represented and examine the feelings conveyed, the scene would most readily seem to denote the realm of the demonic, located between panic and ataraxia.

Besides the division of the painting into three parts we therefore find a threefold development of the subject matter. On the first, or representational, level the development is from the most brutal murder, through struggle, to a renewal of life. On the second, or emotional, level we go from the passive panic of despair, through the consciously demonic, to ataraxia. On the third level, that of the creative method, the formal development leads from purely representational portrayal to a mixture of representation and allegory and then to pure allegory. Here there arises a question crucial for our understanding. Does the emphasis lie in the large middle section, in which the struggle has ended but not the agony, or does it lie in the left section, in the resolution of the conflict by the bull?

The answer may lie in careful interpretation of the woman with the lamp. Whereas the woman at the bottom right provides a physical transition from the right to the center—her escape from panic into struggle—the woman with the lamp provides a more spiritual transition. She is not running but trying to see; the night lamp gives a poor light, however. Held as it is right next to the bomb, it expresses deep irony as well as social criticism: the world being destroyed is as obsolete as the night lamp and the wooden sword; the world in process of being born will not have to cope with dead tradition. We might go further and view the woman, as does Herbert Read, as the allegory of truth [p. 218 above]. Her arm is strong, her grasp firm, and her profile incisive; she suggests something positive, the power of reason and enlightenment. Earlier studies for the painting, where the bull was shown in its full width, indicate a more unmistakable connection between the allegories of truth and fecundity: the woman's arm was level with the bull's back and almost touched it. Is this "truth" throwing light upon the carnage or does it pick out the bull as ultimate hope and certainty? Because the bull has been reduced in size and relegated to the left, and because the horse's head has been moved up, the pure duality between the spiritual and the physical allegory, between truth and fecundity, comes more clearly to the fore. It is characteristic of the great part dualism plays in Picasso's world view.

The other figures and signs in the painting will now have to be reinterpreted accordingly. Take, for instance, the open-beaked bird trying to fly upward but apparently unable to do so. Has it succumbed to the horse's curse or is it deflecting the curse from the bull? Or, if the horse represents not Franco but an innocent victim of the bombing or an allegory of struggle to the death, does the bird transfer to another world the strength of the animal which continues to fight even in its death agony?

4. Cf. the author's *Prehistoric Cave Paintings*, figs. 23, 24. At the time Raphael wrote, the shapes he is speaking of—so-called claviforms—were usually regarded as weapons—cf. ibid., fig. 35 and p. 5—but in more recent scholarship they are interpreted as symbols of the female sex or of fertility. Cf. S. Giedion, *The Eternal Present: The Beginnings of Art* (New York, 1962), pp. 190, 242, 247.

Such action would be in keeping with the symbolic significance the bird of death had in works of paleolithic and archaic times. We might also ask: Is the table an altar of sacrifice? What is the meaning of the arrow, of the seven nails in the horse's hoof, and the seven flames (3 + 4) at the right, near the woman on fire? I shall not try to answer such questions of detail. Their purely formal intent may be to keep the viewer occupied with riddles. But the longer he remains under the painter's magic spell, the less likely is he to be moved to act; the artistic details obstruct and destroy the political effect.

A normal reaction to the above "interpretation" would be to quote Paul Valéry's ironic remark: "Monsieur, votre sens est excellent, je l'adopte" ("Sir, your guess is as good as any; I'll take it"). To produce yet another interpretation, all we need do is turn to the jagged form at the top; Picasso has drawn an electric light bulb inside the "bomb" to suggest how readily a beneficial invention may be transformed into a destructive force in the modern world; or—if you like—that good produces evil and vice versa; or better yet, that good and evil are simultaneously present in any set of facts. If every component of the painting were interpreted according to the principle of *both/and* (rather than *either/or*), we could make of the bull, besides an allegory of nature's inexhaustible vitality or mankind's unshakable moral force, a portrayal of Franco's (and all other "Führers'") impassive sadism: the bull is untouched by the mother's anguish over her child and tells her cynically that the next coitus will produce new cannon fodder. Moreover, the horse might be interpreted, not only as Franco cursing, but as a defiant animal refusing to surrender even after the death of its rider. * * * We would then have to assume that the painting's ambiguities are a necessary consequence of Picasso's axiomatic premise that the function of allegory is to give an appearance of unity to contradictory contents. The viewer would thus be compelled to suspend judgment, since he would not only be able to provide contradictory interpretations for every detail but would even be obliged to do so. But, with all this, allegory does not disappear; i.e., it does not cease to be a mere substitute for form. What we have left in the end is not artistic form, synthesizing meaning and vision—however numerous the meanings—but a split between the concrete and the universal which makes interpretation anybody's guess. Had Picasso succeeded in giving form to the emotional complex of terror, chaos, barbarism, destruction, helplessness in the face of blind social forces, no recourse to the artist's private mythology would have been necessary and the viewer would not have been obliged both to look for interpretations and to suspend judgment. As it is, the viewer is made the victim of an allegory which is not self-evident and must leave him unsatisfied: his emotions and his judgment are being torn apart and set one against the other, so that he is stultified rather than stimulated to creative action.

* * *

We have tried to analyze the painting in terms of its material of figuration, and of the form, content, and allegories it contains. We shall now discuss it in the terms of its effect on the viewer, to cast further light, this time from the outside, as it were, on Picasso's artistic method. (The same method was not necessarily employed in Picasso's other works.)

To begin with sensory perception: the painting appeals to almost all our senses. Although the eye is primarily involved, there are passages in *Guernica* which are not perceivable optically, either because the artist's aim was to keep them out of range of the eye or because they stimulate motor rather than visual sensations. Other passages, which can be seen, cannot be touched, and some of these suggest the domain of the ineffable conscious-being,[5] in which seeing is an intuition or vision of some primal metaphysical phenomenon. Still other places stimulate the sense of touch, as where two diverging planes meet to form a sharp edge, but they lead to visual or motor sensations. Most cases of motor sensation in this work are made explicit: the frantic flight, for example, the outstretched limbs, wide-opened mouths, etc. The bull's posture is the calmest attitude shown, but it is achieved only *after* the abrupt twisting backward of head and forequarters; it is furthermore associated with the flaglike tail, and as a result the viewer is compelled to connect the bull's mouth with its anus. However, though the figures perform all these movements to inspire corresponding sensations in the viewer, the over-all effect is to reduce the viewer to immobility. He is not stimulated to physical activity, to decision, let alone to conscious action. The positive aspect of the effect is not movement but stupor, and the latter is not produced by an optically perceivable chaos of movement but by the chaotic din which the painting seems to give off, so shocking the viewer that he can only assume a passive attitude toward the screaming affects of the canvas.

Picasso makes use not only of various sense perceptions (and their organs) but also of a variety of responses. While the eye is at one point obliged to pursue a lengthy course, at another it must make a leap, and at still another experience a head-on collision. This continual alternation between passivity and activity, between continuity and discontinuity, forces constant reorientation upon the viewer and demands that he be elastic and agile; at the same time Picasso obstructs him at points of collision—in short, he does everything to make active perception, absorption, empathy, contemplation, and enjoyment impossible. These constant changes are designed to prevent the act of perception from being an end in itself and to accelerate it as much as possible; even the frequent repetitions of approximately equal charges of energy serve the purpose of ruling out the repose of simultaneous perception and shortening the time of perception. If perception were encouraged to linger, an accumulation of the viewer's energies would weaken shock and induce aesthetic enjoyment as well as spontaneous activity, freeing him from the artist's control. The degree of shock is in direct ratio to the rapidity with which the viewer is reduced to stupor. Here the senses are stimulated only to be numbed. All this expresses the artist's tyrannical will to power, his attempt to dominate the viewer, whether by compulsive magic or by a kind of shadowboxing with the viewer's mind, consciousness, and freedom.

* * *

Aesthetics, politics, and morality are replaced by a dogma whose value may be enhanced for true believers by its mysteriousness, but which remains valueless for nonbelievers who are not interested in what lies beyond art but only in art itself, or who respect real action in the real world more than the pseudo-intellectual activity of solving riddles, especially riddles that seem vague, antiquated, and petty bourgeois. This is a contrived painting and hence arbitrary and finite. This accounts for its fate, for the fact that the masses—and the anti-Fascist masses most particularly—

5. [To unify the concepts of pure mind, or consciousness, with pure existential being, Raphael coined the term "conscious-being" (*Bewusst-Sein*) by elision—a common practice in German. (See p. 144 of his text.)]

were perplexed by it and quickly lost interest. The literati alone praised it in their turgid fashion because the magnitude of its conception, its boldness, and its inventiveness seemed to justify their own creative impotence. But all this does not change the fact that even Picasso, the greatest artist of our time, was unequal to the challenge of his age, belonging as he did to a class and intellectual climate which had outlived their usefulness. The artist in our modern bourgeois society is both a tragic and a comic figure, rooted in a society whose collapse he *must* desire yet unable to give artistic form to the emerging society he admires. He is condemned by both sides for opposite reasons.

It is perhaps not too rash to assume that Picasso would not object to the first part of the above statement. If he had still believed that painting can serve as a substitute for political action—not at all the same thing as using art to educate a people politically or as an auxiliary to politics (which can and must be done)—or that political problems can be solved by allegorical appeals to the *élan vital* of nature or to rational enlightenment, he would scarcely have joined the Communist party. His work on *Guernica* may have been one of the reasons why Picasso changed his political orientation, for it may have made him aware of the limitations of his former position, the other reasons being the events that followed on Franco's victory and led to the Second World War, which brought the Nazi conquerors to the streets of Paris and even into Picasso's studio. On the other hand, it is unlikely that he would agree with our assertion of *Guernica's* artistic inadequacy (as distinguished from its propagandistic inadequacy), for then he could not stand by his statements that his art and his politics have nothing to do with each other or that *every* painting is political. (Even if it were, it still need not be Communist.) Whatever the reader may think of Marxism or Communism, both have always denied the possibility of divorcing practice (politics) from theory (art). This is particularly true of art, for the whole function of art is to give sensory form to the unity of practice and theory. All Picasso could say in his own defense would be that the artist can give form only to an existing society, not to one still in process of emerging, and that he can therefore give two things: a social criticism of bourgeois society in a bourgeois style and propagandistic support to the Communist party in its struggle to overthrow bourgeois society. From this it appears that Picasso is an inadequate Communist for lack of knowledge (which is naturally his own affair), and that he has not understood the limits of the method which led him to *Guernica*. The latter is a matter of public concern even if art in our disintegrating society is only a luxury product for snobs or an escape for psychopaths.

The method employed in *Guernica* must be regarded as inadequate not because the allegories used by Picasso admit of several contradictory solutions but because he was *compelled* to resort to allegory in the first place. Even if he were one day to give us the banderole with the only correct solution, the fact would remain that the form of this work is not implied in its content. Even if it might be considered too rigorous to place such a work beyond the pale of art, it must be granted that a work of which this can be said is at a lower artistic level than a work in which form and content are indissoluble. For only when such unity is achieved—and it is the specialty of the artist to invent the method by which it can be achieved—does the work transcend historical conditions and individual reactions and attain to suprahistorical, universal human validity. That was what Goethe meant when he said: "Do not talk, artist, create." There is a fundamental difference between the indirect language of allegory and the realization of a conception, idea, or aesthetic feeling in a self-sufficient artistic reality. Both methods are to some extent indirect, in the sense that the artist must go beyond the event or emotion that actually inspired him. But allegorical language actually conceals directness and literalness of approach, the obsession of the artist with what he wants to communicate, and as a result the work created by such a method remains imprisoned in the arbitrary and particular and is only *seemingly* universal; whereas the authentic artistic method raises the particular to the universal, the historical to the suprahistorical, the relative to the absolute, by embodying infinite meaning in concrete and finite appearance. The allegorical method renders the artist's dialogue with himself, and the artist who employs it is trying to tell the world about the discoveries in his self without really revealing them, without really objectifying them. Truly artistic method is a dialogue between the self and the world (or the cosmos), and results in a reality independent of both the artist and the world; whereas allegory creates only new obsessions, unfreedom, and dogma, true art liberates the artist from the prison of self, from his obsession with a particular idea, and creates freedom. The reasons for which Picasso was compelled to resort to signs and allegories should now be clear enough: his utter political helplessness in the face of the historical situation which he set out to record; his titanic effort to confront a particular historical event with an allegedly eternal truth; his desire to give hope and comfort and to provide a happy ending, to compensate for the terror, destruction, and inhumanity of the event. Picasso did not see what Goya had already seen, namely, that the course of history can be changed only by historical means and only if men shape their own history instead of acting as the automatons of an earthly power or an allegedly eternal idea. We must, however, stress the fact that Picasso's *Guernica* expresses a conflict between his great sensibility and need for communication, on the one hand, and his artistic powers on the other. Even if we set aside the elements of allegory, we must recognize that this work stigmatizes the destructiveness of a disintegrating society with a power no other artist has equaled.

John Berger
Success and Failure of Picasso—[1965]*

John Berger demonstrates that the erotic power of the large bronze head (figs. 82 and 86, placed outside the Spanish Pavilion) underlies the intense suffering of *Guernica* and the later etching, *Weeping Woman* (fig. 65). Like Max Raphael, to whom Berger dedicated his study, he subscribes to the Marxist thesis that "when a culture is secure and certain of its values, it represents its artists with subjects. . . . When a culture is in a state of disintegration or transition the freedom of the artist increases but the question of subject becomes problematic for

*Reprinted from *The Success and Failure of Picasso* (Baltimore, 1965), pp. 159–69, by permission of the author and publisher. When the book was reissued in 1980, John Canaday wrote that it "has not only worn well over the past 15 years but has gained in pertinence" (*The New Republic,* 14 June 1980, p. 28). Born 1926 in London, Berger began painting, then writing art criticism (for the socialist *New Statesman* and others), fiction (*A Painter of Our Times,* 1958) and important collections of essays: *The Moment of Cubism* (1969), *Ways of Seeing* (1973), and *The Sense of Sight* (1986).

him: he, himself, has to choose for society'' (p. 134). He concludes that, after the high point of Cubist innovation, Picasso was most effective when two profound personal experiences provided him with subjects: the passionate love affair with Marie-Thérèse and his fight against Fascism. This original and important contribution to Picasso criticism thus diverges from the habitual Marxist condemnation of *Guernica*.

Picasso made several variations of this head [fig. 157] and it is the same head which appears in his etchings of the artist in his studio. It is identified with Marie-Thérèse, but is by no means a portrait. In the etchings it stands there in the studio like a silver oracle, looking at the sculptor and his model who are lovers.[1]

Its secret is a metaphor. It represents a face. Yet this face is reduced to two features: the nose, rounded and powerful, which thrust forward and is simultaneously heavy and buoyant; and below it, the mouth, soft, open, and very deeply modelled. In terms of the density of their implied substance, the nose is like wood and the mouth like earth. These two features emerge from three rounded forms which have been formalized from the cheeks and the bun of hair at the back of the head. The scale of the work is what first offers a clue to the metaphor. It is very much larger than a head—one stands looking at it as at a figure, a torso. Then one sees. The nose and the mouth are metaphors for the male and female sexual organs; the rounded forms for buttocks and thighs. This face, or head, embodies the sexual experience of two lovers, its eyes engraved upon their legs. What image could better express the shared subjectivity which sex allows than the smile of such a face?

Picasso may have arrived at the metaphor unconsciously. But afterwards he deliberately played with the idea of transforming a head into sexually charged component parts. * * *

It is as though—and here Picasso is like most of us—he can only fully see himself when he is reflected in a woman. And it is as though—and here he is rarer—it is almost only through the marvellous shared subjectivity of sex that he can allow himself to be known. The majority of his paintings are of women. There are surprisingly few men. A number of the women are portrayed as themselves. Others are idealizations. But most of them are composite creatures—themselves and he together. In a sense these paintings might be called self-portraits—not portraits of himself alone and untransformed, but self-portraits of the creature he and the woman became as they sensed one another. The relationship is always sexual but the preoccupations of the composite creature may not be. * * *

Thus, on a psychological level, the problem is a similar one to that of finding a subject, of finding the apt vehicle for self-expression. Picasso finds himself in women—and the fact that he had otherwise been so isolated must have increased this need. Through himself, found in woman, he then tries to say things as an artist. Sometimes these things are unsayable because they are essentially outside the scope of the relationship. When they are about the essence of that relationship, when the shared subjectivity that Picasso needs is actually created by sex, then the results are purer

1. [Berger illustrates one of these etchings, *Sculptor and Model Resting* (G. 59, 2 April 1933). Gaile Haessly has analyzed Picasso's innumerable variations of this sculpture in paintings and graphics: "Picasso and Androgyny," unpublished Humanities Ph.D. dissertation, Syracuse University, 1983.]

157. Picasso. *Head of a Woman*. 1932. Bronze, 50⅝ x 21½ x 24⅝" (128.5 x 54.5 x 62.5 cm). S.133. Musée Picasso, Paris

158. David Alfaro Siqueiros. *Echo of a Scream.* 1937. Duco on wood, 48 x 36" (121.0 x 91.4 cm). The Museum of Modern Art, New York (gift of Edward M. M. Warburg)

and simpler and more expressive than any comparable works in the history of European art. Other works may be more subtle because they deal with the social complexities of sexual relations. Picasso abstracts sex from society—there is no hint in the bronze head or *The Nude on a Black Couch*[2] of the role of a mistress, the happiness of marriage, or the attraction of *les fleurs du mal*. He returns sex to nature where *it becomes complete in itself*. This is not the whole truth but it is an aspect of the truth of which no other painter has had the means or courage or simplicity to remind us.

On 26 April 1937 the Basque town of Guernica (population 10,000) was destroyed by German bombers flying for General Franco. * * *[3]

In less than a week Picasso began his painting. He had already been commissioned by the Spanish Republican Government to paint a mural for the Paris World Fair. In June the painting was installed in the Spanish building there. It immediately provoked controversy. Many on the left criticized it for being obscure. The right attacked it in self-defence. But the painting quickly became legendary and has remained so. It is the most famous painting of the twentieth century. It is thought of as a continuous protest against the brutality of fascism in particular and modern war in general.

How true is this? How much applies to the actual painting, and how much is the result of what happened after it was painted?

Undoubtedly the significance of the painting has been increased (and perhaps even changed) by later developments. Picasso painted it urgently and quickly in response to a particular event. That event led to others—some of which nobody could foresee at the time. The German and Italian forces, who in 1937 ensured Franco's victory, were within three years to have all Europe at their mercy. Guernica was the first town ever bombed in order to intimidate a civilian population: Hiroshima was bombed according to the same calculation.

Thus, Picasso's personal protest at a comparatively small incident in his own country afterwards acquired a worldwide significance. For many millions of people now, the name of Guernica accuses all war criminals. Yet *Guernica* is not a painting about modern war in any objective sense of the term. Look at it beside David Siqueiros's *Echo of a Scream*, also painted in 1937 and suggested, I suspect, by a picture of a child screaming in a Spanish Civil War newsreel [fig. 158].[4]

In the Siqueiros we see the materials which make modern war possible, and the specific kind of desolation to which it leads. By contrast, the Picasso might be a protest against a massacre of the innocents at any time. Picasso himself has called the painting an allegory—but has not fully explained the symbols he has used. This is probably because they have too many meanings for him.

Three years earlier Picasso made an etching of *Bull, Horse, and Female Matador*, which, in imagery, is very similar to *Guernica*.[5] But here the matador is Marie-

---

2. [Illustrated in *Picasso 1980*, p. 293.]

3. [In the deleted passage, Berger quotes Steer's account of the bombing (pp. 160–61.]

4. [A reasonable mistake. The crying child in Siqueiros's painting, however, was taken from a photograph of a woman with her baby in Kenya (*The National Geographic Magazine*, Feb. 1925, p. 205). My thanks to Betsy Jones, former MoMA staff member, for sharing Siqueiros's comments that helped me find the photograph.]

5. [Dated 20 June 1934 (G. 85), it is one of the etchings leading up to *Minotauromachy* (fig. 165).]

Thérèse, and the meaning of the scene is wholly concentrated on the movable frontier between sexual urgency and violence, between compliance and victimization, pleasure and pain. That is not to suggest that it is complicated in anything but a sensuous way. It is the body, not the mind, that submits to a kind of death in sex, and an awareness, after love, of feminine vulnerability is the result of an instinctual impulse—an impulse which man shares with many animals.

When Picasso painted *Guernica* he used the private imagery which was already in his mind and which he had been applying to an apparently very different theme. But only apparently—or anyway, only superficially different. For *Guernica* is a painting about how Picasso *imagines* suffering; and just as when he is working on a painting or sculpture about making love the intensity of his sensations makes it impossible for him to distinguish between himself and his lover, just as his portraits of women are often self-portraits of himself found in them, so here in *Guernica* he is painting his own suffering as he daily hears the news from his own country.

The etching the *Crying Woman* [fig. 65] (which is part of the whole cycle of works connected with *Guernica*) is no longer a directly sexual metaphor, but it is nevertheless the tragic complement to the giant bronze head. It is a face whose sensuality, whose ability to be enjoyed, has been blown to pieces, leaving only the debris of pain. It is not a moralist's work but a lover's. No moralist would see the pain so self-destructively. But for the lover, there is still a shared subjectivity. What has happened to his woman's face is like a castration.

Guernica, then, is a profoundly subjective work—and it is from this that its power derives. Picasso did not try to imagine the actual event. There is no town, no aeroplanes, no explosion, no reference to the time of day, the year, the century, or the part of Spain where it happened. There are no enemies to accuse. There is no heroism. And yet the work is a protest—and one would know this even if one knew nothing of its history. Where is the protest then?

It is in what has happened to the bodies—to the hands, the soles of the feet, the horse's tongue, the mother's breasts, the eyes in the head. What has happened to them *in being painted* is the imaginative equivalent of what happened to them in sensation in the flesh. We are made to feel their pain with our eyes. And pain is the protest of the body.

Just as Picasso abstracts sex from society and returns it to nature, so here he abstracts pain and fear from history and returns them to a protesting nature. All the great prosecuting paintings of the past have appealed to a higher judge—either divine or human. Picasso appeals to nothing more elevated than our instinct for survival. Yet this appeal now confirms the most sophisticated assessment of the realities of the modern world, which the political leaders of both the East and the West have been obliged to accept.

VII.
ANALYSIS AND
GENERAL ESSAYS

This part contains but a sampling of the countless articles, books, and chapters written about *Guernica*, that endlessly fascinating and much-discussed painting by the most publicized master of our age. The first American books on *Guernica* published in the 1940s share the laudatory and polemical qualities of the contemporary accounts. Danz responded to the painting somewhat single-mindedly, even naively; Larrea in his equally passionate defense revealed still-painful scars from the recent Spanish trauma.

The early 1960s finally produced two objective, critical works: Rudolf Arnheim forced the viewer to look very carefully indeed at *Guernica*'s many studies and transformations on the canvas; Otto Brendel published the first detailed, iconographical investigation of how Picasso's classical heritage informed the painting. By the later 1960s, however, the younger generation was ready for an irreverent look at this sacred icon: as a graduate student, Joseph Masheck questioned some standard assumptions and Darby Bannard, both critic and serious painter, challenged *Guernica* as a formal problem of composition and painterly touch.

Even with this accumulated literature, *Guernica* in the late 1970s and 1980s was still inspiring original research and publications. Frank Russell, painter/historian and long-time admirer of *Guernica*, created a lovingly designed homage. Sketches newly available after Picasso's death stimulated Reinhold Hohl to fresh insights. And appropriately, this part concludes with Douglas Cooper's appreciation of the new installation in Madrid, *Guernica*'s first home in Spain.

Louis Danz
Personal Revolution and Picasso—
[1941]*

This first Picasso book celebrating *Guernica* emphasizes sensations "poured out in paint" (p. 10); it is written in simplified language indebted to Gertrude Stein and e. e. cummings and intended to evoke childlike emotional responses. It was evidently discussed among American Abstract Expressionists: the sculptor David Smith carefully recorded author and title on a notebook page filled with Picassoid nudes.[1]

Louis Danz achieved his "personal revolution" by approaching modern art emotionally, indeed viscerally. Distrusting intellectual concepts and depicted objects ("nouns"), he stressed modern art's "haptic" energy—a term whose tactile connotation he stretched to include other physical emotional responses. "When somebody great said I think therefore I am the world applauded. But is it not truer to say I *feel* therefore I am," he argued (p. 113).

When I speak of Picasso's *Guernica* I say nothing about the fact that Guernica was a city and a place of great Basque culture. I say nothing that this Guernica was utterly destroyed in three and one half hours of terrific bombing and that its seven thousand people were totally annihilated.

That is history.

That is not art.

I am in search of art and art is like gold and is where you find it and I find it in Picasso's *Guernica*.

However knowing this about the city of Guernica as history makes me understand why Picasso used no color in his picture—no red no blue no green no color.

How could he.

What color is the pain of a bursting bomb. What color is the suffering of everything that is dead. The whole thing is so frightful that the living no longer feel life and so profound that only the dead can suffer.

* * *

But Picasso's colossal superiority as I said lies in that he does not do what he could

*From *Personal Revolution and Picasso* (New York, Longmans, Green & Co., 1941), pp. 2, 4–10, 17–18, 24; reprinted by Haskell House Publ. (Brooklyn, 1974). Danz remains a mystery figure. Publicity for his autobiographical novel of 1943, *It Is Still the Morning,* termed him a self-educated world traveler with many interests, who "settled in California where he lectures on modern art, music, psychology" and remains enthusiastic about "anything modern." In an earlier book, *The Psychologist Looks at Art* (1937), he identified himself as "somewhat a Gestalter."

1. See Rosalind Krauss, *Terminal Iron Works: The Sculpture of David Smith* (Cambridge, MA, 1971), fig. 88.

see and he avoids doing what he does not see. Nothing that is past is carried into the future. In fact for him there is no past and there is not future. Everything is *now*— every line and every color is *now*.

A tragic line such as Picasso feels into his *Guernica* is like the most brutal verb ever unuttered—intensified by the most ghastly unspoken adjectives.

This is what gives Picasso his living line. The line is alive because at that very moment of execution Picasso also is very alive. In this case the case of the *Guernica* Picasso is tragically alive. Every line of his has a birth not a beginning and every line of his has a death not an end.

Living line and living color living form and living content that is what I find in Picasso. In that lies the whole of esthetics and everything—man plant and animal.

I find it in Picasso.

I find it in his *Guernica* most clearly—unmistakably.

* * *

And it is like that now when new men bring us new cargoes and these new men like Picasso and Stravinsky and Joyce and others and others and others are bringing us new cargoes. And I say I found it in the *Guernica* and in *Le Sacre du Printemps* and *Ulysses*.

When I said I wanted to know what is this new thing that I found this new cargo that I found they said go to the dictionary.

Which of course I did.

I found it there.

The word is *haptic*.

I found it. The word haptic it says means actual body experience. I found it in the dictionary like this—the term pertains to the sense of touch. I broadened it out and stretched it over to include all emotive body happenings which take place inside the body.

The word haptic includes all feeling—experiencing. There might be other terms but I feel the power of deep completeness and a sort of inward light in the word haptic and so this word becomes one of the most used and most important words inside me.

* * *

As I say I thought about all this for a long time until I saw that all this is a haptic experience.

It is what I call haptic feeling.

And so when I say haptic I mean exactly the physiology back of an art-act.

It is the *content* of art.

It makes art physiological instead of psychological.

This is one of the most important discoveries ever in art. The value of it cannot be appreciated until it is felt.

Haptic takes the place of such words as intuition or inspiration or instinctive or psychical or creative or spiritual or emotive.

These terms are not synonymous they are superseded by the more inclusive word *haptic*.

The word haptic is primal.

Haptic is as I say physiological. The other words are merely psychological interpretations. What to the philosophers are the intuitive values are in reality the deep haptic values.

So now I have something.

I have something that will help me understand about Picasso and it will help me understand about myself. It is knowing that art is haptic and is not a purely visual event. Quite to the contrary art comes out of haptic experiences—physiological sensations. Real art is bound up with the immediate experiences of body. And here is the paramount condition. It is that real art—that is the actual art-act can only take place simultaneously with the actual experience.

It is like this. You cannot put into your art that which you experienced yesterday or the day before. The haptic experience is something now and must be expressed at its moment. An experience that has turned *cold* will do completely nothing in art.

* * *

Even now I find that when writing I have a haptic experience. Many times like the boy who felt bigger in the dark room—I have an almost irrepressible desire to write the highly emotive feelings in large letters. The less important words shrink up into very small letters in my feelings. It is as if the size of the letters would bring out the feeling lived into my writing at that very moment—adding volume and color and deepening meaning and commanding special attention—and more.

It is like when I am thinking hard my mouth seems to disappear from my body and my eyes grow more solid.[2] And when I am speaking sincerely and energetically my mouth suddenly becomes bigger. And when pain comes and there is that shriek which only pain can bring—then my head is apt to disappear and only my distorted mouth remains. But it is no longer a mouth it is a shriek.

And there you have it.

There you have the agonizing heads in Picasso's *Guernica*—and the head of the horse.

It is like a child painting her own picture reaching hungrily for an apple. She would make the outstretched arm longer. She would accentuate the grasping hand. She would most likely enormously enlarge her mouth. Or again if a child were painting the chase a slow runner might have short legs and a fast runner might have long legs. And just like that Picasso does it.

Body sensations are poured out in paint.

* * *

Art is feeling.

An art-act is feeling in action.

Picasso's painting is always exciting because Picasso paints the path of feeling. I am speaking completely literally. Picasso paints the path of feeling.

Did you ever have a teardrop run down your face.

Sometime have a teardrop run down your face and feel it run. Feel it run and then you will understand Picasso. Picasso paints a teardrop running down the face. He paints a tragic *running down* on *the face*—just as you would feel it. Then at the end of the running he paints the teardrop—as it feels. He paints the path of the teardrop—he paints a path of feeling—he paints the path of every feeling he has at the moment he is feeling. A moment later would be too late.

It is so simple.

2. [Danz's thinking clearly was influenced by Paul Schilder's recently published *Image and Appearance of the Human Body* (London, 1935).]

Picasso paints a teardrop when it is running down the face.

That is all.

Of course he must paint the *when*. He paints it *when* it is running—all the way. He does not paint the teardrop itself until it has stopped running. Then the teardrop hangs suspended from the *when* like it feels on the face.

* * *

Picasso's line is like Martha Graham's dancing. Martha Graham dances the path of feeling as it flows through her body. It flows through her body before it comes out. It is the same with Gieseking playing the piano. He starts in his toes and the line undulates upward through his body and comes out of his fingers. It is like blood— poured out of his body upon the white ivory keys.

Picasso paints like a child paints. Once I saw a painting done by a blind child. It was about a girl chasing a boy and her outstretched hand was trying so hard to grasp his coat. Well that arm was painted about twice its normal length and it had completely left the body and was flying out after the boy.

And like that Picasso paints what he feels not what he sees. And like a child Picasso sees not with his eyes but *feels* with his body.

Plato knew this about art.

Plato said that it is not the eyes that see but the eyes that permit us to see.

The eyes are merely holes for the body to feel through.

* * *

So I mean just what I say.

It is like this that sometimes you have had a hurt. And then the hurt went away. And then later you want to paint and you want to paint this hurt. So you do not paint what you remember made the hurt or how you looked at the time but you again feel the actual hurt in your body as you lived it and put the living hurt down on canvas.

Picasso felt all the hurts that he had ever had in his body when he painted the *Guernica*. Picasso was not in Guernica when he did this. He was in Paris. But he could feel the hurts in Paris because he was in Paris and the hurts were in his own body in Paris.

And when I saw the painting I could feel the hurts in my body.

Look at the hoof of the horse at the bottom of the picture. It is turned toward you because if a horse crushed you that is what you would feel. You would feel the hoof and cold iron shoe. Picasso paints what that hoof would do to you.

* * *

There is no subject matter in the *Guernica*. What is in the *Guernica* is a subject manner. And as I said there is a world of difference between subject matter and subject manner. The *Guernica* is made out of feeling and out of feeling only.

This is a new kind of art.

This art is reborn in our day and is maturing in our day.

It has been in the world a long time ago and at different times and at different places in caves and on monuments and on sarcophagi. But it was never understood except by those few then and these few now.

Picasso's *Guernica* is not at all a representational painting. That is it is not imitative in any part—except the window and except the ear that seems to grow on the top of the Bull's head. These are representational things. And if the ear really grew where it is painted we would not need to include it. How can a picture be representational when nothing in the picture except these two lapses are visual things and all the rest of the picture is pure haptic feeling. I will admit you can if you wish transmute these feelings into things and use nouns and name them—but then you will completely miss the picture.

Picasso did not have a noun image in his mind say like an image of a bull or a horse or a warrior and say inside himself now I am going to put these images down on canvas.

No he did not do this.

He said like this I have hurts endless hurts inside and they want to come out and they must come out. So he put his frightful hurts down on canvas and now when we look at what he did so many of us unfortunately see only a horse or a bull or a woman.

We see only things.

Juan Larrea
The Vision of the Guernica—[1947]*

For fifteen years, this was the only complete book about *Guernica,* with reproductions of all available studies and states (also *Minotauromachy,* and the *Dream and Lie of Franco,* poem and etchings). The essay is written with the passionate convictions of a Spanish survivor, in fact a Basque.[1] These selections also reflect typical intellectual concerns of the 1930s in Paris: Surrealism and Freudian psychology. Larrea added some important interpretations—the personal meaning of the horse—that Picasso shared with this frequent visitor to the studio (p. 200, above).

However overpowering the effect on us of the loudspeaker created by Picasso to release his indignation upon the consciences of his contemporaries, it is impossible to escape the capital enigma presented, in the form of a paradox, by the very existence of the *Guernica.* Here we have the most universally acclaimed painting of the century, and the most effective, because it is the one in which our time best recognized its content; yet it is characterized by the fact that it is not a painting at all. If it is the artist's greatest picture, this is due (as one might again paradoxically claim) to his need to find space in it for a world of absent elements. Everything that has been considered inherent in the art of painting, even by the most advanced schools: light, color, precision or plasticity of drawing—all the more or less outstanding excellences

*This title retains Larrea's, from his *Guernica: Pablo Picasso,* intro. by Alfred H. Barr (New York, 1947), pp. 13–14 (where his text begins), 27, 33, 34, 37, 57–58, by permission of the late author and the executor for Curt Valentin, publisher.

1. Born 1895 in Bilbao, Larrea spent several years in Paris during the 1920s and 1930s, then worked for the Spanish Republic as archivist in Madrid and the Embassy's information and propaganda services in Paris. He wrote *Guernica* in Mexico after emigrating in 1939. Larrea later settled in Argentina, published several volumes of poetry and literary criticism, and taught cultural history at the University of Córdoba.

that have conferred lustre upon the old and the modern masters, are here conspicuously lacking.

The most that can be said to remain is a clean surface upon which we follow the alternate syncopations of blacks with grays and whites, in a mysterious drama of vital disorder, and with a marked tendency toward triangulation. Against such a background, a series of plastic figures composes as it may to fill the space; it resembles the world of the senses as much as a confused mass of twisted iron resembles a building. Not every spectator will be able to make out, at first sight, in the thing like a whirlwind filling the center of the canvas, the body of a horse transfixed by a lance and kneeling on one of its forefeet. One is tempted to think that every kind of fire from heaven is descending here. If it is true (as some books claim) that lightning sometimes indulges in pranks, such as rolling a person's hair into a ball, one might suppose that it was here amusing itself by marking out, with extreme regularity, as a child does when he learns to write, every hair of the horse's mane. In the same manner also, one might explain the terror reflected by the elemental figures, and even the sort of ghastly ectoplasm which intrudes its head through a tiny window, stretching forth its arm so as to place a light in the very center of the scene which at one moment appears to be under a roof, whereas at other moments it is clearly out of doors. The body of the bull in the upper left-hand corner presents to the onlooker the no less unexpected novelty of prolonging itself in the form of a table to which some of the animal's feet belong. On the table a dove is seized by a spasm, like all the other figures, with the sole exception of the bull which, bellowing and nearly bursting with fury, its eyes fixed in their orbits, seems about to charge at the moment least expected. Everything else in this canvas, we repeat, seems beside itself, beginning with the artist, continuing with the scene presented, and ending with the art of painting.

We are here in the presence of an unspeakable tragedy: the culmination of the life and work of a contemporary artist of a calibre to compete with the greatest masters in the field of drawing and painting. None of them, perhaps, found himself better endowed than he, by gifts of the highest order. Suddenly we realize that in this heart-rending tension, in these lacerating mouths, in this extreme negation of artistic values and of his own talents, to say nothing of other details not likely to escape an unbiased eye, a supreme pictorial blasphemy has been given utterance. This is no disavowal of the "cult of appearances, the traditional dogma of painters" in the manner advocated, in the past, by Apollinaire, but an attempt of the artist to free himself altogether from the world of the eyes, to repudiate it as a way of execrating the human order of things which it helped to build up. It is through an unfortunate tendency of the age that the life and work of the most admirable of our artists has had to arrive at the point represented by this horrified shuddering of light, at this gnashing of teeth, at this canvas of sackcloth and ashes. For we can accept only with much reserve the assertion that the master's studies for his *Guernica* began only on May 1st, 1937. To be wholly truthful, it is better to say that Picasso's entire work is composed of a series of studies, essays, sketches, and spectographs whose general justification is rooted in this portentous enigma. May it not be that we are dealing here with *Demoiselles d'Avignon*[2] who have come down in the world and also with the cubist compositions, the big still-lifes, the bull-fights with horses in convulsion,

2. [Picasso's stylistic breakthrough of 1907.]

those strange crucifixions of which there are clear traces in the first stage of the *Guernica*, and the mysterious etchings?—Are we not, even again seeing the compassions of the "blue" period, which at times show such a pronounced tendency toward the triangular and toward the reproduction of the tragic?

In short, does not the *Guernica* climax the procession of scenes of destruction which Picasso has paraded before our eyes, year after year, running up a heavy debt to our sensibility, and finally discharging that debt with its enormous payment in black and white? Even assuming that this painting represents an anticipated projection of the cataclysm of our time, one would have to admit that this cataclysm had been slowly developing in the artist's soul, and from his early youth. Naturally, he had never exhibited a monumental despair such as this but it may be stated that he had carried out an infinite number of partial studies of tortured frenzy, some of them in hardly less strident tones. On the other hand, we have from his brush works of a calmer pathos, though still very close to the *Guernica* in subject matter. We are thinking, in particular, of that incomparable etching known as the *Minotauromachy* (1935) [fig. 165], with much the same elements: the horse in convulsion, the bull, the four women—one of them with bare breasts, the man, the house, the window, the outstretched arm, the beam of light, the sword, the dove, and even the flower, whose place is here taken by the peaceful olive branch budding forth from the hand brandishing the fragment of a sword.—The resemblance is so far-reaching that the *Guernica* could never be completely understood without reference to this preliminary study, likewise in black and white.

Picasso and his time had indeed good reasons to inveigh against, and to despair of, the most primitive aspects of our zoological depths, ignorant alike of proportion and moderation, and to do so incommensurably. The Spanish people had passed almost a year tied to the stake of iniquity and torture, a victim of the deadly sins of all. "Let the day perish wherein I was born And the night which said, There is a man-child conceived"—thundered the pious Job, sitting among the ashes, after being despoiled of all his wealth—as the art of painting is here. To crown it all, the peaceful capital of the Basque democracy, which by the will of fate has given its name to this pictorial mystery, was brutally bombed by Nazi aviation in its first general attempt at extermination, with all the aggravating circumstances of fury and perfidy, while the champions of the so-called Christian civilization and the gentlemen of the City pushed their virtuosity to the point of accusing the Basque defenders of having bombarded themselves! *Ecce mundus*[3]—this title would have been equally fitting for our canvas. We are here in the presence of the rubbish heap of man, as all of his higher exponents, the most illustrious spiritual and temporal powers, have wanted it to be. It is thus clear that the nations making up the non-intervention committee enjoyed to the full their personal opportunities to blaspheme, and then to weep over themselves and their children. And if this *Ecce mundus* at the beginning was Guernica, soon afterwards it was Warsaw, Rotterdam, Nancy, Coventry—down to the day when all of Europe was only one immense material and moral ruin, from east to west and from north to south.

On that terrible day, the *Guernica* turned out to be, of all known paintings, the most European.

3. ["Behold the world".]

* * *

Furthermore Picasso himself seems to encourage us to treat his work with freedom of the imagination, seeing that in the first of his sketches of the *Guernica* he shows us a diminutive winged horse springing forth from the wound of the horse [fig. 6]. Is that the horse's soul, or is it not Pegasus—Picasso, the poetic power of the man?

□ □ □

Thus prepared, let us come to grips with the *Guernica*. As with every dream—and Picasso himself called it thus, two years ahead of time, according to those words of his which head the present study[4] we are very probably in the presence of different orders of things, closely connected, perhaps, with what psychoanalysts call latent content, manifest content, and secondary elaboration.

I am personally certain that Picasso, like other great artists, lives in a forest of symbols on which he draws for the expression of his innermost realities and of his inner conflicts. I remember having heard from his own lips as an *obiter dictum* that in the pictures from a certain period of his artistic development, the horse generally represents a woman who played an exceptionally important part in his life. This is one of the most suggestive vantage points, one which enables us to follow up, in his work, the story of his love life, from those pretty little horses of his youthful years down to the hideous and distorted nags which recur again and again during his pictorial rage of the thirties. It is possibly to his disappointments in love, from which he suffered deeply, that we must ascribe the interest shown by Picasso (though already at a rather late stage of his work) in bullfights. In these paintings he celebrates, on the one hand, the mystery of the *tauromaquia* but on the other finds an easy opportunity to revenge himself, in the picture of the horse, for the vexations of an unrequited passion which is dying down. The symbolic identity of woman and horse (from the sexual viewpoint) is so well known that no further explanations are required. In bullfights, moreover, the horse receives the virile thrust of the bull that gores.

This procedure is pure pictorial magic. In exactly the same manner the wizard operates when transfixing with pins a tiny doll, so that the person represented by the latter may feel the pain inflicted in effigy.

* * *

In the *Guernica*, evidently, [Picasso] goes beyond the intimate considerations connected with the horse. It is true, none the less, that this animal not only dominates the center of the canvas, but also that it differs from the other figures, which are almost flat, since it is distinguished by bulk and by a tortured complexity not found in the rest. It is doubtless the most elaborated feature of the picture, the one on which Picasso has dwelt with a sort of lingering delectation, to the point of conferring upon it the character of a protagonist. The result is enigmatic, since it does not seem credible that the author, having to represent the martyrdom of a people clamoring to heaven, should have chosen the figure of a quadruped usually regarded with hostility, giving it preference, for example, over the figure of the despairing mother on the left, huddling close to the bull. This consideration justifies us in supposing that there is in this horse, as in the Trojan horse, some hidden mystery; the creature represented

4. [Larrea had quoted from Picasso's statements of 1945 and 1935, pp. 152–53 and 143, above.]

may be identified with matters which arouse, in Picasso's soul, reactions similar to those produced in him, formerly, by feminine hostility; to be sure, an understanding of this metaphor will be possible only for those persons who know the explanation given by the artist as to his symbolism.

Putting two and two together, it is easy to conjecture that that horse is the object of an irrepressible desire to inflect harm and to take vengeance. In short, there can be little doubt that the horse transfixed by a lance or pike—a figure that has given rise to the largest number of studies of detail, invariably full of ignoble and depressive features—stands, in the painter's mind, for nothing more nor less than Nationalist Spain. In this figure Picasso's brush bursts out, as it were, in a magic imprecation, calling down upon Franco's Fascism a spasm of agony and its final doom, just as shown in the picture. As, when seized with anger at someone, our first impulse is to insult him by calling him by the name of some ignoble animal, so a painter proceeds, except that he makes use of the picture language. If there remains, in the reader's mind, any doubt about the correctness of this interpretation, suffice it to have a look at one of the etchings of the *Sueño y Mentira de Franco* (*Franco's Dream and Lie* [fig. 110]) which shows the bull close to the horse out of whose gored body, instead of the entrails, there come forth Falangist flags, processional banners, and other repulsive things.

* * *

If in Picasso's previous works the horse stood for a woman, and the bull, in a certain sense, for the artist himself, in the present fantasmagoria, in which the horse symbolizes Spanish Nationalism, the bull seems to be the symbol of the people, and the more so because this animal is almost the totem of the Peninsula, and Spaniards attend its sacrifice with passionate enthusiasm. In the larger part of the notations and sketches which Picasso devoted to it, it appears with a handsome human face, impassive or even glorified. It reappears in the same style and manner in the etchings known as *Sueño y Mentira de Franco*, in which, side by side with the ignoble figure of the *Cabecilla* (leader of rebels), represented as such, we behold the head of the bull in full splendor. One of its constant characteristics is the expression of its powerful and wide-open eyes, contrasting with the convulsed look of the eyes in the other figures. They should be compared, particularly, with those of the horse. Another of the bull's characteristic features is its attitude of Olympic disdain as shown in all sketches, and also in our picture, toward the horse, in whose destruction it is apparently not anxious to intervene, as if afraid of staining itself in so doing. The bull merely fascinates us with its undaunted eyes and with its gesture of protecting the mother and her child. Indeed, this seems to it more important than bothering with that unclean nag which has already received its death blow.

The mother with the child in her arms [fig. 42] is another protagonist of the tragedy, as is proved by the considerable number of sketches devoted to her by the author and by the arrow pointing mysteriously to her heart from the hoofs of the horse. with her mouth almost touching that of the bull (the Spanish people) and sharing, as it were, her breath with the animal's, she possibly represents a characteristic attribute of the Spanish people, the motherhood of Mother Spain. She is the only principal character that did not appear in the early designs. She is first seen on May 8th, on the right-hand side of the general sketch. The child she holds in her arms has bled copiously and is doubtless dead. On May 28th it reappears, transfixed by an arrow. The mother is thus a Mater Dolorosa calling down justice from heaven. During the execution of the *Guernica,* this figure underwent a noteworthy change of form: from a purpose merely of imprecation, it took on one that is also symbolical, a change coinciding with its tranposition to the left side of the picture, while on the right another woman has taken the place left vacant. When it was still on the right-hand side, the child appeared dead. After the transfer to the left, all one can say is that it does show a wound at the neck that is not bleeding. Picasso no doubt thought that this child, indispensable for the symbol of motherhood and imposed, as it were, by the events, symbolized the future, and that representing it dead, to move the consciences of the onlookers, meant jeopardizing all hope for the future of the world. The difficulty was solved by the ambiguous character of the wound. But matters did not stop there: the artist finally suppressed the wound altogether. Thus if, on the one hand, the child ought to have been dead to awaken the memory of the crimes committed by Spanish Nationalism against the childhood of Spain, on the other hand one could not be sure that it had not merely fainted or was asleep. This is the true situation. The role of the bull thus comes out to the full: with its body it protects both mother and child, the present and the future of Spain.

* * *

The fact is that this is no painting due merely to the caprice or the private initiative of Picasso. To understand it in its full objectivity it is necessary to remember that (1) it was a work ordered by the Republican Government of Spain, that is, by the political representatives of the Spanish people, which thus took the initiative; (2) it had an immediate and precise objective: to ornament the Spanish pavilion at the Paris World's Fair of 1937; (3) it is an emotional reflex of the events taking place in the Peninsula at that time, and to these events, therefore, the principal part of the objective phenomena corresponds; (4) it was conceived and executed by the Spanish painter who is the most outstanding in our century and who knows about all centuries, a Spaniard who has gone forth from Spain and vastly broadened his mind; (5) to give body to his Spanish emotion and to his purpose, he did not choose the superficial and anecdotal scenes of the events, but the most deep-rooted symbols of what may be called the national subconscious: the bull fight with all that is involved in such symbols. We are therefore dealing with a work that is four-square Spanish, and with a Spain that exudes *españolismo* from all her pores. As for its emigration to foreign lands, as a result of the political events that gave birth to the *Guernica,* we know today that it was a natural part of its destiny, and the fact permits us reasonably to suppose that the painting is not merely a personal work of Picasso but a revelation of Spain through her natural organ of expression, the most prominent and universal of her painters.

Rudolf Arnheim
The Genesis of a Painting—[1962]*

Noting Picasso's famous suggestions "to preserve photographically, not the stages, but the metamorphoses of a picture,"[1] Professor Arnheim proceeded to analyze Picasso's raw materials for *Guernica*—the preparatory studies and photographic states. With scientific care that reveals his initial training as a Gestalt psychologist, Arnheim precisely described his visual data, asking probing questions, testing Picasso's various reasons for changes made, and then formulating his conclusions and interpretations. This is a technique well worth mastering to discover Picasso's "visual problem solving," or—to use the artist's phrase—to follow his brain along the path "in materializing a dream."[2]

The Sketches for the Mural[3]

1 [Figure 1]

Picasso's first sketch for *Guernica* contains much of the final basic form; the small drawing on a piece of blue paper certainly comes closer to the composition of the mural than anything else the painter put down before he started on the actual canvas. We discern the bull on the left, in his final location. Not only the head but the entire body is turned away from the scene—as though this turning away was the basic thought, later refined when the bull was made to face the event but with his head averted. The bird sits on the bull, at the exact spot where it will later hover on the table. The horse seems to lie dead on its back, thereby representing the extreme effect of the murderous assault—a function later transferred to the dead child. The horse's raised hindlegs are significant as the early establishment of a central rising vertical, which later caused much experimentation. The woman is pushing the lamp through the window; she, too, is in her final place. The horizontal base of prostrate bodies underlies the entire principal scene, more radically and simply than the warrior will finally do it. A vertical element is clearly indicated at the extreme right—is it a part of the building, or a figure, or are there two figures?

We cannot tell how much Picasso's image went beyond what he hastily penciled on this piece of paper. From what we see we can infer that there were four basic elements to the concept and that they stood starkly for four basic positions: the

---

*Reprinted from *Picasso's Guernica: The Genesis of a Painting* (Berkeley and Los Angeles, The University of California Press, 1962) by permission of author and publisher, pages 30–31, 46–47, 124, and 133. (Reissued in paper, *The Genesis of a Painting: Picasso's Guernica*, 1973, and 1980). Arnheim has been professor of the psychology of art at Sarah Lawrence College and Harvard University; among his other important books are *Art and Visual Perception* (1954, new version 1974), *Toward a Psychology of Art* (1966), *Visual Thinking* (1978), and *New Essays in the Psychology of Art* (1986).

1. Arnheim began his chapter III (p. 30) by quoting from Picasso's 1935 statement, p. 143, above.

2. Idem.

3. [Arnheim continued quoting from Picasso's 1935 interview, observing that probably both statements are pertinent: "the first vision remains almost intact," and "a picture is not thought out and settled beforehand" but "changes as one's thoughts change".]

upright bull, the light bearer, the sprawling victim, the inert base of destroyed bodies. The first and fundamental role assigned to the feminine element was that of making light; the lamenting women began to appear a week later. The rival luminary is not yet at the ceiling.

The sheet of paper is of the ratio 1 to 1.2, and the composition itself is approximately of the same format. Is this more squarish shape accidental, determined simply by the shape of the first piece of drawing paper which came to hand? Or did Picasso in the beginning think of a more compact pattern? The light is already placed in the center, but it tops no triangle as yet. Instead, there is a large circular curve, for which the final composition would have no room and which is obviously designed to pull the vertical and horizontal dimensions together in order to produce a more tightly unified whole. The cast of characters is still small, and demands little floor space. The arrangement of the scene is closer to the classical pictorial tradition than the final mural will be. It is less "modern."

10 [Figure 10]

Done on the same day as the heads of the horse—either before or after them—this new attempt to outline the total work progresses considerably beyond sketch 6. The cast of characters is pulled together: neither the bull nor the dead soldier remains an indifferent outsider. Radical steps have been taken to eliminate the intertwining of limbs. The bull's leap serves the formal purpose of lifting him bodily above the rest of the scene. His outline is entirely unbroken. Also he has become most active; but does the action suit the purpose? Is he running away from the light, similar to his predecessor, the bull-man of the *Minotauromachy*, who shielded his eyes with his hand? Or is he inspired by it? The light-bearing woman has been retrieved from the background. But her exclusive interaction with the bull seems no more appropriate than was her equally exclusive connection with the horse in sketch 6. It is as though the painter were trying out the possible pairings one by one.

If this were the final composition, the simplest interpretation might assume that the bull is the enemy, frightened away by the spirit of light after riding roughshod over the horse and the human victims. In fact, no wounds or projectiles indicate here that the destruction is caused by any other aggressor. Did Picasso waver in his concept of the bull? In the final mural, the steady frontality of the bull's glance is modified by a profile turn of the head, as though the animal, while steadfast, were also shying away from the scene. Is that subtle final gesture a remnant of the straightforward flight from revelation displayed in the present sketch?

The figure of the light-bearing woman is an impressive demonstration of visual problem solving. From one drawing to the next, the painter has attained all but the final solution. The static horizontality of sketch 6 has been changed to a goal-directed downward swing. The stiff stump of the arm has been freed from its tie to the architecture: its shape has been lengthened, and enriched by animating swellings. Lamp and fist, considerably more substantial, have been moved to their central location. The squeezed head has become a full, compact volume, and the stray arm has been clipped off. The bull's tail, a mere space filler in sketch 6, has been assigned the temporary task of playfully accompanying the forward thrust of the woman.

The horse is bent out of the bull's way. This visual simplification considerably affects its role, which now becomes that of the collapsing victim, bowing to fate and engaged in close dialogue with the soldier, the representative of death. The horse has joined a passive mass of vanquished bodies—a defeatist turn of thought. There is still considerable confusion of limbs in the lower right quarter of the picture. A dead woman has been introduced—the first splitting of the feminine element, which stands now for both light and death. This new woman's function is, however, not yet unique. She appears as a duplication of the soldier, which indicates that he, too, is not yet conceived in his final uniqueness.

There is a beginning, though, in that the warrior has now been decapitated smoothly and symmetrically—a change which announces his transformation into a statue. This fragmentation serves, first of all, to clean up the visual promiscuity. Observe the corridor of empty space it creates for the horse's foot and head! We realize further that a cut-off head of flesh and blood would have appeared as a mere inert leftover from a dreadful physical mutilation. The head of a statue is another matter. Although its place in the picture does make it a product of destruction, a sculptured head is not necessarily incomplete; and it speaks, even when it is only a fragment of a broken marble figure.

The head speaks, yet at the same time the figure is in pieces. Its aloofness is different from that of the bull in the final mural. It is a broken ideal, defeated, out of commission. Being a statue, however, it represents not only material defeat or the pain of it but rather the abstract fact and idea of defeat. Stone does not suffer as horses do. The transformation of the warrior into a statue tempers the heat of the physical catastrophe. It increases the abstractness of the reality level in the whole picture. But even at the more abstract level, the difference between horse and statue remains—the difference between war as organic suffering and as military, historical fact. And while the suffering is alive in the struggling horse, the statue lies dead.

Fourth State [Figure 37]

Any vacancy is an invitation to invention. The empty space at the extreme left was filled with a crescent in the third state. Little meaning seemed to be attached to this new celestial body; it looked as though it simply answered the demand that something ought to be there. Did the need for a filler suggest the turning around of the bull? This need may well have been what the logicians call the proximate cause, which, however, could hardly have brought about the action, had it not solved the problem of the bull's position. The gain is remarkable. With one strategic move, the painter refines the attitude of the animal: the bull now faces the scene, yet his head is turned away; the empty space at the left is filled with the eloquent tail; mother and child are enveloped and bolstered by the protective torso; the animal's hindquarters are removed from the center. Truly an ingenious invention.

The shifting of the bull's body has, in turn, created a vacuum. Again, as did the crescent, a neutral object occupies the space. Again, we may ask whether this emptiness invited the invention of the bird, which will finally fill it, and further, whether the newly cleared breathing space made the horse raise its head. And again, the answer must be that in the creative process material openings or obstacles constantly interact with the demands of meaning, and that the work gains from proceeding at these different levels of the problem situation simultaneously. Meaning required that the horse raise its head, so that the call of suffering would occur at the same proud level at which the bull holds his imperturbable, watchful head and so that the appeal would be addressed and transmitted to that remote yet spatially near monument of survival. But the horse could not raise its head unless there was space in which to put it.

The organization of space in itself can never be the final purpose of an artist, because space is only a means to an end. But to ignore formal problems and opportunities or to dismiss them as inferior is to forget that the artist thinks in shapes.

Conclusions

I have taken pains to show that formal considerations lead to solutions that are always more than formal. When an object had to be moved, the formal change entailed a change of meaning. When a foot was taken away from the falling woman and assigned to the fugitive, the result was an extension of the central compositional triangle into the right corner. This change accomplished more than the formal symmetry of the left and the right corners. It created a strong base for the leftward and upward rush of the whole central group. It anchored in a cornerstone at the right the movement toward the bull, basic to the meaning of Picasso's statement; and, by reducing the area occupied by the falling woman, it reduced the catastrophe of her fall to its proper secondary status. When the bull's body was removed from the center and placed behind mother and child, the result was not simply a "compositional" improvement but a far-reaching change of meaning, which if inappropriate or senseless would have argued against the rearrangement of the shapes.

Formal resemblances invited the painter frequently to let one element of subject matter take over the function of another. But these opportunities for visual puns prevailed only when the replacement changed the meaning favorably. Thus, when in sketch 12 the tail of the bull adopted the visual function of the light bearer's arm the result impoverished the meaning, and therefore the move had to be discarded. But when the raised arm of the warrior in the first state of the mural was replaced by the raised neck and head of the horse in the fourth state, the gain in significance was such that the formal improvement passed muster.

It is for this reason that I objected earlier to the notion that creativity consists in the readiness of a nimble mind to make new combinations. Surely such flexibility is indispensable, but it is no more than a prerequisite. We observed the painter trying a given sentiment on different characters: the theme of the upward outcry was first assigned to the horse and later to the mother. A given location was filled with one character after another, and a given character moved from place to place and from sentiment to sentiment. Also, Picasso experimented with various possible groupings of characters: he paired the horse with the light bearer, the light bearer with the bull, the warrior with the horse; but these trial combinations were under the strict control of the basic vision, which used them in the search of the final form.

Visual thinking, then, was goal-directed throughout. However, the goal was neither perceptual harmony nor originality. Harmony was needed to provide the work with readable, unified sense. Originality was needed to make the work correspond exactly to the particular painter's concept and to provide it with fresh, striking expression. But, as always in the arts, beauty and originality were only means to the end of making a vision visible.

Was this vision given from the beginning? Or did it emerge only gradually? We gained the impression that the basic "mood" of the work and the main ingredients of its expression were already present when the first sketch was made. Perhaps the aggressor was in the beginning an active part of the concept of *Guernica*. Certain ambiguities in the early presentations of the bull suggest this possibility. But the aggressor was soon reduced to indirect presence by effect, and the role of the antagonist, supplementing the passivity of the victims, was assumed by the victims themselves, by the aggressive *élan* of their complaint and appeal and the challenging resistance embodied in the bull.

While the work was going on, there were changes of emphasis and proportion, and there were many experiments in trying to define the content by working out its shape. A germinal idea, precise in its general tenor but unsettled in its aspects, acquired its final character by being tested against a variety of possible visual realizations. When, at the end, the artist was willing to rest his case on what his eyes and hands had arrived at, he had become able to see what he meant.

Otto J. Brendel
Classic and Non-Classic Elements in Picasso's Guernica—[1962]*

Professor Brendel uncovers in *Guernica* some unexpected and not-always-serene elements in the classical tradition. He sees the tragic mask behind the pure profile of the woman with the lamp, the crumbling academic tradition in the broken warrior-statue, and the Minotaur—demonic hybrid—behind *Guernica*'s bull. This noted classicist and humanist deepens our appreciation of "the uncanny persuasiveness of the mythical symbol"[1] enriching our response to *Guernica* and Picasso. For the artist was most at home along the Mediterranean's classical shores: in his native Málaga, in Barcelona, and in his last estate above Cannes.

My contention here is not only that classic elements are included in the painting, now so famous, which Picasso first showed in the Spanish Government Pavilion at the Paris World's Fair of 1937, and named *Guernica*; but that this painting more than any other elucidates what "classic" means, and indeed what this term can possibly mean, in a modern work of art. For whatever we call "classic" of course has its ultimate roots in some ancient thought, either Greek or Latin, or in some ancient artistic monument. But the "classic is also a living tradition and, as such, a part of the contemporary scene. In its modern phase tradition is no longer concerned solely

---

*Reprinted by permission of the late author and the publisher from Whitney J. Oates, ed., *From Sophocles to Picasso: The Present-Day Vitality of the Classical Tradition* (Bloomington, Indiana University Press, 1962), pp. 121–23, 126–55 (extensive footnotes abridged, updated, or deleted). Brendel (1901–1973) taught Greek, Roman, and Etruscan art at Columbia University and prepared an important survey of Etruscan painting and sculpture (Pelican History of Art, 1978).

1. From "The Classical Style in Modern Art," his preceding essay in the Oates anthology, p. 107.

with the ancient exemplars, as was the classicism of the Renaissance. It has since acquired many new saints to worship and new models to contend with. For one thing, the Renaissance has meanwhile made its own contribution and left an unforgettable impress on the Western mind. Raphael is now a part of the classical tradition; so is the art of Poussin, of Ingres, though obviously the latter two are "classical" in a somewhat different sense. "Classical" is today confronted with, and distinct from, "neoclassic." Another complicating factor has appeared in our evaluation of the ancient materials themselves, since we have become acquainted with many facets of ancient art to which the attribute "classical" is commonly denied. Greek archaic, much Etruscan, much Roman art are "ancient" but not "classic." It is no longer possible to expound in a simple statement the role of classicism in modern thought, nor the range of its contents. One cannot even assert that the contemporary forms of classicism are always readily recognized.

Accordingly, the term "classical" has during the last century and a half tended to develop three dimensions of meaning, of rising complexity. All are aspects of the same intellectual problem. The primary function of the term was, and still is, as a synonym of "Greek and Roman," generally speaking. At the same time, "classical" retains something of a selective connotation, in the sense of "exemplary." This meaning for the most part underlies that current of contemporary thought which for the sake of brevity I have earlier called "academic"[2] In this selective sense certain models and manners of art are "classical." The term thus acquires a rather definite if restricted content, traditionally established. Thirdly, beyond the confines of such traditionalism, the same word can also be used in a much broader sense. It then is likely to express a special quality of art and thought, a specific attitude, not easily describable by any other term, toward the forms into which we cast the human experience and toward the definition of form itself. Only in the latter sense is "classical" truly a critical term, with a postulated meaning to be actualized in many different ways. By necessity, in this sense it must also become a controversial term, dealing not with a set evaluation of ancient or of any other art but with an essential aspect of all art; exemplified chiefly but not exclusively by the arts of ancient Greece and Rome, and known by experience if not by definition.

* * *

Yet by 1937, the year of *Guernica*, all this was a matter of the past;[3] and it is a strange fact in itself that so much past memory should once more be conjured up and incorporated in this large and extraordinary painting, which thus seemed from the outset destined to epitomize the end of an era, while at the same time signalizing the beginning of a new one. * * * Although painted on canvas entirely in black, white, and grey this monumental work may well be called a wall painting. It has in every respect the character of a public proclamation, in scale as well as style. Yet its terrifying imagery remains startling and inexplicable like a dream. That is to say, the signs and images are not too difficult to name, each for itself. Only their context, the way in which they relate to one another if at all, is difficult to determine. * * * As a documentary report of an event the images assembled hardly seem to make sense.

2. [In his preceding essay (pp. 71–118), Brendel had focused on other major works by Picasso.]

3. [In the deleted pages, Brendel had discussed Picasso's academic training and youthful oeuvre, fully illustrated now by Cirlot (Nos. 405, 465, 467–84); *Picasso 1980*, pp. 20–21; or Palau i Fabre, *The Early Years*.]

They do not add up to a naturalistic description of content, for instance, of an episode of war. They must not be read literally and objectively, like a report in a newspaper. In other words, the observer must soon become aware of the fact that the painting does not offer him simply the representation of a unified theme, as he may have been led to expect by its title; that it does not in any ordinary sense represent the destruction of a town, but something else, far more complex.

This conclusion is corroborated by the preparatory sketches which by their established sequence permit us to follow quite clearly the growth of the composition. Three stages can be distinguished. From the beginning four elements are present: the woman with the lamp, the wounded horse, the bull, and the prostrate warrior. Of these four, solely the woman with the lamp, leaning out of a window, appears at once in a pose resembling her final form [fig. 1]. Only the kind of light which she is holding differs from case to case: it may be a burning candle, or a different type of lamp. On the other hand the images of the horse, the bull, and the prostrate warrior, which are likewise found in the initial sketches, undergo considerable change almost to the last. In the second stage the woman with the dead child appears near either the bull or the horse. Finally in the third stage emerges the present, tripartite composition in which the bull and the woman with the dead child form a group of their own on the left. Also the two women at the right seem to have been added at this stage. The horse was placed definitely at the center. From this evidence one must conclude that precisely the comparatively realistic, illustrative items in the composition were added later, as the work progressed; while the original thought first crystallized around the elements to which a symbolic rather than direct narrative value must be ascribed, as will have to be shown presently. This original symbolic group comprises the bull, the horse, the prostrate warrior, and the woman with the lamp. Now it is certainly a point of importance here that in at least three of these figures the very reminiscences or connotations of the classical which we set out in this paper to investigate come again to the fore. A certain relation seems to exist between the symbolical functions of these images and the varying aspects of classicism which each incorporates. In the following paragraphs each shall be explored separately, yet all three must also be considered together, for their impact upon one another. As symbols they have no independent existence. As in a dream they owe their existence to one another, because they came into being by implementing each other's meaning.

We shall first concern ourselves with the woman holding a lamp. Her large head in profile and long outstretched arm, rushing across the canvas like a sudden gust of wind, are beautifully invented. Together this head and arm form perhaps the most impressive detail of the entire painting, the one which we are likely to notice first and remember longest. They also constitute the first thought which assumed definite shape in the artist's own sketches, and must be regarded as one of the germinating ideas of the entire composition, much as a sequence of words suddenly occurring to a writer may in its aboriginal perfection become the nucleus of a whole poem. Yet the action of this woman, while forming a most memorable gesture, is not easily explained. Why should she wish with her poor lamp to light the street? The lamp would not avail her much on this horrible afternoon. Actually I do not think that this image represents a matter of realistic interpretation at all but draws its meaning from a different and more hidden context. For this context, we must first turn to an altogether different series of representations.

A few years before *Guernica,* in 1934, Picasso created a number of very interesting compositions dealing with bullfights. In these the bull has turned aggressor, a cruelly wounded horse is the victim. Interest focuses entirely on this group. Usually, the arena is shown rather dimly, but in some instances certain large faces in profile, apparently of women, detach themselves from the background as they bend forward to follow the scene of slaughter more closely with a mien of earnest if somewhat factual scrutiny, not unlike the tense attention with which the physicians in Rembrandt's painting follow the demonstrations of Dr. Tulp. In one case only a single onlooker, holding a burning candle, is so shown, but she seems to shy away with an expression of sudden disgust[4] [fig. 108]. These compositions culminate in the *Minotauromachy* of 1935, perhaps Picasso's most important etching [fig. 165]. From the bull ring the scene has been transferred to a mythological setting, near a seashore and a tower. The bull has become half humanized, in the form of a Minotaur looming darkly above the doomed horse, which, curiously enough, he attacks with the sword of a *toreador.* But the onlookers have not been omitted. Two rather pretty young women observe the mythological nightmare from the window of the tower. The third is a child: a little girl. She stands near the scene of horror, which she watches intently yet without any outward signs of fear. In her raised left hand she, also, holds a burning candle. The connection between all these fantasies is obvious; so is the fact that they have a bearing on the *Guernica* mural.

We cannot here discuss the bullfight scenes in full; the bullfight, after all, is a separate subject inviting many different thoughts. But a few remarks are in order, especially about the way in which, in these compositions, reality becomes transformed. The series starts with a live situation, the arena. It ends with a situation which seems half myth, half dream. Yet in spite of all transformations the main themes remain constant. The group of the horse and the bull renders an act of brutality committed, it appears at first, in the name of a bullfight; but it is treated eventually as a subject in its own right. This group carries many and far-reaching connotations, implying among other characteristics a contrast of sex. It has been stated by others, and I think correctly, that in these compositions the horse is associated with feminine attributes.[5] For instance in the *Minotauromachy* the horse carries on its back the lifeless figure of a female matador. It is of course entirely possible to describe the brutal power of will as an essentially masculine, at the same time destructive, quality, and to assume that by contrast suffering is the fate of women and of the passive. This statement of the case indeed reconfirms a polarity of classical conception, built into the core of many Greek tragedies in which a comparable contrast provides the mainspring of action. To name only one instance, it certainly is not incidental that in Sophocles' drama the king, Creon, is a man, Antigone a woman. On the other hand the very realism of the tragic concept itself must warn us that no single statement of this kind can possess ultimate validity. The unwillingness to love is likely to turn into hatred at any time, with any individual. In Euripides' *Bacchae* the king becomes the slain victim and the bull-god is on the side of the frenzied women.

Be this as it may, a knowledge of Picasso's bullfight compositions provides us

4. [Brendel also notes Zervos VIII: 212; other examples in *Picasso 1980,* pp. 314–15 and 318.]

5. D. E. Schneider, "The Painting of Pablo Picasso: A Psychoanalytic Study," *College Art Journal* VII (1947–48), pp. 86 ff. [See also Larrea, p. 284, above.]

with a most valuable background for his *Guernica* painting. The least we can now say is that clearly these earlier compositions, which seem so fraught with private meaning, set the standard of the imagery and determined the broad scope of thought and feeling, which *Guernica* transformed into a more monumental style and a more public manifestation. We become acquainted with the interdependence of the members of the symbolic group of bull, horse, and onlooker. And we are led to recognize the same protagonists also in the *Guernica* painting, although there the bull is not visibly the aggressor and the horse was wounded by a weapon from above. True symbols have a long life and, like dreams, fit many different situations. In this sense I should say that in *Guernica,* the woman with the lamp replaces the onlooker of the former compositions. She fulfills much the same functions. Even stylistically, in the context of *Guernica,* she is an exception. If we compare her face to other details of the same painting it looks as if conceived in a different key. The reason is, obviously, that it was cast in a classical form, alien to the rest of the composition. With mouth wide open, eyes large with horror, this woman herself resembles an ancient masque of tragedy more than an ordinary, living face. Around her all creatures suffer, but hers is the only face in which, over and above the terror, we read a reaction of reason: powerless, certainly, like her useless lamp, but still expressing a certain energy of judgment, of sorrow, of outrage. The event which she witnesses is a moment of panic, turmoil beyond comprehension. Yet as an onlooker, however much involved in what she sees, as far as her stern unflinching gaze surveys the scenes of slaughter she remains a stranger to the event. She takes the part of the Chorus in a Greek tragedy, who can by the same token be described as an onlooker. It is an interesting fact that for this one face, Picasso chose the grand and, to our contemporary world, alien manner of a classic style.[6]

Yet the idea of the classic presents quite diverse facets to the modern artist, as we remarked earlier in this essay. And the other aspects of the problem have not been forgotten in the *Guernica* painting. * * * One rather curious circumstance is the fact that almost all the victims represented in the *Guernica* are women. Again in this selection the painting need not be taken literally—as if there had been no men in the town of Guernica. Rather the seemingly one-sided emphasis on the women followed quite logically from the previously established symbolism of the wounded horse which, as we have seen, with its markedly feminine overtones set the keynote also for the *Guernica* painting. There is only one obvious exception to the rule, and this quite characteristically consists in a figure which did not originally belong to the symbolic group of the horse and the Minotaur: namely, the prostrate warrior. The idea of this figure can be traced to the earlier sketches, but its form went through numerous metamorphoses. In its final shape it was reduced to three large fragments: a left arm with open palm, a head, and, severed from both, a right arm clutching a broken sword. Perhaps not without intent we are left in doubt as to whether these fragments ever belonged to a live person. They may have; but especially the arm with the sword, by way of a grim paradox, also reminds us of the academic plaster casts.

6. It appears that the woman with the lamp in the *Guernica* painting has her antecedents primarily in French neoclassic art; especially the figure of Nemesis in Ingres' *L'Apothéose de Napoléon Ier* and preparatory sketches. * * *

A bent arm, drawn from plaster, can be found among Picasso's earliest academic exercises from La Coruña.[7] Later, plaster arms appear as studio equipment occasionally combined with a sculptured head, in a series of still lifes culminating in the rather temperamental "studio" of Juan les Pins, painted during the summer of 1925 [fig. 105]. They now look decidedly threatening, carrying a stick or clenching their fists. But they also make us realize what strange objects they really are, torn limbs rendered harmless only by the deadly pallor of their plaster existence. * * * In one of the early drawings for *Guernica*, likewise, the prostrate warrior wears a Greek helmet, thus resembling a statue toppled over rather than a real person [fig. 6]. In the final painting only the three disconnected fragments of this figure have remained. But their association with the world of the academic plaster casts can now hardly be overlooked. They look like casts, especially the head and the arm with the broken sword. Yet if indeed they carry these connotations, it also seems that they are viewed here with rather more sympathy than previously: they form so clearly a part of the epoch which perished on that fateful afternoon of spring, 1937. The arm has lost its authoritarian terror. The sword which it wielded, academic or otherwise, has proved a sadly obsolete weapon against the airplane.

After the victims, the victor. The bull has entered from the left, and now casts his cold attentive glances over the field of destruction. Obviously this bull, also, is no ordinary animal. His presence in the *Guernica* painting had been planned from the start, and the earlier sketches place him right in the center of the composition, near or above the horse. On the other hand, his form and attitude change continually in the many preliminary studies. Only one important characteristic remains constant. The head always appears more or less humanized. But even if it is entirely human, its expression and character differ from drawing to drawing. In one drawing it looks bearded, stupid, and somewhat brooding, as if its animal dullness had been translated into a human form [fig. 21]. Again in another drawing it appears youthful and noble; in still others, hideously monstrous [figs. 23 and 29]. In the final version the animal form has prevailed, but in such a manner as to leave on the face a semblance of human expression, as of cruelty and triumph. The overall evidence thus permits no doubt that the bull here is only half animal, that to an extent he has become personified if not fully humanized; in short, that he belongs to the large family of Picasso's Minotaurs.

The importance and frequency of the Minotaur theme in the art of Picasso between 1933 and 1937 constitutes a most remarkable fact. As a general rule mythological subjects are extremely rare in modern art after the Impressionists. Science has no room for myths. * * *

The Minotaur was a monster of Greek mythology, shaped as a man with a bull's head. Therefore, his every appearance, in a work of modern art, constitutes in itself a revival of an ancient symbol, regardless of whether or not the interpretation agrees with the ancient myth. Obviously the role which the Minotaur plays in the art of Picasso is a matter of considerable interest, for this special reason: it opens up a new aspect, not so far mentioned here, of the contemporary awareness of the classical. For in this instance the question is not of the merits or demerits, as the case may be, of the classical as a critical category and a mode of form, nor of the academic plaster

---

7. [Brendel illustrates a pencil drawing of 1893–94; Zervos, *Dessins*, No. 4.]

casts and their function or lack of function in a living art. Instead the problem of the classical moves here into the focus of modern discussion by way of a third category, not as form but as content. * * *

And as a rule this content runs counter to a benevolent, optimistic interpretation. The Greek tragedies with all their lucid formal order do not tell pretty things. They deal with crimes, failures, and suffering; indeed with the inevitability of crime, failure, and suffering. They were the consummate expression of that realism inherent in all Greek thought. As gradually during the past two centuries more Greek literature became known and the myths were studied more perceptively, the result was inevitable. Much was unearthed from the very core of the classical heritage which could not meet the test of Olympian serenity, nor of Apollonian reason; which, by these standards, could hardly be called classical. This split within the explanations of the classical itself, caused by a more intimate knowledge and a more realistic appraisal of the classical contents, appears to have been of considerable importance for modern thought. It certainly accompanied, and even preceded, the non-academic and anti-neoclassic trends of the nineteenth-century romanticism and realism. I am inclined to assume that the early discovery of the unclassic elements in ancient daemonology or, in other words, the unclassical character of much classical lore, had its share in the formation of these trends; that is to say, of modernism.

But now to return to the Minotaur and Picasso. The monster of Greek mythology lived in a dark and devious cave called the Labyrinth, on the island of Crete. Each year a group of young people was sent to him from Athens and held captive in the cave. One year the prince, Theseus, was among them. He slew the monster and freed the captives with the help of a Cretan princess, Ariadne, who followed Theseus on his way home but was deserted by him on the island of Naxos. The story of the group of young people, the year's crop, as it were, being sent to a dark cave has anthropological parallels in other continents. On the other hand, the legend of the deserted princess who then became the bride of a god, Dionysos, seems to belong to a different, less primitive level of thought and feeling. However the fusion of these two motives into one single story may be taken as a rather typical example of the often irrational foundations, the age-old fantasies on which rested Greek intellectualism. The Greek mind remained forever sensitive to the store of symbolism which in these ancient tales stayed so peculiarly alive. Moderns were no less attracted by them whenever they realized that many truths can be expressed more fully, and certainly more compactly, in the seeming impossibilities of an ancient symbol than by discursive reason. The myth has always retained its high place in poetic content, in spite of the fact that it is conventional matter, or perhaps precisely because of that circumstance. It invites new interpretations continually. * * *

In 1933 Picasso drew a Minotaur for the cover of a then new magazine, entitled *Le Minotaure* [fig. 114]. It is obvious that the theme began to interest him very much. During the same year and the years immediately following, quite a few other representations of it appear in his works, mostly drawings and prints. The etching of the *Minotauromachy* was created in 1935. Soon afterward, in the years 1936 and 1937, he executed the splendid series of Minotaur compositions which still represents easily the most comprehensive, as well as the most interesting, treatment of an ancient mythical content in modern art.[8] None of these compositions tells literally a known

8. Frequently illustrated. [For recent reproductions, see *Picasso 1980*, pp. 334–35; color illustrations in *Marina Picasso 1981*, Nos. 171 and 187.]

story. On the contrary, each is a free fantasy. Yet together these fantasies form a chain of variations on a common mythical theme. We may well call them a series of *Capricci,* borrowing the term from Tiepolo and Goya. They possess the extravagance and obscure reality of dreams, and as in dreams, one thinks to perceive among the incredible happenings familiar elements: the elements of myth. There is the veiled bride, an apparition unattainable. There are moments of peril and rescue; the sea, the boat, and the departure. There is, in addition, the Minotaur. He moves through these visions as a hero of fiction moves through the passing situations of a novel. The novel in this case is a rather surrealistic one, to be sure, and he a dark hero, an infinitely threatening image composed of animal powers paired with a human will; but while he causes terror and suffering, he also suffers. Once we see him before his cave, carrying a limp and frightened horse.[9] The images of bull and Minotaur, Man-Bull and Bull-Man, have merged into one; and again the horse is the substitute victim of his violence. However, the theme is capable of variations. It happens that the horse escapes and the Amazon with it; or that in anguish, its body bursting, it becomes transformed into the benign bearded form of the rescuer raising the strong protective arm, which we also know.[10] There seems to be no end to the flow of images and their strange amalgamations. A mythical content, originally Greek, has thus been explored, and the myth found endless. Certainly the interpretations are new and arbitrary. But while the academic concepts and traditional classicism are bursting in their seams, something else instead emerges: the enduring truth, the protean life, and perhaps most important, the inherent realism of mythical symbols. This truth, this realism are always present, and their resurrection in a personal experience can happen at any time: *quod erat demonstrandum.*

When in the *Guernica* painting the Man-Bull enters, his presence remains unexplained; neither does it explain anything in the painting, expressly. Nevertheless its impact on the composition is very great. It entirely alters the tenor of meaning in the painting, revealing more clearly than any other detail the essentially symbolic, not episodic character of the latter. For now we know the violence of the bull and the blind rage of his destructive will. We have come to understand that since pure will must impose itself, its triumphs become moments of destruction. We are made to see that this is the hour when the Bull feasts on his triumph, and that he has come to survey the work completed which, as in the tragic paradox of a Greek drama, was the work of Necessity operating through human wills. The horse still is his victim. Beyond these obvious connotations, derived from the image itself and the context of Picasso's own art, I should not suggest a more definite name or denotation for the bull. Any such suggestion would be mere guesswork, and I doubt that much could be gained by it. For instance we may name this an image of war, or as Henry Kahnweiler did, of the invincible Spanish people.[11] Clearly in inventing definitions of this kind we have entered into an area where, as the road signs say, everyone travels at his own risk. The truth is that with a symbol connotations often matter more than denotations, because the same group of thought associations can fit quite diverse names and circumstances in reality. What matters first of all is the image which we

---

9. [Brendel illustrates *Minotaur and Dead Mare before a Grotto,* 6 May 1936; see *Picasso 1980,* p. 334, and color reproduction in *Picasso, Paris 1979,* p. 279, or *London 1981,* p. 98.]

10. Zervos, *Dessins,* fig. 125.

11. [Kahnweiler, reprinted p. 220, above.]

see, and all possible names which one might devise can be true only as analogies of that image. They would, in the present case, only denote different instances of actuality in which the power of the Minotaur can be recognized. He himself requires no other name.

What must rather interest us is the fact itself which is beyond reasonable doubt, that a symbol of this kind, namely a mythical character in all its unmitigated strangeness, was here introduced into the representation of a real, contemporary event. Such mythical symbolism is very nearly unheard of in modern art. The symbol itself was old, of primitive, even prehistoric origin. Even the Greek Minotaur is only one of its later, mythical incorporations. Newborn children were sacrified to another, the Phoenician Moloch. One remembers the distorted figure of the mother with the dead child, so placed before the bull in the *Guernica* painting as to form almost a group with him, although the one hardly notices the other. We know of bull-masks in primitive dances, and of highly complex impersonations of the bull-god, like the Greek Dionysos, in whom the good and the perilous aspects of the creative passion have become so unaccountably united. There is, over and above the known mythological connotations, the ambiguous part which the bull plays in the severely ordered drama of the Spanish bull-games, now a hero, and then again a dark and deadly enemy.[12] The life of a symbol feeds on the associations with which we connect it, yet mutely it contains them all, as if they were so many foregone conclusions. Thus the myth must teach us that the world of primitive experience is not excluded from the classical but absorbed by it, as the living organism absorbs nourishment. It is very likely that the Man-Bull in the *Guernica* painting had Hellenic antecedents but he certainly also stems from other, less classic ancestors. This is not the only instance where by accepting mythological images into his art, Picasso seems to have discovered for himself the primitive roots of a classical content.

There remains for us to say a word about style. In a work of art, style and meaning affect each other mutually; they are inseparable. In the *Guernica* painting, also, the use of symbolic imagery is a matter of style as much as of content. It is equally unusual on either level, if compared to the prevailing habits of modern art where even symbolism is likely to be expressed in common and natural rather than mythical images. The formal composition of the painting itself is very interesting. It is oblong yet centered, as are many monumental compositions of ancient art. Thus even the formal order carries classical overtones, and produces comparable results. The effect is a certain static monumentality seemingly in contradiction to the vehement movements in which it becomes established, thereby creating a strong feeling of formal tension. Needless to say, with Picasso, any reference to other art or a certain manner of style, no less than references to nature, must undergo radical formal transformations. For the creation of images at which his art is aiming is not compatible with copying, nor is the creation of a picture the same as "composition." Yet from the severe isolation of forms and fragments of forms, which characterizes this style, and from the transformations which permit these shapes to enter into a purely compositional context, the images draw their peculiar strength. Their test of truth is the degree to which they become memorable. The symbolic selection of the images, suggesting possible rather than representing actual meanings, enhances this

12. Marrero, pp. 32 ff. [See also p. 173, above.]

effect. One may doubt if any more episodic approach, in the manner of a journalistic report, could have served the purpose as well. It is remarkable how many elements which one might deem essential have been omitted from this representation. Not a single airplane appears in it. Indeed the electric street lamp in its unrelieved bareness is the most modern thing in the entire painting. Obviously the mechanics of the destruction do not matter here, only their human causes. Yet it is precisely this transforming selection that lifts the accident from the plane of an episodic record of a deplorable event to the level of thought where the event reveals another, paradigmatic meaning. No more common imagery could have given the same effect of concise monumentality. The *Guernica* painting by Picasso is not only an artistic reflection on a given subject matter. It is also a reflection on art itself.

Darby Bannard

Bannard brings a painter's insights and sensibilities to his art criticism.[1] He considers *Guernica* a "culture-hero painting" that "is *liked* for the wrong reasons," while its faults are glaring, discussable, and hardly ever taken into account."[2] In these excerpts from two longer articles, Bannard courageously tackles *Guernica*'s "structural weakness," its problems with "touch and scale"—while admiring the related drawings and etchings (a view not exceptional among contemporary painters and critics). He concludes that Jackson Pollock and his generation succeeded where Picasso had failed and "took Cubist style up to a very large scale."

How Guernica Fails:
Applied Cubism—[1968]*

Early Cubism required the incising, cutting stroke made by a small brush, loaded with paint, worked by the wrist and fingers. In this way it kept some of the sensuality of oil paint as a hedge against its radical intent. But large scale Cubist painting, until Abstract Expressionism, *excluded* paint handling of this kind because the wrist-finger

1. Born 1931, Bannard attended William Seitz's informal studio classes at Princeton University, and was included in Clement Greenberg's color-field painting exhibition of 1964, "Post-Painterly Abstraction." At the time that he won a Guggenheim Fellowship and National Foundation of the Arts Award for painting in 1968–69, he also was teaching, lecturing, and writing criticism for *Artforum*.

2. Letter of 7 June 1974 to ECO; he admitted twice criticizing *Guernica* in lectures "and got roundly hissed each time."

*From "Cubism, Abstract Expressionism, David Smith" *Artforum* VI (April 1968), pp. 24–25, by permission of author and publisher.

technique was inadequate for the size. When Cubist painting got big, then the "pieces" got big. When the pieces got big, they had to be filled with paint; and so they were, with flat, evenly painted areas, pieces cut with a saw, not a knife. When the Cubists painted big they gave up the vigor of early Cubism, and went to what I called "applied" Cubism, that is, the use of the forms developed by early Cubism, laid down, straightened out, and filled evenly with paint—Cubism used on its own terms, and not as a means of abstraction. ∗ ∗ ∗ To make a painting like *Guernica* as large as he wanted it, Picasso was forced (or so he thought) to make it out of large flat pieces that would have to be built from scratch, because they could not be made quickly by a few strokes of the brush, as was possible on a smaller scale. For Picasso this meant taking on a liability; it meant that he could not "handle" the materials, and Picasso's brilliance is in his hands. He usually has trouble with large scale, and he is always best when his *touch* is most directly involved, for example, his drawings and etchings, and some of his sculpture and ceramics. Even the great early Cubist paintings are very tactile, like clay bas-reliefs. Also, Picasso has trouble with conception, with thinking something out, and a mural-size painting must be planned with great care and a regard for the dynamics of scale. He never had this quality of thought, and I think it is one thing which has led him into failure in his later years. Even the early Cubist paintings were not really *thought out;* they were produced by an intense and aggressive visual imagination, by doing rather than thinking. *Guernica* is about 25 feet long, way beyond the reach of any means of touch or stroke available to Picasso, and he was not the radical of 1910, ready to fall back on his visual intuition to solve art-making problems. Besides, he was not thinking visually, he was thinking about non-art things. The bombing of Guernica was a big thing for him, so he decided to make a big painting of it. To make this painting, with the equipment he had available to him, he had to *apply* Cubism, to build the painting out of Cubist building blocks. There was very little *invented* for *Guernica;* the painting was unsupported by anything brought in as new.

When Cubist "pieces" are enlarged and painted flat they get *hollow* and *thin.* This is because big flat things, seen in space in depth, look hollow and thin, like paper, cut lumber or tabletops. Picasso could have enlarged his *stroke* to fit the scale confronting him, but that did not occur to him. Instead he went ahead and built the painting out of thin sheets, blew it up, like a slide projector would, without the support of color—thin means indeed to carry the strength of his feeling, which the painting was designed to express. Picasso tried to paint a huge painting by extending small-painting technique. It did not work because he was not willing to make the accommodations to scale that his style demanded. *Guernica* remains a pathetic monument, impressive for its huge size and for the "human content" which flickers over its surface, through the desperate overstatement.

The drawings and small studies for *Guernica* were typical of what Picasso could do well. A drawing for something demands more gesture than thought, and is small, "handleable," and normally without color. Picasso could sit down with a soft pencil or crayon, the paper half an arm's length away, and quickly draw some of the figures, moving swiftly from one to the other, sometimes without lifting the crayon from the paper. Cubism stood in the background, coming forward now and then to correct and adjust, maintaining its discipline while hidden, like the director of a play.

Abstract Expressionism did not spring from these drawings; its roots were widespread. However, as Abstract Expressionism grew and developed, it *looked* like these drawings, and expressively they were cousins. Abstract Expressionism simply added scale, and, less important, color; it expanded the size of the Cubist painting, and developed a method of painting consistent with this expanded size. *Guernica* fails, in part, because it is a mammoth painting done with small-scale means.

How Guernica Fails:
Touch and Scale—[1971]*

Apparently the only way to use Cubism in very large scale, retaining full touch, is to alter the terms of the style, as Pollock did, or one step further, as Olitski has. It may be possible to take Cubism up to very large scale by deliberately excluding touch; perhaps it could be shown that this is what Newman and Noland have done, but their styles are so rid of Cubist effect that it would be stretching a point. The great example of the misapplication of very large size to the Cubist style is the famous *Guernica*, which I have discussed before [excerpt above] and which I pick on not because it is any worse as art than many other bad, oversize Cubist paintings but because it is such a perfect example by way of its many extreme exaggerations, particularly size and theatricality, because it is so familiar to so many, and because of all paintings of this century it is specially, in a very modern way, *meretricious*.

In making *Guernica* Picasso applied the mechanics of original Cubism doggedly. The composition is carefully controlled, centered and made symmetrical, darks and lights are pushed to extremes to provide "air" for over-and-under connection, hue difference is abolished, all edges are Cubistically modified—everything in the Cubist bag of tricks is ground into the picture to force coherence on the huge surface. But as so often happens in art-making, perspiration and inspiration don't mix. The painting fails in two ways, one depending on the other: it fails structurally, and, partly as a result of the structural failure, it fails expressively. *Guernica* should be the casebook example of the misunderstanding of the demands of large scale and of the failure of theatricality to overcome pictorial weakness.

Guernica is built on the terms of original Cubism, so an analysis of its structural weakness bears comparison with the strength of the earlier style. Though simultaneous in creation, fundamental coherence seems not to be a factor of quality; it appears, at least to the intellect, to *support* the spirit or quality of a painting, and be necessary for it, but it never guarantees it. Coherence is visual *gestalt*, the rendering of a surface so that the surface has sufficient visual integrity to seem plausible as a picture. * * * Cubism evolved a method of picture-making which guaranteed immediate visual coherence, not only by rendering the insides of the painting in terms of the edge, which is the strongest factor of design of the rectangular canvas, and by the resulting interconnection of line, but also by following through with

*Reprinted from "Touch and Scale: Cubism, Pollock, Newman, and Still," *Artforum* IX (June 1971), pp. 61–63, by permission.

everything else, forcing everything into conformity with design-by-edge. For a comparison with *Guernica,* it is necessary to see original Cubism as a style of *compression.* If in the process of evolution Cubism seems analytic, "reducing" realist depiction to a simplified alphabet of forms, its spirit, the force behind it, aimed for complexity, density and richness so muscular and opaque that we can only conclude that the "bones" of the Cubist style came up not as pictorial end products but as a support for the immense superstructure of inspiration. The original Cubist picture holds a concentrated intensity which, unlike most Impressionist paintings, is immediate because there are no distractions, no overlay of nicety. (This is not a value judgment; the fresh, easy "blanket" of perfect realism of the Impressionist painting is a fine part of its quality.) All other attributes of the Cubist painting succumbed to this force, conformed to it, and by their disposition are the record of the path it took, as the fossil is the evidence of past life. The picture stayed small, as a kind of tight "belt," to force formal integration; it stayed (usually) vertical because our habits of seeing, derived from the facts of gravity and materials, let us assume that a vertical *construction* has more integral strength than a horizontal one. As the surface evolved into abstraction, figures were cut up into Cubist units because the conformation of real objects did not fit the Cubist scheme, until finally subject matter itself—guitars, bottles, glasses, pipes—was chosen for its Cubist-like formal regularity. The illusion of depth was shallow, extending only enough for the necessary connection-to-the-center; the painting was massed at the center. The subject was "destroyed" to bring it in line with demands made by the picture; touch, the quick electric dots and dashes, the rough and ready shading and over-painting allowed so easily on a surface small enough to show the quick work of the wrist and fingers—Picasso's strength—was the final forceful flourish of the Cubist painting. *Guernica,* though it uses the elements of design and the forms of original Cubism as a foundation, reflects none of the pictorial attributes given to the Cubist picture as the style evolved. This does not prove that *Guernica* is failed art—the proof is in the pudding, of course—but tracing these things in the huge painting helps us see the failure of coherence, helps us feel, finally, the failure of the whole. *Demonstrating* the integral weakness of *Guernica* is easy enough; take a reproduction of the painting and fold it in half vertically—you will see that either half is compositionally stronger than the full painting. Folding it in half vertically again yields four compositions, each stronger than the halves [fig. 159].[3]

Compared to the original Cubist painting, excepting touch, the immediate internal difference seen in *Guernica* is expansion and dispersal, the immediate external difference size and horizontality. The forms and constructive methods remain pretty much the same. We see, then, that an art-making method devised to handle the overloading and compression of original Cubism will not meet the needs of a very large mural-like space. The structural failure of original Cubism in the scale of *Guernica* is failure of connectivity, a problem Pollock later solved by altering the Cubist method to eliminate the things which stood in the way of expansion. Picasso correctly saw that the paper-thin space of the small Cubist picture would not work for a huge one because the parts would come up flat against the surface and render the

3. [Or see this book's cover.]

painting incoherent, so he pushed back the background and brought up the foreground by the use of extreme, almost black-white, value differences. But he kept the flat forms of original Cubism; the same forms which squeeze, shuffle and jockey about in the pinched space of the original Cubist picture are blown up, pulled apart and cast into the airy, barn-like interior of *Guernica*. The depth was needed to set the painting up rigid, like a box, but the figures do not have volume adequate for it. They inhabit the space like cardboard characters in a stage set. It seems a shame that *Guernica* was not actually constructed, rather than painted;[4] the use of real space would have brought out Picasso's gift for sculpture, and would have avoided the weakness he has usually shown for large painting. Though these figures inhabit the same painted space there is not enough pictorial connection between them. The composition is muralized; they are dispersed horizontally, as real figures would be, but they lack the automatic relationship of volumetric figures in deep space because their substance is all surface, and this surface is all offered frontally. The sense of

159. *Guernica* divided in half; divided in quarters

4. [See Hohl's discussion of *Guernica* as drama (pp. 317–20), or Enrico Baj's huge and partly three-dimensional construction, fig. 136A.]

dispersal with inadequate connection is heightened by the individuality of the figures, each with its own form and place, and by the extreme difference of character between the picture-edge and the figure-edge, which frustrates the edge composition which is the organizing principle of the Cubist style. The massing of incident, so much a part of the original Cubist picture, which counted so much for coherence, is just about impossible for the muralized canvas, which must have individuation, discrete scenes and the horizontality to accommodate these scenes. (The few horizontal original Cubist pictures were severely massed at the center, and I can recall one or two of the later collages which were horizontal *and* dispersed.) The free, floating figures are too flimsy and spread out to give convincing structure to the picture. Like a bridge too long for its supports, *Guernica* buckles despite the contrived, flaccid, central pyramid. Its component lines switch from figure to background with no objective reason, and they are loose and rubbery because, in the spirit of the "hand-made" work of art, they have not been measured off.

It might be answered, to all I have said about *Guernica*, that all this is not really important—why not take it simply as a mural, forget all the problems of structure and let the "emotion" of the painting come across. Well, a painting must push itself into existence as a painting, and if it doesn't it fails. Nevertheless, the expressive failure of *Guernica*, even if it could be taken separately from its structural failure, is more directly felt and is more tragic, and has more of the quality of meretriciousness than that structural failure. Feeling is the proclaimed point of *Guernica*, and it is in feeling that its failure is most poignant. The picture lacks touch, the mark of the brush, at least from proper viewing distance, and touch is what carries such liveliness into original Cubism, and gives such vitality to the small realist or semi-realist works of Picasso, especially the drawings and etchings, and, ironically, the studies "for" *Guernica*, many of which were done *after* the large painting.[5] *Guernica* lacks touch because of scale; it is simply too large to show the wrist-and-finger work of the compact Cubist picture. The huge size of the painting also makes the figures look plotted and deliberate. These are not the distortions forced by the impacting pressure of Cubist invention, but are applied, partly to keep in line with the style borrowed for use in this unfamiliar territory, partly to echo the horror of the event commemorated by the painting. The unfortunate effect is that of vulgar cartooning. The bright lamp at the top of the picture, for example, gives off a jagged body of light just like a "kaboom" in a war comic. The grotesquerie advertises itself, calls attention literally, saying "I am wounded, I am screaming, I am contorted by grief." But the emotion is not felt, unless supplied by the imagination and knowledge of the viewer, because the forms are not adequate to convey it. The figures are posed, the emotion is applied, the effect is false.

As an artist I can feel the frustration Picasso must have known painting *Guernica*. I can almost taste it in some of the small sketches made during and after the work on the painting. He was stymied, and he scrawled these beautiful drawings not as studies but as a kind of "working out," as a dream works out the frustrations of the day. Here the bewilderment at the failure imposed by scale comes up raw and biting as Picasso feels the power of his hand and eye. But as a critic I must point to

---

5. [Bannard was thinking of *Weeping Woman* variations created after *Guernica* was completed, such as figs. 58–62, 65–67, and 74, or the much-admired drawing of 28 May (fig. 42) made well after the mother-and-child motif had been outlined on the canvas itself.]

the failure of invention which plagued Picasso in large scale despite the incredible ambition he turned to painting and the genuine feelings he wanted to bring to the world through his art. *Guernica* stands as a triumph of empty theatricality over pictorial quality. Go any time to the Museum of Modern Art to see the reverent group before the painting, or read its praises in a dozen books, then go see the empty floor before another mural-size painting—Monet's *Water Lilies*—which is as fine and true in feeling as *Guernica* is coarse and dissembling.

About 10 years after *Guernica* was painted, Jackson Pollock became the artist who successfully took the Cubist style up to very large scale.

Joseph Masheck
Grandeur Mobilized—[1967 and 1981]*

This irreverent view of *Guernica* began as a lecture for the Graduate Art History Union of Columbia University where Joseph Masheck was a 25-year-old student. Since completing his Ph.D., he has taught art history at Columbia University, Barnard College, and Harvard University. Author of numerous articles on contemporary art and contributing editor of *Artforum* magazine, Masheck has published *Duchamp in Perspective* (1974) and *Historical Present: Essays of the 1970s* (UMI Research Press, 1984).

In Memoriam: Rudolf Wittkower (1901–1971)

Sweeping and passionate though it obviously is, Picasso's *Guernica* may seem too familiar to be really disturbing, yet too disturbing to be simply beautiful. A rust of obviousness obscures it from view. The painting, only some 40 years old and as polemical as a poster, has altogether blatant "meaning." So, instead of working out iconographical crossword puzzles, let us look at the picture and reflect upon it broadly, here and now (during the war in Vietnam) and in relation to the Grand-Manner tradition of moral and artistic sublimity.

We approach the work with what, for a modern painting, is a curious awe, which cannot be for its colossal size alone—thanks, since, to Abstract Expressionism, not to mention the monumental painting of earlier times. This must be a largely intellectual respect, however worthy the object remains visually, though for *Guernica* to have taken on even the antiquarian dignity of grand history painting is hardly inappropriate. As a result, however, we may fail to acknowledge the true historicism, however radical, of the work itself. We can be so ready to concede to *Guernica* traditional rank and glory that we overlook its active revision of tradition, whether or not such a categorical superstructure can still justify artistic merit. More plainly,

*Condensed and revised by the author for this anthology from *Guernica* as Art History," *Art News* LXVI (December 1967), pp. 32–35, 65–68.

this is an overexposed image: *Guernica,* the modern *Mona Lisa,* is used as *the* stock artistic illustration of modern culture.[1]

Why, then, should *Guernica* seem passé, and is that all bad? The picture engages the collapse of individual, chivalric combat as a modern possibility. It testifies to the end of heroism and mercy, virtue and glory, as possibilities once as real in warfare as suffering and death, and to the beginning of a kind of war, newly re-barbarized, in which the only passions are whatever sufferings engineering and chemistry can inflict—regressive wars where noncombatants die in random groups and the dignity of a personal death is denied even to the soldier. In this sense, *Guernica* seems rightly passé, partaking of a dignified nostalgia. But we, now, a hardened audience, find Picasso's image neutralized in typicality: Guernica might as well have been a village in Vietnam, as seen, live, on television. Hence the Grand-Manner treatment of its subject can seem forced or idiomatically outmoded, like a symphony orchestra condescendingly playing jazz.

So, too, if *Guernica* resembles a newspaper photograph, "black-and-white" and pictorially brash, Andy Warhol has in the meantime taught us about our passivity before the spectacle of industrialized brutality with his "Death in America" paintings of the mid-1960s: *29 Die* monumentalizes a tabloid front page showing a plane crash; *Electric Chair,* 1965, also based on a newspaper image, shows that device as unabashedly as any gadget (Warhol also silk-screened it on T-shirts). This is the spirit in which *Guernica* may seem "uncool": whereas Warhol ironizes complacency itself, *Guernica* is traditional in conveying high moral chagrin.

Obviously I am not handling this picture in the usual (worshipful) way. Instead of rehearsing yet again the series of preparatory sketches, and the photographs by Dora Maar of the work in the stages of its execution, I would rather examine some of the painting's major motives from a fresh historical viewpoint. The historical strength of such explication, of course, depends on manifest visual conviction and appropriateness, even as, from the modern side, past culture reveals itself less as a debt than as an inheritance.

In *Guernica* the power of war (Mars) and death *(thanatos)* entirely dominates the spirit of life (Venus, *eros,* maternal instinct).[2] Like Picasso's painting, in this regard, is a great composition by Rubens (in two nearly identical versions), *The Consequences of War,* 1637–38 [fig. 160; also p. 87, note 70, above], where the allegorical theme is precisely the domination of Mars's over Venus's power—a vision of discord and cultural destruction that is the antithesis of anything like, say, Mars and Venus United by Love. Two ideal figures, Mars and Venus, personifying war and love, occupy the central zone of Rubens's *Consequences* (as in *Guernica,* rather left of center), accompanied by their more naturalistic counterparts, a man who seems more beastly than martial and a woman almost silly under the sway of love. This makes for a progression in four intensities from left to right that is not unlike the

1. Lawrence Ferlinghetti satirized the sanctimonious fame often bestowed on *Guernica* in a funny poem, "Special Clearance Sale of Famous Masterpieces," in his *Starting from San Francisco* (San Francisco, 1961).

2. An astrologer, Roger Parris, noted the cosmic situation at the time of the Guernica bombing, on 26 April 1937 at 4:30 P.M. Briefly, Taurus (a feminine sign, and that of Hitler, whose horoscope was widely published in the 1930s) was opposed to Scorpio (the sign of Spain and Picasso both), and the horoscope showed even less chance of survival than that of Hiroshima under attack; everything, Venus especially, was subject to Mars. On revivals of astrology as symptomatic of a loss of faith in reason, see Fritz Saxl, "The Revival of Late Antique Astrology," in his *Lectures* (London, 1957), vol. I, pp. 73–84.

306

leftward drift of *Guernica* (might Picasso have known a reversed, engraved version of Rubens's composition?). The progression is expressive, too: the vertical axis of each Rubens figure tilts further to the right as each is successively more under the "sway" of violent impulse. Compare also the woman with upraised arms at the far left of the *Consequences of War* with her counterpart at the far right of *Guernica*. Both take the same dramatic position, emerging from an open door. What is more, they share the same anguish, except that what was once a posture of barest hope, of human supplication, is now like the motor response of an animal facing up at its tormentors (here the unseen Fascist bombers).

While the woman at the open door argues that this part, at least, of Picasso's painting looks back to Rubens, other motives in *Guernica* suggest prototypes that are also significant. I owe to Dustin Rice the idea that there is a relation between the horse and fallen warrior in *Guernica* and another (earlier) Baroque painting, Caravaggio's *Conversion of St. Paul*, 1600–1601. The dispositions of the figures correspond, but so does even the spatial complication, in each work, of horse's legs and fallen man. Rudolf Wittkower stressed this very feature of Caravaggio's painting,[3] and the equivalent area of *Guernica* is likewise spatially ambiguous. What does the parallel with Caravaggio imply? According to Rice, the notion of traumatic conversion, the first signs of Picasso's "Conversion" to Communism, in analogy with the conversion of the formerly persecuting Saul (become "Paul") to Christianity. "Pablo," of course, *is* "Paul," and Picasso made the first sketches for *Guernica* on May Day.[4]

160. Peter Paul Rubens. *The Consequences of War*. 1637–38. Oil on canvas, 81 x 135⅞" (206 x 345 cm). Palazzo Pitti, Florence (Alinari Reference Bureau)

3. Rudolf Wittkower, *Art and Architecture in Italy 1600–1750,* 2nd ed. (Baltimore, 1965), p. 26: "It is impossible to tell where the saint's lower right leg would be or how the attendant's legs can possibly be joined to his body." [When the article was written in 1967, Dustin Rice taught art history, and Wittkower was chairman of the department at Columbia University.]

4. For Picasso, Catholic (he was Max Jacob's godfather) and Marxist, to put Christian iconography (St. Paul, the Holy Innocents) at the service of radicalism, has its own Pauline aspect: a Jew himself, St. Paul argued (*Acts* 15) that gentile converts should not be obliged to conform to Jewish Law.

Significantly, the theme of the Conversion of St. Paul would be given a Marxist interpretation by Brecht—while Eisenstein had already used the bull as an image of human massacre in his first film, *Strike*, 1924.[5] Writing on a *Conversion of St. Paul* by Pieter Brueghel the Elder, Brecht observed, *"The Conversion of Saul*. The fall was from a horse: i.e., the conversion of an upper-class person."[6] *Guernica*, too, may refer to chivalry, for the fallen warrior has the guise of a fractured immortalization or idealization, as, specifically, the broken *statue* of an equestrian figure.[7] As such, it memorializes not one legendary hero but the entire chivalric mode, now fractured, dismembered and reduced to hardly more than archaeological remains.

Another great early Baroque sacred-history painting may help to account even for an otherwise seemingly arbitrary "distortion" in *Guernica*, the form of the woman leaning out the window with a lamp in her hand, which remains close to its original conception from Picasso's first sketch onward. The form itself keeps a firm hold on the imagination, even when we are only remembering the painting. Perhaps, as with the man and horse, it has little to do with "distortion"; again, it may amount to a revivification of an apt motive from past art. For the molten, veritably Surreal, tear-drop-shaped head of this figure recalls a similar woman with her baby under attack in the *Massacre of the Innocents* of Guido Reni, c. 1612 [fig. 98]. The whole form of that head, with its pulled hair and stretched face, is remarkably like the head of Picasso's woman, including painfully expressive eyes and knit brow, the profile of the nose and the open mouth. There could be a whole study of *Guernica* as a Massacre of the Innocents.

As it happens, these various motives all find antecedents in grand moralistic painting of the early 17th century, specifically in certain masterpieces of Counter-Reformation propaganda art (even if this is only one approach to *Guernica*).[8] Yet the splendor of the painting is not borrowed but earned anew, ransomed even: its moral and artistic sublimity is as real as anything in the old Grand Manner, however also ironic is its painfully purgative withdrawal from beauty. Addressing itself to civilized humanity, in particular to lovers of great European art, *Guernica* both qualifies for high respect and also rules out uncritical esthetic satisfaction, subverting bourgeois neutralization as *mere art*—as though crying out to Europe to wake up.

Since *Guernica*, Picasso's painting has affected artists concerned not only with related themes but even with specific artistic qualities of the work, especially its earnest tonal reductiveness. The black-and-white aspect of the picture, *along with its association with the Spanish Civil War*, is thus taken up by Motherwell in his series of abstract *Elegies to the Spanish Republic* [fig. 122]. Jack Youngerman extended the political modernism of Picasso and Motherwell alike with *Elegy for a Guerrilla*, 1965, in which a lyrically individualized abstract figure interacts in give-and-take with its surrounding ground. So sure a place, finally, has Picasso's image in the

5. At the beginning and end of the final sequence of *Strike*, shots of a bull's slaughter are interspliced in montage with shots of a crowd under police attack; see the script excerpted in Sergei Eisenstein, *The Film Sense* (New York, 1947), pp. 234f.

6. Bertolt Brecht, "Alienation Effects in the Narrative Pictures of the Elder Brueghel" (1957), in *Brecht on Theater: The Development of an Aesthetic*, ed. and trans., John Willett (New York, 1964), p. 158. Brecht, a Communist, is said to have died in the arms of the Church.

7. The black-and-whiteness of *Guernica* also resembles traditional *grisaille* painting (all in grays), often used for pictures of sculpture (especially reliefs).

8. Gertrude Stein, in her lively contemporary book on the painter (1938), compares the 20th century with the 17th for its "splendor": *Picasso* (Boston, 1959), pp. 48f.

culture of our age that it is only natural to see it quoted in a peace march poster [figs. 128A and 128B], perfectly in keeping with its original intent and mode.

Whenever we defer to *Guernica* in the passive spirit of monument worship we neglect its own true grandeur, betraying its own radically valid claims on tradition. Even inductively, however, there must be greatness in a painting that so effectively subsumes the past in the service of the future. What more, in the end, can we ask of a work of art than that it move us to feel, to reflect, and to act?

Frank D. Russell
An Epilogue—[1980]*

Here are Russell's concluding pages to his rich study of *Guernica*'s structure, multiple sources, and imagery—observations illustrated with several hundred photographs and diagrams highlighted to make a point, like a cinematic survey or a generously illustrated slide lecture. How does Russell explain *Guernica*'s continuing hold over us? For one, we recognize Picasso's presence and ourselves in *Guernica:* "we find a resonance of strengths and contests within ourselves." And if the painting leaves some critics dissatisfied and uneasy, if it lacks "that unquestionable quality" of earlier masterpieces, "surely it is the uneasiness of the times." Picasso has given us the painting for our age.

Gathering our impressions of a picture we look first to see something of the artist's first and inevitable subject, himself. It is this subject which we have guessed to be stamped across the face of the Guernica like so many Chinese seals, halted in the bull, seizing in the swordbearer and again in the lightbearer. The lightbearer's lamp, the meagre light-maker whose rays are painted nonetheless undiminished into the teeth of a hard daylight—and similarly the scrap which succeeds somehow as a sword, a nothing gripped and extended to shake the world—these may be seen as disguises of that insubstantial weapon of the artist, his brush. Surely it is Picasso who pushes through to us, seen from a certain angle of vision.

The Guernica is of course more than a posting of the artist's likeness. We have sifted rubbles, the remains of histories—we have dug along the outlines of architectures. Yet histories and architectures recede behind some still closer meaning, for the mural clamors through as something more insistent than a clay tablet, or an outline of walls and towers.

---

*Reprinted from *Picasso's Guernica: The Labyrinth of Narrative and Vision*, Montclair, N.J., 1980, pp. 271–75, by permission of author and publisher. Russell's interest in *Guernica* goes back to his school days in the 1930s when he "followed the news from Spain religiously," and found the painting exciting yet puzzling when it first arrived in New York (Oct. 1979 letter to ECO). While teaching at Rutgers University during the 1950s, he began studying *Guernica* both as painter (MFA from Temple University) and historian (MA from the Institute of Fine Arts, NYU). He is professor of art at The Maryland Institute, College of Art.

A headline, an outcry against blood-letting, undoubtedly the picture's orchestration includes that. Yet little is insisted on literally in the way of death, nor is there any death-dealing to be seen; no image of an outward adversary, none to be seen or named.

We see the general image of life in contest with death. Life holds its own; and the agony in the picture, so conspicuous on the surface, goes to force the link between past and future; throughout the mural in its theme of resurrection and in its close fugal organization we see a harmony and a hard logic in the last extremity, and in its gestures, a signaling and handing over of life. And in all of this the Guernica shows us things which we ourselves possess, or hope that we possess. Even the Guernica bull, its brutality and darkness, not fascism but a tragic idleness—an inward adversary—this, too, we can recognize and own. More than a painter's signature, more than an architect's outlines, and more than the catastrophies of the archives, we find a resonance of strengths and contests within ourselves. Here then as in all art which holds and tests our imagination, we see the artist's last and most lasting subject, a portrait of ourselves, made from some difficult interior angle.

"I saw an old peasant standing alone in a field: a machine gun bullet killed him." (Father de Onaindía [see p. 164, above].)

Who was it, after all, that Father de Onaindía saw?

But the poet has reminded us not to ask for whom the bell tolls. No distance can divide us finally from an occurrence such as Guernica, or from the artist's relocations of the old peasant who stands while he can. In each of Picasso's protagonists we see a separateness, each figure "alone in a field," a likeness, if you will, of the human state. Life goes on, but contends with our isolations and our self-destruction. Over and above the sense of external catastrophe we see in the Guernica the tragic exchanges common to all life, the tragedy of mind which is not brought into focus with physical force, and, in the bull, the tragedy of force which is not governed in the mind. How much, then, of all life is tragically summarized in Picasso's picture! In its re-growth out of the mangled roots of histories, in its taking up of scraps and pressing into service of human fragments, surely in this mountain of improvising we discover something of the texture of our own lives, no less than in the architectures which must lend a predestined shape to that texture.

The artist has given us a picture which transcends incident and time, a work whose relevance lies within issues of peace at least as much as within those of war. "If a work of art cannot live always in the present, it must not be considered at all."[1]

Like much challenging art, like life, the Guernica is not apt to stay one thing steadily. We see a piece of ourselves, ourselves stood up roughly and blistered with light—and now all at once something unfamiliar, something merely heroic, distant. All at once no part of our known experience seems any match for it; craning upward, we calculate the authority of the horse, the passion of the bereaved mother, the reach of the warrior's arms. Our own hands remain full of life and of dealings with the middle of it, theirs, with the extremities of life, and with death. A crag towers over us, and yet as with other tragedies and with all intense life, at its most extreme the crag comes down and is again ourselves, newly seen and named, enlarged.

---

1. [Picasso's comment, which Russell had quoted earlier (p. 77); from the famous 1923 interview reprinted by Barr, p. 271, or Ashton, p. 4.]

□   □   □

How enduring a work, then, do we feel Picasso's clifflike monument to be? Hitherto our attitude toward the picture, like that of the majority of its observers, has been what might be called telescopic: scanning towering heights. The Guernica is a towering height, but is telescopic awe the only useful approach to a height?

The future will not lose sight of the Guernica, we are convinced. We look to it to take its place in the mountain ranges of the past. But despite the picture's huge authority, its timeliness, its timelessness, its eloquence and mystery, its relevance to ourselves—despite the things that it is, at occasional intervals there intrudes for many of us an uneasiness, an uncomfortable rattling as of stray pebbles slipping from the summit. Why, for instance, must the picture be eternally argued, searched? Why is there not, we ask when all is said, that unquestioned, that unquestionable quality we find in some earlier tragic expressions, expressions addressed, like the Guernica, in grand programmatic terms to a general public—Bach Passions, Giotto?

This way and that we may argue this point, according to the urging of the moment. It is natural, for example, for the Guernica to pose problems, because our taste has gone beyond Picasso; or has not yet arrived at him; and no art has ever been entirely self-sufficient within itself, all art is dependent on life, which is to say on history. . . . still the Guernica will not simply be dismissed, taken for granted. Some irritant, it may be, excites us, or, just at the height of our response, chills us, slightly. When the mural's eloquence does not seem needlessly obscure, it may present itself now and then as slightly forced. Some maverick piece of us at an awkward moment strays to the sidelines and declines to be awed by the mural's elaborate structure—a dissatisfaction we never experience in relation to Giotto or to Bach. We seem to sense when all is said, a volatile heat, an emotion thrown off perhaps too close to the moment of its causing. We ask ourselves—not while under the direct spell of the picture, but in retrospect—whether we have experienced the full catharsis which comes of an emotion wholly subdued in life and in wisdom.

Do we sense these negative things: do we ask such questions—or do we not? We return to the picture. We are not sure.

But Picasso was the illustrator of an unsure age. One of his difficulties, in particular, was that the present age is not one in which artists are born to illustration, especially illustration of passion and of large occurrence. Picasso rushed in where other painters since at least as early as the 1930's, warned by many casualties, fear to tread. Illustration in our century, if it ventures into the open, has learned to protect itself behind a slightly sarcastic warmth, or else a suspicious coldness. "Love and death," as Virginia Woolf said of the works of a clever modern writer, "like damp fireworks, refuse to flare up. . . ." It is of course the discouraging atmosphere of the times, the general rubble of iconographies and faiths; all credit to Picasso, who almost alone among artists of his time has seized both love and death clothed in their visible flesh, and compelled them (outside the Guernica) if not always to climb to a heroic height, at least to rise to an authentic level. Where does this leave our scanning of the special heights attempted in the Guernica uniquely? Has the painter tried, this time, for something more Himalayan than the century can allow—has he kept his footing to the end of his hazardous ascent? Do we find him slightly out of breath?

Picasso rushed in: the press of time was precisely one of the difficulties. Picasso was certainly too close to the event which aroused him, to treat it with serenity.

Classical illustrators such as Giotto and Bach, along with those of Elephanta, Athens, and Chartres, took for their heroic themes the collective memories of centuries, where Picasso's May project was triggered by an occurrence in late April. No contemporary artist, plucked at by newspapers, has at his command those broad distances which tended to enlarge the artists of earlier times, and which, giving them their authority in relation to the past, gave them their authority in relation to the future. Both in theme and in ways of seeing, they steered securely within tradition, for tradition was everything; a lesser artist could polish its brass and scrub its decks, while a strong artist could turn it in some new direction, a ship which needed guidance but which supported, and which contributed a deep impulse of its own. The new ships, those afloat, leave it to the artist to steer his course in any direction at all; he is invited to tear the decks apart under his feet; the old ships are dried hulks which the artist is at liberty to pick at as he pleases, joining or scattering the pieces as he chooses. Such freedom is of course intolerable to humankind, and we see some artists, among them the most advanced, clinging to one another in formations as closely knit as ever they were in the middle ages—others, like Picasso, circling around the old hulks, wresting planks. Picasso, like the others, has had to be shipwright, crew, and pilot. It is precisely a part of the buoyancy of Picasso's ship—we might well argue—that its borrowed planks of tradition are not self-sufficient, do not stick out superficially for us to count and to name, but must be searched, flashlighted below its surface where they have taken their place among its innermost workings. The ship stays afloat. The Guernica with its obstacles to casual understanding, its origins invisible below decks, its improvisations, its metamorphoses unlikely and unpredictable, its traditions chopped up and scattered, begged and borrowed—all this is good sound living material, it is after all none of it of Picasso's making, it is ourselves. If the ship proceeds uneasily, rears up, strains, surely it is the uneasiness of the times, the unsteadiness of the winds. Picasso has done what can be done, he has given us in full measure what one man can. No ship, we feel, could get across these waters between the past and the future with greater sureness than his.

Reinhold Hohl
Picasso's Guernica: A Drama of Truth and Cruelty—[1978–81]*

In his essay especially prepared for this anthology, the Swiss art historian discusses Picasso's little-known and highly personal projects that preceded *Guernica* as possible compositions for the Spanish Pavilion. After demonstrating that Picasso became intensely concerned with expressing the truth about the Guernica bombing, Hohl interprets Picasso's painting as a modern psychodrama intended to involve its viewing audience emotionally.

To Leo Steinberg

Despite all the studies and photographs of its different states documenting Picasso's work on *Guernica,* we know little about his initial plans for the great painting. How was it possible that the most private and even egocentric artist of his time would deliver the most effective history painting of our century? What gave his entirely mythical imagery the political and humanitarian charge and multiple meanings that, to this day, provoke controversial reactions and contradictory interpretations? Viewing *Guernica* in a museum [fig. 139A], we miss some crucial elements for an adequate understanding: the time and place in which and for which it was painted, but also the circumstances against which it was created.

Picasso's participation had been secured in January 1937. What, then, were his preliminary ideas for this commission—before the bombing of the Basque town of Guernica prompted him to choose *Guernica,* the dedicative but not descriptive title, inscribed on the frame [fig. 89]?

Christian Zervos tells us how, since the beginning of the civil war in 1936, the painter was torn between his passionate reactions to the destructive and cruel events in Spain, and his concern as an artist of his exceptional status to do something that in itself, as an act of creation, and by its theme would counter the horrors (p. 56, above). "I stand for life against death," Picasso later declared about his public com-

---

*The text summarizes the author's three essays: " 'Die Wahrheit über Guernica,' " *Pantheon* (Munich), vol 36, No. 1, January–March 1978, pp. 41–58; "Ein Weltbild der Grausamkeit: Picassos *Guernica* und Artauds Théâtre de la cruauté," *Frankfurter Allgemeine Zeitung,* No. 280, 1 December 1979, and " 'Ich stehe für das Leben ein gegen den Tod'—'Guernica' und die Vorprojekte für den spanischen Pavillon von 1937," *Neue Zürcher Zeitung,* No. 247, 24/25 October 1981.

Dr. Hohl received graduate degrees from the Sorbonne and the University of Basel, has taught in New York and Wisconsin, currently teaches architectural history at the Swiss Federal Institute of Technology in Zurich, and is curator of the Institute's Print Collection. Author of highly respected monographs and articles on Alberto Giacometti (Stuttgart 1971, New York 1974), his recent publications include articles on Cubist painting (in *Kubismus,* Kunsthalle Cologne, 1982), Picasso's Cubist constructions and his late sculptures (in *Sculpture in the Twentieth Century,* Basel, 1984), and "Matisse and Picasso" (in *Matisse,* Zurich, 1982).

mitment.[1] It is quite possible that such a painting which "stands for life" was on his mind when he accepted the commission for the Spanish Pavilion. In his etchings, the *Dream and Lie of Franco,* Picasso in January had given in to his hatred and passion. His contribution to the International Exposition would be something more universally meaningful.

An idea of 9 February devising the installation of a monumental *Bather* painting within a hall might belong to the early stages of the conception as well as other, seemingly more private themes.[2] Yet the definitive pre-*Guernica* project—until now sometimes mentioned but never documented—was a composition of the painter and his model in the studio. Only since Picasso's death have studies for it become known. They develop the idea of a stage set representing the large studio of an artist, a door on the right-hand wall near a spiral staircase leading to an upper floor, and a window to the right of the back wall. In the center would stand a huge, triangular construction on which the artist's easel and his work-in-progress were to be painted, comparable to the large canvas in Velázquez's *Las Meninas.* The artist in front of it and the reclining nude model on a sofa (left stage) were also conceived as cut-out constructions. Studies for wooden boxes hiding real stagelights to illuminate the three-dimensional tableau complete this set of drawings, all done on 18 April 1937.[3]

The following day, a Monday, Picasso must have gone to the construction site in the Trocadéro gardens, since he sketched on the front page of *Paris-Soir* of 19

161. Vera Mukhina. *Young Worker and Collective-Farm Woman.* Spring 1937. Stainless steel, approx. 80' (24.5 m) high. Moscow. (See also Nos. 81A and 81B.)

1. At the Third Peace Congress in Sheffield, England, in November 1950, Picasso declared: "I stand for life against death; I stand for peace against war" (Penrose [1958] p. 329). It was a poignant reference to the Falangists' password during the Spanish Civil War: "Viva la muerte!"

2. Z.VIII:336 (dated 9 Feb. 37, dedicated to Dora Maar) a monstrous woman standing in shallow water between cliffs and beach cabins, with barbed wire jump rope, and Z.VIII:337, under barbed wire clouds—images of innocent and painfully vulnerable existences. Also Z.VIII:338, a woman (Marie-Thérèse?) in an interior—the epitome of peaceful privacy. On 1 May 1937—the day of the first *Guernica* sketches—Picasso painted two terrified bathers (Z.IX:217).

3. Dominique Bozo, director of the Picasso Museum in Paris, discovered them, recognized them for what they are, and will publish all of them: MP 1178–1189 and 1191. [Our figs. 162A and 162B (MP 1177 and 1190) are dated "19 A. 37." They have been graciously made available by the Picasso Museum director; ECO.] After conversation with the author in November 1980, Werner Spies brought them to public attention in *Marina Picasso 1981,* p. 21 [See also Sidra Stich's brief discussion (*Arts,* Oct. 1983, p. 117 and figs. 10 and 11) of our two illustrations.]

162A. Picasso. Untitled ink drawing on newspaper, *Paris-Soir*, 19 April 1937. Not in Zervos. Musée Picasso, Paris

162B. Picasso. Untitled ink drawing on paper, 19 April 1937. Not in Zervos. Musée Picasso, Paris

April 1937 something which he could only have seen there—or rather, an imaginative paraphrase of it. He rendered Vera Mukhina's two-figure sculpture for the Soviet Pavilion [fig. 161; as one cartoon-like person with an outstretched left arm holding a handle with a hammer on the left and a sickle on the right side of the fist [fig. 162A]. This emblematic figure reappears the same day on a sheet with sketches for the stage-project, "The Artist's Studio," together with the detail of the arm and the fist holding up the combined tools [fig. 162B].

This, then, is the date when, triggered by another work of art, the private and the political iconography merged for the commission of the Spanish Republic. Myth and manifesto will be combined again in the first and second state of the *Guernica* canvas (between May 11 and 20; figs. 18 and 27), but in a very different conception, since meanwhile, Guernica had been bombed on 26 April 1937, by the German Condor Legion.

Or hadn't it?

Our question is not rhetorical, since this was exactly the topical question of the day, May 1st, when Picasso made the very first sketch for what would become the painting called *Guernica*.

We do, of course, know that Guernica *was* bombed, and why and by whom it was bombed,[4] and so did great parts of the newspaper-reading world after 27 April.[5] But schemes to suppress this truth were initiated by the Condor Legion on the very evening of the terror bombing; beginning 27 April, they were systematically pursued by General Franco's Nationalist Spain, and by the German government after 28 April: Basque extremists and *dinamiteros* were accused of having blown up and set fire to their historic capital.[6]

Basque eyewitnesses and officials reacted immediately and repeatedly to these enormous accusations. They made known detailed accounts and pronounced solemn declarations, exemplified by the urgent entreaty of President José de Aguirre of Euzkadi (the autonomous Basque state), issued on 28 April 1937:

> We appeal to the civilized world and to all those who wish that Truth and Justice shall prevail. In order to establish the facts, we are ready to receive all commissions, persons, and institutions who desire to investigate on their own the deeds that have been done on Basque territory. Our doors are open to everyone.

Endorsing this statement on the same day, the Basque government added that "the world should learn in all details about the acts of extreme savagery that have victimized the Basque population." These declarations reached the French public through different channels, including a press conference with representatives of the Spanish Republic in Paris, reported on the eve of May Day (e.g., by *L'Humanité* on

---

4. The responsibility falls to Wolfram von Richthofen, then chief of staff of Goering's Condor Legion and previously head of a special German airforce section that developed new strategies, tactics, and weapons for a future war. Among these were the complete destruction of a town from the air, with a mixture of incendiary and explosive bombs, and the terrorizing of a given population for political and strategic reasons—in the case of Guernica, to intimidate the Basques (to secure a separate peace?) and to break their determination to defend Bilbao. [For documentation, see pp. 165–68, above.]

5. E.g., *L'Humanité*, 30 April / 1 May, front page. Southworth's detailed examination of press coverage *(Guernica! Guernica!)* is fundamental for understanding Picasso's *Guernica* in contemporary context.

6. For instance, this commentary in a German newsreel of mid-May 1937:
Here are the ruins of the old Spanish town of Guernica a few hours after Nationalist troops had forced the criminal Bolshevist arsonists to leave. The Jewish press-liars ["jüdische Lügenpresse"] maintained that German airplanes had bombed the town, but the international press soon branded their coverage as propaganda maneuvers by the Bolshevists, who themselves had burned down the entire town, house by house, before evacuating it.

the front page of its 30 April / 1 May edition). This was precisely the moment when Picasso started his sketches for *Guernica*.

In its eloquence and general content, the Basque proclamation matches Picasso's myth-making art more closely than any war photograph. Neither airplanes nor bombs are mentioned; instead, it cites destruction and terror on Basque soil, the victims, and truth which shall prevail. The main theme of *Guernica*, then, is the appearance of Truth above the site of horror, so that the suppressed truth about the destruction of Guernica shall be revealed to the whole world at the International Exposition in Paris. Indeed, while visiting the Spanish Pavilion, President Aguirre and members of his government had their official photograph taken in front of Picasso's *Guernica*.[7]

To plead the Republic's urgent and desperate cause was also the purpose of the other exhibits and installations. A stage and open-air auditorium [fig. 90], for instance, was to serve for the presentation of documentary films about the war and the Nationalists' brutality, and for various political and cultural manifestations.

At an early date, Josep Lluis Sert, architect of the pavilion, had explained to Picasso his painting's emplacement: the large side wall of the entrance hall that led to the patio auditorium [figs. 88 and 89]. But what caught Picasso's eyes—studying the blueprints, or visiting the construction site—must have been the pavilion stage. It is possible that his pre-*Guernica* project, "The Artist's Studio," with the movable cut-out canvases on a stage counted on the availability of this pavilion stage while not in use for other performances: a grandiose solution suited to the exhibition pavilion as well as to Picasso's self-image. Yet even if our supposition could be proven wrong, we have to retain the stage-idea, since it had a crucial impact on the elaboration of *Guernica* as a wall painting placed in the entrance hall. Picasso must have recognized that the public, entering or leaving the building through the main gate, would pass by his work and even turn its back while watching events on the stage. This situation presented a challenge to him, as well as a clearly defined artistic problem.

Painting *Guernica*, Picasso committed himself to giving public and permanent visual form to the quest for truth with the immediacy and inescapability of a mythical representation, like a Surrealist *mise-en-scène*.[8] This interpretation is apt to reconcile all the seemingly contradictory elements in the finished painting, which have always defied rational interpretations. But before we analyze the imagery of the painting as a whole, and in parts, as a stage event of sorts, we must first draw an art-historical parallel.

Among the many allusions to older art discovered by critics and art-historians, *Guernica*'s scenes are comparable most fruitfully to Raphael's and Giulio Romano's *Fire in the Borgo* of 1515 [fig. 163]. Painted in the Vatican Palace for Leo X to legitimate the Pope's power to end recent schisms, *The Fire in the Borgo* is as much a political proclamation as is *Guernica*. More than once the Vatican fresco has been

7. For a recent reproduction, see "Spain: Artistic Avant-Garde and Social Reality, 1936–1976," *La Biennale di Venezia*, exhibition catalogue, 1976, vol. 1, fig. 1, p. 177.

8. With such contributions as *Parade* (1917), *Antigone* (1922), and *Mercure* (1924), Picasso occupies an important place in the history of the Surrealist *mise-en-scène*. Cf. Douglas Cooper, *Picasso Theater* (New York, 1968) and his observations about *Guernica* (p. 80):

> The stark setting of houses and walls (both internal and external) which enclose the pictorial space is conceived like a stage decor, and the sense of theater is increased by the attitudes and gestures of the figures as well as by the temporal ambiguity produced by an electric light hanging in the center of an apparently outdoor scene.

163. Raphael. *Fire in the Borgo.* c. 1514. Fresco, 22'1" base (6.73 m). The Vatican, Rome (Alinari Reference Bureau)

described as a dramatic event staged like a theatrical performance, with columns from the temples of Mars Ultor and Saturn as painted wings and Old St. Peter's basilica as a backdrop in the center. There, in his elevated loggia, Pope Leo IV is extinguishing the fire of 847 A.D. with a gesture of his hand—a deed more allegorical than real. (Likewise, the allegory of Truth in *Guernica* dominates the scene.) Imploring the Pope with outstretched arms, some women in Raphael's fresco rush from side to center, some are shown far back, against the atrium of Old St. Peter's. These rectangular openings seem to be echoed in Picasso's scenery in the 9 May drawing, from and in front of which arms are stretched out, sometimes without being attached to a visible body, as if appearing from behind stage sets [fig. 15]. Their fists, of course, refer to the actual political context: the gesture of the Popular Front. They also parallel Vera Mukhina's sculptural group and Picasso's caricature of it drawn on 19 April—partisan allusions the artist deliberately and characteristically dropped in state III of the *Guernica* canvas [fig. 28].[9] But many reminiscences of Raphael prevail. The most obvious one is the woman in the foreground rushing to the left. In *The Fire in the Borgo,* her trailing robe creates the triangular shape that characterizes *Guernica*'s running woman. Other corresponding but transformed motifs can easily be discovered. For our argument it is sufficient to suggest that Raphael's composition has influenced the elaboration of *Guernica,* specifically its stage characteristics.

9. In an unpublished lecture in Berlin, Otto Karl Werckmeister in June 1981 linked Picasso's elimination of the raised fist to the Communists' new predominance in the Spanish Republican government; Picasso did not want to be involved in factional partisanship. See also Hélène Parmelin's quotation of Picasso's statement to her: "If, instead of adhering to the [Communist] Party in 1944, I would have done it earlier, I would not have been Picasso" ["Je n'aurais jamais été Picasso"], from *Voyage en Picasso* (Paris, 1980), p. 214.

The stage idea perhaps is not clearly visible in the first preparatory drawings for *Guernica*. Until 8 May, the sketches with mythological, allegorical, and historical figures are more or less square in format: the bull carrying a bird or a winged horse, the dying horse releasing Pegasus—iconographically reminiscent of Picasso's drop curtain for *Parade*—the classical woman holding a light, a dead soldier with an antique Roman helmet. This is still true of the main motif in the 8 May drawing, although the paper is now of more oblong shape and the figure of a running woman with a dead child is added on the right. The compositional study of 9 May brings a complete change: the central motif is flanked on both sides by architectonic elements resembling stage sets. The ratio of the paper dimension is now 5:9; this ratio will become 5:11 for the final canvas, thus approximating the proportions of the pavilion stage.

By 9 May, therefore, Picasso had found the compositional framework suited to the emplacement *and* to the purpose of the painting in the pavilion. He now needed to incorporate the various thematic elements; to reconcile the various levels of reality (from myth to allegory to real scenes of distress and their witness); and to dramatize his subject to its highest pitch. This was possible with the concept of the painting as a staged drama.

Looking at *Guernica* we are participating, so to speak, in one of those theatrical events that Antonin Artaud envisioned in his manifesto of 1932, "The Theater of Cruelty." To be experienced as much more than a play, these events were designed to create Total Theater, fusing reality, poetry, and myth. The audience was bombarded with inescapable, realistic shock effects from all sides, from on stage and in front of it: piercing screams, the sight of blood, and blinding spotlights.[10] The underlying philosophy of it was Artaud's conviction that cruelty is Man's basic and even life-enforcing drive—a concept that Picasso himself had expressed in the same period with the myth of the Minotaur.

One of the last elements that Picasso added to the nearly finished painting [in state VII, fig. 52] was the orthogonal design of the floor which opens on a shallow pictorial space and corresponded to the square tiles of the pavilion's concrete floor [fig. 89]. It is as if the painting illusionistically prolonged the entrance hall; as if the painted lamp—whose light bulb was also one of the last additions—mirrored the real lamp in front of the painting; as if Picasso on the flat wall had created his own stage. Viewing *Guernica* as a stage presentation, we can understand the pictorial space as the theater building in which stage sets represent Spanish houses, with interiors and exteriors. The electric light is a visible stage light; the lamp nearby which sheds no light and casts no shadow is a stage prop, as is the shattered warrior, apparently made of plaster, with a broken sword in his hand.[11] The half-open door at the extreme right leads onto the stage where the running woman has just appeared to implore Truth. The burning and falling woman, the agonizing horse, and the Unholy Family of bull, mother, and dead child represent three separate, expressive tableaux.

10. Antonin Artaud, "Le théâtre de la cruauté" (1932), English trans., *The Theater and Its Double* (New York, 1958). The drama *Les Cenci*, staged May 1935 in Paris, most closely realized Artaud's revolutionary and influential concepts.

11. See Picasso's *Studio with Plaster Head* [fig. 105] and William Rubin's analysis (*Picasso in MoMA*, pp. 120–22, and note 1, p. 221) for Picasso's description of this toy theater he made for his son.

But all these figures are, of course, not actors: they are images and myths. The running woman, for instance, is metaphorically and literally "the woman from the street"—from the streets of Guernica, as well as the streets of Paris—reminding us of Aguirre's statement: "Our doors are open to everyone." (In states IV and VI [figs. 37 and 45] Picasso had even experimented with pinned-on patterns for her dress.) Note that the painted door at the right corresponded to the entrance of the pavilion; the painted opening on the left matched the nearby window in the enclosing wall. Acknowledging the comings and goings of visitors, Picasso designed the painting so that it could be approached from the left as well as the right, and from up front. Were it not for its apocalyptic content, one could call Picasso's *Guernica* a "sideshow."

What it really is, I think, is a painted "sideshow" or, to use the French term, a painted "parade." Let's not forget that since *Parade*, done in 1917, all of Picasso's work intended for public exposure (as was *Guernica*) were works for the stage. Since he could not contribute to the pavilion stage, Picasso painted a sideshow announcing what was presented in the pavilion. The most famous painted sideshow is, of course, Seurat's large, oblong painting of 1887–88, *Invitation to the Side-Show (La Parade)*.[12]

Visitors to the Spanish Pavilion thus were not only viewing a painting, but were drawn into a drama: a psychodrama about Man's cruelty, despair, and his appeal for truth. After his private, mythical *Minotauromachia* of 1935, Picasso had created this universal *psychomachia* (a battle of the soul) as a public concern (a *res publica*), for the *Republic* of Spain and the whole world. And, while we have no proof that *Guernica* aroused the general public in 1937, we now do know that this painting remained a political case for half a century, and that it still can move new generations to take upon themselves the causes of Humanity, Justice, and Truth.[13]

12. Picasso certainly knew this painting, which was exhibited in Paris *nine* times between 1900 and 1930 before Stephen C. Clark acquired it in 1933; see *French Paintings: A Catalogue of the Collection of the Metropolitan Museum of Art*, vol III, pp. 197–200 (Bequest of Stephen C. Clark, 1961).

13. Some sense of theater characterizes *Guernica*'s installation in Madrid since 1981 [fig. 139B]. Were it not for the unabated demand for Basque autonomy, which necessitates that the painting be protected by armed guards, bomb detectors, and a huge bullet-proof showcase, I would say that the present *mise-en-scène* of *Guernica*—separate visitors' space, proscenium, stage lights, and back doors "in the wings"—is indeed appropriate for its dramatic content.

Douglas Cooper
Guernica Installed in the Prado—[1982]*

The British art historian and critic, author of the important study, *Picasso Theater,* and a long-time friend of Picasso's, shares his recollections of *Guernica*'s various settings. Having seen the painting in Picasso's studio and at the Spanish Pavilion in 1937, in New York and in several traveling exhibitions, Douglas Cooper was one of the international consultants for its initial installation in Madrid.[1] There, he felt as if he were "truly seeing *Guernica* for the first time . . . one of the rare absolute masterpieces of the twentieth century."

The wall chosen for *Guernica* was the back wall of the ballroom in the Casón del Buen Retiro, which forms part of the Prado ensemble, a large high space created as a ballroom * * * and it is possible to see the whole canvas from about eighty feet away. The painting has been set within a glass and steel structure, like a greenhouse, and the entire canvas can be seen framed within a special, protective glass panel nearly as large as the painting and not traversed by parts of the metal structure [fig. 139B].[2] The painting is admirably lit, there being no shadows, no reflections and no distortions. Never in its history has *Guernica* been displayed so beautifully or so entirely to its advantage.[3] It was always cramped on the walls of MoMA, badly lit, and a certain confusion was caused by the more than forty associated drawings which were hung closely around it. In the Casón, *Guernica* stands alone and, even when a considerable number of people are in the gallery at the same time, the visitor's view is not blocked. One can approach to within one metre of the protective glass screen, which stands one metre from the canvas. Related drawings and paintings are hung separately behind a glass panel on the walls of two long side-galleries which open directly from the main ballroom.

On this occasion I felt as if I were truly seeing *Guernica* for the first time since I watched it evolving through many phases in Picasso's studio in the rue des Grands-Augustins in Paris throughout May 1937. Today, I have no doubt not only that it is Picasso's major achievement, but indeed that it is one of the rare absolute master-pieces of the twentieth century. At the time that it was painted, *Guernica* came as a blinding shock, as an imaginative, visionary and highly dramatic document of the time. One was more obsessed by seeking the meaning of the mysterious symbols which are built into the composition than by analysing the composition, looking for the underlying streak of creative genius and deep feeling which had inspired it, or

*From the conclusion, pp. 291–92, "Picasso's 'Guernica' Installed in the Prado," *The Burlington Magazine,* May 1982, pp. 288–92.

1. Ibid., p. 291; Cooper (1911–1984) was a trustee of the Prado. His essay lucidly summarizes the complex documentation in *Guernica–Legado.* For subsequent installation plans, see p. 44, above.

2. [Except when seen from an angle, as in the news photograph.]

3. [Opinions differ, of course, and *Guernica* thus again arouses controversy. Many Americans, accustomed to the intimate and unimpeded MoMA setting (fig. 139A) dislike the new formal installation with its necessary emphasis on security (p. 134, above).]

by reacting to the quality of the painting itself and the essentially pictorial nature of its conception. In the Spanish pavilion the painting was at a disadvantage, for it covered the right-hand wall of the space through which the public entered, while right in front of it stood a massive iron toy, designed by Calder, which was kept in motion by a flow of mercury shipped to Paris from a Spanish mine. I saw *Guernica* again in London, and then in May 1939 in the Valentine Gallery in New York: it looked lost, sadly out of place and uninspiring in both galleries. In neither place did I experience a new and unexpected thrill, a feeling of seeing and discovering significant aspects of the whole which had hitherto passed unobserved. Somehow, even though the declaration of war was imminent, one was still too close to the birth of this vast composition to be able to see it and discourse with it on a plane of emotional detachment. My first shock of "discovery" of its incalculable importance came when I saw it standing amid the bomb-damaged marble and elaborate plasterwork décor of the great hall in the erstwhile Royal Palace in Milan alongside the Duomo. It had just arrived from New York, rolled, had been restretched and was at that moment being surface-cleaned, touched up and having certain areas in the canvas repaired by the restorer Pellicioli. He had just finished working on the paint surface of the *Last Supper* by Leonardo, after the removal of its protective wartime covering of an elaborate piling-up of sacks of sand.

In that melancholy, but once grand décor, *Guernica*, carried out in black, white and grey exclusively, dominated the scene by its horrifying and forceful presence. For the first time, I saw it as an overwhelming pictorial achievement, as a picture rooted in more traditions than one. It had both a contemporary and an eternal significance, and was executed in an expressive formal language invented by Picasso. It was then that I first saw clearly the classical nature of the composition, and became aware of its indebtedness to Poussin. Expressionist distortions of form, movement and gesture are used here to evoke human tragedy, helplessness and sense of panic, while by making several of the figures represent broken lives, and using others to convey horrific depths of experience and pain, Picasso manages to draw the spectator into his ambiguous inside/outside spatial setting and force him to relate to the event on the purely human plane.

I saw *Guernica* again many times after 1953: at Paris in 1955 and, off and on until 1980, hanging in MoMA. Yet I never again experienced the deep thrill of Milan until I saw the canvas in place at last in the Casón in Madrid in October 1981. There I was more overwhelmed and convinced than ever before by its extraordinary purity of invention, the absence of any sort of anecdote or sentimentality and its strictly pictorial imagery. This is a painting which brings tears from the heart, arouses belief in the courage and endurability of human beings, and inspires one to take up arms and demolish the forces of evil, whenever, wherever and in whatever guise (fascist or not) they manifest themselves, before they can succeed in suppressing the manifold forms of liberty which civilized man has won for himself, or in destroying the world around us. That Spain, the country whose Civil War provided the basic spark of inspiration, which set Picasso's pictorial imagination to work to produce this amazing masterpiece, should today be able to present *Guernica* in a more perfect setting than ever before, is in itself ironical. But it is true. And *Guernica* is there in Madrid, which it will never leave again, as a noble but no less frightening successor to the *Dos* and *Tres de Mayo* by Goya [fig. 149].

VIII.
WORKS RELATED TO GUERNICA

To create *Guernica*, Picasso drew on some forty years of artistic experience, incorporating from his other works the imagery of bullfights or of the women he loved, using Expressionist, Cubist, and Surrealist techniques. A closer scrutiny of several specific related works thus illuminates and enriches our study of *Guernica* in a special, intimate way.

It is well known that *Guernica*'s composition is the mirror image of the mystifying large etching, *Minotauromachy*. Does this earlier work perhaps bear an elusive message about *Guernica*'s private significance for Picasso? In January 1937, months before Picasso could face *Guernica*'s huge canvas, his rage—later generalized and purified—first erupted in angry scrawls onto the etching plate for the *Dream and Lie of Franco*. With four scenes derived from *Guernica* drawings, he finished the etching cycle at the very moment when he was completing the mural. The many drawings for *Guernica* are also worthy of separate study. Finally, *The Charnel House*, painted in 1945, is filled with tragic resonance of *Guernica*'s protest against war and inhumanity. Far more than just a postscript, it is a significant and impressive work in its own right.

Alfred H. Barr
Minotauromachy: A Private Allegory— [1946]*

The first director of the Museum of Modern Art here introduces Picasso's great etching of 1935, whose dreamlike personages—mirror-image reversed by the printing process—return as *Guernica*'s protagonists. The brief essay typifies Alfred Barr's exemplary method: close description of visual facts, scholarly and imaginative insight, a lucid and often poetic writing style.

In Memoriam (1902–1981)

Picasso's most remarkable composition of 1935—and possibly the most important of all his prints—is the *Minotauromachy* [fig. 165].[1] This large etching is so rich in Picasso's personal symbolism and so involved with the iconography of his previous and subsequent work that it requires some analysis, however brief. The bison-headed Minotaur advances from the right, his huge right arm stretched out toward the candle held high by a little girl who stands confronting the monster fearlessly, flowers in her other hand. Between the two staggers a horse with intestines hanging from a rent in his belly. A female matador collapses across the horse's back, her breasts bared, her *espada* held so that the hilt seems to touch the left hand of the Minotaur while the point lies toward the horse's head and the flower girl. At the left a bearded man in a loin cloth climbs a ladder to safety,[2] looking over his shoulder at the monster. In a window behind and above two girls watch two doves walk on the sill. The sea with a distant sail fills the right half of the background.

*Reprinted from *Picasso: Fifty Years of His Art* (New York, The Museum of Modern Art, 1946), pp. 192–93 (internal references to illustrations deleted), by permission of the museum. This monograph set the highest standard for Picasso studies, just as did Barr's book, *Matisse* (1951), and the trail-blazing exhibitions and catalogues of 1936–37: *Cubism and Abstract Art* and *Fantastic Art, Dada, and Surrealism*. (See obituaries and appreciations, *The New York Times*, 16 Aug. 1981, front page, and 23 Aug. 1982, D–23; also *Art News*, Nov. 1981.) A striking photograph of Barr seated before *Guernica* became the dustjacket of his posthumous *Defining Modern Art: Selected Writings of Alfred H. Barr*, ed. Irving Sandler and Amy Newman (New York, 1986).

1. [See also *Picasso 1980*, pp. 328–29, for the five states of the etching that reveal increasing complexity and ambiguities].

2. [An example of ambiguous drawing: one can argue that the man is descending, his left foot grasping one ladder rung while his right is reaching for another below; see also Russell, pp. 290–91.]

The flower girl appears several times in Picasso's earlier work—in 1903 and 1905; in the large Grecoesque *Composition* of 1906 and its studies—but never before in such a crucial role. The ladder, usually in the left-hand side of the composition, occurs in the 1905 paintings and etchings of acrobats; is climbed by a monkey in the curtain for *Parade;* by a man with a hammer in, significantly, the *Crucifixion* of 1930 [fig. 112]; by an amorous youth in a gouache of 1933;[3] by a shrieking woman in a *Study for the Guernica* [fig. 16 or 17].

One of the earliest of the bullring series of the previous years shows a female matador falling from a horse which is borne, like Europa, on the back of the bull, though her sword has been plunged, ineffectually, into the bull's neck.[4] The agonized, disemboweled horse bares his teeth in many of these same bullfights, and in 1937, after dying in the *Dream and Lie of Franco* [fig. 110], revives to become the central figure of *Guernica.*

Minotaur himself appears as a decorative running figure in 1928[5] but takes on his true character in 1933 when Picasso designed the cover for the first issue of the magazine *Minotaure,* and made numerous etchings and drawings in which the monster holds a dagger like a sceptre [fig. 114] or makes love.[6] In a drawing of April 1935 he struts with hairy nakedness across the bullring toward a frightened horse.[7]

As a kind of private allegory the *Minotauromachy* tempts the interpreter. But explanation, whether poetic or pseudo-psychoanalytic, would necessarily be subjective. It is clear that the ancient and dreadful myth of the Minotaur which originated, together with the bullring, on the island of Crete, has here been woven into Picasso's own experience of the modern Spanish *toromachia*. To this he has added certain motives associated with his theatre pictures and his *Crucifixion.*

Apparently the scene is a moral melodramatic charade of the soul, though probably of so highly intuitive a character that Picasso himself could not or would not explain it in words. Of three extraordinary allegories it is the first: it was followed, in 1937, by a nightmare comic strip and a great mural painting.

3. [For several illustrations of cited works, see Rubin 1972, p. 231. also pp. 36 and 194.]
4. [*Picasso 1980*, pp. 314 and 319.]
5. [Ibid., p. 270.]
6. [Ibid., p. 312.]
7. [Rubin 1972, p. 231.]

Brigitte Baer
Minotauromachy: A Private Allegory Revealed?—[1983]*

Brigitte Baer has accepted the challenge of interpreting *Minotauromachy,* the image that Barr and others have considered Picasso's "private allegory" filled with personal symbolism. Perhaps she has found the key to this labyrinth in specific events of Picasso's private life. She is well equipped for her task: a classical education and work in psychoanalysis; experience in journalism, and six years spent sorting and studying the treasures of Picasso's estate—paintings, drawings, and graphics, books and letters—for distribution to his several heirs. Especially fascinated by the graphics, she found some of the printers who had worked with Picasso, and is continuing Bernhard Geiser's *catalogue raisonné* of the graphic works.[1]

The Blind Minotaur Guided by a Little Girl [Fig. 164].

The Blind Minotaur, who has been compared with reason to Picasso's series of blind people of 1903, is being guided just as Theseus was guided by Ariadne's thread and as Oedipus was guided by Antigone towards Colonus, where in fact he would meet Theseus and his death. The little girl has Marie-Thérèse's face and carries the bunch of flowers which is her symbol. A young sailor is leaning against a wall in a posture which repeats exactly the ritualized stance which Oedipus always assumes before the Sphinx, thus obliging us to associate the two myths. He is the spectator, the Minotaur's double, the one who has replaced the sculptor, Theseus. In the background, fishermen are hauling down their sail and bringing in their nets full of fish. The color of the boat's sail, black or white, is of vital importance in the Theseus myth, as seen below. The fish are an evident symbol of masculinity. On the left, we can see the *Death of Marat,* upside down and cancelled.

* * *

[*inserted from p. 87*] Olga's jealousy took the same road as Picasso's passion for Marie-Thérèse, if we judge from his work, i.e. from bad to worse, and the situation became increasingly intolerable. In one of his most famous drawings, made on the 7th of July [1934] (Z.VIII:216), the artist has drawn his inspiration from David's *Death of Marat* repeating the subject in a small print from July (G.430; B.282). It is Marie-Thérèse who lies in the bath with her head thrown back as in the David. But Picasso adds a Charlotte Corday, in the guise of a delirious sorceress, the epitome of murderous revenge, who hurls herself at the woman in the bath while brandishing a butcher's knife. Scholars have always seen here a depiction of Olga's jealous fury and the artist's fears for his mistress.

*From Brigitte Baer, *Picasso the Printmaker: Graphics from the Marina Picasso Collection.* Exhibition catalogue, Dallas, 1983, pp. 91, 87, 95, 96, 98, by permission of author and publisher.

1. See Marilyn August's biographical sketch, "Brigitte Baer: A New Perspective on Picasso," *Art News,* March 1984, p. 77, supplemented by Mme. Baer's May 1984 letter to me.

328

164. Picasso. *Blind Minotaur Led by Girl with Bouquet of Flowers* (Vollard Suite 94). 22 September 1934. Etching and engraving, 9¹⁵⁄₁₆ x 13⁵⁄₈″ (25.3 x 34.5 cm). B.94. The Museum of Modern Art, New York

165. Picasso. *Minotauromachy.* Spring (March) 1935. Etching and scraper, 19½ x 27⁷⁄₁₆″ (49.5 x 69.7 cm). B.288.V. The Museum of Modern Art, New York

* * *

The inference to be drawn from the autobiographical aspect is clear. His love for Marie-Thérèse, watched over by Oedipus/Theseus, is leading him on blindly. Is it not towards Olga's jealous violence, repressed but latent, that the Minotaur is walking? But also the anguish inherent in the femininity of the Minotaur is an important factor here, that anguish present both in the Cretan cycle of the Theseid as well as in Picasso's iconography. Femininity has two contradictory aspects: on the one hand, the weak child, gentle and full of affection, and on the other, the witch armed with a murderous knife. Primary femininity (a product of the primary relationship with the mother and the defense mechanisms provoked by it) is impotence (the impotence of an infant) and also the inherent destructive rage which always attacks the best loved and most vital object of its affections.[2] This destructive rage, present during the preceding months in the iconography of the Minotaur, is intolerable to look at in the "mirror" which is the other, the mother and the wife (here Olga), just as Perseus needed the gift of Athena, the polished shield, to use as a double mirror in order to kill Medusa. The Minotaur prefers to be blind and his shield is the child. But when a man allows himself to become weak and dependent, to be led, it means that once again destructive fury is not very far away. Theseus will abandon Ariadne (herself rather witch-like) pregnant on the beach at Naxos, because it is better to run off than to kill. What will the Minotaur/Picasso do?

Let us now examine more closely our proof of the *Minotauromachy* [fig. 165]. Clearly there is violence, but so restrained that it is easy to overlook. The characters seem to have been petrified in the middle of their gestures as through the fairy from *Sleeping Beauty* or the lava of Pompeii. * * * On the left, a serious and "human" man, bearded like the sculptor and dressed like the crucified Christ, is calmly climbing a ladder with a lingering backward look. (There is an obvious visual reference here to the iconography of the Crucifixion, where in the scenes of the Descent from the Cross, Joseph of Arimathea is shown on a ladder as he unnails the body of Christ.) Toward the upper corner, on the ramparts of the tower, thus out of reach, stands the doubled Marie-Thérèse, calm and serene with her two doves. In the center, the main action comprises a mare, with her entrails hanging out of a gaping hole, carrying across her back a Marie-Thérèse torera, whose bared stomach and breasts are already swollen. In a dead faint she seems to be drawing her sword against herself, but this is not immediately clear as the sword against herself, but this is not immediately clear as the sword also touches the Minotaur's left hand. On the left, the little girl with the bunch of flowers is holding aloft a feeble candle whose pure light nevertheless manages to blind the Minotaur. The little girl is wearing the hat that Marie-Thérèse had on when photographed as an adolescent girl on October 20, 1922.[3] This photograph was in the artist's possession and now belongs to Maya Picasso. Finally, on the right, the Minotaur. His fear of the light betrays his anguish and, we

---

2. [These misogynist-seeming definitions of "femininity" derive from the psychoanalytic theories of neo-Freudians, such as Melanie Klein, whom Baer cites in her parenthetical explanation (Kleinian fantasy), below. See, for instance, Klein's *Love, Hate, and Reparation* (New York, 1975; 1st ed., London, 1937). In her letter to me, Baer further acknowledged her indebtedness to the French psychoanalyst André Green. Picasso may well have been aware of current psychoanalytic thought since he used the young psychiatrist Jacques Lacan—later to become renowned and controversial—as his general physician and to treat Dora Maar during her breakdown in 1945 (Gilot, pp. 89–90 and 159–60, where he interprets Gilot's dreams).]

3. [Baer published (p. 96) the uncropped photograph with a legible date; reproduced without its inscription in *Picasso 1980*, p. 254, and dated c. 1927.]

are tempted to say, his aggressive fantasies. He carries a bundle in a big, knotted red handkerchief (known from the colored proofs), red as a bullfighter's cape, red as blood. He has come to find something, to steal something, before escaping like the man on the left. The distant boat will carry him away. He is ready for the voyage with his belongings on his back. They are not heavy, however, since the arm which carries them is very small. The bundle, in fact, seems almost empty. Thus Marie-Thérèse is depicted five times: doubled, a spectator, unconscious of the passions unleashed by her condition; a little girl hardly younger than when Picasso met her (at least in the eyes of a man who was 53 and easily old enough to be her father), seen as childish and pure, trusting and naive, capable because of this very naivety of protecting her other persona; the wounded Marie-Thérèse, symbolized by the mare; and the torera about to transfix herself with her own sword. (The fact that it is difficult to distinguish whose hand is holding the sword is clearly not without significance.) What the mare is losing out of the hole in her belly, what is already in the Minotaur's bundle or what he desires to put there, is quite simply the baby of which he is madly jealous, and which he wants to destroy, and/or to wrench away so that he can have it for himself alone. (Here, we refer to the Kleinian fantasy, often misunderstood, but nonetheless true, which joins up with the theme of destructive rage and envy inherent in primal femininity.) His double, the man, understanding like Christ, prefers to leave. He does not run away, however, but cedes his protective role to the innocent child, which is enough to prevent the tragedy. On the other hand, he, in his persona of the sculptor, cannot but be envious: what price a lump of dead stone when compared with a living child? Therefore, we are given the destructive jealousy of the child/Minotaur whose place has been taken, the jealousy of the man/Minotaur who wants to carry off what he can never possess, and the jealousy of the sculptor who is unable to compete.

If we look carefully at the wound in the mare we realize full well that it is a baby pouring out. It is not a wound gored by a bull, but rather, a birth or miscarriage. There can be no doubt that there is a direct reference to the female gential organs.[4]

It is a crisis, but it is the final crisis. The Minotaur's mad urge to destroy had been exorcized by the immense toil of the print.[5] Evidently, the mad passion for Marie-Thérèse has been exorcized as well. She stays the Muse, but she is about to be a mother, and, from the very instant of birth, Picasso made no distinction between the mother and daughter, Maya, calling them both "my girls." It will not be long before he goes off,[6] just like Theseus, just like the sculptor, just like the Minotaur who will rapidly vanish from the scene and gradually turn into a humanized faun.

* * *

But a faun, even one as handsome as a god, is not a Minotaur. As we have seen

4. [Although the depicted forms are not distinct enough to leave "no doubt," Baer's reading nevertheless is persuasive in view of Picasso's famous painting and preparatory drawing of April 1936, *Minotaur Moving His House*. A blue-green mare gives birth to a bright red foal: "And the horse isn't gored—she's having a baby!" was Picasso's exasperated explanation to the puzzled Duncan (*Picasso's Picassos*, p. 87; color plate, p. 86). Marie-Thérèse on Christmas Eve 1934 had told Picasso of her pregnancy; their daughter Maya was born on 5 September (Baer, pp. 95 and 210; see also Pierre Cabanne, "Picasso et les joies de la paternité," *L'Oeil*, May 1974, p. 7).]

5. [*Minotauromachy* is Picasso's largest etching, developed through several proofs. *Picasso 1980* reproduces five states, pp. 328–29.]

6. [Laporte twice recalled Picasso's explanation: "You see, getting a woman with child is for me taking possession, and helps to kill whatever feelings existed" (p. 36). And, "I know that the birth of a child will be the end of my love for her" (p. 74).]

in the series of gouaches which antedate our aquatint[7] by a month, the Minotaur dies and takes his leave. A large gouache, a project for the drop-curtain of Romain Rolland's *Le 14 juillet* [fig. 116], shows us the Minotaur as a hollow doll, dressed in the costume of Harlequin and slung over the arm, like an overcoat, of a figure with the head of a griffon. That destructive passion that Picasso felt for Marie-Thérèse is now changed into love and tenderness. A new love affair is not far away. Like Theseus, Picasso made his choice: he found a solution for the anguish and the crisis, but in human terms, this is both a victory and a defeat. Doubtless his art, a new inspiration, a new stimulus, called him away.

Herbert Read
Minotauromachy and Guernica:
The Form of Things Unknown—[1952]*

After Barr began exploring Picasso's mysterious etching, Herbert Read, the British art historian and critic, discovered in *Minotauromachy* "a picture so rich in symbolic significance, that one is almost persuaded that Picasso at some time made a study of Jung" (p. 333, below). Some of these same Jungian archetypes reappear in *Guernica* as symbols of "collective or traditional significance," working their magic through Picasso's forms.

Whatever the theoretical justification for the use of such symbols,[1] their predominance in the history of art is inescapable, and Picasso is merely reverting, in this respect, to a predilection which was evident enough in Mycenaean and Minoan art, and is recurrent in the plastic arts, in myth and poetry, throughout the history of western civilization. The bull as a symbol, and the equally archaic symbol of the horse, were embodied in the ritual of the *tauromachia* or bullfight, a pagan ritual that has maintained, in the hearts of the Spanish people, a hold as strong as the Christian ritual. The art of Picasso, in the course of his development, builds up to the most complete revelation of the unconscious sources and symbolic significance of this same rite. I am referring to his painting called *Guernica*, regarded by some critics of art as Picasso's greatest achievement: it is certainly, in scale and execution, his most monumental work.

7. [In the deleted passages, Baer had been discussing *Faun Unveiling a Woman* of 12 June 1936; see also *Picasso 1980*, p. 332.]

*Excerpts reprinted from *The Form of Things Unknown* (New York, 1960), pp. 65–71, by permission of the publisher. Read prepared this talk for one of the Eranos conferences at a Swiss estate, frequently attended by Carl Jung, where "a sympathetic contact of minds takes place, with an interflow of very various cultural traditions" (preface, p. 12). The entire paper originally was published in *Eranos Jahrbuch 1952*, vol xxi; all footnotes have been updated to the standard works of Jung, Bollingen Series XX.

1. [Read's introduction distinguished between eidetic images—naturalistic signs for outer appearances—and symbols that capture "the subjective reality of the artist's imagination".]

Let me recall the origins of this painting. On 28th April 1937 the world was shocked to hear that the Basque town of Guernica had been destroyed by bombs dropped by German aeroplanes in the service of General Franco. Picasso began to paint his picture two days later, on 1st May, and worked on it with maniacal intensity until it was finished some weeks later. During the course of the work he declared: "In the panel on which I am working which I shall call *Guernica*, and in all my recent works of art, I clearly express my abhorrence of the military caste which has sunk Spain in an ocean of pain and death." [See p. 224, above.]

The motive of the painting is therefore not in doubt. How is that abhorrence expressed?

By symbols—by the traditional symbols of the bull and the horse, with a number of minor symbols in association with them. Before commenting on the use of these symbols in *Guernica*, let us note that two years before the town of Guernica was bombed, before there was any question of expressing abhorrence for a particular deed, Picasso had used virtually all the same symbols in a large etching which he called *Minotauromachy* [fig. 165].

There is a significant omission in the later picture—the figure of the bearded man who, in *Minotauromachy*, is climbing up a ladder on the left edge of the picture, as if to escape from the scene. It is the archetypal image of the wise man—"the saviour or redeemer" who, as Jung says, "lies buried and dormant in man's unconscious since the dawn of culture," and who is "awakened whenever the times are out of joint and a human society committed to a serious error."[2]

The scene that the Wise Man abandons shows the Minotaur advancing with uplifted arms towards a child who, with a light uplifted in one hand and a bunch of flowers in the other, surveys a horse uprearing, under the threat of the Minotaur, with a woman, apparently dead, stretched on its back. From an opening in the tower-like building in the background, which may be intended as the labyrinth of the Minotaur, two figures in loving embrace, and associated with doves, look down on the scene.

It is a picture so rich in symbolic significance, that one is almost persuaded that Picasso has at some time made a study of Jung and Kerényi! In addition to the figure of the Wise Man, already mentioned, we have the Minotaur, representing the dark powers of the labyrinthine unconscious; the sacrificial horse, bearing on its back the overpowered libido; and confronting them the divine child, the culture bearer, the bringer of light, the child-hero who fearlessly confronts the powers of darkness, the bearer of higher consciousness.[3] How easily a Jungian interpretation can be given to this picture may be judged from the following passage from Jung's contribution to an *Introduction to a Science of Mythology*:

> It is a striking paradox in all child-myths that the "child" is on the one hand delivered helpless into the power of terrible enemies and in continual danger of extinction, while on the other he possesses powers far exceeding those of ordinary humanity. This is closely related to the psychological fact that though the child may be "insignificant," unknown, "a mere child," he is also divine. * * * The "child" is born out of the womb of the

---

2. "Psychology and Literature," *The Spirit in Man, Art and Literature,* The Collected Works of C. G. Jung, Bollingen Series XX, vol. 15 (Princeton, 1966), p. 103. [Hereafter: Jung, Bollingen 15, etc. The essay was reprinted in *Modern Man in Search of a Soul*.]

3. "The Psychology of the Child Archetype," *The Archetypes and the Collective Unconscious,* Jung, Bollingen 9 (Princeton, 1968), pp. 169–70. [Published in London with Karl Kerényi as *Introduction to a Science of Mythology* (1950).]

unconscious, begotten out of the depths of human nature, or rather out of living Nature herself. It is a personification of vital forces quite outside the limited range of our conscious mind; of possible ways and means of which our one-sided conscious mind knows nothing; a wholeness which embraces the very depths of Nature. It represents the strongest, the most ineluctable urge in every being, namely the urge to realize itself.[4]

The *Minotauromachy* may therefore be regarded as Picasso's affirmation of the grandeur and invincibility of the "child," a child holding the light of revelation and not at all terrified by the powers of darkness confronting it. An obvious allegory, it might be said, of no great interest because it "nowhere oversteps the bounds of conscious comprehension";[5] but then this dominant theme by no means exhausts the symbolical significance of the picture. If the dead or unconscious woman represents the libido, why does she carry a sword in her right hand? And what is the significance of the maidens and doves who lovingly look down on the strange scene? All these symbols, no doubt, would yield to rationalistic explanation, but I must be forgiven if I do not dwell on them because what matters, in my present context, is not the interpretation of meaning, but the fact that the artist has employed universal symbols of this kind.[6] Before making any general comment on this process of symbolization I would like to return to *Guernica*.

We are lucky to possess photographs which show the evolution of this painting in Picasso's studio—not only the various stages in the composition of the canvas itself, but also a considerable number of preliminary sketches of details.[7] This preliminary material shows that the constituent symbols of the painting—the bull, the horse, the woman with a dead child, the light-bearer, the figure representing the sacrificed republic—were present in Picasso's mind from the beginning as discrete phenomena. He began with these symbols—the bull, the horse and the woman bearing a light. In some of the composition studies, pencil sketches on gesso made on 1st and 2nd May 1937, a Pegasus is introduced, at first perching on the bull's back, but next day emerging from a wound in the horse's flank. But this symbol was quickly discarded, and others were introduced, notably the one of the victim, at first the traditional republican figure with helm and spear. These traditional accessories are gradually discarded, and in general there is a tendency to get away from literary or historical associations and to let the symbols tell by their inner expressive power. The artist is seen, in these preliminary sketches, exploring the expressive tensions of distortion and exaggeration, until he has substituted his own symbols of power, sacrifice, terror, death and resurrection.

As in the *Minotauromachy*, the horse is the sacrificial animal of the Upanishads, where it signifies a renunciation of the universe. "When the horse is sacrificed," comments Jung,

> then the world is sacrificed and destroyed, as it were . . . The horse signifies the libido, which has passed into the world. We previously saw that the "mother libido" must be sacrificed in order to produce the world; here the world is destroyed by the repeated

---

4. Ibid., p. 170.

5. Ibid., p. 173.

6. In a drawing made two years later, entitled, *The End of a Monster,* Picasso shows a sea goddess emerging from the sea to hold up a mirror to the Minotaur, who lies on the beach transfixed by an arrow [Barr, p. 211.]

7. [Read reproduces our figures 6 and 10.]

sacrifice of the same libido, which once belonged to the mother. The horse can, therefore, be substituted as a symbol for this libido, because, as we saw, it had manifold connections with the mother. The sacrifice of the horse can only produce another state of introversion, which is similar to that before the creation of the world.[8]

This is only a casual comparison, but Picasso's use of these symbols is unerringly orthodox, and the question is whether he is orthodox because he is learned in the history of symbolism, or because he allows his symbols to emerge freely from his unconscious. They not only emerge as orthodox symbols, but in significant association: the sacrificial horse with the figure representing the sacrificed republic, the bull with the horse, the light-bearer with the bull, minor symbols like the flower that grows by the side of the broken sword, and the dove of peace that flies above the carnage.

The question could only be settled by a direct approach to the artist, and this I feel too diffident to make—it would be to invite a confession that in the estimation of psychologists would be damaging to the dynamic force of the work of art. It is generally known, however, that Picasso is not a naïve artist: he is a man of culture, who reads voraciously. It is not inconceivable, therefore, that the traditional symbols he uses are used with deliberate intention. Such symbols are activated by surface emotions, and not by the unconscious. But as Jung has said,

> A symbol loses its magical power . . . as soon as its dissolubility is recognized. An effective symbol, therefore, must have a nature that is unimpeachable . . . its form must be sufficiently remote from comprehension as to frustrate every attempt of the critical intellect to give any satisfactory account of it; and, finally, its aesthetic appearance must have such a convincing appeal that no sort of argument can be raised against it on that score.[9]

In the past I have praised *Guernica* as a work of art [p. 218, above] and even now I am not going to suggest that it can be dismissed as a work of art merely because its symbols are traditional—that criterion would exclude the best part of all the visual art ever created by man. But I would maintain that there is a stage in the evolution of symbolism at which the symbols become clichés, and clichés can never be used in a work of art. A dead or exhausted symbol is just as much a cliché as a stale epithet or a hackneyed metaphor. The situation obviously is not improved by beginning with the clichés and then deliberately disguising them. Artistic creation, to the same degree and in the same manner as effective symbolism, implies spontaneity: the artistically valid symbols are those which rise, fully armed by the libido, from the depths of the unconscious.

What redeems this picture, to a degree I would not now venture to determine, is what saves any painting of the past that makes a conscious use of traditional symbolism—any painting making use of the symbols of the Christian faith, or a painting by Poussin making use of the symbols of classical mythology: I mean the fact that every line, every form, every colour, is dominated by the aesthetic sensibility of the artist. What the symbols import into this aesthetic organization is a certain element of collective or traditional significance. * * *

One way of putting it (it is Jung's way) is that "humanity came to its gods through

8. "The Sacrifice," *Symbols of Transformation,* Jung, Bollingen 5 (Princeton, 1956), pp. 421–22. [First published in 1916 as *Psychology of the Unconscious.*]

9. "The Problem of Types in Poetry," *Psychological Types,* Jung, Bollingen 6 (Princeton, 1971), p. 237.

accepting the reality of the symbol"; but equally one might say that it was only possible to accept the reality of the symbol because the artist had succeeded in giving it *living form*.

The complex but deliberate symbolism of works like *Minotauromachy* and *Guernica* has simplified our task, which is to show the interrelations between the forms of art and the energies of the psyche. I have admitted that to the extent the symbols used by Picasso in these two pictures are deliberate and allegorical, to that extent we may suspect that they have been fished from waters that are relatively shallow; but *Minotauromachy* and *Guernica* occupy a small place in the copious repertory of images created by Picasso throughout his career, most of which resist any attempt at rationalistic explanation. Other images are vital, and their vitality comes, not from any identity with the outward world of visual appearances, but from a fidelity to an inner world where vision is archetypal.

Joseph Campbell
Minotauromachy and Guernica:
Creative Mythology—[1968]*

Joseph Campbell's monumental publications on comparative religions and mythology include observations on Picasso's iconography; his comments on *Minotauromachy* are excerpted here. Campbell also wrote poetically of "Picasso's apocalyptic *Guernica*" which, despite its great size, suggests to him a puppet stage: "the figures are two-dimensional cut-outs, without depth, as we all are now supposed to be in this self-moving machine world: mere masks of nothing beyond."[1]

In Figure 165, his etching called *Minotauromachy* (1935), the same monster[2] appears from the watery abyss, shading his eyes from the light, in polar contrast to the figure of the sage at the left (Nietzsche's "Socratic Man"), climbing aloft to escape the reality of the Dionysian terror, while the Graces Three with their dove (the bird of Venus-Aphrodite) calmly regard the apparition: the youngest of them, innocent Thalia, holding in one hand the flowers of life-abundance and in the other the light of consciousness, which are here the foci of the composition, equidistant from the eye of the sage and left eye of the bull. The sword of the overcome matador is pointed not

*From *The Masks of God: Creative Mythology* (New York, 1968, Viking paperback, 1970), pp. 668–9, 671, by permission of author and publisher. This fourth volume concludes the *Masks of God* series covering primitive, oriental, and occidental religions and myths (1959–68); among his earlier studies are *A Skeleton Key to Finnegans Wake* (1944) and *The Hero with a Thousand Faces* (1949).

1. *Creative Mythology*, p. 215; also pp. 209 , 211–12, 215–18. Other critics have noted this stage-like quality of *Guernica*: Hohl, p. 317, and Bannard, p. 303, above, for instance.

2. [Campbell had been discussing the "monster" of the *Minotaure* cover, fig. 114.]

at the bull but at the eviscerated horse, and the matador is revealed as a woman. Clearly the *Guernica* (1937) is a reorganization of the same mythological motifs, recognized as implicit in a monstrous act of war and rendered as a moment equally of rapture and of pain (terror-joy), with the figure in flames at the right marvelously falling and rising at once, both from and toward the window at the upper right, which, like the end of *Finnegans Wake,* opens to the void.

"The bull is a bull and the horse is a horse," Picasso is reported to have said, "These are animals, massacred animals. That's all, so far as I am concerned."[3] Which is obviously untrue: horses are not of papier-mâché, nor do bulls have an eye in the middle of the forehead. Such deliberate prevarication is justified, however, by the fact that mythic symbols point beyond the reach of "meaning," and even in the sphere of meaning have many "meanings." To define and fix authoritatively any consciously conceivable set of final "meanings" would be to kill them—which is, of course, what happens in dogmatic and historicizing theology, as in both didactic and pornographic art. Symbols of the mythological order, like life, which they unfold from dark to light, are there, "thus come" from beyond "meaning," on all levels at once.

Accordingly, as James Joyce's title, *Ulysses,* refers us from the Waking level of the action of his novel to the mythic, so Picasso's title *Guernica,* from the mythic order of his imagery to the Waking of historical event. Such double-talk, uniting history and geography *(land náma)* and the archetypes of the psyche, is of the essence of creative art-as-myth; the prime function of the Muses being to serve as the channel of communication between the spheres of daylight knowledge and the seat of life, between the earthy order below of silent Thalia, and that aloft of Apollo and the Graces:[4] the Lord of Light (consciousness) and the Goddess of Life (creative energy) in her triadic manifestation as future, present, and past: "Anna was, Livia is, Plurabelle's to be."[5]

In art, in myth, in rites, we enter the sphere of dream awake. And as the imagery of dream will be on one level local, personal, and historic, but at bottom rooted in the instincts, so also myth and symbolic art. The message of an effective living myth is delivered to the sphere of bliss of the deep unconscious, where it touches, wakes, and summons energies; so that symbols operating on that level are energy-releasing and -channeling stimuli. That is their function—their "meaning"—on the level of Deep Sleep: while on the level of Waking Consciousness the same symbols are inspirational, informative, initiatory, rendering a sense of illumination with respect to the instincts touched, i.e., the order subliminal of nature—inward and outward nature—of which the instincts touched are the life.

3. [See page 102, above.]

4. [Campbell refers to fig. 13 in his *Creative Mythology*: an Italian Renaissance image of "The Music of the Spheres," dated 1496.]

5. James Joyce, *Finnegans Wake* (New York, 1939), p. 215.

Patricia Failing
Dream and Lie of Franco: Picasso's "Cries of Children . . . Cries of Stones"— [1977]*

Picasso created his etchings, *Dream and Lie of Franco* (figs. 109 and 110), in January 1937, just before he received the commission for *Guernica*; he added the last four scenes in early June (fig. 55) as he completed the large painting. While most critics comment on the imagery that these two very different works share, the etchings have been overshadowed by the vast canvas. They have not received the attention they deserve as independent works of art and as political statement. In this article developed from studies begun in a graduate seminar, Failing draws on contemporary sources and newspaper coverage to illuminate Picasso's famous etching.

Within Picasso's oeuvre, the *Dream and Lie of Franco* is the single work in which propagandistic considerations outweigh artistic ones. It is important, therefore, to look at the details of the etchings in relation to specific historical circumstances. The central character in the *Dream and Lie* suite is a sluglike monster, the "evil-omened polyp" named in the poem accompanying the etchings (p. 184, above). The origins of this polyp form can be traced to studies of biomorphic, Surrealist forms Picasso drew in April 1936. These forms, marked with a characteristic mustache, resurface in the *Dream and Lie* as symbolic respresentation of General Francisco Franco. Short (5'3"), plump, and often photographed in Legionnaire's attire, Franco was an ideal and frequent target for caricature.

Once introduced, the monster is treated as the main character in a violent and obscene graphic *commedia dell'arte* using simplistic symbolic mechanisms that sympathetic viewers could readily perceive. One must underline that the propagandistic potential of Picasso's solutions was apparent not just to an elite group of Paris intellectuals. Copies of Picasso's work were stockpiled by the Republican Ministry of Foreign Affairs in Valencia, and offered to its representatives as anti-Franco propaganda on the local level.[1]

A scene-by-scene explanation will make the connections clearer. The scenes will be numbered here in reverse order. Picasso characteristically etched as if he were drawing—that is, without regard to the flop-effect produced by the etching plate; also, it would have been unnecessary to draw in reverse, given that the sheets were designed to be cut up and sold as individual scenes. Thus for purposes of

---

*Shortened for this anthology by the author from her article, "Picasso's 'Cries of Children . . . Cries of Stones,'" *Art News*, September 1977, pp. 57–62 and p. 64. Failing is a contributing editor of the magazine.

1. Luis Mongió, Professor Emeritus of Spanish, University of California at Berkeley, confirmed that, as Republican diplomatic representative to Morocco, he received the *Dream and Lie* portfolio for such use.

166. Picasso. Details from *Dream and Lie of Franco*. (See Nos. 109 and 110.)

discussion each row of illustrations will be numbered from right to left, moving from the top row to the bottom, starting with the sequence dated 8 January 1937 (fig. 166).

In scene 1, the "evil-omened polyp" enters astride a caricature of a disemboweled horse, carrying a sword and religious banner and wearing a crown, atop which rests a crescent moon. The image connects with a specific event: the assault on Madrid in November 1936. Rebel forces announced victory in advance and following suit, Radio Lisbon broadcast a description of Franco's triumphal entry into Madrid astride a white horse even though, in fact, the rebels did not penetrate beyond the outskirts of the city.

In a more general sense, the entire scene is an obvious parody of equestrian portraits of Spanish nobility, the most famous of which are those of the 17th-century Catholic king Philip IV and his court by Velázquez.

This association, however, is more than just purely art historical. When the war broke out, most of the middle class was attracted to the Falange, the Spanish fascist party. The grinning sun on the monster's right relates it to the Falange, whose party anthem was "Cara al Sol" ("Face to the Sun").

As a political body, the Falange aligned its ideology specifically with the nationalist policies of Spain's Catholic kings of the 16th and 17th centuries, among the most prominent of whom were Velázquez's clientele. Picasso, in parodying Velázquez, thus illustrates the aspirations of Franco and his party to the policies and privileges of Catholic monarchy.

The image of the Virgin, which appears here and in a majority of the scenes, serves as a reminder that unlike fascism anywhere else, the Spanish version was uniquely linked with Catholicism. In drawing up the new constitution in 1931, the Republican government proposed the abolition of state subsidy to the clergy, the dissolution of convents and monasteries, and the striking down of Catholicism as Spain's official religion. It is little wonder, therefore, that church leaders characterized the war as a holy crusade, and that bishops and priests all over the world implored the protection of the Virgin for the rebel Nationalist troops.

Another relationship merits special emphasis: the crescent moon atop the monster's crown is the one symbol Picasso carefully includes in every scene. As the national symbol of Morocco, the crescent moon was the official insignia worn on the lapel or hat by the native Moorish troops who were the backbone of Franco's army.

Picasso may have known about Franco's association with the Moors and Foreign Legion even before it became apparent that Franco was relying on Moorish troops in 1936. In October 1934, the year of Picasso's last visit to Spain, General Franco, then army chief-of-staff for the Republican government, used the Foreign Legion and Moorish *Regulares* to suppress a miner's rebellion in Asturias. Franco had commanded the Foreign Legion from 1923 until 1927, and returned clandestinely to Morocco in July 1936 in order to gather military support for his coup. Franco's association with the Moors was thus long-standing and well known.

In scene 2, Franco's relationship with the Moors is again stressed: the half-moon appears, but this time the monster also wears a hat which combines two others customarily worn by Moorish *Regulares*—a tasseled fez encircled by wrapping known as a tarbush. The three-cornered hat under the half-moon is a schematic representation of a priest's ritual headdress (and is rendered in more detail in other scenes). This allusion to religious institutions is reinforced by a processional banner decorated with a traditional conical form of the Madonna, in which her female shape is purposely disguised by her costume.

The huge genitals of the Franco monster in scene 2, besides being a reference to traditional army "machismo" and a reminder of the penis preoccupation of Moorish troops (who habitually castrated the corpses of their victims), were probably also intended to parody the propaganda of the Nationalist general Queipo de Llano, whose notoriety was exceeded only by that of Franco himself.

De Llano had gained control of Seville in the July coups, immediately seized the local radio station, and began nightly broadcasts which made him famous throughout Western Europe. In one of the broadcasts, on 23 July 1936 for example, Queipo declared that:

> Our brave Legionnaires and Regulares have shown the red cowards what it means to be a man. And incidentally, the wives of the Reds too. The Communist and Anarchist women, after all, have made themselves fair game by their doctrine of free love. And now they have at least made the acquaintance of real men and not the milksops of militiamen.[2]

Costumed in a bishop's mitre and the boots, buttons, and sword of Velázquez's aristocrats, the Franco monster in scene 3 attacks a classical sphinx with a pickaxe. Here the theme is Franco as enemy of the arts. The classical female statuary type is drawn from Picasso's etchings, "The Sculptor's Studio" of 1933. Profaning the sculptor-sculpture relationship, Franco approaches the bust not with sculptor's tools but with an instrument of destruction, comparable to the bombs his airmen dropped near the Prado.

To understand the significance of scene 3, the distorted and inflammatory nature of international press reports must be taken into account.[3] Of the atrocities commited by both sides in summer and fall 1936, those perpetrated in the name of the Republic received the most press attention. Reports of church burnings and destruction of religious art were repeated again and again by rebel propagandists, who cast the Nationalists as saviors of culture. In fact, Nationalists' incendiary bombs in November had ignited such art repositories as the Madrid townhouse of the Duke of Alba. Loyalist militiamen rescued numerous artifacts from the flames while the Duke, in London to escape the turmoil, publicly blamed the destruction upon "red vandalism."

2. Arthur Koestler, *Spanish Testament* (London, 1937), p. 31.

3. Emphasized by Dr. Hershel Chipp, Professor Emeritus of Art History at Berkeley. [See also Bibliography for his 1974 article.]

Such charges prompted Picasso to a rare public statement in July 1937:

The ridiculous story which the Fascist propagandists have circulated throughout the world has been exposed completely many times by the great number of artists and intellectuals who have visited Spain lately. . . . Everyone is acquainted with the barbarous bombardment of the Prado Museum by Rebel airplanes, and everyone also knows how the militiamen succeeded in saving art treasures at the risk of their lives. . . . On the one hand, the rebels throw incendiary bombs on museums. On the other, the people place in security the objectives of these bombs, the works of art.[4]

In scene 4, the mustachioed monster appears in a traditional Spanish woman's costume, wearing a *peineta* [large ornamental comb] and mantilla, and waving a sword in one hand and fan in the other. On the fan is the conical Madonna which decorates the banners in earlier scenes.

The outline of a city looming in the background links several ideas: monstrosity masquerading as tradition, a transvestite allusion to cowardice, and a specific historical situation. In January 1937, Franco's troops had yet to penetrate beyond the outskirts of Madrid, and civilian resistance to the Nationalist siege was a principal source of hope, optimism, and positive propaganda.

The optimistic note that distinguishes scene 5 from the earlier four is related to the same civilian determination to resist. Here the monster, obviously surprised by the attack of a noble and ferocious bull—the traditional symbol of Spain—loses his crown and sword as he is knocked off his feet. The action of the noble and human-eyed bull, Franco's adversary in this scene of confrontation, parallels that of the Popular Front who clearly surprised Franco with the tenacity of their resistance.

Scene 6 is more complex. The Franco monster, wearing so many hats that one must be tied on with a string, kneels to pray before an altar upon which, instead of a religious image, is a coin labeled "I duro." Religious references are strengthened with details: besides tarbush and fez, the monster wears a flat-brimmed padre's hat and at its neck, in place of the traditional crucifix, hangs a sword. Besides illustrating the standard critique of capitalists as "worshippers of money," this scene comments upon the formidable economic power of the Spanish Church.

In scene 7, the Franco creature gives birth behind barbed wire, through a hairy orifice, to an army of snakes and slimy beasts. Hanging in the position where male genitals were found in the previous scene are schematic representations of breasts and nipples which again suggest the monster's dual sexual attributes and illustrate its role as "mother" of the disgusting creatures who populate the trenches. That the "mother" gives birth in the name of religion is indicated by the three-cornered priest's hat and religious banner.

4. See Barr, pp. 202 and 264, and Ashton, pp. 143–44. [Cf. pp. 224–25, above.]

In number 8, the monster arrests and strangles Pegasus while stabbing him with an arrow-tipped banner. As Picasso still emphatically maintained when he composed an *Open Letter to a Young Spanish Artist* in 1952,[5] Franco should be recognized and exposed as oppressor of worker and peasant, and of creative energy and freedom. In the 1937 *Dream and Lie* etchings, Picasso employs a strangled symbol of the Muses to make the same statement.

The arrow-shaped lance that wounds Pegasus in scene 8 is again featured in scene 9, an equestrian portrait in which the monster tilts the Falangist sun in a manner recalling Don Quixote. Arrows gathered under a yoke were the official symbol of the Falange party, as they had been for the Catholic sovereigns Ferdinand and Isabella, to whom the Falange paid homage with their choice of emblem. The parody of Don Quixote, the literary character who embodied the aspirations of the Golden Age Catholic warrior, illustrates Picasso's reaction to Nationalist propaganda such as that by the rightwing poet José Maria Pemán in August 1936. "Twenty centuries of Christian civilization are at our backs," proclaimed Pemán. "We fight for love and honor, the paintings of Velázquez, for the comedies of Lope de Vega, for Don Quixote and El Escorial!"[6]

In scene 10, the first in the upper right on the second plate, the monster consumes the entrails of Pegasus in an appropriately monstrous fashion, another expressive variation on the theme "Franco versus the Arts."

Scenes 11 and 12 depart radically in style and content from the previous ten. In number 11, a bleeding woman with the face of the sphinx (scene 3) lies wounded in a field with burning buildings in the background—a reference to incendiary bombing and to Spanish women who fought and suffered as warriors and victims. Scene 12 has no overt political reference. Although it obviously held private meanings for Picasso, who repeated the interwined horse and fallen man motif in *Guernica*, the tender embrace of the "classical hero" of several other mid-1930s etchings and the graceful horse contrast with the broad depictions of violence in the other scenes.

5. Ashton, pp. 146–47.
6. Thomas, *The Spanish Civil War* (1977) p. 416.

The style of scenes 1–10 returns in number 13. Here a particularly grotesque and hairy version of the Franco-monster confronts a Spanish bull so noble and intelligent that rays emanate from his head.

In scene 14, the Franco-creature metamorphoses into a horse wounded by a humanoid bull in a manner familiar to all aficionados of the *corrida*. Among the entrails spilling from the belly of the horse is a religious banner, the crescent moon, a sword, and the monarchist flags which had officially replaced the Republican flag in mid-August 1936. At a ceremony in Seville, Franco kissed the flag many times, as did the Cardinal of Seville, shouting to the crowd with tears in his eyes, "This is our flag, one to which we have all sworn, for which our fathers died, a hundred times covered with glory!"[7]

The transformation of the "evil-omened polyp" into a gored horse in this scene serves as a reminder of the essential connection between Picasso's imagery in the *Dream and Lie* and certain ideas he shared with the Surrealists.

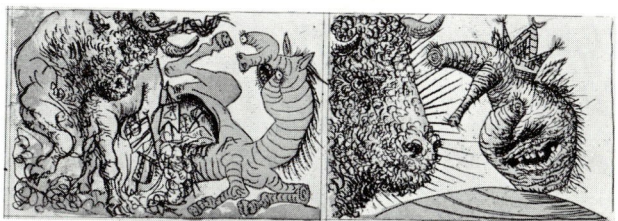

Like the Surrealists, Picasso exploits in this series the fascination which deformity and monstrousness hold for the human psyche. The polyp that turns into the horse reflects the Surrealist concept of metamorphosis. The incongruous juxtaposition of the monstrous and the beautiful is another Surrealist device. Picasso's links with Surrealism, however, are most clearly expressed in his poem accompanying the etchings. Poetic images of "evil-omened polyps standing naked," of a "commedia dell'arte of poor weaving and dyeing of clouds," of "teeth driven into . . . horse wide open to the sun," of "banners," of "clouds tied by its [sic] feet," of "entrails," and of "broken wings" appear simultaneously in poem and etchings, which are not therefore illustrations of the poem, but visual forms of similar imagery. John Golding concludes that "perhaps more than any other work by Picasso, the *Dream and Lie of Franco* breaks down, as the Surrealists so passionately wanted to do, distinctions between thought, writing, and visual imagery."[8]

The emotional and poetic rapport is perhaps strongest between the last lines of the poem (composed in January) and the final four *Dream and Lie* etchings which derive from a series of studies that followed the painting of *Guernica*. What these final four etchings express, in fact, seems to be exactly this: "—cries of children cries of women cries of birds cries of flowers cries of timbers and of stones—" [fig. 55].

* * *

7. Ibid., p. 414.
8. *Picasso in Retrospect*, p. 119.

To assume, as many authors, have,[9] that Picasso's approach to symbolism in the *Dream and Lie* etchings matches that of *Guernica* ignores the fact that the etchings were intended as a money-making, propagandistic statement of marketable appeal; a certain obviousness thus was required for which there is no parallel in *Guernica*. Certainly the two works are related in emotion and spirit, but not necessarily in terms of specific iconography. To make this assumption fails to do justice both to the propagandistic effectiveness of the *Dream and Lie of Franco,* and to the more universally expressive visual power of *Guernica*.

Robert Motherwell
The Drawings: Universal Language of Children's Art—[1970]*

Like other American artists and critics, Motherwell values the spontaneous and emotionally charged *Guernica* studies more highly than the finished canvas.[1] These brief observations from a lecture are of special interest, furthermore, in suggesting the many intellectual and philosophical concerns of this important Abstract Expressionist. Accepting the challenge of Picasso's problematic composition, Motherwell since the late 1940s has created an eloquent response: the many versions of *Elegy to the Spanish Republic* (fig. 122 and p. 117, above).

Part of the enterprise of modern art is to strip away from painting the costumes, the masquerades, the status symbols of church and state and politics—hence, its so-called abstraction, which is actually a humanly felt universalism. This universalism is not unparallel to that of small children, as when the French Fauves and the German Expressionists began to paint more and more directly, colorfully, immediately and expressively, or when Kandinsky in Munich began to understand the significance of the scribble (before he fell into logic in Paris), or Klee in Germany began turning his own scribbles into the fairyland of his magical art, as did Miró and the

9. [Among others, Failing discusses Larrea and Carla Gottlieb. She debates whether Picasso planned the *Dream and Lie* as a sequential series (and it was decided, later, to divide and reproduce the images as postcards) or whether, from the start, Picasso planned for separate postcards. Failing argues convincingly for the latter: the individual vignettes are just under French postcard dimension (10 x 15 cm in the 1930s), are marked by double lines to facilitate cutting, and can be understood individually and separately from each other.]

*Reprinted from "The Scholar Cornered: The Universal Language of Children's Art," *The American Scholar,* winter 1970, pp. 26–27 (from opening address, 29 April 1970, conference on International Exchange in the Arts), kindly brought to my attention by Mr. Motherwell.

1. See the essays by Bannard and Greenberg; also Spender, p. 217, above. Already in 1944, Motherwell had brilliantly discussed "the relative failure" of *Guernica* from a Marxist viewpoint, in contrast to the preliminary drawings that he termed "a question of Picasso's own genius" ("The Modern Painter's World," *DYN,* November 1944, pp. 9–11; reprinted in Barbara Rose, *Readings in American Art Since 1900* [New York, 1967]).

French Surrealists in Paris, and as later the American Abstract Expressionists in New York used the scribble in the interests of a more sublime or tragic art than the intimacy of prewar Paris. Or, as Picasso quite consciously did in those great drawings during the Spanish Civil War after *Guernica,* drawings much greater than the painting itself. While in his picture he relied on Cubism, which is essentially a lyrical, and not a dramatic or tragic, mode of expression, in the drawings he relied some on Goya—natural enough for a Spanish painter during those terrible days of the rise of Fascism—but, above all, on the directness of children's line drawings; for the world of the tragic is not alien, any more than the world of joy or anxiety or any other mode of feeling, to children's expressions.[2] Still, in those Picassos, there is a maturity and a freedom of choice that is more exhilarating than children's art, which, after all, seems to be inherent in them, in an Aristotelian (or perhaps Jungian) sense, whereas Picasso's freedom is hard-won, in that spirit-breaking struggle against everything that is provincial, parochial, ironclad conventional in the traditional classes and the nationalisms that surround every grown man, and which he may never conquer, but to which he dare not succumb without distorting the most valuable part of his inheritance, his universal humanity.

Clement Greenberg
The Charnel House: Picasso's
Last Masterpiece?—[1966]*

Greenberg's description of *Guernica* in 1957 must have shocked readers into viewing the famous painting for the first time as a problematic, abstract composition quite apart from its political message: "With its bulging and buckling, it looks not a little like a battle scene from a pediment that has been flattened out under a defective steam roller—in other words, as if conceived within an illusion of space deeper than that in which it was actually executed."[1] In a more positive vein, he discussed here *The Charnel House* (fig. 167) as a successful resolution of Picasso's formal problems.

Picasso's painting started to fall off in quality after 1925, but it continued to count in the history of art for another dozen years or so. It continued to germinate during this

---

2. [Indeed! See pp. 244–46, above.]

*Reprinted from "Picasso Since 1945," *Artforum,* V (Oct. 1966), pp. 28–29, by permission of author and publisher; the essay reviewed Picasso's postwar works exhibited in Washington in 1966. Clement Greenberg (b. 1909) has been an influential formalist critic since the 1940s when, writing for *The Nation* and the *Partisan Review,* he first championed the new "American-type painting," as he termed the art of Jackson Pollock and other Abstract Expressionists (see his anthology, *Art and Culture,* Boston, 1961, 1965).

1. Greenberg, "Picasso at Seventy-Five," *Arts,* XXXII (Oct. 1957), p. 45.

time even if it could no longer realize. During that same time, in 1930 and 1931, his sculpture came to a climax, of realization as well as invention, in the wrought-iron constructions he did with Gonzalez's technical help. (This climax might have been prolonged had he executed some of the sketches for sculpture he did in the year or two following—for example, the pencil drawings he made in February 1933 that are grouped under the title "An Anatomy.")[2] But his sculptures, too, began to fall off a short while after that. The real turning point, for his sculpture no less than his painting, came, however, around the time of *Guernica*, in 1937. It does not matter so much that since then Picasso's failed works far exceed his successful ones in number; what does matter is that the terms of success themselves were from then on pitched a good deal lower than before. Picasso's art ceased being indispensable. It no longer contributed to the ongoing evolution of major art; however much it might intrigue pictorial sensibility, it no longer challenged and expanded it.

I know of only one painting that Picasso has done within the last thirty years which is an exception to what I have just said. It is the *Charnel House* of 1945 [fig. 167] * * * and I am tempted to say that it may be Picasso's last unqualified masterpiece in any medium.[3]

It is not its quality alone that makes *Charnel House* a surprise (and I don't want to exaggerate that quality: Picasso did greater things before 1925); it is also the way in which it revises *Guernica*. To judge from photographs, the latter's first and exclusively linear state was better than any subsequent one. Without being entirely linear itself, the later painting recaptures something of the quality of that first state and improves on it. *Charnel House* was finished and brought off by being left unfinished. The whole upper third of the canvas on which it was painted contains nothing but black lines on priming. The uncovered priming also runs along the other three sides of the canvas to form a narrow and irregular internal frame broken only here and there by extensions of the painted surface. And the priming reappears, crisscrossed by incompletely erased lines in charcoal, among the patches and wedges of black, grey, and grey-blue that fill the middle and bottom of the picture. In *Guernica* it's precisely the upper part of the picture that goes out of kilter most: the white shapes there fail to stay in place and relate themselves in a binding way to the pyramid of interlocking shapes below. And it's as though the "unfinished" state of the upper part of *Charnel House* betrayed a recognition of this. This is suggested further by the fact that *Guernica*'s central pyramid is more or less retained (along with the upturned face of the dead man in the lower left). It seems to me that in *Charnel House* Picasso also makes a specific correction of the color scheme of the earlier picture by introducing a pale grey-blue amid the blacks and greys and whites. This works, along with the use of priming instead of applied white, to give the later painting more ease of space, more air. *Guernica* suffers from being boxed-in, too compressed for its size.

2. [Examples of "An Anatomy" are illustrated in *Picasso's Picassos* (1981), pp. 179–81. Referring to the realization of earlier sculptural ideas, Greenberg cited Picasso's sculpture for the Chicago Civic Center, "monumentally executed in steel and installed in front of a new building in downtown Chicago. The result is magnificent." (Letter of 18 June 1974 to me.)]

3. [In his 1974 letter, Greenberg requested addition of this note:

I'm no longer of the opinion that *Charnel House* is an "unqualified masterpiece." Renewing acquaintance with it at The Museum of Modern Art in New York, I find myself slightly—if only slightly—dissatisfied with it; it doesn't "sit" in quite the same way that it did at first sight. Right now I'd say that Picasso's last unqualified masterpiece in any medium would have to be sought among his graphic works.]

167. Picasso. *The Charnel House*. 1945. Oil and charcoal on canvas, 78⅝ x 98½" (approx. 2 x 2.5 m). Z.XIX:76. The Museum of Modern Art, New York

Charnel House has a more original as well as an easier relation to the proportions and size of its canvas. This is an effect of design, too, of the way in which the staccato rhythms in the lower left center open out into larger, arabescal ones as the main axis of the composition swings up into the upper right-hand corner.

Charnel House is a much smaller painting than *Guernica,* and Picasso's Cubism or neo-Cubism has never been comfortable in a very large format.[4] *Guernica* tends to be jerky; it stops and starts, buckles and bulges. *Charnel House* flows, and flows throughout. *Guernica* aims at the epic and falls into the declamatory (though there are parts of it, but only parts, that are better than that—the central pyramid is one). *Charnel House* is magnificently lyrical—and Picasso at his best is usually lyrical. And it is fitting that this picture should be lyrical, for it is an elegy, not an outcry or even a protest, and it is fitting that an elegy should chant rather than intone.

William Rubin
The Charnel House—[1972]*

For a decade after 1971, *The Charnel House* hung diagonally across from *Guernica* and next to related studies. They transformed this museum gallery into a worthy memorial: eloquent witnesses to the horrors of war. Rubin, a trained art historian who knew Picasso, examines *The Charnel House* and makes us respond to its poignant forms and to see connections with Picasso's other works, including of course *Guernica.*

Picasso usually relies on personal experience and the given of his immediate environment as the point of departure for his art. The pressures of external circumstances tend to be communicated indirectly—in terms of style and mood—the subjects remaining nominally familiar, even conventional. "I have not painted the war," Picasso was quoted as saying in autumn 1944, "because I am not the kind of painter who goes out like a photographer for something to depict."[1]

However, in the months following that remark, precisely under the impact of photographs of concentration-camp abominations, Picasso began his awesome *Charnel*

---

4. [Cf. Bannard's criticism, pp. 299–305.]

*Reprinted from *Picasso in the Collection of the Museum of Modern Art* (New York, The Museum of Modern Art, 1972), pp. 166–69, by permission of the author and publisher (some internal references and notes deleted). Director of the Department of Painting and Sculpture, William Rubin earned a Columbia Ph.D., is adjunct professor at New York University, and author of many important books: *Dada and Surrealist Art* (1968); *Cézanne: The Late Work* (1977) and *"Primitivism" in 20th-Century Art* (1984), both with other contributors; and the two Picasso catalogues (1972 and 1980), which benefited from several visits with Picasso (see *Art News,* summer 1973).

1. Barr, *Picasso,* p. 223, quoting a 3 Sept. 1944 press report, "Picasso Is Safe."

House [fig. 167].[2] It represented only the second time that the urgency of collective social distress had drawn him from the more familiar, personal paths of his art.[3] One of his largest and most searingly intense pictures, *The Charnel House* transcends the pure horror in the photographs, converting reportage into tragedy.[4] Its grisaille harmonies distantly echo the black and white of newspaper images but, more crucially, establish the proper key for a requiem.

Like *Guernica*, *The Charnel House* is a Massacre of the Innocents—an evocation of horror and anguish amplified by the spirit of genius. It marks the final act in the drama of which *Guernica*—with which it has affinities of style as well as iconographic cross-references—may be said to illustrate the beginning. Both works submit their vocabulary of contorted and truncated Expressionistic shapes to a compositional armature derived from Cubism. *The Charnel House*, in particular, derives its visual tautness from the acute contention between these antagonistic modes. Its forms twist, turn, bulge and buckle but finally adjust themselves to what is almost an inner frame of whitish priming and to the rectilinear accents that echo this device in the interior of the composition. This ultimately endows the picture—for all its turbulence—with a kind of classical Cubist "set," absorbing the screaming violence of the morphology into the silent and immutable architecture of the frame.

The Charnel House depicts a pile of dead bodies on the floor of a room that also contains a table with a pitcher and casserole on it. From the tangled bodies the forms of a man, a woman, and a child can be disengaged. Flamelike patterns rising toward the upper right corner of the composition allude to death by fire. The man, whose head hangs as if his elongated neck were broken, is stretched almost horizontally across the picture space. His feet emerge from the mass of limbs at the left of the picture field; his rib cage has been rotated clockwise in relation to his chest and navel; and his wrists have been tied behind him, keeping his arms suspended in a kind of enforced rigor mortis. The woman is stretched in the opposite direction, her feet emerging in the lower right corner of the canvas. Both of the man's eyes are open; one of hers is closed while the other—displaced to her chin—is open and seemingly alive. Blood pours from a gash above her breast into one and then the other hand of the child, who lies obliquely to the picture plane, his body foreshortened. Although the child's eyes are closed, his right arm and open hand, raised as if to stanch his mother's wound, suggest that he might still be living.

The lifeless man is reminiscent of the dead soldier of *Guernica* as that figure was laid out in the mural's first stage [fig. 18], i.e., with his feet in the lower left of the canvas. Indeed, the raised arm of the dead man in *The Charnel House* also recalls

2. [Chronology of *The Charnel House* is problematic. It is often dated 1944–45 and Zervos published the first state of the canvas, dating it February 1945. Yet writers close to Picasso have always linked its origins to published newspaper images of Nazi concentration camps—which Allied troops liberated in April 1945. Picasso's composition surely resembles horrendous photographs of emaciated corpses piled up in mass graves (*Time* magazine, 30 April 1945, "Common Grave [Belsen]," p. 40, and Van deren Coke, *The Painter and the Photograph* [New York, 1972], pp. 110–11].) In the Chronology for *Picasso 1980*, William Rubin (with Jane Fluegel) published new evidence explaining the earlier date, entry for February 1945, p. 380: "Zervos photographs *Charnel House* in early state. Dora Maar later recalls that image is based on contemporary Spanish film showing the annihilation of a family in its kitchen."]

3. [*Guernica* being the first.]

4. As in *Guernica* where Picasso eschewed such details as contemporary weapons, which might have attached the image directly to the time and place of the Fascists' bombing, or even more generally to modern war (Schapiro, lectures at Columbia University), so he ensured the universality of *The Charnel House* by avoiding those references which would link it specifically with the concentration camps.

that of the dead soldier; his clenched left fist echoes the soldier's Loyalist salute; and the open fingers of his right hand recapitulate the petal pattern of the "sunflower" radiance that haloed the soldier's fistful of grain in *Guernica*'s second stage [fig. 27]. But the raised hand of the dead man of *The Charnel House* is empty, and his arm is not self-supporting like the *Guernica* soldier's phallic limb, which symbolized rebirth; it remains aloft only through its fastening to the other arm.

This latter motif is directly related to the bound legs of the lamb in the many studies for the *Man with the Lamb,* which Picasso executed during 1942–43. The pathos expressed by this motif is reinforced by the manner in which the lamb's head is turned in contrapposto to its bound legs, and by the elongation of its neck—both of which characteristics also appear in the figure of the man in *The Charnel House.*
* * *
Among Picasso's many drawings of the bound lamb are some in which its head resembles that of the horse in *Guernica.* Indeed, the horse's neck and head in the finished mural acquire expressiveness from the same kind of stretching and turning. By these indirect but characteristically Picassoid associations, the man of *The Charnel House* becomes linked to the suffering equine innocent of *Guernica.* As with the lamb, the symbolism of the *Guernica* horse is potentially both pagan and Christian, for he is at once the innocent but often slaughtered member of the corrida and, by virtue of the spear thrust into his side, also the crucified Christ.[5] Moreover, the horse in some studies for *Guernica,* which show him stretched out horizontally across the field [fig. 19], bears a family resemblance to the man in *The Charnel House.*

The association of the man in *The Charnel House* to the bound lamb, and to the soldier and horse of *Guernica,* may be said to endow the work with secondary symbolic dimensions. But unlike *Guernica,* which is openly symbolic, these are never made explicit, and remain subordinate to the more directly given realism of the work. That realism is rooted in the commonplace associations of the imagery of *The Charnel House,* which revolve around the immediate aspects of Picasso's daily life and work. The presence of a family group, for example, relates to the many intimate images central in his painting during the two years prior to *The Charnel House*— especially those of children, including his own daughter Maya. Nor are we surprised that the face of the man in *The Charnel House* should bear a strange resemblance to Picasso's own, while that of the woman has its antecedents in pictures inspired by Dora Maar.

This personal dimension of *The Charnel House* is most obvious in the still life in its upper left, set on a table similar in form and composition to the one in *Guernica,* and as surprising and irrational a presence.[6] The pitcher and casserole are virtually identical in design with those in *Pitcher, Candle, and Casserole,* painted in February 1945 while work was under way on the larger canvas. *Pitcher, Candle, and Casserole* is one of numerous still lifes that recall the darkest days of the occupation—the lack of electricity and the meager meals cooked in Picasso's studio on the rue des Grands Augustins. In transposing it into *The Charnel House,* Picasso suppressed the candle, probably lest it be read as a symbol of optimism. Other still lifes

5. [See Rubin, *Dada and Surrealist Art* (pp. 290–309).]

6. [Author's addition, August 1981: For illustration of *Pitcher, Candle, and Casserole,* see *Picasso 1980,* p. 386.]

painted while *The Charnel House* was being elaborated significantly include a series in which Picasso juxtaposed a pitcher, some leeks, and a skull. Here, the equation of "still" life with death implied in *The Charnel House* is rendered explicit in a manner well expressed by the French term *nature morte*. Taken together, these references to Picasso's intimate world give a sense of the iconography of *The Charnel House* that might be expressed as: I am this man; these are the woman and child I have loved and painted here during the last few years; these are our pitcher and casserole; it is incredible that we human beings should be as dead as these objects— reduced to the state of things.[7]

Picasso began *The Charnel House* in the last month of 1944 and worked on it over a period of at least a year and perhaps much longer.[8] In the earliest state in which it was photographed (by Zervos) in February 1945, it already contained numerous pentimenti. Some of these erasures, such as the flamelike form in the upper right, would be reinstated. * * *

In the third progressive photograph, of May 1945, the pole to which the man's wrists had been tied at the outset has been suppressed, the flamelike forms reinstated and the table with its still life introduced. The details of the man's feet have been filled in, and Picasso seems to have worked a great deal over the region of the woman's upper torso and the child's legs without making, finally, more than marginal changes.

Up to this point Picasso had worked exclusively in charcoal. In all probability it was sometime in July that he began to heighten certain of the lines with black paint and to fill in the planes with unshaded black and gray. The photographer Brassaï saw *The Charnel House* during or just after these changes. He reports Picasso as saying: "I'm treading lightly. I don't want to spoil the first freshness of my work. . . . If it were possible, I would leave it as it is, while I began over and carried it to a more advanced state on another canvas. Then I would do the same thing with that one. There would never be a 'finished' canvas, but just different states of a single painting. . . . To finish, to execute—don't those words have a double meaning? To terminate, to finish but also to kill, to give the *coup de grâce?*"[9] * * *

[Zervos] was apparently unaware that Picasso had made a number of small additions at some point during the many years that he continued to keep the picture in the studio [see note 8]. These primarily involved filling in some previously white areas (i.e., primed canvas sometimes shaded with erased charcoal) with a light blue-gray. * * * The blue-gray panels added a fourth value—between the gray and white in intensity—to the light-dark arrangement of the picture, making smoother the visual assimilation of its often abruptly contoured shapes; the blueness also gave a mortal

---

7. Robert Rosenblum has pointed out an affinity in regard to the juxtaposition of dead bodies and still-life objects between *The Charnel House* and Goya's "Ravages [or Wreckage] of War" from *The Disasters of War* [fig. 150A]. The latter image, certainly familiar to Picasso, contains six dead figures in a wrecked house in which a chair plays a role somewhat analogous to the still life in *The Charnel House.*

8. [Cf. note 2.] The date Picasso ceased work on *The Charnel House* is not known. The work could not possibly have been halted before July 1945, when Brassaï reports his painting it. It was first publicly exhibited in February 1946 in *Arts et Résistance.* * * * When the picture was exhibited at the Palazzo Nazionale of Milan in 1953, the catalog entry indicated that the final changes were made as late as 1948. The picture was purchased in 1954 by Walter P. Chrysler, Jr., from whom the museum acquired it [in 1971]. [For illustration of the states and pentimenti, see Rubin 1972, pp. 240–41.]

9. Brassaï, *Picasso and Company*, p. 182.

chill to the tonality; distinguishing it from the somewhat warmer gray of *Guernica* without fundamentally changing its funereal noncolor scheme.[10]

Like *Girl with a Mandolin*,[11] *The Charnel House* is nominally unfinished in the sense that it was abandoned short of Picasso's having carried all its parts to the standard of finish prevailing in his work at the time. * * * However, we may presume that since Picasso kept *The Charnel House* about him for some time and then signed and released it, he felt that the work was, in its own interior terms, as good and as complete as he could make it. Indeed, the incompleteness at the top of the picture adds to its poetry by giving the still life a different level of reality; its spectral quality makes it like a fugitive thought, a passing association to the main subject of the work. The unpainted areas also enhance the picture's composition by making it more open and unexpected, sidestepping a patness that might have resulted from filling out the patterning. * * * It is no doubt true, as has been observed with acuity, that *The Charnel House* "was finished and brought off by being left unfinished."[12]

As they could easily have been removed, there is no doubt that Picasso wanted us to see the many charcoal traces of the pentimenti which haunt *The Charnel House* like ghosts, thus allowing us to recapitulate, in a sense, the integration of the image. Picasso's manifest and titanic struggle to realize the work pictorially becomes a metaphor for the difficulty of realizing emotionally and intellectually the enormity of the event depicted.

10. See Greenberg, p. 346, above.
11. [Rubin 1972, pp. 66–67.]
12. Greenberg, p. 346.

Selected Bibliography

NOTE: Excerpts included in this anthology are marked *

BIBLIOGRAPHIES

Kibbey, Ray Anne. *Picasso: A Comprehensive Bibliography*. New York and London, 1977. Some omissions, many typographical errors; more useful than Gaya Nuño.

Gaya Nuño, Juan Antonio. *Bibliografía Crítica y Antológica de Picasso*. San Juan, 1966. Incomplete for English-language materials, better for French and Spanish sources.

See also Alfred Barr (p. 354, below), excellent up to 1946; and Catherine Freedberg (p. 357, below).

RECENT EXHIBITION CATALOGUES AND CATALOGUES RAISONNÉS

Bloch, Georges. *Pablo Picasso: Catalogue of the Printed Graphic Work*. 4 vols. (vol I: 1904–1967), Berne, 1968–1979. Informative text in French, German, English.

Geiser, Bernhard C. *Picasso: peintre-graveur*. 2 vols. (vol I: 1899–1931; vol II: 1932–1934), Berne, 1933, 1968. Superior, more complete for graphic work to 1934.

Guernica–Legado Picasso. Museo del Prado, Madrid, 1981. Statements and essays by Joan Miró, Josep Renau, Josep Lluis Sert, Javier Tusell, and Herschel B. Chipp. Complete catalogue raisonné of *Guernica* and its studies in the Prado (Casón) collection; superb color plates.

Musée Picasso: Catalogue sommaire des collections. Dominique Bozo and staff. Paris, 1985. This first volume comprises paintings, paper collages, sculpture, and ceramics, but not drawings. *The Picasso Museum, Paris*. Abrams, New York, 1986.

Musée Picasso: Catalogue. Marie-Laure Besnard-Bernadac, ed. Paris, 1985. This full catalogue by the museum's curator includes commentary on the *Weeping Woman with Handkerchief* (fig. 72A) and a related drawing and watercolor.

Pablo Picasso: A Retrospective. William Rubin, ed. The Museum of Modern Art, New York, 1980. Fully illustrated (many color plates), carefully documented, 464-page catalogue of the vast exhibition (May–Sept. 1980); extensive chronology by Jane Fluegel with detailed commentary, quotations.

Pablo Picasso: Eine Ausstellung zum hundertsten Geburtstag—Werke aus der Sammlung Marina Picasso. Werner Spies ed., with contributions by Reinhold Hohl and others. Important catalogue with intelligent commentary, good selective bibliography; the artistic inheritance of the surviving child of Picasso's legitimate son Paulo (see also Schiff and *Picasso the Printmaker*, below).

Pablo Picasso: Meeting in Montreal. Montreal Museum of Fine Arts, June–November 1985. Catalogue of 82 paintings Picasso gave to Jacqueline, fully illustrated in color, with selection of superb photographs of the artist; several important essays, including translation of such classics as Breton's "Picasso Poet" and Eluard's "I Talk about What Is Good."

Picasso from the Musée Picasso, Paris. Minneapolis, 1980. Catalogue of the exhibition at the Walker Art Center with essays by Martin Friedman (director); Dominique Bozo, "The Picasso Legacy"; Robert Rosenblum, "Ten Images"; Sir Roland Penrose, "Reminiscences." Excellent smaller (144 pp.) catalogue, stylistic chronology, selected bibliography.

Picasso: Oeuvres reçues en paiement des droits de succession. Paris, 1979. Dominique Bozo, ed. Catalogue of the exhibition, Grand Palais, October 1979–January 1980; fully illustrated; the core of the future Picasso Museum in Paris.

SELECTED BIBLIOGRAPHY

Picasso, 1881–1973: Exposición Antólogica. Museo Español de Arte Contemporáneo, Madrid, November–December 1981; Museo Picasso, Barcelona, January–February 1982. The first major retrospective in Spain; excellent reproductions; new documentation.

*Picasso the Printmaker: Graphics from the Marina Picasso Collection. Brigitte Baer, ed. Dallas, 1983. Excellent catalogue of exhibition in Dallas, Brooklyn, Detroit, Denver (Sept. 1983–May 1984); see part VIII for Baer essay.

Picasso: Todesthemen. Ulrich Weisner, ed. Kunsthalle Bielefeld, January–April 1984. Fascinating exhibition catalogue focusing on Picasso's lifelong obsession with death; important essays, such as Chipp's "Die Todesthematik in *Guernica:* Der Tod und Spanien."

Picasso at Work at Home: Selections from the Marina Picasso Collection. Gert Schiff, ed. Center for the Fine Arts, Miami, November 1985–March 1986. Fully illustrated in color with perceptive introduction and commentary.

Spies, Werner. *Sculpture by Picasso, with a Catalogue of the Works.* trans. Maxwell Brownjohn from German. New York, 1972 (London, 1971, title: *Picasso Sculpture*). Rev. ed. *Das plastische Werk.* Stuttgart, 1983. Basic reference, fully illustrated.

Zervos, Christian. *Pablo Picasso.* Cahiers d'Art, Paris, 1932–1978. Volume IX: *Oeuvres de 1937–1939* covers *Guernica* material, introductory essay, black-and-white plates, very little documentation. Last vol. XXXIII published 1978. The essential *oeuvre catalogue* for work after 1916 is by Pierre Daix (see below).

———. *Dessins de Pablo Picasso,* 1892–1948. Paris, 1949. Supplements the above.

PICASSO—GENERAL STUDIES, ANTHOLOGIES

Ashton, Dore. *Picasso on Art: A Selection of Views.* (The Documents of 20th-Century Art.) New York, 1972. Includes Picasso's statements of 1933 and 1935, excerpts of interviews with Téry and most of Seckler; selections arranged by themes; good bibliography.

**Barr, Alfred H. Jr. *Picasso: Fifty Years of His Art.* The Museum of Modern Art, New York, 1946. Reprinted 1966, paperback 1974. Fundamental and influential monograph; important Picasso texts; superb bibliography (538 items). See part VIII.

**Berger, John. *The Success and Failure of Picasso.* Harmondsworth and Baltimore, 1965. Paperback reissued 1978. Fresh observations, Marxist viewpoint; see part VI.

Brassaï [Gyula Halász]. *Picasso and Company.* trans. Francis Price from French; preface Henry Miller; introd. Roland Penrose. Garden City, New York, 1966. Recollections primarily of 1932 when Brassaï photographed Picasso's sculpture, and the early postwar years.

Cabanne, Pierre. *Pablo Picasso: His Life and Times.* trans. Harold J. Salemson from French (1975). New York, 1977. Highly readable, detailed, not always precise, candid (hence controversial).

Chipp, Herschel B. *Theories of Modern Art: A Source Book by Artists and Critics.* With contributions by Peter Selz and Joshua C. Taylor. Berkeley, Los Angeles, London, 1968. Most useful paperback anthology for background on Cubism and Surrealism; includes Picasso statements of 1923, 1935, Seckler interview, Téry quotation. (Chipp's articles are cited in the next section.)

Daix, Pierre. *La Vie de peintre de Pable Picasso.* Paris, 1977. Reliable biography by Picasso's friend and author of the truly comprehensive, scholarly *catalogues raisonnés: Picasso: The Blue and Rose Periods, 1900–1906* (New York, 1967) and *The Cubist Years, 1907–1916* (New York, 1979).

Dominguín, Miguel Luis, and Boudaille, Georges. *Pablo Picasso: Toros y Toreros.* trans. Edouard Roditi. New York, 1961. Facsimile reproductions of three Picasso sketchbooks, with commentary by Picasso's bullfighter friend.

Duncan, David Douglas. *Picasso's Picassos.* New York, 1961. Important picture book, superb Picasso-approved color photographs, frequently amusing and enlightening commentary quoting Picasso's responses.

———. *The Silent Studio.* New York, 1976. The last photographic study of Picasso's studio-home, Notre-Dame de Vie in Mougins; of special interest: the cluttered work areas; vast sculpture gallery; high quality black-and-white.

Fermigier, André. *Picasso.* Paris, 1969. Excellent small "Livre de Poche" paperback.

Gasman, Lydia. *Mystery, Magic and Love in Picasso, 1925–1938: Picasso and the Surrealist Poets.* Ph.D. diss., Columbia University, New York, 1981. Important, exhaustive study (4 vols., 1,920 pp.); imaginative interpretations. Revised publication forthcoming.

Gilot, Françoise, and Lake, Carlton. *Life with Picasso.* New York, Toronto, London, 1964; 1981 paperback reprint. Controversial book by Picasso's mistress (1944–1955) and mother of Claude and Paloma; to be used with care: possibly unreliable "quotations" of long talks with Picasso, but vivid descriptions of Picasso's working methods, daily life.

*Kahnweiler, Daniel-Henry. *Confessions Esthétiques.* Paris, 1963. See part IV.

———. *My Galleries and Painters by Daniel-Henry Kahnweiler with Francis Crémieux.* (The Documents of 20th-Century Art), trans. Helen Weaver, introduction John Russell (*Entretiens avec Francis Crémieux,* Paris, 1961). New York, 1971.

Leymarie, Jean. *Picasso—The Artist of This Century.* New York, 1977. Handsomely illustrated monograph documented with statements by Picasso, his friends, and major critics.

Lipton, Eunice. *Picasso Criticism, 1901–1939: The Making of an Artist-Hero.* Ph.D. diss., New York University, 1975, and Garland Publishing, New York, 1976. Very useful study, with evaluation and translation of important texts.

*Marrero, Vicente. *Picasso and the Bull.* trans. Anthony Kerrigan from Spanish (Madrid, 1951). Chicago, 1956. See part II.

McCully, Marilyn. *A Picasso Anthology: Documents, Criticism, Reminiscences.* Princeton, 1982. Outstanding anthology translates many little-known sources; includes excerpts of Raphael, Zervos.

*Penrose, Roland. *Picasso: His Life and Work.* New York, 1958. Rev. ed., Icon paperback, 1973. Indispensible biography by Picasso's English friend, painter, collector, museum director. See part IV.

——— and Golding, John, eds. *Picasso in Retrospect.* New York, 1973. Best collection of essays by leading Picasso scholars, from the Blue Period to the late works; especially relevant for *Guernica:* Golding, "Picasso and Surrealism," and Penrose, "Beauty and the Monster."

Rubin, William. *Dada and Surrealist Art.* New York, 1968. Excellent for background, with interpretation of *Guernica* "myths."

———. *Pablo Picasso: A Retrospective.* See catalogues.

*———. *Picasso in the Collection of the Museum of Modern Art.* New York, 1972. Excellent documentation, commentary frequently includes discussions with Picasso; see part VIII.

Runnquist, Jan. *Minotaurus. En studie: förållandet mellan ikonografi och from i Picasso konst 1900–1937.* Stockholm, 1959. Important early iconographical study, psychosexual emphasis; summary in French, pp. 187–192.

Sabartés, Jaime. *Picasso: An Intimate Portrait.* A. Flores, trans. New York, 1948. Emphasis on childhood and youth, mid-1930s and early wartime, but unfortunately not *Guernica* period.

Schiff, Gert. *Picasso in Perspective.* Englewood Cliffs, N.J., 1976. Valuable anthology of selected texts and interpretive essays; includes Herbert Read, Vernon Clark.

*Zervos, Christian. "Conversations avec Picasso," CdA X, 7–10, 1935, pp. 173–178; see parts I and IV. Translation by Myfanwy Evans published by Barr, frequently reprinted.

PICASSO—GUERNICA

*Arnheim, Rudolf. *Picasso's Guernica: The Genesis of a Painting.* Berkeley, California, 1962. Paper editions, 1973, 1980, entitled *The Genesis of a Painting: Picasso's Guernica.* See part VII.

Blunt, Anthony. *Picasso's Guernica.* New York, Toronto, 1969. Useful brief (32 pp.) overview, Whidden lecture at McMaster University, Ontario. Paper edition.

*Brendel, Otto J. "Classic and Non-Classic Elements in Picasso's *Guernica.*" In Whitney J. Oates, ed., *From Sophocles to Picasso: The Present-Day Vitality of the Classical Tradition.* Bloomington, 1962. See part VII.

Cantelupe, Eugene B. "Picasso's *Guernica,*" Art Journal XXXI/1, Fall 1971, pp. 18–21. English professor, dean of humanities department, emphasizes classical tradition in *Guernica* sources, composition; summarizes bibliography.

*Clark, Vernon. "The *Guernica* Mural—Picasso and Social Protest." *Science and Society*, Winter 1941, pp. 72–78. See part VI.

Chamberlain, Ken. "*Guernica:* Poster and Painting," *Arts Canada* 24, March 1967, pp. 5–10, 15–16. Cogent arguments that *Guernica* succeeds as art, but not as political poster.

Chipp, Herschel B. "*Guernica:* Love, War and the Bullfight," *Art Journal* XXXIII, Winter 1973–1974, pp. 100–115. Well illustrated, documented essay, citing contemporary press reports for historical background.

———. "*Guernica:* Once a document of outrage, now a symbol of reconciliation in a new and democratic Spain," *Art News*, May 1980, pp. 108–112. Emphasis on *Guernica's* role in 1937, upon 1939 arrival in America (*New York Times* news reports); revised, translated for Chipp's essay in *Guernica–Legado Picasso.*

———. *Picasso's Guernica: History, Transformations, Meanings.* Berkeley, California; forthcoming. Promises to become the major contribution to *Guernica* studies. (See also *Picasso: Todesthemen.*)

*Cooper, Douglas. "Picasso's 'Guernica' installed in the Prado," *Burlington Magazine*, May 1982, pp. 288–92; see part VII.

*Danz, Louis. *Personal Revolution and Picasso.* New York, Toronto, 1971. Reprinted 1974 with misleading title, *Revolution and Picasso*, since book is extremely personal, even idiosyncratic response to *Guernica*; see part VII.

Darr, William. "Images of Eros and Thanatos in Picasso's *Guernica*," *Art Journal* XXV / 4, Summer 1966, pp. 338–46. Interesting though debatable interpretations, Freudian, anthropological orientation.

Ferrier, Jean-Louis. *Picasso, Guernica—Anatomie d'un chef-d'oeuvre.* Paris, 1977.

Gedo, Mary Mathews. "Art as Autobiography: Picasso's *Guernica*," *Art Quarterly*, Spring 1979, pp. 191–210. Highly questionable methodology, with some valid use of sources, new interviews, "psychoanalytical" interpretation. Chapter from book, *Picasso: Art as Autobiography* (Chicago, 1980), based on author's "Picasso's Self-Image; a Psycho-Iconographic Study of the Artist's Life and Works," Ph.D. diss., Northwestern University, 1972.

Gottlieb, Carla. "The Meaning of Bull and Horse in *Guernica*," *Art Journal* XXIV / 2, Winter 1964–1965, pp. 106–12. Good summary, especially of political background, but unusual and debatable interpretation of symbolism.

Granell, Eugenio Fernandez. *Picasso's Guernica: The End of a Spanish Era.* Ann Arbor, 1981. Revision of Ph.D. dissertation, New School for Social Research, 1967, by Spanish Republican (b. 1912); valuable background, politics, bullfight; very little about *Guernica*, with eccentric interpretation as Christian Nativity.

Guernica: Kunst and Politik am Beispiel Guernica. Neue Gesellschaft für Bildende Kunst. Berlin (West), 1975. More than a catalogue for traveling exhibition (Berlin, Schwäbisch Hall, Ingolstadt, Erlangen); didactic materials for use in schools; wide-ranging essays, commentary, illustrations. New ed., *Guernica: Picasso und der spanische Bürgerkrieg*, Berlin (West), 1980.

Jordan, John O. "A Sum of Destructions: Violence, Paternity, and Art in Picasso's *Guernica*," *Studies in Visual Communication* 8, No. 3, Summer 1982, pp. 2–27. Occasionally debatable but very well-written, subtle application of psychoanalytical approach.

Kern, Edward. "Cry of Anger: *Guernica*," in *Life* Magazine, special double issue on Picasso, LXV, 27 December 1968, pp. 86–94B. Oriented to general readers; outstanding photographs throughout.

*Larrea, Juan. *Guernica: Pablo Picasso.* Trans. Alexander H. Krappe, edited by Walter Pach, introduction by Alfred Barr. New York, 1947. See part VII.

Markham, James M. "A New Battle for *Guernica*," *New York Times Magazine*, 26 November 1978. Good summary of personal, political, diplomatic maneuvers around *Guernica* "repatriation," with new interviews by this *Times* journalist in Madrid.

Marzorati, Gerald, "*Guernica* will hang in the Prado as Picasso wished," *Art News*, May 1977, pp. 65–67. Based on statements to the press by Picasso's lawyer, Roland Dumas. See part I.

356

*Masheck, Joseph. "*Guernica* as Art History," *Art News,* December 1967, pp. 32–35. See part VII.

Proweller, William. "Picasso's *Guernica:* A Study in Visual Metaphor," *Art Journal* XXX / 3, Spring 1971, pp. 240–48. Summarizes and attacks (especially Masheck) *Guernica* articles, offers own eccentric interpretation in terms of Mérode Altarpiece (c. 1425) by Master of Flémalle. Masheck's responses, *Art Journal* XXXL / 3, Spring 1972, p. 366.

*Raphael, Max. *The Demands of Art.* Trans. Norbert Guterman from German, preface by Herbert Read. Princeton, 1968. See part VI for selections from his *Guernica* chapter V.

*Russell, Frank D. *Picasso's Guernica: The Labyrinth of Narrative Vision.* Montclair, N.J., 1980. Artistically designed monograph with original, personal observations; see part VII.

*Seckler, Jerome. "Picasso Explains," *New Masses,* 13 March 1945, pp. 4–7; frequently reprinted, in Barr, Chipp, Ashton. See part I.

*"Symposium on *Guernica.*" The Museum of Modern Art, New York, 25 November 1947, unpublished typescript made available at the museum library. Moderator, Alfred Barr; participants: Sert (reprinted in part IV), Seckler, Larrea, and artists Jacques Lipchitz and Stuart Davis, with questions from the audience.

Tuchman, Phyllis. "Guernica and 'Guernica,' " *Artforum,* April 1983, pp. 44–51. Good political background, illustrations, no footnote documentation; from "*Guernica, L'Humanité,* and the Spanish Pavilion," unpublished M.A. thesis, New York University, 1973.

HISTORICAL, POLITICAL, CULTURAL BACKGROUND

Bolín, Luis. *Spain: The Vital Years.* Philadelphia, 1967; London, 1968. Fascinating memoirs by General Franco's propaganda chief, with a Nationalist's version of what he termed "the Guernica Myth."

Brenan, Gerald. *The Spanish Labyrinth.* New York, 1943. Highly respected background study of the civil war.

*Campbell, Joseph. *The Masks of God: Creative Mythology.* Final volume of studies of comparative religion and mythology. New York, 1968; 1970 paperbound. See part VIII.

Documents on German Foreign Policy, Series D, 1918–1945, Volume III, *The Spanish Civil War.* London, Paris, Washington, 1951. Reproduces confiscated German documents of the Nazi period. See part II.

Egbert, Donald D. *Social Radicalism and the Arts: Western Europe* (New York, 1970). Important background material for part VI; bibliography.

Fernández-Quintanilla, Rafael. *La odisea del "Guernica" de Picasso.* Barcelona, 1981. Admirable detective work by Spanish diplomat who tracked down documents (reproduced here) that facilitated *Guernica*'s "repatriation"; many previously unpublished photographs.

Freedberg, Catherine Blanton. *The Spanish Pavilion at the Paris World's Fair.* Ph.D. diss., Harvard University, 1981, and Garland Publishing, New York, 1986. Outstanding scholarly study and essential reference (992 pp. and nearly 300 ill.). Chapters on the Spanish and other pavilions; exterior and interior design and installations; art works by Picasso, Gonzalez, Miró, Calder, Albert Sánchez. (Fully available to me only after this manuscript entered production.)

Gershman, Herbert S. *The Surrealist Revolution in France.* Ann Arbor, 1969. Emphasis on politics, art and literature; useful chronology.

Jackson, Gabriel. *A Concise History of the Spanish Civil War.* New York, 1974.

*Maier, Hans A. *Guernica 26.4.1937: Die deutsche Intervention in Spanien und der "Fall Guernica.*" Freiburg im Breisgau, 1975. Includes contemporary documents and later recollections by *Luftwaffe* aviators, compiled by an officer of the West German Military Research Office. See part II.

*Payne, Robert, ed. *The Civil War in Spain, 1936–1939.* New York, 1962. Important anthology of primary sources compiled by writer who covered the civil war; includes eyewitness report by Father Alberto de Onaindía, reprinted in part II.

*Southworth, Herbert Rutledge. *Guernica! Guernica! A Study of Journalism, Diplomacy, Propaganda, and History*. Berkeley, Los Angeles, London, 1977. Outstanding study; comprehensive documentation, bibliography. See part II.

Sperber, Murray A. *And I Remember Spain: A Spanish Civil War Anthology*. New York, 1974. Excellent survey of British and American writers: volunteers, reporters, tourists, and the "literary homefront."

*Steer, George L. *The Tree of Gernika*, London, 1938. Expanded version of his newspaper reports from Spain; included also in Sperber. See part II.

Talón, Vicente. *Arde Guernica*. Madrid, 1970. A journalist's daring search, during the Franco era, for the truth about the Guernica raids; extensive documentation, excellent photographs.

Thomas, Gordon, and Witts, Max Morgan. *Guernica: The Crucible of World War II*. New York, 1975. Dramatized, fictionalized history; documentation includes material from Maier and independent interviews.

Thomas, Hugh. *The Spanish Civil War*. New York, 1961; Harper paperbound, 1963; revised, enlarged third ed., London, New York, 1977. Considered the most documented, carefully researched history (over 1,100 pp.); extraordinary bibliography; important revisions of Guernica story in 3rd ed.

Weintraub, Stanley. *The Last Great Cause: The Intellectuals and the Spanish Civil War*. London, New York, 1968.

Index